1995

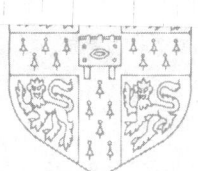

The Tanner Lectures on Human Values

THE TANNER LECTURES ON HUMAN VALUES

15

1994

Oz, Korsgaard, Keller, Stern,
Hoffmann, Renfrew

Grethe B. Peterson, *Editor*

UNIVERSITY OF UTAH PRESS
Salt Lake City

Copyright © 1994 University of Utah Press
Copyright © 1994 Amos Oz
Copyright © 1994 Colin Renfrew

All rights reserved
ISBN 0-87480-450-7
ISSN 0275-7656

∞ This symbol indicates books printed on paper
that meets the minimum requirements of
American National Standard for Information Services —
Permanence of Paper for Printed Library Materials,
ANSI A39.38–1984.

THE TANNER LECTURES ON HUMAN VALUES
was composed in Intertype Garamond with Garamond Foundry display type
by Donald M. Henriksen, Scholarly Typography, Salt Lake City.

THE TANNER LECTURES ON HUMAN VALUES

The purpose of the Tanner Lectures is to advance and reflect upon scholarly and scientific learning that relates to the entire range of human values.

To receive an appointment as a Tanner lecturer is a recognition of uncommon capabilities and outstanding scholarly or leadership achievement in the field of human values. The lecturers may be drawn from philosophy, religion, the humanities and sciences, the creative arts and learned professions, or from leadership in public or private affairs. The lectureships are international and intercultural and transcend ethnic, national, religious, or ideological distinctions.

The Tanner Lectures were formally founded on July 1, 1978, at Clare Hall, Cambridge University. They were established by the American scholar, industrialist, and philanthropist, Obert Clark Tanner. In creating the lectureships, Professor Tanner said, "I hope these lectures will contribute to the intellectual and moral life of mankind. I see them simply as a search for a better understanding of human behavior and human values. This understanding may be pursued for its own intrinsic worth, but it may also eventually have practical consequences for the quality of personal and social life."

Permanent Tanner lectureships, with lectures given annually, are established at nine institutions: Clare Hall, Cambridge University; Harvard University; Brasenose College, Oxford University; Princeton University; Stanford University; the University of California; the University of Michigan; the University of Utah; and Yale University. Other international lectureships occasionally take place. The institutions are selected by the Trustees.

The sponsoring institutions have full autonomy in the appointment of their lecturers. A major part of the lecture program is the publication and distribution of the Lectures in an annual volume.

The Tanner Lectures on Human Values is a nonprofit corporation administered at the University of Utah under the direction of a self-perpetuating, international Board of Trustees. The Trustees meet annually to enact policies that will ensure the quality of the lectureships.

The entire lecture program, including the costs of administration, is fully and generously funded in perpetuity by an endowment to the University of Utah by Professor Tanner and Mrs. Grace Adams Tanner.

Obert C. Tanner was born in Farmington, Utah, in 1904. He was educated at the University of Utah, Harvard University, and Stanford University. He served on the faculty at Stanford University and was a professor of philosophy at the University of Utah for twenty-eight years. Mr. Tanner was also the founder and chairman of the O. C. Tanner Company, the world's largest manufacturer of recognition award products.

Harvard University's former president Derek Bok once spoke of Obert Tanner as a "Renaissance Man," citing his remarkable achievements in three of life's major pursuits: business, education, and public service.

Obert C. Tanner died in Palm Springs, California, on October 14, 1993, at the age of eighty-nine.

GRETHE B. PETERSON
University of Utah

THE TRUSTEES

James J. Duderstadt
President of the University of Michigan

David Pierpont Gardner
President Emeritus of the University of California
President Emeritus of the University of Utah

The Rev. Carolyn Tanner Irish
Washington, D.C.

Gerhard Casper
President of Stanford University

Anthony Low
President of Clare Hall, Cambridge

O. Don Ostler
Chief Executive Officer, O. C. Tanner Company

Jack W. Peltason
President of the University of California

Chase N. Peterson
President Emeritus of the University of Utah

Neil L. Rudenstine
President of Harvard University

Richard C. Levin
President of Yale University

Harold T. Shapiro
President of Princeton University

Arthur K. Smith, CHAIRMAN
President of the University of Utah

Lord Windlesham
Principal of Brasenose College, Oxford

CONTENTS

The Tanner Lectures on Human Values v

The Trustees vii

Preface to Volume 15 ix

Amos Oz	The Israeli-Palestinian Conflict: Tragedy, Comedy, and Cognitive Block — A Storyteller's Point of View	1
Christine M. Korsgaard	The Sources of Normativity	19
Evelyn Fox Keller	Rethinking the Meaning of Genetic Determinism	113
Fritz Stern	I. Mendacity Enforced: Europe, 1914–1989	141
	II. Freedom and Its Discontents: Postunification Germany	185
Stanley Hoffmann	The Nation, Nationalism, and After: The Case of France	215
Colin Renfrew	The Archaeology of Identity	283

The Tanner Lecturers 349

Index to Volume 15 357

PREFACE TO VOLUME 15

Volume 15 of the Tanner Lectures on Human Values includes lectures delivered during the academic year 1992–93.

The Tanner Lectures are published in an annual volume. A general index to Volumes I through V is included in Volume V; beginning with Volume VI, each volume has its own index.

In addition to the Lectures on Human Values, Professor Tanner and the Trustees of the Tanner Lectures have funded special international lectureships at selected colleges and universities which are administered independently of the permanent lectures.

*The Israeli-Palestinian Conflict:
Tragedy, Comedy, and Cognitive Block —
A Storyteller's Point of View*

AMOS OZ

THE TANNER LECTURES ON HUMAN VALUES

Delivered at

University of Michigan
November 12 and 13, 1992

AMOS OZ, who is currently Professor of Hebrew Literature at Ben-Gurion University of the Negev, was educated at the Hebrew University of Jerusalem. He has taught at St. Cross College, Oxford, the University of California at Berkeley, Hebrew University, Colorado College, and Boston University. His fifteen books — seven novels, three short story collections, four books of essays, and one children's book — have won numerous awards. His novel *Black Box* (1987) received the Prix Femina Étranger, France's top annual literary award for best foreign novel, in 1988, the same year it was awarded the Wingate Prize (London). His children's novel *Soumchi* (1977) received the Hans Christian Andersen Medal, and the Ze-ev Award, the Luchs Prize (Germany), and the Hamore Prize (France) for children's books. Other recent works include *The Silence of Heaven* (1993), *The Third Condition* (1991), and *To Know a Woman* (1989). Since the Six Day War, Professor Oz has been actively involved in the Israeli Peace Movement, and has been one of the leading figures of Peace Now since its founding in 1977.

Remember the last scene of Hamlet? The one where the tragedy suddenly turns into a farce? When everyone seems to be stabbing the wrong person with the wrong sword? Well, the Israelis and the Palestinians are now almost ready to swap the poisoned swords. At the same time, they are almost ready for an uneasy compromise and for a sad and sober peace.

Let us look into the tragic-grotesque option first: the Palestinians, adopting traditional Zionist arguments, insist that they will not rest unless their historic rights are restored. The Israelis, for their part, relinquish the weapon of historical rights to replace it with what used to be a traditional Palestinian argument: "the natural case of a native." An Israeli, born in a predominantly Jewish Haifa, possibly born there to parents and grandparents who were also born in a predominantly Jewish Haifa, can hardly be expected to relinquish Haifa to some strangers who have never even been there, but claim that Haifa is where their ancestors came from. In short, "the right of memory" might once again clash with the "right of being there," except that the Israelis can resort to a former Palestinian argument and vice versa. The poisoned swords are swapped, the bloodshed continues — unless we all realize that wherever there is a clash between right and right, a value higher than right ought to prevail, and this value is life itself: "And Death shall have no Dominion" (Dylan Thomas).

Let us consider the term that all sides have been using abundantly: "rights" — "historical rights," "natural rights," "legitimate rights," "ancestral rights." Israelis and Palestinians have been claiming for at least 100 years now that they are the rightful owners of the country that we call the Land of Israel and they call Palestine. Even the pragmatists on both sides are sure of the axiomatic validity of their respective right to the land, but ready perhaps to consider forfeiting part of it for the sake of a peaceful compromise. Let us ponder on this term "right to the land," thus adding another drop to the ocean of arguments that have been used, misused, refuted, reformulated, or turned upside-down during the course of those "100 years of solitude." I have said many times since 1967 that the clash between Israelis and Palestinians is a tragic one because it is a clash between right and right — between one very strong case and another. Perhaps rather than "right and right," it is better to speak of "claim against claim."

The term "right," at least in its secular sense, stands for something that is recognised by others, not for something that someone feels very strongly about. You may have the deepest conviction that a beloved person, place, or object is exclusively your own, but as long as this is not the way others see it what you have is a claim, not a right. If you gain partial support then you have a stronger claim; more support would turn this claim into a disputed right. Further recognition still would turn it into an established right. The line between "claim" and "right" can only exist where there is an accepted law or where there exists a standard system of values. The case of the Land of Israel, or Palestine, as it stands after almost a century of struggle and upheavals is roughly as follows: the whole world recognizes Israel's rightful existence in the Land of Israel, but nobody supports an Israeli claim over the whole Land of Israel. At the same time, although everyone supports the Palestinians' right to self-determination in Palestine, there is only a very marginal support for a Palestinian claim over the whole of Palestine. This situation is a reasonable starting point for a possible compromise. I believe in a two-state solution: an Israeli recognition of the Palestinian right of self-determination, in return for Palestinian and Arab readiness to meet Israel's legitimate security provisions, to reach a comprehensive agreement, and to renounce all further claims on all sides.

Possibly the worst patch of the Israeli-Arab conflict is now over. I am not implying by this that we will not be seeing any more bloodshed. Oh yes, I am afraid we will. But the good news is that the cognitive block, which existed, in different ways, on both sides, is beginning to dissolve at last: for too many years, in fact for decades, the Arabs believed that if they were only to rub their eyes hard enough, Israel would go away, like a nightmare; go away like a mobile exhibition, perhaps, that can be transferred elsewhere. Many Israelis, for their part, have believed for too long that the entire Palestinian issue is not a real one — that Palestine is nothing but an invention by a vicious Pan-Arabic propaganda machine, aimed at eroding Israel's integrity and damaging her reputation abroad. Now both sides are beginning to sober up. Both sides are opening their eyes to face reality. And it isn't easy for either of them. This is not the beginning of a honeymoon. If anything, it's like a patient awakening from an anaesthetic slumber only to discover with pain and frustration that, after surgery, things are never going to be the same again. There is a lot of rage and disillusionment, sadness and insecurity on both sides. But I think they both now realize that the other side is real, is not about to go away, and, in fact, is here to stay. Many people on all sides are now aware of the fact that it's not enough to call Washington, D.C., long distance and say: Will you please get those terrible people off my back! This phase of the conflict is over. Gone are the days when Arabs, by and large, refused even to pronounce that "dirty" word "Israel," preferring to resort to self-deceiving expressions, such as "the Zionist entity." Gone, too, are the days when Israelis, by and large, preferred to refer to the "country's Arab inhabitants" or "locals," in order to evade the term "Palestinians." Yes, we have all made considerable progress in the last decade. What Mr. Arafat is now proposing to the Israelis, although too late and too little, would still have been enough to cause Mr. Arafat of the past to shoot today's Mr. Arafat in the head. What the Israelis are now proposing to the Palestinians, again, too little and to late, is enough to make Socialist Golda Meir turn over in her grave. Despite the suspicion, frustration, and rage on both sides, let us not be blind to the fact that the progress we have all made recently is very significant indeed, considering our respective stances of ten, twenty, or fifty years ago. Now the Israeli-Arab conflict is at long last becoming a dispute about real estate, not a theological dispute, nor an ethnic clash, although some fanatics on both sides are trying to turn it into a holy war. Essentially, it is now a dispute over real estate: whose house? Who is going to get how much? Such conflicts can be resolved through a compromise. And I am not suggesting that the compromise can be reached overnight or over a few months. The issues are very real and very painful: security, settlements, water, boundaries, a comprehensive Middle Eastern security system, and so on. Nevertheless, from now on, Israelis and Arabs are no longer talking about who is going to go away altogether, but, rather, about who is going to get what. This is what I would call "normalizing" the conflict. Unlike former Yugoslavia, unlike Northern Ireland, probably unlike Lebanon, the Israeli-Palestinian clash is *an international conflict and not a civil war* — an international conflict and not a civil rights issue. In 100 years of tension and violence, these two societies have remained two societies — this making the choice somewhat easier. This observation does not, however, refer to Israel's Palestinian citizens: theirs is not a case of divorce, but of legal equality, democratic plurality, and multiethnic coexistence within Israel.

Naturally, both sides are now apprehensive; both of them have to undergo a major change. But let me, for a moment, be the advocate of the Hawks in Israel, although I resent them wholeheartedly. Still, I would like to give them a fair hearing. The Hawks feel that whereas Israel is expected to relinquish real estate, to give land, to forfeit strategic assets, the Palestinians and the Arab nations are only expected to produce a piece of paper, a nice document, which may so easily be torn to shreds the following day. This, say the Israeli Hawks, is an uneven deal, bearing in mind the instability of the Middle East, the rise of Islamic fundamentalism, and the violent nature of disagreements in the Arab world. But some of the apprehensions of these sincere Israeli Hawks (as opposed to fanatic and demagogic Hawks) *can* be alleviated, if the contract contains an element of time as well as one of space: the Palestinians *will* gain sovereignty over the West Bank and the Gaza Strip, although they won't do so overnight. It will happen phase by phase — the fulfillment of Palestinian national rights will be deployed over a period of several years and delivered not mile by mile, but one attribute of sovereignty after another. In this way, Israel will not simply be relinquishing land in return for a cheque. Israel will have the time necessary to find out if this cheque is valid. Are the Palestinians and the Arab nations able to deliver peace? Will they be able to contain their extremists and zealots? Is an effort being made to create a new atmosphere? Are there evident syndromes of emotional deescalation?

You may be sure that the Palestinians, too, are apprehensive. They, too, are having to change some of their dogmas, some of their basic concepts; and Israel, in turn, is going to have to exhibit significant changes in her attitude toward them. First and foremost, perhaps, toward her own Arab citizens.

As both sides are uneasy and worried about the impending progress, now is time for the "outside world" to help calm both sides down. It would be a stupid mistake for public opinion makers to cause the parties even more anxiety and paranoia by calling this or that party names. Let people of goodwill and well-meaning governments outside the region stop wagging their fingers in disapproval, like old-fashioned Victorian schoolmasters. Instead of finger wagging, they might consider some scheme to incorporate a future peaceful Middle East into a international security system or a European security system or a Mediterranean one. This could help both sides overcome some of their fears. One could conceive of a plan for incorporating a peaceful Middle East into the European economic system or maybe a Mediterranean economic system. One could devise a Marshall Plan for the Middle East to help resettle about 1 million Palestinian refugees as well as some million Jewish refugees from the former Soviet Union and elsewhere. This would certainly be a worthwhile contribution. And by the way, don't worry about the cost; I believe that within some fifteen years a peaceful Middle East would be in a position to fully repay the sponsors of such a Marshall plan, or better still to initiate its own Marshall Plan for less privileged parts of the world — for Africa, for example, or for Latin America. Potentially, the Middle East is a very rich region.

I believe the Gulf War has been an extremely sobering lesson for many on all sides. At a painful cost, I think some Palestinians have learned that there is no hope for them in just sitting around expecting some Saladin to come riding up from the East, on a white horse, throwing the Jews into the ocean and ridding Palestinians of the need to compromise. The Israeli Hawks have learned, at a no less painful cost, that the extra forty kilometers, which is what the occupied territories are all about, do not necessarily grant the country absolute security in an age of ballistic missiles.

I don't expect the two parties to fall in love with each other. Let's not be sentimental. Even after peace is achieved, both parties will still disagree as to who was to blame for the whole conflict. They will disagree about the past. They will almost certainly remain divided as to who was David and who was Goliath in this conflict. And, by the way, the issue is not an easy one: the question of which is David and which is Goliath depends on framing. If you focus on the West Bank and Gaza, then the Israelis are a clumsy Goliath, and the stone-throwing Palestinians are poor little David; yet if you change the zoom and put the frame on the conflict between Israel with her 5 million citizens and over 100 million Arabs, or, worse still, between Israel and many hundreds of millions of Muslims, you'll get a totally different notion as to who is David and who is Goliath. Fortunately, there is no need for the parties to agree on this issue: peace is still possible even between parties who have different notions of the past.

In order to understand the Israeli psyche, you must bear in mind the Israelis' legitimate fears and apprehensions: for seventy years now Israel has more or less lived out the experience of a collective Salman Rushdie. For seventy years there has been a collective death sentence hanging over our heads, issued by Islamic fundamentalist leaders and by Arab politicians. It is only understandable that the Israelis have grown untrusting, even neurotic. Such a Salman Rushdie experience would be enough to drive even the sanest society insane and I can hardly claim that Israel is the sanest society. So we really do have good reason to be nervous, frightened, and even neurotic about our security. I know that Palestinians have equivalent feelings, having, for decades, been hearing many Israelis describing the country, as it was before the Jews started to settle it, as "an empty land."

It is of utmost importance to realize that one of the things both parties *do* have in common is that both of them, in two different ways, are victims of Christian Europe. The Arabs have been victimized by Europe through colonialism, imperialism, oppression, and exploitation. The Jews have been victimized by Europe through discrimination, pogroms, and, ultimately, mass murder. According to the mythology of Bertolt Brecht, victims automatically develop a sense of mutual solidarity, becoming brothers and starting to love each other. Together they march to the barricades, chanting Brecht songs. But in real life, as we know, some of the worst conflicts develop precisely between victims of the same oppressor. Two battered children of the same cruel parent do not necessarily love one another; they sometimes hate each other bitterly, as each of them, looking at the other, sees the image of his or her past oppressor. So it is between the Israelis and the Arabs. On the one hand, the Arabs look at us Israelis and can't see us as what we really are: a bunch of half-hysterical refugees and survivors. What they see when they look at us is a nightmare image, an extension of the white, oppressing, sophisticated, colonizing Europe, coming back to the Middle East with the purpose of, once again, oppressing and humiliating the Arabs. When we Israelis, on the other hand, look at the Arabs, we often fail to see them as victims of colonialism, paralyzed by identity crises and tyrant regimes, an oppressed people. What we see is nothing but an incarnation of our past oppressors: Cossacks, pogrom-makers, Nazis. They have grown mustaches this time and wrapped themselves up in kaffiyehs, but they are still out to do the same old thing: cut Jewish throats. This tragic inclination, on both sides, to see the others not as what they are but as the old enemy incarnate calls for a removal of stereotypes; for learning each other's culture and history, for an imaginative literary dialogue.

Yet I have never shared the somewhat sentimental view that it is necessary first to change hearts then to make peace. Throughout history, things tend to work the other way around: make peace first, then work toward changing hearts and removing the conflictual stereotypes. Time and again, I receive these invitations from well-meaning European and North American institutions to come and spend a few days in idyllic retirement with Palestinian artists and intellectuals, in order to get to know and like one another. It seems that many people in the West have completely forgotten that conflicts *do* exist. These people seem to believe only in "misunderstandings" that may somehow be settled through group therapy, or marriage counselling, in quiet, pleasant surroundings. Well, I've got some news: there are no basic misunderstandings between Israelis and Palestinians — there is a very real conflict: they want the land because they think it belongs to them; we want it because we think it belongs to us. This provides for sufficient understanding between the parties, and for a tragic clash between them. This conflict can be resolved through compromise, through a partition, but not by simply having a nice cup of coffee with the enemy. Rivers of coffee cannot extinguish the tragedy of two peoples loving the same homeland. I don't need to go somewhere for a *tête-à-tête* with my Palestinian colleagues in order to get to like them — I like them, and yet they are my enemies, and it is precisely because they are my enemies that I believe I need to make peace with them.

This perhaps is a suitable point at which to distinguish between our own Israeli peace movement, Peace Now, and what I would call the sentimental Left, the oversimplistic dovish Left that constitutes some of the peace movements in the West. The Israeli peace movement has little in common with a tradition in which peace and love and compassion and brotherhood and reconciliation are synonymous. Actually, they are not synonymous. The opposite of war is not love; the opposite of war is peace. Hence my own attitude toward the Palestinians is make peace, not love. Anyway, I do not believe in love between nations, which is a very naive concept. As the Beatles lamented, "there just isn't enough love to go around." I am a peacenik, I am not a pacifist. To me, the ultimate evil is aggression, rather than war itself. Israel's most pragmatic prime minister, Levi Eshkol, used to say: "There is one thing that is even worse than using violence, and this is: capitulating to violence." I don't want Israel to be the Jesus Christ of the nations, forever turning the other cheek. I will fight again, as I did in 1967 and in 1973, if anyone tries to kill me or my people, fight like the devil, and I'll fight if anyone tries to turn me or my people into slaves. But nothing short of that would ever make me or my colleagues in the peace movement take up arms: we will not fight over resources or national interests or ancestral rights or an extra bedroom for the country. Life and freedom, yes, but nothing else.

In certain sections of the sentimental Left in Europe and North America, they are forever in the business of good guys and bad guys. Who are the good guys and who are the bad guys? They have this inclination to give the Third World a certain moral discount: "After all, those people have suffered a lot, you really ought to forgive them," etc. I don't think anyone in this world is worthy of a moral discount. Ever. Material assistance, yes; political fairness, definitely; equal standards, by all means, but no moral discount. By the way, for some time I have been hearing something like this from Western intellectuals: well, the Palestinians you must understand, they have suffered a lot, they've been oppressed and humiliated, they *are* a part of the Third World, after all, so it's only natural for them to become a bit violent; what else do you expect? But the Jews, they've suffered so much, they've been oppressed and discriminated against, how on earth can they, having experienced all this, behave violently? Now this, I believe, is giving double standards a bad name. It may derive from a certain simplistic Christian sentiment — Jesus bled on the cross and then became God. Consequently every Jew who bleeds on the cross should become an angel. Well, in real life, some victims of oppression and discrimination and racism indeed become more tolerant, more receptive, more sensitive to the sufferings of others. Whereas other victims of the same horrible experience tend to become more vindictive, more angry, and more suspicious. Let me tell you, both these contradicting responses to suffering are equally human. They may not be equally humane, but they are equally human. The Nazi gas chambers showered their victims not with some moral-cleansing liquid, but with Cyclone-B. I don't even want to mention the grotesque pro–Third World sentiment, which turns Saddam into a good guy, simply because he is against America, and turns Israel into the bad guy, simply because she is associated with America — and being associated with America is the same as being "Rosemary's Baby," which, by definition, is diabolical. Saddam Hussein is friends with Libya and China, and Libya and China are friends with Fidel Castro, and Fidel Castro has been married to Che Guevara, and Che Guevara is Jesus Christ, and Jesus is love, and therefore let us all love Saddam. Well, I was one of those Israelis who endorsed the need to get Saddam Hussein out of Kuwait during the Gulf War, by force, if necessary, which was a very uneasy stance for a peacenik to take and did not make me very popular among some dogmatic Western peaceniks. Kuwait had been a bad guy, I have no doubt in my mind about this: a corrupt regime, an oppressive, feudalistic system, stinking of oil and injustice. But I maintain that even a bad guy does not deserve to be violated and the violator be allowed to get off scot-free. Had

Saddam Hussein been permited to get away with the "Anschluss" of Kuwait, a very dangerous precedent would have been set for all small nations in the Middle East.

I do not share the sentiment of some well-meaning people who always seem to agree with the Third World's every whim and wish, whether right or wrong, "for the sake of world peace."

Nor do I admire the Palestine National Movement, which I have always regarded as one of the most extremist and uncompromising national movements of our times. I do not harbour a soft spot for Mr. Arafat. I would shake his hand tomorrow, if I thought that this would help bring about peace, but nothing in the world would ever make me endorse him. He is no Ho Chi Minh, and I am no Jane Fonda, and even Ho Chi Minh is no longer Ho Chi Minh, as Jane Fonda is no longer Jane Fonda. And anyway, ours is not a Vietnam-like conflict. One of the reasons I am angry with the PLO and its predecessors in the Palestine National Movement is the amount of misery and tragedy they have caused, not only to us Israelis, but especially to their own people, by taking such an uncompromising stance for decades, by endorsing the Nazis in the 1930s and 1940s, and by blatantly intending and attempting to exterminate Israel, a purpose they openly proclaimed for several decades. They might have blinded themselves to reality by misdiagnosing Zionism, by conceiving of it as a colonial phenomenon — but Zionism is not a colonial phenomenon.

Actually, the early Zionists who came to the land of Israel at the turn of this century had nothing to colonize there. It's one of the few countries in the Middle East with no resources. In terms of colonial exploitation, the Zionists have involved themselves in the worst bargain of all times, as they have brought into the country thousands of times more wealth than they could ever hope to get out of it. Wrong diagnosis begets a wrong perception and a wrong treatment. So I think that Palestinian ideologists as well as some of the world Left should set about revising their concept of Zionism. It's not a form of colonialism; neither is it a form of racism. It is a national liberation movement, and, like other national liberation movements, it has its own ugly, selfish, narrow-minded, and fanatic components. It is equally crucial for many Israelis to revise their view of the collective Palestinian identity and to reach the realization that Palestinian freedom is morally inevitable and undeniable and that, as long as the Palestinians have no freedom, our own freedom is doomed to remain crippled. Regardless of my criticism of Zionism, however, and of the Palestinian National Movement, I think it is time to make a peace based on compromise. Neither the Palestinians nor the Israelis are lucky enough to have the privilege of choosing their enemy. And it is your enemy you have to make peace with; not because the enemy is "nice," not necessarily because you feel one of you has wronged the other. You make peace with your enemy simply because this *is* your enemy.

Self-determination is not bestowed only upon nice and well-behaved people. It's not a decoration for excellent behaviour or for a wonderful record. Had this been the case, half the nations of the world should already have been stripped of their independence. If it was a question of good record, then Germany and Austria ought perhaps to have been stripped of their independence. But good record is not the name of the game. Survival is the name of the game. Survival for both sides.

I am fully aware of the fact that many well-meaning people in the West, indeed in Israel, are somewhat disenchanted and disillusioned with the reality of Israel. Our record on civil rights is not good, though not the worst one in the Middle East. Some of our internal conflicts are painful and sometimes ugly. The disagreements about our identity and where do we go from here are sometimes very dramatic, sometimes very melodramatic. Some of Israel's realities could not possibly be as magnanimous as her initial dreams. Israel was born out of the monumental visions and huge expectations not only of her founding fathers and mothers, but also of millions of other people all over the world. With all due respect to Charles Dickens, I would say that, on Israel's visiting card, "Great Expectations" is her middle name. Various visions and master plans were conceived for Israel. But, by definition, some of those initial master plans collided with others, as did some of those early visions. There was no way for all of them to have been fulfilled. Moreover, to some extent, unlike communism, unlike many other political visions, Israel is a dream come true. As such, it is bound to be flawed and imperfect. The only way to keep a dream intact is never to try to fulfill it. This is true of an initial vision for a novel, for family life, for a sexual encounter, or for planting a garden, and indeed for building a nation. Israel is flawed and imperfect, precisely because she is a dream come true. Let me add right away that I think that internal questions such as the place of religion in the state, the implementation of civil rights, and the attitude to minorities cannot be satisfactorily resolved before resolving the issue of the Israeli-Arab conflict. No nation has ever been very good on civil rights while at war with a deadly enemy. We have to resolve the Israeli-Arab conflict first, and then work on some of our painful internal divisions. Moreover, questions of state and church, in Israel's case state and synagogue, and the position of minorities are issues that took Europe centuries of blood and fire to resolve. Many nations, allegedly civilized nations, including this blessed America, have only been able to establish their rules of the game through bloody civil wars, rivers of blood and fire. At least in Israel our perpetual internal civil war is essentially a verbal one. In a clash between Israeli and Israeli, the casualties are verbal, and so are the ammunition and artillery. Rather than shoot at each other, we Israelis are constantly giving each other ulcers and heart attacks by calling each other terrible names. This provides for perpetual sound and fury, but also serves as a safety-valve against internal violence. I guess I am trying to convey the fact that although, at the moment, I dislike many aspects of Israel, I love her nonetheless.

I think the Israeli-Palestinian conflict, as opposed to the Israeli-Libyan or Israeli-Iraqi conflict, is a tragedy in the exact sense of the word. It is a clash between one very powerful claim and another no less powerful. And it is high time for honest people outside the region to conceive of it as a tragedy and not as some western movie, with "good guys" and "bad guys." Tragedies can be resolved in one of two ways: there is the Shakespearean resolution and there is the Chekhovian one. On the one hand, at the end of a Shakespearean tragedy, the stage is strewn with dead bodies and maybe there's some justice hovering high above. A Chekhov tragedy, on the other hand, ends with everybody disillusioned, embittered, heartbroken, disappointed, absolutely shattered, but still alive. And I want a Chekhovian resolution and not a Shakespearean one for the Israeli/Palestinian tragedy.

These, in a nutshell, are my politics.

Perhaps the very first joint project to be created by Palestinians and Israelis, as soon as peace between them is established, should be a monument to our mutual stupidity. After all, in the end, the Palestinians are only going to get a fraction of what they could have had with peace and honour back in 1948, forty-five years ago, five wars ago, and some 150,000 dead ago, ours as well as theirs. The Israelis, too, will get less than they could have had, had they been imaginative, generous, or even realistic back in 1967, and since. Only the dead will get nothing except for some wreaths and a flood of high-flown rhetoric. However, it is feasible that, before long, a two-state solution will materialise. Obviously, we all have to remember that there are different sets of clocks at work in the world and in the Middle East. The clock of common sense and pragmatism is only one of many. Fear, despair, and zeal for uncompromising justice are also on stage. Conflicts, whether individual, intercommunal, or international, do not usually resolve themselves through a miraculous formula that sends rival parties falling into each other's arms like long-lost brothers in a Dostoyevsky novel; rather, most conflicts tend to fade away gradually, as a result, simply, of exhaustion on all sides. I think this blessed exhaustion is a syndrome recently observed among several Israelis and Arabs.

Let all of us, primarily we Israelis, realize now that the present Palestinian leadership is the most moderate one, and the most willing to compromise, that the Palestinian people are able to produce today — or tomorrow. At the same time, let us all, although primarily the Palestinians, Syrians, and other Arabs, realize that the present Israeli government is the most moderate one, and the most willing to compromise, that Israel can produce today — or tomorrow. Let's take it from there. Above all, we mustn't forget that Shakespeare might still take over, and that we must work doubly hard for Chekhov...

The Sources of Normativity

CHRISTINE M. KORSGAARD

THE TANNER LECTURES ON HUMAN VALUES

Delivered at

Clare Hall, Cambridge University
November 16 and 17, 1992

CHRISTINE M. KORSGAARD is currently Professor of Philosophy at Harvard University. She was educated at the University of Illinois at Urbana-Champaign, and at Harvard, where she received her Ph.D. degree in philosophy in 1979. She has taught at several schools in the University of California system, including UC Santa Barbara, UCLA, and UC Berkeley, and at the University of Chicago. She is a member of the American Philosophical Association, the North American Kant Society, the Hume Society, and the American Society for Political and Legal Philosophy. She has published and lectured extensively on Immanuel Kant, including "Kant," in *Ethics in the History of Western Philosophy*, edited by Cavalier, Gouinlock, and Sterba (1989), "Kant's Analysis of Obligation," in *The Monist* (1989), and "Aristotle and Kant on the Source of Value," in *Ethics* (1986). In addition, her articles "Immanuel Kant," "John Rawls," and "Richard Price," were published in *The Garland Encyclopedia of Ethics*, edited by Becker (1992). A longer version of her Tanner Lecture, *The Sources of Normativity*, with commentary by G. A. Cohen, Raymond Geuss, Thomas Nagel, and Bernard Williams, and edited by Onora O'Neil, is forthcoming from Cambridge University Press.

Lecture I: The Normative Question
Introduction

In 1625, in his book *On the Law of War and Peace*, Hugo Grotius asserted that human beings would have obligations "even if we should concede that which cannot be conceded without the utmost wickedness, that there is no God, or that the affairs of men are of no concern to Him."[1] But two of his followers, Thomas Hobbes and Samuel Pufendorf, thought that Grotius was wrong. However socially useful moral conduct might be, they argued, it is not really *obligatory* unless some sovereign authority, backed by the power of sanctions, lays it down as the law.[2] Others in turn disagreed with them, and so the argument began.

Ever since then, modern moral philosophers have been engaged in a debate about the "foundations" of morality. We need to be shown, it is often urged, that morality is "objective." The early rationalists, Samuel Clarke and Richard Price, thought that they knew exactly what they meant by this.[3] Hobbes had said that there is no right or wrong in the state of nature, and to them, this implied that rightness is mere invention or convention, not something real.[4] Hobbes meant that individuals are not obligated to obey the laws of social cooperation in the absence of a sovereign who can impose them on everyone.[5] But the rationalists took him

---

[1] Grotius, *On the Law of War and Peace*, Schneewind I, p. 92. I owe a great debt to Jerome Schneewind for drawing my attention to this stretch of the historical debate, and especially for encouraging me to read Pufendorf.

[2] See Hobbes, especially *Leviathan*; and Pufendorf, *On the Law of Nature and of Nations* and *On the Duty of Man and Citizen according to Natural Law*.

[3] See Clarke, *A Discourse concerning the Unchangeable Obligations of Natural Religion, and the Truth and Certainty of the Christian Revelation: The Boyle Lectures 1705*; and Price, *A Review of the Principal Questions in Morals*.

[4] Hobbes, *Leviathan*, I.13, p. 90.

[5] Ibid., I.15, p. 110.

to mean what Bernard Mandeville had later ironically asserted: that virtue is just an invention of politicians, used to keep their human cattle in line.[6]

But what exactly is the problem with that? Showing that something is an invention is not a way of showing that it is not real. Moral standards exist, one might reply, in the only way standards of conduct *can* exist: people believe in such standards and therefore regulate their conduct in accordance with them. Nor are these facts difficult to explain. We all know in a general way how and why we were taught to follow moral rules and that it would be impossible for us to get on together if we didn't do something along these lines. We are social animals, and probably the whole thing has a biological basis. So what's missing here, that makes us seek a philosophical "foundation"?

The answer lies in the fact that ethical standards are *normative*. They do not merely describe a way in which we in fact regulate our conduct. They make *claims* on us: they command, oblige, recommend, or guide. Or at least, when we invoke them, we make claims on one another. When I say that an action is right I am saying that you ought to *do* it; when I say that something is good I am recommending it as worthy of your choice. The same is true of the other concepts for which we seek philosophical foundations. Concepts like knowledge, beauty, and meaning, as well as virtue and justice, all have a normative dimension, for they tell us what to think, what to like, what to say, what to do, and what to be. And it is the force of these normative claims — the right of these concepts to give laws to us — that we want to understand.

And in ethics, the question can become urgent, for the day will come, for most of us, when what morality commands, obliges, or recommends is *hard*: that we share decisions with people whose

---

[6] See Mandeville, *The Fable of the Bees: or, Private Vices, Public Benefits*, especially the section "An Enquiry into the Origin of Moral Virtue," pp. 41–57. Mandeville himself denied that he meant either that virtue is unreal or that it is not worth having. See for instance "A Vindication of the Book," pp. 384ff.; and also *An Enquiry into the Origin of Honor*, Schneewind II, pp. 396–98.

intelligence and integrity don't inspire our confidence; that we assume grave responsibilities to which we feel inadequate; that we sacrifice our lives or voluntarily relinquish what makes them sweet. And then the question *why?* will press, and rightly so. Why should I be moral? This is not, as H. A. Prichard supposed, a misguided request for a demonstration that morality is in our interest (although that may be one answer to the question).[7] It is a call for philosophy, the examination of life. Even those who are convinced that "it is right" must be in itself a sufficient reason for action may request an account of rightness that this conviction will survive. The trouble with a view like Mandeville's is not that it is not a reasonable explanation of how moral practices came about, but rather that our commitment to these practices would not survive our belief that it was true.[8] Why give up your heart's desire, just because some politician wants to keep you in line? When we seek a philosophical foundation for morality we are not looking merely for an explanation of moral practices. We are asking what *justifies* the claims that morality makes on us. This is what I will call "the normative question."

Now it is often thought that the normative question poses a special problem for *modern* moral philosophers. The Modern Scientific World View is supposed to be somehow inimical to ethics, while, in different ways, the teleological metaphysics of the the ancient Greek world and the religious systems of medieval Europe seemed friendlier to the subject. It is a little hard to put the point clearly and in a way that does not give rise to obvious objections, but both of these earlier outlooks seem to support the idea that human life has a purpose that is or only can be fulfilled

[7] Prichard, "Does Moral Philosophy Rest on a Mistake?" and "Duty and Interest." Prichard's argument is discussed in detail below.

[8] Actually, as Hume and Hutcheson both argued, there are also problems about the explanatory adequacy of Mandeville's view. For Hume's discussion, see the *Enquiry concerning the Principles of Morals* (1751), p. 214. For Hutcheson's, see the *Inquiry concerning the Original of Our Ideas of Beauty and Virtue* (1725), Raphael I, p. 291. Neither Hume nor Hutcheson names Mandeville, but he is clearly their target.

by those who live up to ethical standards and meet moral demands. And this is supposed to be sufficient to establish that ethics is really normative, that its demands on us are justified. They are justified in the name of life's purpose. The Modern Scientific World View, in depriving us of the idea that the world has a purpose, has taken this justification away.

Whether this is true or not, the moral philosophy of the modern period can be read as a search for the source of normativity. Philosophers in the modern period have come up with four successive answers to the question of what makes morality normative. In brief, they are these:

(1) Voluntarism. According to this view, moral obligation derives from the command of someone who has legitimate authority over the moral agent and so can make laws for her. You must do the right thing because God commands it, say, or because a political sovereign whom you have agreed to obey makes it law. Normativity springs from a legislative will. This is the view of Pufendorf and of Hobbes.

(2) Realism. According to this view, moral claims are normative if they are true, and true if there are intrinsically normative entities or facts that they correctly describe. Realists try to establish the normativity of ethics by arguing that values or obligations or reasons really exist or, more commonly, by arguing against the various forms of skepticism about them. This kind of argument has been found in the work of rational intuitionists ever since the eighteenth century. It was advanced vigorously by Clarke and Price in the eighteenth century and by Prichard, G. E. Moore, and W. D. Ross in the early twentieth century.[9] It is also found in the

---

[9] Clarke, *A Discourse concerning the Unchangeable Obligations of Natural Religion, and the Truth and Certainty of the Christian Revelation: The Boyle Lectures 1705*; Price, *A Review of the Principal Questions in Morals*; Prichard, *Moral Obligation and Duty and Interest: Essays and Lectures by H. A. Prichard*; Moore, *Principia Ethica*; and Ross, *The Right and the Good*.

work of some contemporary moral realists, including Thomas Nagel.[10]

(3) I call the third view "Reflective Endorsement." This view is favored by philosophers who believe that morality is grounded in human nature. The philosopher's first job is to explain what the source of morality in human nature is, why we use moral concepts and feel ourselves bound by them. When an explanation of our moral nature is in hand, we can then raise the normative question: all things considered, do we have reason to accept the claims of our moral nature or should we reject them? The question is not "are these claims true?" as it is for the realist. The reasons sought here are practical reasons; the idea is to show that morality is good for us. Arguments with this structure can be found in the tradition in the work of Francis Hutcheson, David Hume, and John Stuart Mill, and in contemporary philosophy in the work of Bernard Williams.[11]

(4) The Appeal to Autonomy. This kind of argument is found in Immanuel Kant and contemporary Kantian constructivists, especially John Rawls.[12] Kantians believe that the source of the normativity of moral claims must be found in the agent's own will, in particular in the fact that the laws of morality are the laws of the agent's own will and that its claims are ones she is prepared to make on herself. The capacity for self-conscious reflection about

---

[10] In *The Possibility of Altruism* and *The View from Nowhere*. But see note 44 below.

[11] See Hutcheson, *Inquiry concerning the Original of our Ideas of Beauty and Virtue* and *Illustrations on the Moral Sense*; Hume, *A Treatise of Human Nature* and *Enquiry concerning the Principles of Morals*; Mill, *Utilitarianism*; and Williams, *Ethics and the Limits of Philosophy*. More specific references for Hutcheson, Hume, and Williams will be found in Lecture 2. Mill's argument appears in chapter 3, "Of the Ultimate Sanction of the Principle of Utility."

[12] See Kant, *Foundations of the Metaphysics of Morals* and *Critique of Practical Reason*; Rawls, *A Theory of Justice* and "Kantian Constructivism in Moral Theory: The Dewey Lectures 1980."

our own actions confers on us a kind of authority over ourselves, and it is this authority that gives normativity to moral claims.

During the modern period, each of these accounts of normativity developed in response to the prior one, sometimes as a result of criticism, more often when the implications of the earlier view were pressed a little harder. In this lecture and the next one I am going to describe this historical process, comparing earlier versions of these accounts with those on the contemporary scene. The Kantian account was the culmination of this historical development. In the third lecture I will present an updated version of that account that I believe to be true.

In the rest of this lecture I will discuss the first two theories of normativity: voluntarism and moral realism.

Voluntarism

As I mentioned at the beginning of this lecture, Grotius asserted that human beings would have obligations even if God did not exist to give us laws. Because of that remark, he is often identified as the first *modern* moral philosopher.[13] But the credit for that should really go to Hobbes and Pufendorf. For they were the first to identify clearly the special challenge that the Modern Scientific World View presents to ethics and to try to construct ethical theories in the face of that challenge.

According to Pufendorf, the actions of human beings, like every other form of physical motion, are in themselves morally indifferent. Values are not found in the world of nature at all. Instead, Pufendorf says, intelligent beings must *impose* moral values on nature. He tells us that what he calls "moral entities" — values and obligations — are "superadded" to physical entities — such as actions — at "the will of intelligent entities."[14] Hobbes opens his most famous ethical treatise with the apparently unpromising reflection that since to be alive is simply to be a self-

[13] I owe this point to Schneewind. See Schneewind I, pp. 88–89.
[14] Pufendorf, *The Law of Nature and of Nations*, Schneewind I, p. 171.

moving object, we may as well say that watches and engines and other self-moving objects have an artificial life, and that we ourselves in turn are just a kind of machine.[15] And he proceeds to construct a completely mechanistic explanation of how human beings work and an ethics that is based upon it.

Their question is how nature, an indifferent and mechanical world of matter in motion, can come to be imbued with moral properties. Interestingly, both Pufendorf and Hobbes traced obligation ultimately to divine command, not because they hung on to a medieval or religious conception of the world, but rather because they had *adopted* the Modern Scientific World View. They believed that it *takes* God or a Godlike sovereign to impose moral properties on the indifferent world of nature. Pufendorf held that "since . . . moral necessity . . . and turpitude . . . are affections of human actions arising from their conformity or non-conformity to some norm or law, and law is the bidding of a superior, it does not appear that [they] . . . can be conceived to exist before law, and without the imposition of a superior."[16] And Hobbes of course maintained that there is no obligation until a sovereign capable of enforcing the "laws of nature" is in power. Obligation must come from law, and law from the will of a legislating sovereign; morality only comes into the world when laws are made.

Pufendorf and Hobbes shared two other views of which their critics sometimes failed to see the importance. First, voluntarism is often criticized on the ground that the sovereign can make anything right or wrong. And many theological voluntarists have held that that is true. But Pufendorf and Hobbes thought that the *content* of morality is given by reason independently of the legislative will. They agreed that good and evil, prudence and imprudence, and in a way even justice and injustice, are objectively identifiable attributes of states of affairs and of the actions that produce them. What is good is what is naturally beneficial to a person; what is

---

[15] Hobbes, *Leviathan*, introduction, p. 9.
[16] Pufendorf, *The Law of Nature and of Nations*, Schneewind I, p. 175.

right and just is what makes harmonious social life possible. So no legislator is needed to give content, at least in a general way, to the ideas of the good and the right. Most human beings in most circumstances have reason to want what is good and, at least as a group, to do what is right, independently of law or obligation. But in the absence of God, Pufendorf wrote, the precepts of morality might "be observed for their utility, like the prescriptions doctors give to regulate health" but ". . . would not be *laws*." [17] And Hobbes, after laying out his laws of nature, says: "These dictates of Reason, men use to call by the name of Lawes; but improperly: for they are but Conclusions, or Theorems concerning what conduceth to the conservation and defence of themselves; whereas Law, properly is the word of him that by right hath command over others." [18] So the role of the legislator is to make what is *in any case* a good idea into *law*.

Second, both Pufendorf and Hobbes believed that no one could be a legislator without the power to impose sanctions to enforce his law. And it is frequently inferred that the point of these sanctions is to provide the subjects of the law with motives to obey it. Actually, however, both of these philosophers thought that morally good action is action that proceeds from what we would now call the motive of duty.[19] Morally good actions are done from what Pufendorf calls an "intrinsic motive" rather than from interest or fear.[20] Pufendorf says that this marks the difference between obligation and compulsion; and Hobbes, similarly, that it marks the difference between mere counsel and command.[21] A just man, as

[17] Pufendorf, *On the Duty of Man and Citizen*, p. 36.

[18] Hobbes, *Leviathan*, I.15, p. 111.

[19] While Pufendorf is almost ignored by contemporary moral philosophers, there is a great deal of controversy about Hobbes's views on moral motivation and obligation and susbtantial recent literature on the topic. For references, see Tuck's Introduction to *Leviathan*, p. xliii. While a complete defense of the view I set forward here would require taking on the issues raised by that controversy, this is not the place for that.

[20] Pufendorf, *On the Law of Nature and of Nations*, Schneewind I, p. 180.

[21] Ibid.; Hobbes, *Leviathan*, II.25, pp. 176–79.

Hobbes put it, is one whose will is "framed" by justice, not by fear or benefit to himself.[22] One does the right thing because it is the right thing, because it is the law, and for no other reason.

Why, then, are sanctions needed? The answer is that they are necessary to establish the authority of the legislator. Pufendorf and Hobbes thought that the legislator's power to enforce the law is necessary to give moral commands the special force of *requirement*. A homely example will illustrate their point. Suppose you are a student in my department. Then my colleagues and I are in a position to require you to take a course in logic. We are in this position because we have authority over you, and we have authority over you in part because we can impose a sanction on you. If you refuse to take the logic course, you will not get a degree from us. Now I want you to notice several things about this. First of all, the scenario does not in the least imply that our decision to make you study logic is arbitrary. It may be a very good idea for philosophy students to study logic, and that may be why we require it. If we are good at our jobs and worthy of our authority, we will have some such reason. In a similar way the laws that God or the Hobbesian sovereign requires us to obey are precepts of reason, determined independently of any arbitrary legislative will. Yet it is not merely their reasonableness that obligates us to obey them, just as it is not merely the benefit of studying logic that obligates students in my department to take the logic course. For if you are a philosophy student but are not in my department, I can give you all sorts of excellent reasons why you should take a course in logic, and you will not thereby be required to take one. And that is why authority requires a sanction.

Let me play out the analogy a moment longer. Suppose again that you are a student in my department and consider your motive for taking the logic course. There are three possibilities. First, you might take it because you grasp the reasons why we require it. You see that it is a good idea and you are moved by that fact.

[22] Hobbes, *Leviathan*, I.15, p. 104.

Second, even if you think the requirement arbitrary and unnecessary, you may take the course out of fear of being denied your degree — because of the sanction. Or, third, you may take it simply because it is a required course. The important point is that the third motive is appropriate here. While you may very well grasp the reasons why we require the course, and it may even be true that for those reasons you would have taken it anyway, there is something a little odd about saying that this is your motive. Since it is required you would have to take it in any case. But there is no reason to suppose that therefore you only take it out of fear of being denied your degree, as it were cringingly. It's being a required course is, under the circumstances, itself a reason. This is the picture of obligation, and of what it is to act from the moral motive, that Hobbes and Pufendorf have in mind. And according to this picture neither moral obligation nor its proper and characteristic motive, the motive of duty, are possible unless there is a legislator backed by the power of sanctions who can lay down the law.

Let me sum up. Hobbes and Pufendorf believed that the content of morality is given by natural reason. What morality demands of us is what it is reasonable for us, at least as a group, to do. The rules of morality are the rules that make social life possible, and social life is necessary for human beings. Hobbes and Pufendorf clearly supposed that in many cases this consideration could be motivationally sufficient as well. Pufendorf, especially, says that in the absence of obligation we would still do what is right because it is useful. The legislator is not invoked to supply the content of morality or to explain why people are often motivated to do what is right. The legislator is necessary to make *obligation* possible, that is, to make morality normative.

Realism

Samuel Clarke, the first defender of realism, was quick to spot what he took to be a fatal flaw in the view I have just described.

Hobbes, Clarke complains, tries to derive obligation from the social contract, from our agreement to obey the laws of a sovereign who will make social cooperation possible. But why are we obligated to conform to the social contract? Clarke says: "To make these *compacts* obligatory [Hobbes] is forced . . . to recur to an antecedent *law of nature*: and this destroys all that he had before said. For the same law of nature which obliges men to *fidelity*, *after* having made a compact; will unavoidably, upon all the same accounts, be found to oblige them, *before* all compacts, to *contentment* and mutual *benevolence* . . ."[23] If the need to establish a cooperative system can obligate us to conform to a social contract, why doesn't that same need obligate us to behave ourselves in cooperative ways in the first place? Or, if we say obligation comes from the fact that the laws have been made by the sovereign, then what are we to say about why we are obligated to obey the sovereign? Again Clarke complains that "compacts ought to be faithfully performed, and obedience to be duly paid to civil powers: the obligation *these things* [Hobbes] is forced to deduce entirely from the internal reason and fitness of the things themselves..."[24]

Pufendorf tries to *explain* why we are obligated to obey the sovereign, by defining a notion of legitimate authority. He stipulates that the superior who is able to obligate us must have these two attributes: "not only the strength to inflict some injury upon the recalcitrant but also just cause to require us to curtail the liberty of our will at his discretion."[25] He goes on to explain that another has the right to claim our obedience if he has conferred exceptional benefits on us; or if he is able to look out for us much better than we can look out for ourselves; or of course if we have contracted to obey him. So the authority of the legislator springs not only from his power to impose sanctions, but also from our

---

[23] Clarke, *A Discourse concerning the Unchangeable Obligations of Natural Religion,* Raphael I, p. 219.

[24] Ibid., p. 221.

[25] Pufendorf, *On the Duty of Man and Citizen,* p. 28.

gratitude for his benefits or from his benevolent wisdom or from our own contractual acts. But the difficulty with this solution is obvious. If we have no antecedent obligation to be grateful to benefactors, or to submit to the guidance of benevolent wisdom, or to honor our agreements, how can these things confer legitimate authority on the legislator? And if we do have a natural obligation to these things, then why may we not have other natural obligations as well? The very notion of a legitimate authority is already a normative one and cannot be used to answer the normative question.

Hobbes has a way of avoiding this last problem, but it is at a serious cost. He says flatly that God's authority does not depend on our gratitude or on His graciousness, but simply on His irresistible power.[26] And he concludes that this is true of the authority of the political sovereign as well. But this gives rise to a problem. The sovereign's authority now consists entirely in his ability to punish us. Although sanctions are not our motive for obedience, they are the source of the sovereign's authority and so of our obligations. I am obligated to do what is right only because the sovereign can punish me if I do not. Well, suppose I commit a crime and I get away with it. Then the sovereign was not able to punish me. And if my obligation sprang from his ability to punish me, then I had no obligation. So a crime I get away with is no crime at all. If irresistible power is just power unsuccessfully resisted, then authority is nothing more than the successful exercise of power, and things always turn out right. For no one can ever do what he lacks the power to do.[27]

The problem here is a general one, which applies to any attempt to derive normativity from a natural source of power. Suppose the authority of obligation derives from the power of our

[26] Hobbes, *Leviathan*, II.31, p. 246.

[27] Strictly speaking, crime is still possible. If the sovereign catches me and punishes me, then I did something wrong. But wrongdoing is always punished, for if it is not, then it was not wrongdoing after all. So although not everything that happens is right, in one sense everything turns out all right.

sympathetic motives. Then if you lack sympathetic motives, you lack obligations. Your obligations vary along with your motives, and so you can do no wrong. Suppose, as Hume sometimes seemed to think, that the authority of our reasons for action must be derived from the strength of our desires. Then you will always do what you have reason to do, and you can do no wrong. As Joseph Butler would later point out, this sort of argument shows that authority cannot be reduced to any kind of power. And the relation in which moral claims stand to us is a relation of authority, not one of power.[28]

So we are faced with a dilemma. If we try to derive the authority of morality from some natural source of power, it will evaporate in our hands. If we try to derive it from some supposedly normative consideration, such as gratitude or contract, we must in turn explain why that consideration is normative, or where its authority comes from. Either its authority comes from morality, in which case we have argued in a circle, or it comes from something else, in which case the question arises again, and we are faced with an infinite regress.

The realist's response is to dig in his heels. The notion of normativity or authority is an irreducible one. It is a mistake to try to explain it. Obligation is simply there, part of the nature of things. We must suppose certain actions to be obligatory in themselves if anything is. According to Clarke, it is a fact about certain actions that they are *fit to be done*. Richard Price argues that unless we may say that some actions are *in themselves* right or wrong it is impossible that we should have any obligations; and in turn that if some actions *are* intrinsically right or wrong it is senseless to ask why we are obligated to do or avoid them.[29] Because of these views, Clarke and Price were primarily polemical writers.

---

[28] See Butler, "Upon Human Nature," Sermon 2 of the *Fifteen Sermons Preached at the Rolls Chapel* and of the *Five Sermons*, pp. 39–40.

[29] These positions are defended throughout in Clarke, *A Discourse concerning the Unchangeable Obligations of Natural Religion*; and Price, *A Review of the Principal Questions in Morals*.

They could not prove that obligation was real and instead devoted their efforts to rebutting what they took to be skeptical attacks.

Early twentieth-century rational intuitionism, represented by the work of Prichard, Ross, and Moore, follows a similar pattern. It is clearest in Prichard's classic essays: "Does Moral Philosophy Rest on a Mistake?" and "Duty and Interest." Prichard argues that it makes no sense to ask why you should be moral. If I give you a moral reason — such as, "it is your duty" — then my answer is circular, since it assumes you should be moral. If I give you a self-interested reason — such as, "it will make you happy" — then my answer is irrelevant. That is not the reason why you should be moral; you should be moral because it is your duty. If a question admits only of answers that are either circular or irrelevant then it must be a mistake to ask it. And if that is the question of moral philosophy, Prichard thinks, then moral philosophy rests on a mistake. Obligations just exist, and nobody needs to prove it.

As these arguments show, realism is a metaphysical position in the exact sense criticized by Kant. We can keep asking why: "Why must I do what is right?" — "Because it is commanded by God" — "But why must I do what is commanded by God?" — and so on, in a way that apparently can go on forever. This is what Kant called a search for the unconditioned — in this case, for something that will bring the question "Why must I?" to an end. The unconditional answer must be one that makes it impossible, unnecessary, or incoherent to ask why again. The realist move is to bring this regress to an end by fiat: he declares that some things are *intrinsically* normative. Prichard joins Clarke and Price in asserting this about obligatory actions, while Moore thinks there are intrinsically good states of affairs.[30] The very nature of these intrinsically normative entities is supposed to forbid further questioning. Having discovered that he needs an unconditional answer, the realist straightaway concludes that he has found one.

[30] See Moore, *Principia Ethica*, and also "The Conception of Intrinsic Value."

A comparison will help to show why this is metaphysical. Consider the cosmological argument for the existence of God, which purports to prove God's existence by proving that there must be a necessarily existent being. It runs this way: Somewhere there must be an Entity whose existence is necessary in itself. For if an Entity is contingent, it can either exist or not exist. How then can we explain its existence? Well, some other Entity must have brought it into being, have made it exist. What then about this other Entity? Is it necessary or contingent? And if it is contingent then what in turn made it exist? In this way we generate a regress, which can only be brought to an end if some Entity exists necessarily, that is, if there is some Entity about which it is impossible, unnecessary, or incoherent to ask why It exists. So there must be such an Entity, and that is God.

As Hume pointed out in his *Dialogues concerning Natural Religion*, there are two problems here.[31] First of all, so far as the argument goes, *anything* could be the necessary being. It could be matter, or the universe, or the sun. In placing the necessity in God, the cosmologist has simply placed it where he wanted to find it. And second, unless you assume that even contingent beings must in some sense be necessary — that is, that there must be an explanation that shows that they must have existed — the argument cannot even get started.[32]

Moral realism is like that. Having discovered that obligation cannot exist unless there are actions that it is necessary to do, the realist concludes that there must be such actions and that they are the very ones that we have always thought were necessary, the

---

[31] Hume, *The Dialogues concerning Natural Religion*, part IX.

[32] It may not be obvious that Hume makes this second argument, but it is implied by one he does make. Hume has Cleanthes say, "In such a chain too, or succession of objects, each part is caused by that which preceded it, and causes that which succeeds it. Where then is the difficulty?" (p. 190). That of course amounts to a denial that the items in the "chain" need be in any sense necessary. It is worth noting that the cosmologist Cleanthes explicitly quotes in the course of his criticism is Samuel Clarke.

traditional moral duties. And the same two problems exist. The realist like the cosmologist places the necessity where he wanted to find it. And the argument cannot even get started, unless you assume that there are some actions that are necessary to do.

But when the normative question is raised, these are the exact points that are in contention — whether there is really *anything* I must do, and if so whether it is *this*. So it is a little hard to see how realism can help.

Yet realism is seen by many as the only hope for ethics, the only option to skepticism, relativism, subjectivism, and all the various ways of thinking that the subject is hopeless. There are, I think, two reasons for this. One is clear from the arguments that I have just reviewed. It can look as if granting the existence of intrinsically normative entities is the only way to bring the endless question "why" to an end and still save obligation. The other is based on a confusion. Realism may be defined in a way that makes it look like the *logical* opposite of skepticism — say, for instance, as the existence of moral truth. But considered as a substantive position, realism actually involves more than that.

Let me explain. There is a trivial sense in which everyone who thinks that ethics isn't hopeless is a realist. I will call this *procedural* moral realism, and I will contrast it to what I will call *substantive* moral realism. Procedural moral realism is the view that there are answers to moral questions; that is, that there are right and wrong ways to answer them. Substantive moral realism is the view that there are answers to moral questions *because* there are moral facts or truths, which those moral questions ask *about*.

To see the difference, it helps to consider normative realism more generally. The procedural normative realist thinks that when we ask practical questions like "What must I do?" or "What is best in this case?" or "How should I live?" there are correct and incorrect things to say. This is not just a view about morality. Suppose the correct answer to the question "How should I live?" is "Just as you like." Then people deluded by duty who don't live as they like would be making a *mistake*. The view that there is *no* normative truth about action is the view that it is impossible to fail to do what you have reason to do, or should do, or ought to do: it is the view, more or less, that it doesn't matter what you do. Procedural realism isn't completely trivial, for it does have an opposite, but that opposite is a kind of nihilism. The denial of procedural normative realism says that there is no ought, should, must, or reason at all.

But procedural realism does not require the existence of intrinsically normative entities, either for morality or for any other kind of normative claim. It is consistent with the view that moral conclusions are the dictates of practical reason, or the projections of human sentiments, or the results of some constructive procedure like the argument from John Rawls's original position.[33] As long as there is some correct or best procedure for answering moral questions, there is some way of applying the concepts of the right and the good. And as long as there is some way of applying the concepts of the right and the good, we will have moral and more generally normative truth. Statements employing moral concepts will be true when those concepts are applied correctly.

Perhaps an example will help here. Most people suppose that the means/end relation is normative, in the sense that the fact that a certain action is a means to your end provides you with a reason to do it. Very few people have ever supposed that this requires an adjustment in the metaphysics of the Modern Scientific World View, say, by the introduction of intrinsically normative entities into our ontology. But how then do we establish that this relation is normative? One plausible answer comes from Kant. Kant tells us that the means/end relation is normative because of a principle of practical reason that he calls the hypothetical imperative. The hypothetical imperative tells us that if we will an end, we have a

---

[33] See *A Theory of Justice*, part I. Rawls characterizes his conception of justice as a "Kantian constructivist" one in "Kantian Constructivism in Moral Theory: The Dewey Lectures 1980."

reason to will the means to that end. This imperative, in turn, is not based on the recognition of a normative fact or truth, but simply on the nature of the will. To will an end, rather than just wishing for it or wanting it, is to set yourself to be its cause. And to set yourself to be its cause is to set yourself to take the available means to get it.[34] So the argument goes from the nature of the rational will to a principle that describes a procedure according to which such a will must operate, and from there to an application of that principle that yields a conclusion about what one has a reason to do. And Kant of course thought that in a similar way moral principles could be shown to be principles of practical reasoning that are based on the nature of the will and yield conclusions about what we ought to do. There are then facts, moral truths, about what we ought to do, but that is not because the actions are intrinsically normative. They inherit their normativity from principles that spring from the nature of the will — the principles of practical reasoning.

What distinguishes substantive from procedural realism is a view about the relationship between the answers to moral questions and our procedures for arriving at those answers. The procedural moral realist thinks that there are answers to moral questions *because* there are correct procedures for arriving at them. But the substantive moral realist thinks that there are correct procedures for answering moral questions *because* there are moral truths or facts that exist independently of those procedures, which those procedures track.[35] Substantive realism conceives the procedures for answering normative questions as ways of *finding out* about a certain part of the world, the normative part. To that extent, substantive moral realism is distinguished not by its view about what kind of truths there are, but by its view of what kind

[34] *Foundations of the Metaphysics of Morals*, pp. 414–17; in Beck's translation, pp. 31–35.

[35] Substantive realism is a version of procedural realism, of course; what distinguishes it is its account of *why* there is a correct procedure for answering moral questions.

of subject ethics is. It conceives ethics as a branch of knowledge: knowledge of the normative part of the world.

Substantive moral realism has been criticized in many ways. It has been argued that we have no reason to believe in intrinsically normative entities or objective values. They are not harmonious with the Modern Scientific World View, nor are they needed for giving scientific explanations. Since the time of Hume and Hutcheson, it has been argued that there is no reason why such entities should motivate us, disconnected as they are from our natural sources of motivation. Many of these criticisms have been summed up in John Mackie's famous "Argument from Queerness." Here it is in Mackie's own words:

> If there were objective values, then they would be entities or qualities or relations of a very strange sort, utterly different from anything else in the universe. Correspondingly, if we were aware of them, it would have to be by some special faculty of moral perception or intuition, utterly different from our ordinary ways of knowing everything else. . . .
>
> Plato's Forms give a dramatic picture of what objective values would have to be. The Form of the Good is such that knowledge of it provides the knower with both a direction and an overriding motive; something's being good both tells the person who knows this to pursue it and makes him pursue it. An objective good would be sought by anyone who was acquainted with it, not because of any contingent fact that this person, or every person, is so constituted that he desires this end, but just because the end has to-be-pursuedness somehow built into it. Similarly, if there were objective principles of right and wrong, any wrong (possible) course of action would have not-to-be-doneness somehow built into it.[36]

And nothing, Mackie suggests, could be like that.

Of course Mackie doesn't really prove that such entities couldn't exist. But he does have a point, although I think it is not the point

[36] J. L. Mackie, *Ethics: Inventing Right and Wrong*, pp. 38 and 40.

he meant to make. If someone falls into doubt about whether obligations really exist, it doesn't help to say, "Ah, but indeed they do. They are *real* things." To see this, imagine a case where morality requires you to face death rather than do a certain action. You ask the normative question: you want to know whether this terrible claim on you is justified. Is it really true that this is what you must do? The realist's answer to this question is simply "Yes." That is, *all* he can say is that it is *true* that this is what you ought to do. This is of course especially troublesome when the rightness of the action is supposed to be self-evident and known through intuition, so that there is nothing more to say about it. If the realist is not an intuitionist he can go back and get you to review the reasons why the action is required. Prichard says explicitly that it is only because people sometimes need to do this before they can see the necessity of an action that the question "Why should I be moral?" appears to make sense when actually it does not.[37] So we need to remind ourselves that the action promotes pleasure, or is called for by a universalizability criterion, or fosters social life. But this answer appears to be off the mark. It addresses someone who has fallen into doubt about whether the action is really required by morality, not someone who has fallen into doubt about whether moral requirements are really normative.

Now, to be fair to Prichard, it is clear from his essays that he takes words like "right" and "obligatory" to imply normativity by definition. These terms, as he sees it, are normatively loaded, so that it is incorrect to *say* that an action is right or obligatory unless we are already sure that we really have to do it. In one sense, that's fine: it is six of one, half a dozen of the other, whether we ask, "Is this action really obligatory?" or "Is this obligation really normative?" If we take obligation to imply normativity, then the first question is the same as the second. The trouble with Prichard's way of talking about these matters is more a heuristic one. The question "Is this action really obligatory?" can be understood as

[37] See Prichard, "Does Moral Philosophy Rest on a Mistake?" p. 8.

a question about whether moral concepts have been applied correctly in this case — whether, for instance, the requirement can really be derived from the categorical imperative or the principle of utility or some other moral principle. And that is a different question from the question how this obligation or any obligation can be normative. Prichard's way of approaching the matter therefore leads us to confuse the question of correct application with the question of normativity. And this actually happened to Prichard himself. For it led him to think that once we have settled the question of correct application, there can be nothing more to say about the normative question.[38]

And that is the problem with realism: it refuses to answer the normative question. It is a way of saying that it cannot be done. Or rather, more commonly, it is a way of saying that it need not be done. For of course if I *do* feel confident that certain actions really are required of me, I might *therefore* be prepared to believe that those actions are intrinsically obligatory or objectively valuable, that just is a property they have. Just listen to what Samuel Clarke says: "These things are so notoriously plain and self-evident, that nothing but the extremest stupidity of mind, corruption of manners, or perverseness of spirit, can possibly make any man entertain the least doubt concerning them." [39] Well, obviously *he* isn't worried. But suppose you are? Perhaps his confidence will make you take heart, but it is hard to see how else this could help.

The difficulty here is plain. The metaphysical view that intrinsically normative entities or properties exist must be *supported by* our confidence that we really do have obligations. It is because we are confident that obligation is real that we are prepared to believe in the existence of some sort of objective values. But for that very reason the appeal to objective values cannot be used to

---

[38] See Lecture 2, note 30, for discussion of a parallel problem in Prichard's attitude toward skepticism about belief. The point is perhaps even clearer in that case.

[39] Clarke, *A Discourse concerning the Unchangeable Obligations of Natural Religion*, Raphael I, p. 194; Schneewind I, p. 296.

support our confidence. And the normative question arises when our confidence has been shaken, whether by philosophy or by the exigencies of life. So realism cannot answer the normative question.

Some contemporary realists, such as Thomas Nagel, have argued that realism need not commit us to the existence of curious metaphysical objects like Plato's Forms or Moore's nonnatural intrinsic values. According to Nagel, we need only determine whether certain natural human interests, like our interest in having pleasure and avoiding pain, have the normative character that they appear to us to have. The point is not to look for some sort of specially normative *object*, but to look *more objectively* at the apparently normative considerations that present themselves in experience. That you are, say, in pain, *seems* like a reason to change your situation; the question is whether it is one.[40] Utilitarianism itself can be seen as a naturalistic form of realism, and versions of it have been defended as such by contemporary realists like David Brink and Peter Railton.[41] Contemporary realists argue that there is no need to make the right and the good into mysterious entities. Nothing seems more obviously normative than pleasures and pains, or desires and aversions, or our natural interests. So the realist need not assume, as Mackie supposes, that believing in objective values is believing in some sort of peculiar entities. We need only believe that reasons themselves exist.[42]

But if we take Mackie's point in the way that I have suggested, this leaves the problem in place. For how do we determine that these reasons exist? Like his rationalist predecessors, Nagel asserts that all we can do is rebut the skeptical arguments against the reality of reasons and values. Once we have done that, there is no special reason to doubt they exist.[43] And then when you see some-

---

[40] Nagel, *The View from Nowhere*, p. 157.

[41] Brink, *Moral Realism and the Foundations of Ethics*, especially chapter 8; and Railton, "Moral Realism," pp. 189ff.

[42] Nagel, *The View from Nowhere*, p. 144.

[43] Ibid., pp. 143–44. Nagel says: "It is very difficult to argue for such a possibility [the reality of values], except by refuting arguments against it" (p. 143).

thing that appears to be a reason, such as, say, your desire to avoid pain, the best explanation of this appearance is that that's what it is — it's a reason.[44]

And there's nothing wrong with that. But it is an expression of confidence and nothing more. Just listen to what Thomas Nagel says: "In arguing for this claim, I am somewhat handicapped by the fact that I find it self-evident."[45] Nagel's manners are better than Samuel Clarke's, but his predicament is the same. He isn't worried.

Now I'd like to pause for a moment and say something that I hope will be helpful about why the normative question slips so easily through our fingers. Earlier I said that in a sense Prichard *is* asking the normative question. For him "obligation" is a normatively loaded word. If "obligation" is a normatively loaded word, then the normative question is whether certain actions are really obligatory. If "reason" is the normatively loaded word, as Nagel thinks, then the normative question is whether obligations give us reasons, or more generally whether we have any moral reasons. If "objective" is a normatively loaded word, as Mackie seems to

---

[44] Ibid., p. 141. He actually says: "The method is to begin with the reasons that appear to obtain from my own point of view and those of other individuals; and ask what the best perspectiveless account of those reasons is." Because Nagel believes in the existence of reasons, rather than Forms or Non-Natural properties, it would be easy to suppose that he is only what I have here called a "procedural realist." Actually the issue is a bit complicated. I categorize him here as a substantive realist because he seems to believe, as the passage quoted shows, that our relation to reasons is one of seeing or knowing that they are there. As I have just argued, there is a way in which this view of ethics as an epistemological subject is the essential characteristic of substantive realism. But in §II of my paper "The Reasons We Can Share: An Attack on the Distinction between Agent-Relative and Agent-Neutral Values" I argue that it is *possible* to understand the projects Nagel prosecutes in both *The Possibility of Altruism* and *The View from Nowhere* as constructivist projects and that Nagel himself wavers between that way and a realist way of construing his own work. If we read Nagel as a constructivist then he is only a procedural realist.

[45] Nagel, *The View from Nowhere*, pp. 159–60. Actually he says this about the idea that pain and pleasure provide "agent-neutral" rather than "agent-relative" reasons. But he says things pretty much like this about whether reasons exist at all. For instance on p. 157 he says that if there is no special reason to doubt the existence of reasons then denying that pain provides a reason to change your situation "seems meaningless."

think, then the normative question is whether obligations are objective, and so on.

Discussions of normativity often founder because of unexamined assumptions about the normatively loaded word. There are two problems here. First, philosophers making different assumptions about which is the normatively loaded word may fail to understand each other. The second and perhaps more serious problem is that all of the ways of formulating the normative question that I have just mentioned suffer from the fact that they are readily confused with different questions. As I pointed out in my discussion of Prichard, the question whether the action is "really obligatory" can be confused with the question whether the moral concept really applies. In a similar way, the question whether an obligation really provides a reason can be confused with the question whether it provides an adequate motive. Again, the question whether the obligation is *objective* can be confused with the question whether the moral concept is one whose application is determinate or sufficiently "world-guided." In all of these cases, the philosopher is led to think that settling the other question, whatever it is, is a way of settling the normative question. And in all of these cases it is not.

Part of what I have tried to do in this lecture is to raise the normative question in a way that is independent of our more ordinary normative concepts and words. No doubt this has sometimes been confusing as I have tried to describe and compare the views of philosophers who use different terms to imply normativity. The point is not that I think that there is no normatively loaded word. Of course we will have to use some words to imply normativity, but we can choose any of the above ways of talking or others. All that matters there is that we agree, so that we will understand each other. But the interesting question is not how we decide to talk about the issue. The interesting question is why there should be such an issue: that is, why human beings need normative concepts and words. And substantive realism — to get back now to my argument — is not merely the view that "obligation" (as Prichard thinks) or "good" (as Moore thinks) or "reason" (as Nagel thinks) are normative words that we know how to apply correctly. It is a view — and a false one — about why human beings have normative words.

What is really wrong with substantive realism is its view about the source of normativity. Why do we use normative concepts like good, right, reason, obligation? According to the substantive realist, it is because we grasp that there are things that have normative properties. Some things *appear* normative, and there is no reason to doubt that they are what they seem. We have normative concepts because we've spotted some normative entities, as it were wafting by.

According to substantive realism, then, ethics is really a theoretical or epistemological subject. When we ask ethical questions, or normative questions generally, there is something about the world that we are trying to find out. The world contains a realm of inherently normative entities, whose existence we have noticed, and the business of ethics, or of practical philosophy more generally, is to investigate them further, to learn about them in a more systematic way. But isn't ethics supposed to be a practical subject, a guide to action? Well, the realist will grant that the eventual point is to apply all this knowledge in practice. Look at the result of that view: according to the substantive realist, the moral life is the most sublime feat of technical engineering, the application of theoretical knowledge to the solution of human problems. And in general human life and action consist in the application of theories, theories about what is good. Now that is surely wrong.

I've just been criticizing moral realism for asserting that we have moral concepts because we have noticed some moral entities in the universe. There's another argument on the contemporary scene that makes what looks like a similar criticism, but takes this criticism as a reason for moral skepticism. Since I am not arguing for skepticism, I want to say something about that. This other argument is that we have no reason to believe in the existence of moral entities or facts, because we do not need to assume the existence of such entities or facts in order to explain the moral phenomena. We need to assume that physical entities and facts exist in order to explain our observations of and beliefs about the "external world," but we do not need to assume that moral facts or entities exist in order to explain our moral beliefs and motives. Explanations of those can proceed in entirely psychological terms. So, the argument suggests, the best explanation of why I see a rock is that there is one. But the best explanation of why I disapprove of killing is that I was brought up in a certain way.[46]

A more carefully formulated version of this argument has some force against substantive moral realism, and this is a point I will come back to. But I want to start by saying what I think is wrong with this argument. As it is stated, this argument looks as if it should work against *any* form of normative realism. It should have just as much force against the existence of *theoretical* normative truth (that x is a reason to *believe* y) as it does against *practical* normative truth (that x is a reason to *do* y). We can after all explain the occurrence of people's beliefs merely in terms of the causes of those beliefs and leave their reasons out of it. Even if people's beliefs are caused by their thoughts about what reasons they have, we can explain the beliefs simply as caused by those thoughts. This does not commit us to saying that the reasons that appear in the contents of those thoughts are real. I may tell the truth because I think lying wrong, but in order to explain my honesty you need not suppose that my reason is real. It is enough that I think so. In the same way, I think that I am mortal because I am human, but in order to explain why I believe I am mortal you need not suppose that my reason is real. Again it is enough that I think so. So we don't need to assume that theoretical reasons exist in order to explain the occurrence of beliefs.[47] But we

---

[46] The locus classicus is perhaps Gilbert Harman, *The Nature of Morality: An Introduction to Ethics*, chapter 1.

[47] Actually, however, there is a problem explaining how human beings could come to have the illusion that there are such things as theoretical and practical rea-

cannot coherently take that fact as a *reason* to doubt that there is any such thing as a reason for belief. For if there is no such thing as a reason for belief, there is *ipso facto* no reason for believing this argument. And — to echo Clarke himself — if instead we admit that there are reasons for belief, then why not admit that there are reasons for action as well?

The trouble with drawing skeptical conclusions from the fact that a belief in normative truth is not needed to explain what people think or do is that it assumes that explanation and description of the phenomena is the sole or primary function of human concepts. That amounts to supposing that the business of human life is the construction and application of theories. And the reason the argument has some force against substantive realism is that substantive realism implicitly shares that assumption. The substantive realist assumes we have normative concepts because we are aware that the world contains normative phenomena, and we are inspired by that awareness to construct theories about them.

But that is not why we have normative concepts. The very enterprise we are engaged in right now shows why we have those: it is because we have to figure out what to believe and what to do. Normative concepts exist because human beings have normative problems. And we have normative problems because we are self-conscious rational animals, capable of reflection about what we ought to believe and to do. That is why the normative question can be raised in the first place: because even when we are inclined to believe that something is right and to some extent feel ourselves moved to do it we can still *always* ask: "But is this really true?" and "Must I really do this?"

Normative concepts like right, good, obligation, and reason are our names for the solutions to normative problems, for what it is we are looking for when we face them. And if we sometimes succeed in solving those problems, then there will be normative

---

sons if no such things exist at all. But the reason why we have the concept of a "reason" does not therefore have to be that we *notice* that they exist.

truths: that is, statements that employ normative concepts correctly. So it is true that the assumption of a realm of inherently normative entities or objective values is not needed to explain the existence of normative concepts or the resulting existence of a category of normative truths. It is not because we notice normative entities in the course of our experience, but because we are normative animals who can question our experience, that normative concepts exist.

Conclusion

Contemporary defenses of substantive moral realism almost always arise in the same way. They are always initiated by *somebody else*, a self-proclaimed spokesperson for the Modern Scientific World View. Armed with the distinction between facts and values, or brandishing Ockham's razor like a club, the spokesperson for the Modern Scientific World View declares that there cannot be ethical knowledge, that we can explain the moral phenomena without positing the existence of moral entities or facts, or that intrinsically normative entities are just too queer to exist. And the moral philosopher, frantic with the sense of impending loss, rushes to the defense of ethical knowledge. And nobody pauses to ask whether ethical knowledge, or indeed any sort of knowledge at all, is what we really want here in the first place.

Is the normative question a request for knowledge? To raise the normative question is to ask whether our more unreflective moral beliefs and motives can withstand the test of reflection. The Platonic realist thinks that we can answer that question by taking a closer look at the *objects* of our beliefs and motives, to discover whether they are really the True and the Good. Nagel thinks we should take a closer look at the beliefs and motives themselves, to discover whether they are really reasons. But no such *discovery* is ever made. The realist's belief in the existence of normative entities is not based on any discovery. It is based on his *confidence* that his beliefs and desires are indeed normative. But if confidence can support a metaphysics that in turn is supposed to support the claims of morality, why can't confidence support the claims of morality more directly?

In the next lecture I will examine the views of some philosophers who reject the idea that knowledge is what we need for normativity and put something more like confidence in its place. According to these philosophers, morality is not grounded in our apprehension of truths about objective values. It is grounded in human nature and certain natural human sentiments. The normative question is then whether it is good to have such a nature and to yield to its claims. Normativity will be established, not by knowledge, but by our own reflective endorsement of our moral nature.

Lecture II: Reflective Endorsement

Introduction

At the end of the last lecture I argued that normativity is a problem for human beings because of our reflective nature. Even if we are inclined to believe that an action is right and even if we are inclined to be motivated by that fact, it is always possible for us to call our beliefs and motives into question. This is why, after all, we seek a philosophical foundation for ethics in the first place: because we are afraid that the true explanation of why we have moral beliefs and motives might not be one that sustains them. Morality might not survive reflection.

The view I am going to describe in this lecture takes its starting point from that thought. It applies one of the best rules of philosophical methodology: that a clear statement of the problem is also a statement of the solution. If the problem is that morality might not survive reflection, then the solution is that it might. If we find upon reflecting on the true moral theory that we still are inclined to endorse the claims that morality makes on us, then morality will be normative. I call this way of establishing normativity the "reflective endorsement" method.

The reflective endorsement method has its natural home in theories that reject realism and ground morality in human nature. In the modern period it makes its first appearance in the work of the sentimentalists of the eighteenth century. They explicitly rejected the realism of the rationalists and argued that the moral value of actions and objects is a projection of human sentiments. As Hume famously says:

> Take any action allow'd to be vicious: Willful murder, for instance. Examine it in all lights, and see if you can find that matter of fact, or real existence, which you call vice. In whichever way you take it, you find only certain passions, motives, volitions and thoughts. There is no other matter of fact in the case. The vice entirely escapes you, as long as you consider the object. You can never find it, till you turn your reflexion into your own breast, and find a sentiment of disapprobation, which arises in you, towards this action. Here is a matter of fact; but 'tis the object of feeling, not of reason. It lies in yourself, not in the object.[1]

Strictly speaking, we do not disapprove the action because it is vicious; instead, it is vicious because we disapprove it. Since morality is grounded in human sentiments, the normative question cannot be whether its dictates are true. Instead, it is whether we have reason to be glad that we have such sentiments and to allow ourselves to be governed by them. The question is whether morality is a good thing for us.

Of course the sentimentalists were not the first to ground morality in human nature. Some of the classical Greek philosophers, in particular Aristotle, did so as well. So it is not surprising that the reflective endorsement method has reemerged in some recent moral thought of Aristotelian inspiration, namely that of Bernard Williams.[2] Like Hume, Williams rejects realism and defends in

---

[1] Hume, *Treatise of Human Nature*, III.1.i, p. 469.

[2] These remarks will naturally raise the question whether Aristotle himself used the reflective endorsement method. In chapter 3 Williams makes a good case for the

its place a theory that grounds morality in human dispositions. And like Hume, he finds that the answer to the normative question rests in whether those dispositions are ones we have reason to endorse.

My purpose in this lecture is to explain this method of establishing normativity in more detail and to defend it against certain natural objections that arise from the realist camp. My aim will not be to criticize this view. Instead, I will end by saying why I think the logical consequence of Hume and Williams's theory of normativity is the moral philosophy of Kant.

David Hume

The choice of Hume as the major traditional representative of a theory of normativity might seem perverse. The pose Hume strikes in his moral philosophy is that of the scientist, whose task is to explain the origin of moral ideas. In his essay "Of the Different Species of Philosophy," Hume firmly separates two different ways of treating moral philosophy, which we may call "theoretical" and "practical." Theoretical or "abstruse" philosophers regard human nature as a subject of speculation and are concerned to discover the principles that regulate our understanding, excite our sentiments, and cause us to approve and disapprove as we do.[3] Practical philosophers, by contrast, are interested in inciting us to good conduct. Their work, as Hume puts it, is to paint virtue in "amiable colors, borrowing all helps from poetry and eloquence, and treating their subject in an easy and obvious manner, and such as is best fitted to please the imagination and engage the affections."[4] Hume compares the theoretical philosopher to an anato-

---

claim that reflective endorsement is at least involved in Aristotle's method of justifying morality. (See below). But Aristotle's teleological conception of the world adds another element to his conception of normativity. In these lectures I am addressing modern methods of establishing normativity, so I have not discussed Aristotle's views directly. What I think about them will, however, become apparent in the course of Lecture III.

[3] Hume, *Enquiry concerning Human Understanding*, p. 6.
[4] Ibid., p. 5.

mist and the practical philosopher to a painter.[5] The business of the anatomist is to explain what causes us to approve of virtue; the business of the painter is to make virtue appealing. And Hume styles himself a theoretical philosopher: his aim is to reveal the elements of the mind's "anatomy" that make us approve and disapprove as we do.

The odd thing about this way of dividing up the philosophical enterprise is that the normative question seems to fall between the cracks. Neither the anatomist nor the painter seems to be interested in the *justification* of morality's claims. The theoretical philosopher is concerned only with providing a true explanation of the origin of moral concepts. The practical philosopher is a preacher or a Mandevillian politician. His task is to get people to behave themselves in socially useful ways, and he is prepared to use "all helps from poetry and eloquence." So we have explanation on the one hand and persuasion on the other, but no branch of moral philosophy that is concerned with justification.

It is not that Hume takes it for granted that morality's claims can be justified to the individual. He explicitly denies that the truth of his theoretical account depends at all on "its tendency to promote the interests of society." He thinks it is conceivable that knowledge of the true moral theory would undermine the commitment of individuals to moral conduct. Yet he also asserts that "a man has but a bad grace, who delivers a theory, however true, which . . . leads to a practice dangerous and pernicious." As he says: "The ingenuity of your researches may be admired, but your systems will be detested; and mankind will agree, if they cannot refute them, to sink them, at least, in eternal silence and oblivion. Truths which are *pernicious* to society, if any such there be, will yield to errors which are salutary and *advantageous*." But although he admits that this could happen, he thinks that it doesn't. Although he is not supposed to be a practical philosopher, Hume

---

[5] Ibid., pp. 9–10; *A Treatise of Human Nature*, III.iii.6, pp. 620–21. I owe a debt to Charlotte Brown for many useful discussions of this issue.

cannot resist pointing out that his account of the origin of moral ideas *does* make virtue attractive. According to his theory, he points out, virtue asks nothing of us but "gentleness, humanity, beneficence, and affability." And he urges: "She talks not of useless austerities and rigours, suffering and self-denial. She declares that her sole purpose is to make her votaries and all mankind, during every instant of their existence, if possible, cheerful and happy . . ." [6] So Hume thinks that his account of morality, though itself theoretical and abstruse, can be used by the practical philosopher to good effect.

One can, of course, take Hume to be saying merely that his theory is a gold mine for practical philosophers. But I think he has something more in mind. Normativity is not the provenance of either the theoretical or the practical philosopher because it will emerge, if it does emerge, in the way the two sides of philosophy interact. If the true account of our moral nature were one that made us want to reject its claims, then practical philosophers, as the guardians of social order, would have to make sure that the truth was not known. But if practical philosophers can get people to accept the claims of morality simply by telling them the truth about the nature of morality, then the claims of morality are *justified*. Hume is claiming that his theory is normative — or so I will now argue.

According to Hume, moral judgments are based on sentiments of approval and disapproval that we feel when we contemplate a person's character from what he calls "a general point of view."[7] Taking up the general point of view regulates our sentiments about a person in two ways. First, we view the person not through the eyes of our own interests, but instead through the eyes of our sympathy with the person herself and her friends, family, neighbors, and colleagues.[8] We are sympathetically pleased or pained

---

[6] All of the quotations in this paragraph are from Hume, *Enquiry concerning the Principles of Morals*, p. 279.

[7] Hume, *A Treatise of Human Nature*, III.3.i, pp. 581–82.

[8] Ibid., p. 582.

by the good or bad effects of her character on those with whom she usually associates, the people Hume calls her "narrow circle."[9] Second, we judge her characteristics according to the usual effects of such characteristics, rather than according to their actual effects in this or that case. As Hume puts it, we judge according to "general rules."[10]

These two regulative devices bring a kind of objectivity to our moral judgments. Judging in sympathy with the narrow circle and according to general rules, we are able to reach agreement, in the sense of a convergence of sentiments, about a person's character. We all approve and disapprove of the same characteristics, and as a result we come to share an ideal of good character. A person of good character, one whom we judge to have the virtues, is one who is useful and agreeable to herself and her friends. Since people love those who have useful and agreeable qualities, and since the perception of a lovable quality in ourselves causes pride, virtue is a natural cause of pride, and vice in the same way of humility. And since pride is a pleasing sentiment and humility a painful one, we have a natural desire to be proud of ourselves and to avoid the causes of humility. This gives us a natural desire to acquire the virtues and avoid the vices. The normative question, then, is whether we really have reason to yield to these desires and to try to be virtuous people.

I think this is the question Hume is raising in the last section of the *Enquiry concerning the Principles of Morals* when he says: "Having explained the moral *approbation* attending merit or virtue, there remains nothing but briefly to consider our interested *obligation* to it, and to inquire whether every man, who has any regard to his own happiness and welfare, will not find his account in the practice of every moral virtue."[11]

---

[9] Ibid., III.3.iii, p. 602.

[10] Ibid., III.3.i, p. 585.

[11] Hume, *Enquiry concerning the Principles of Morals*, p. 278.

Hume proceeds to detail the ways in which the practice of virtue contributes to the moral agent's happiness. His fourfold division of the virtues into qualities useful and agreeable to self and others enables him to do this in very short order. No argument is needed to defend the qualities that make you useful and agreeable to yourself, for those contribute to your happiness by definition. Almost as little is required to defend the qualities that make you *agreeable* to others, for we all want others to like and admire us. To defend the qualities that are *useful* to others, Hume borrows a famous argument from Joseph Butler.[12] In order to be happy, we must have some desires and interests whose fulfillment will bring us satisfaction. And other-directed desires and interests are just as good for this purpose as self-absorbed ones. Indeed, in many ways they are better. Hume reminds us that any desire, "when gratified by success, gives a satisfaction proportioned to its force and violence." But benevolent desires have the additional advantages that their "immediate feeling . . . is sweet, smooth, tender, and agreeable" and that they make others like us and make us pleased with ourselves.[13] To be a morally good person, then, is conducive to your happiness or at least not inconsistent with it.

Now it might be thought that this argument is not intended to show anything about the goodness of being subject to motives of moral *obligation* and that therefore it cannot show anything about the normativity of obligation. For according to Hume's account a *naturally* virtuous person is one who acts, not from the motive of duty or obligation, but simply from some natural motive, such as benevolence, that a spectator would approve. No reason why you are *obligated* to perform virtuous actions has been given by the argument or is required by it; you perform virtuous actions because you have natural motives to do so; and the argument has simply shown that this is a good way for you to be.

---

[12] Butler, "Upon the Love of Our Neighbor," sermon 11 of the *Fifteen Sermons Preached at the Rolls Chapel*; sermon 4 of the *Five Sermons*.

[13] Hume, *Enquiry concerning the Principles of Morals*, p. 282.

But this would not be correct. For first, Hume admits that in a case where a person is aware of lacking a virtuous moral motive, he "may hate himself upon that account, and may perform the action without the motive, from a certain sense of duty." [14] And second, it turns out that in the case of what Hume calls the *artificial* virtues such as justice, this sense of duty is the motive that is normally operative.[15] According to Hume, the first or natural motive for participating in a system of justice is self-interest. But this is not the usual motive for performing just *actions*, for just actions, taken singly, do not necessarily or even usually promote self-interest. What promotes self-interest is the existence of the *system* of justice. But the connection between individual just actions and the system is too "remote" to sustain interested motivation.[16] Instead, Hume argues, sympathy with the public interest causes us to disapprove of all unjust actions on account of their general tendency to bring down the system.[17] And this sympathy grounds a sense of duty that motivates us to avoid injustice. We avoid injustice because we would disapprove of ourselves — that is, we would feel humility — if we did not.

Furthermore, there are cases in which this sense of duty is the *only* available motive, for it can happen that an action, while it is of the type that tends to bring down the system of justice, will not in fact do that system any harm at all, and that the agent knows that. This is the plight of the famous "sensible knave" who poses the most difficult challenge to Hume's account of "interested obligation." The sensible knave, as Hume describes him, "may think that an act of iniquity or infidelity will make a considerable addition to his fortune, without causing any considerable breach in the social union and confederacy." [18] So why shouldn't he do it?

---

[14] Hume, *A Treatise of Human Nature*, III.2.i, p. 479.
[15] Ibid.
[16] Ibid., III.2.ii, p. 499.
[17] Ibid., pp. 499–500.
[18] Hume, *Enquiry concerning the Principles of Morals*, p. 282.

This is, of course, a version of the familiar free-rider problem. The sensible knave wants to know why he should not profit from injustice when it will not damage his interests by endangering the system of justice. And here is Hume's surprising answer:

> I must confess that, if a man think that this reasoning much requires an answer, it will be a little difficult to find any which will appear to him satisfactory and convincing. If his heart rebel not against such pernicious maxims, if he feel no reluctance to the thoughts of villainy or baseness, he has indeed lost a considerable motive to virtue; and we may expect that his practice will be answerable to his speculation.... Inward peace of mind, consciousness of integrity, a satisfactory review of our own conduct; these are circumstances, very requisite to happiness, and will be cherished and cultivated by every honest man, who feels the importance of them.[19]

There's an old joke about a child who's glad he doesn't like spinach, since then he'd eat it, and he hates the disgusting stuff. Hume appears at first sight to be giving us that sort of reason for being glad we don't like injustice. *Of course* integrity will be cherished by honest people who feel the importance of it. But the sensible knave is questioning exactly that importance. The fact that we disapprove of injustice and therefore of ourselves when we engage in it can hardly be offered as a reason for endorsing our own disapproval of injustice.

Actually, however, in Hume's theory it can. Hume's theory of sympathy allows him to argue that an individual is likely to experience humility when he acts unjustly regardless of whether or not he believes that there is good reason to disapprove of the unjust action in the case at hand. For it follows from Hume's account of sympathy that the sentiments of others are contagious to us. And their sentiments about ourselves, in particular, have a tendency to get under our skins. So the fact that *other people* will disapprove

[19] Ibid., p. 283.

and dislike the sensible knave will be sufficient to provide him with feelings of disapproval and dislike of himself. Of course a knave will try to keep his knavish actions secret. But unless he is very hardened indeed, even the knowledge that others *would* hate him if they knew what he is up to will be enough to produce humility and self-hatred when he acts unjustly. As Hume says:

> By continual and earnest pursuit of a character, a name, a reputation in the world, we bring our own deportment and conduct frequently in review, and consider how they appear in the eyes of those who approach and regard us. This constant habit of surveying ourselves as it were, in reflection, keeps alive all the sentiments of right and wrong, and begets, in noble natures, a certain reverence for themselves as well as others, which is the surest guardian of every virtue.[20]

So Hume's reply to the sensible knave is not circular. Morality provides a set of pleasures of its own, a set of pleasures that the knave loses out on. Because of sympathy, the sense that you are lovable and worthy in the eyes of others makes you lovable and worthy in your own. For the same reason, the sense that you are detestable in the eyes of others makes you detestable in your own. And morality provides these feelings regardless of whether you think that morality is justified or not. This fact enables Hume to add the familiar claim that virtue is its own reward to his list of the ways in which virtue promotes self-interest without any circularity at all. Together, all of these arguments establish what Hume calls our "interested obligation" to be moral.

The arguments I've just detailed give rise to two closely related criticisms, which issue from the realist camp. First, you might think that Hume is not giving an account of the normativity of morality, but simply an account of our motives to be moral, and one that falls afoul of Prichard's famous argument at that.[21] We

[20] Ibid., p. 276.
[21] For a discussion of Prichard's argument, see "Realism" in Lecture I.

should not practice virtue because it is in our interest, but rather for its own sake, so Hume's argument is irrelevant. But it is clear that Hume is not saying that we should perform *particular* virtuous or obligatory actions because it serves our own interest to do so. He is saying that it is in our interest to be *people who practice virtue for its own sake*. This is especially clear in the Butlerian argument used to defend the virtues that are useful to others. Neither the immediately agreeable sensations of benevolence nor its gratifications are available to anyone who is not genuinely and wholeheartedly concerned about others. The Butlerian argument is not meant to show that morality promotes some set of interests you already have, but rather that moral interests are good ones to have. What the argument establishes is the harmony of two potentially normative points of view, morality and self-interest.[22]

The second realist objection carries Prichard's worry to a higher level. This time the objector grants that Hume's argument is not offered to us as a wrongheaded theory of moral motivation, but rather as an attempt to establish normativity by showing that morality is good. But it says that even as such it fails. An argument that shows that virtue is good from the point of view of self-interest only shows that morality is extrinsically good or extrinsically normative. But what we need for normativity is to show that morality is intrinsically good or intrinsically normative. And now we come back to a thought familiar from our encounter with realism: that only something intrinsically normative can satisfy the demand for unconditional justification.

At this point it will help to turn to an earlier view Hume held about normativity. The arguments I have been detailing until now are for the most part from the *Enquiry concerning the Principles of Morals*. In *A Treatise of Human Nature*, Hume appealed to a

[22] The argument can therefore be seen as establishing what Rawls calls "congruence." See *A Theory of Justice*, p. 399. Rawls's own argument that justice is a good for the just person, in §86 of that work, is a congruence argument. On the use of congruence arguments among the eighteenth-century British Moralists, see Charlotte Brown, "Hume against the Selfish Schools and the Monkish Virtues."

more specific version of the reflective endorsement account, which I call "normativity as reflexivity." This view can help to answer the realist's worry.

Since Hume does not set this view out explicitly, I will start by explaining the grounds on which I attribute it to him. Book 1 of *A Treatise of Human Nature* ends in a mood of melancholy despair and skepticism, while book 3 concludes in a mood of triumphant affirmation. And this is because at the end of book 1 Hume finds that "the understanding, when it acts alone, and according to its most general principles, entirely subverts itself, and leaves not the lowest degree of evidence in any proposition, either in philosophy or common life."[23] Whereas at the end of book 3 Hume concludes that the moral sense "must certainly acquire new force, when reflecting on itself, it approves of those principles, from whence it is deriv'd, and finds nothing but what is great and good in its rise and origin."[24] The understanding, when it reflects on itself, falls into doubt about and so subverts itself. But the moral sense approves of and so reinforces itself. Therefore skepticism about the understanding is in order, but skepticism about morality is not.

These facts suggest that Hume is relying on an account of normativity that is completely general, applying to any kind of purportedly normative claim. Let me define two terms that will help express the view. Call a purportedly normative judgment a "verdict" and the mental operation that gives rise to it a "faculty." The faculty of understanding gives rise to beliefs, which are verdicts of conviction. The moral sense gives rise to moral sentiments or verdicts of approval and disapproval. The faculty of taste gives rise to verdicts of beauty. According to this theory, a faculty's verdicts are normative if the faculty meets the following test: *when the faculty takes itself and its own operations for its object, it gives a positive verdict.*

[23] Hume, *A Treatise of Human Nature*, I.4.vii, pp. 267–68.
[24] Ibid., III.3.vi, p. 619.

Now Hume clearly thinks that the understanding fails this test. A belief, according to Hume, is a sentiment of conviction, a lively idea of the thing believed. He argues that the harder we press the question whether we ought to believe our beliefs or whether they are likely to be true, the more the degree of our conviction — that is, the liveliness or vivacity of the ideas — will tend to diminish. So the more we reason about whether reasoning is likely to lead us to the truth, the less confidence in the results of reasoning we will end up having.[25] The understanding in this way "subverts itself" when it reflects on its own operations.

But the moral sense passes the reflexivity test. In the conclusion of the *Treatise*, Hume asserts that, in explaining our moral judgments as arising from sympathy, he has traced them to a "noble source" and has given us a "just notion both of the generosity and capacity of our nature." He says:

> It requires but very little knowledge of human affairs to perceive, that a sense of morals is a principle inherent in the soul, and one of the most powerful that enters into the composition. *But this sense must certainly acquire new force, when reflecting on itself, it approves of those principles, from whence it is deriv'd, and finds nothing but what is great and good in its rise and origin.* . . . not only virtue must be approv'd of, but also the sense of virtue. And not only that sense, but also the principles from whence it is deriv'd. So that nothing is presented on any side, but what is laudable and good.[26]

Reflection on the origin of our moral sentiments only serves to strengthen those sentiments. The moral sense approves of its own origins and workings and so it approves of *itself*.

I believe that Hume got the idea for this theory of normativity from the moral sense theorist Francis Hutcheson. In his *Illustrations on the Moral Sense*, Hutcheson imagines a rationalist who

---

[25] See ibid., I.4.i, pp. 180–85.

[26] Ibid., III.3.vi, p. 619 (my emphasis).

objects that judgments of good and evil cannot come from a moral sense, because we judge our senses themselves to be good or evil.[27] For instance, we approve of a benevolence-approving moral sense, while we would deplore a malice-approving moral sense. These judgments would be trivial if they came from the benevolence-approving moral sense itself. The argument is a variant on one familiar argument against theological voluntarism — that if God determines what is good and evil then we cannot significantly judge God himself to be good — and like that argument it is intended to drive us to realism. Hutcheson replies that the goodness of a sense must be assessed from some point of view from which we make judgments of good and bad and that we have a limited number of such points of view to which we can appeal. We can judge the moral sense from the point of view of the moral sense itself; we can judge it from the point of view of benevolence toward others; or we can judge it from the point of view of our own self-interest.[28] What we cannot do is get outside of all of the points of view from which we judge things to be good or bad and still coherently ask whether something is good or bad. There is no place outside of our normative points of view from which normative questions can be asked.

The same argument can of course be made about the normativity of the verdicts of the understanding. If we fall into doubt about whether we really ought to believe what we find ourselves inclined to believe — that is, if we fall into doubt about whether our beliefs are true — we cannot dispel the doubt by comparing our beliefs to the world to see whether they are true. We have no access to the world except through the verdicts of the understanding itself, just as we have no access to the good except through the verdicts of the various points of view from which we make judgments of goodness. The only point of view from which we can

[27] Hutcheson, *Illustrations on the Moral Sense*, p. 133.
[28] Ibid., pp. 133–34.

assess the normativity of the understanding is therefore that of the understanding itself.

It is this line of thought, I believe, that gave Hume the idea for the reflexivity test. It is, of course, complicated in the moral case by the fact that there is more than one point of view from which we can assess things as good or bad. This is what, in the later work, leads Hume to use the more general reflective endorsement test instead. But we can see reflexivity and reflective endorsement as working together. For one of the reasons that the moral sense approves of itself *is* that morality contributes to our happiness, and the moral sense approves of anything that contributes to people's happiness.

Now let's go back to the more general form of the realist's objection. This was that the reflective endorsement test only shows that morality is extrinsically normative, whereas what we want to show is that it is intrinsically normative. The addition of the reflexivity test does show that or, rather, shows something that is very close. It shows that *human nature*, including our moral nature, is intrinsically normative, in a negative version of the sense required by the realist argument: there is *no intelligible challenge* that can be made to its claims. Within human nature, morality can coherently be challenged from the point of view of self-interest, and self-interest from the point of view of morality. Outside of human nature, there is no normative point of view from which morality can be challenged. But morality can meet the internal challenge that is made from the point of view of self-interest, and it also approves of itself. It is human nature to be governed by morality, and from every point of view, including its own, morality earns its right to govern us. We have therefore no reason to reject our nature and can allow it to be a law to us. Human nature, including moral government, is therefore normative and has authority for us.

Perhaps a comparison will make this thought seem more familiar. According to the teleological ethics of the ancient world, to be virtuous is to realize our true nature, to be the best version of what we are. So it is to let our own nature be a law to us. And the Greeks thought that, since our own good would be realized in being the best version of what we are, we have every reason to be virtuous. Sentimentalism can be seen as a kind of negative surrogate of the teleological ethics of the ancient world. According to the sentimentalists, we have *no reason not to be* the best version of what we are.

Bernard Williams

This brings us to a recent attempt to revive the virtue-oriented ethics of the ancient world. In chapters 8 and 9 of *Ethics and the Limits of Philosophy*, Bernard Williams argues that there is a contrast between the kind of objectivity we can hope to find in science and that which we can hope to achieve in ethics. Williams accepts a form of realism in the case of science, but rejects it in the case of ethics.

Williams frames this contrast in terms of convergence, that is, in terms of what might lead us to the best kind of agreement. In science, the ideal form of convergence would be this: we come to agree with one another in our beliefs because we are all converging on the way the world really is. In ethics, this sort of convergence is unavailable, and so another must be found.[29] This, as we will see, is where reflective endorsement comes in.

Williams begins by solving a problem in the formulation of his contrast. The problem is essentially the same as the one that drove Hume to suppose that only a reflexivity test could establish the normativity of belief: we can't go outside of our beliefs in order to determine whether they match the world or whether they correctly capture "the way the world really is." Williams puts the problem this way. We have a certain way of conceptualizing the world, a conceptual scheme. One thing we might mean in talking about "the way the world really is" is whether we have applied

[29] Williams, *Ethics and the Limits of Philosophy*, p. 136.

our concepts correctly. If we say that grass is green we have and if we say that it is pink we have not. This notion is unproblematic, but it leaves us no room to query our way of conceptualizing the world itself.[30] Is our conceptual scheme adequate? Is it the correct one or the best one or the one that captures the most or the one that captures what is "really true" about the world? Philosophers will of course disagree on whether any of these questions are coherent and, if so, which one of them is the right one to ask. But since science leads us to modify our conceptual scheme, and we think of these modifications as improvements, it does appear that some such question is in order.

Williams proposes that we can capture the distinction between the way the world really is and the way it seems to us by the formation of a kind of limiting conception that he calls "the 'absolute conception' of the world." [31] The idea involves a contrast between concepts that are more and less dependent on the particular perspective from which we view the world. For instance, we use color categories because we are visual, so color concepts like "green" and "pink" are dependent on something about our own perspective. The concept of a certain wavelength of light might be less dependent.

Williams associates two other properties with a concept's greater independence from our particular perspectives. First, our use of concepts that are more dependent on our own perspectives will be explained in terms of a theory that employs concepts that

---

[30] It is interesting that Prichard (on pp. 14–15 of "Does Moral Philosophy Rest on a Mistake?") argues that this is correct — there *is* no room to query our way of conceptualizing the world. Just as the only way to resolve a doubt about whether we are "really obligated" — whether obligation is normative — is to review the reasons why the action is right, so the only way to resolve a doubt about whether our beliefs are true is to review the reasons for those beliefs — in the language I am using here, to make sure the concept has been applied correctly. The problem here is the same as the one I discussed in "Realism" in Lecture I. By asking the normative question in the form "Is my belief really true?" Prichard is led to confuse it with the question whether my concepts have been applied correctly. But the normative question is a question about the status of the concepts, not about whether they have been correctly applied.

[31] Williams, *Ethics and the Limits of Philosophy*, p. 139.

are less dependent. So, for instance, our use of color concepts might be explained by a theory of vision that employs wavelength concepts. Relatedly, and importantly, this theory (or some yet more absolute theory in which it is embedded) will also *justify* our belief that color vision is a form of *perception*, that is, a way of learning about the world, by the way that it explains it.[32] Color vision is a way of learning about the world because it gives us information about wavelengths, or something yet more ultimate, which we take to be part of reality. Second, the more independent of our own perspective a concept is, the more likely it is that it could be shared by investigators who were unlike us in their ways of learning about the world. Suppose that there are rational creatures on Jupiter who cannot see colors but do something more like hear them or perhaps feel them in the form of vibrations. They could not use color concepts, but they might be able to use wavelength concepts. The more independent concepts are more shareable.

Williams thinks that the nearest thing we have to a conception of the way the world really is is the conception of the world that is maximally independent of our own perspective. And if we and the alien investigators actually began to converge on such a conception (and of course to agree on what judgments are correct within it) then we would have reason to believe we were converging on what the world is really like. This would be the best case of convergence for science: our theories would come to converge with the theories of other investigators because all of us were converging on the way the world is.

Now consider what the parallel would be in ethics. Here too we must deal with a possible objection — namely that there is nothing analogous to perceptual judgments in ethics. Seeing the facts is one thing, and evaluating them in a certain way is another. This sort of argument was popular among early and mid-twentieth-century emotivists and prescriptivists. To counter it, Williams

[32] Ibid., p. 149.

notices, we may appeal to the existence of what he calls "thick" as opposed to "thin" ethical concepts. Thin ethical concepts — like right and good and ought — do not appear to be world-guided, in the sense that their application does not appear to be guided by the facts. Pure in their normativity, they are like those little gold stars you can stick on anything. But thick ethical concepts — Williams's own examples are coward, lie, brutality, and gratitude — are world-guided and action-guiding at the same time.[33] Only an action that is motivated in some way by fear can be called cowardly, and yet to call an action cowardly is to suggest that it ought not to be done.[34]

Of course the prescriptivist or emotivist has his own account of these concepts. He thinks that their world-guidedness is one thing and that their action-guidingness is another. The facts tell us which actions are motivated by fear, and when we disapprove of those actions or want to discourage others from doing them, we project our pejorative feelings onto them. So the word "cowardly" is just a pejorative way of describing an act motivated by fear, used when we want to express our feelings or influence our neighbors.

The difficulty with this analysis is that it suggests that it would be possible to use a thick ethical concept with perfect accuracy even if you were completely incapable of appreciating the value it embodies. Williams argues that this is implausible. Of course he does not mean that we can only use evaluative concepts when we ourselves actually endorse the values in question. But we apply such concepts by entering imaginatively into the world of those who have the values, not merely by applying a set of factual criteria.[35] We have to see the world through their eyes. This makes

---

[33] Ibid., pp. 140–41.

[34] Williams says that thick concepts often provide reasons for action (or refraining), but of course, strictly speaking, this is not true of "cowardly." To say that an action is cowardly is to suggest that there is a reason not to do it but not to mention what that reason is. Something in the situation is worth overcoming human fearfulness for, but the term doesn't tell us what. This is because courage is a so-called executive virtue. Williams's other examples are of more directly reason-providing concepts.

[35] Williams, *Ethics and the Limits of Philosophy*, pp. 141–42.

it natural to think of judgments employing thick ethical concepts as perceptual ones. And that in turn makes it natural to think that, like other perceptual judgments, they are a kind of knowledge.

I say that the sky is blue, and my visitor from Jupiter says that it makes a humming noise. Are we agreeing? Certainly we don't *mean* the same thing, since I am talking about how the sky looks and she is talking about how it sounds. Yet when we reflect on these views we find that the things we both say have implications that are expressible in terms of a more absolute concept, that of wavelengths. And when we look at those implications our judgments are found to converge. Here we find grounds for confidence that both of our perceptions are guiding us rightly: they are ways of knowing about the world. Now take this case. The medicine man says that killing the black snake will charm away the evil spirit. And we take "charming away the evil spirit" to have implications expressible in terms of what *we* take to be a more absolute concept, let's say that of curing an illness. And probably we think he is wrong: killing snakes is not a way of curing illnesses.[36]

What would the parallels be in ethics? They might look something like this. The monk says that lying is sinful, and the knight says that it is dishonorable. Certainly they do not *mean* exactly the same thing, for the monk is saying something about the lie's effect on his soul and about how it relates him to his God, while the knight is saying something about the lie's effect on his reputation — on his "character" in the older, more public sense of that word — and how it relates him to his social world. But we take both of their remarks to have implications for what *we* think is a more absolute concept—the lie is wrong and ought not to be told—

---

[36] He *might* be right, of course. There might be some story to tell about placebo effects — perhaps killing the black snake really works because the patient believes it will. Or perhaps the patient knows that if killing the black snake doesn't work the medicine man will try to frighten the evil spirit off by doing something dreadful to the patient, and this prospect frightens the patient into getting well. We don't know enough about medicine to know — and all that matters for the point is that we know roughly how such stories would have to go in order for us to be convinced by them.

and here we find that they converge. And we may think, in this case, that the convergence shows that their concepts are guiding them toward what we take to be a moral truth or that they correctly reflect a moral reality: say, that there are certain kinds of actions that you cannot do without being personally diminished or disfigured, and that this is related to their wrongness.

On the other hand, suppose the knight says that he will be dishonored unless he fights a duel with the man who has insulted him. If we take this to have the implication that trying to kill someone who has hurt your feelings is required, or even all right, we shall have to disagree. But now this is a conclusion that we should be uncomfortable with, and this is precisely because there is a world-guided side to the idea of dishonor. The knight's reputation, his position in his social world, may be damaged in *exactly* the ways that he foresees and has in mind when he says he will be dishonored. What is *for him* his identity may be diminished and disfigured just as it would have been by telling the lie. Facts of this sort should give us pause about whether he is, after all, using the idea of dishonor in a way that has implications for what is morally right or wrong in *our* sense of those words.

Thinking about such cases may lead us to conclude that after all the analogy with the scientific case doesn't hold. We may see the medicine man as trying to cause health, but we should not see the knight as trying to figure out what it is morally right to do. We should not even, according to Williams, assume that we share with the knight any general sense of what it is right or all right to do, about which our views and the knight's both have implications. Instead Williams proposes a different way in which we might look at the ethical beliefs of others:

> On the other model we shall see their judgments as part of their way of living, a cultural artifact they have come to inhabit (although they have not consciously built it). On this, nonobjectivist, model, we shall take a different view of the relations between that practice and critical reflection. We shall

> not be disposed to see the level of reflection as implicitly already there, and we shall not want to say that their judgments have, just as they stand, these implications [that is, implications about what it is right or all right to do].[37]

The proposal is that we should see their values not as their best approximations of the truth about value, but rather as a kind of *habitation*. Their values form a part of the structure of the social world in which they live.

But this does not mean that we cannot make any evaluative judgments about their values. We can ask whether their social world — that is, the world that is made of those values — is a good place for human beings to live. This is still, in a broad sense, an ethical question, but our resources for answering it are not tied to any particular system of values. Questions about the suitability of a habitat are answered with reference to the health and flourishing of the creatures who live in it. Williams suggests that a theory of human nature, drawing on the resources of the social as well as the physical sciences, could guide our reflections about what makes for human flourishing. And those reflections in turn could enable us to assess whether a given system of values promoted human flourishing.[38] Williams mentions psychoanalytic theory as one such resource, and of course it is impossible not to think of Freud in this context, with his gloomy view that "the cultural superego ... does not trouble itself enough about the facts of the mental constitution of human beings."[39] It does seem natural to say that societies in which girls wish passionately that they had been born boys, or in which suicide motivated by feelings of personal worthlessness is common, or in which large segments of the population are sexually dysfunctional are suffering from their values.

Williams proposes that if we did find that a social world promoted the best life or at least a flourishing life for human beings,

---

[37] Williams, *Ethics and the Limits of Philosophy*, p. 147.
[38] Ibid., pp. 45ff, 152–53.
[39] Ibid., p. 45; Freud, *Civilization and Its Discontents*, p. 90.

this would justify the values embodied in that social world. The structure of justification would be very different from the realist structure he thinks we can find in the case of scientific belief. The justification would not be that we find upon reflection that the values are true or that they are reliable guides to the truth about morally right action the way colors are reliable guides to wavelengths. Williams suggests that the only ethical belief that might survive at the reflective level would be the belief "that a certain kind of life was best for human beings."[40] The justification of other ethical beliefs would be that it is good for human beings to lead a life that is guided and governed by those beliefs.

So far, in detailing Williams's view, I have been talking, as Williams does, as if from the point of view of an outside observer of an alien society. But when we imagine this same reflective exercise being carried out by a member of the society in question, it becomes clear that the structure of justification here is one of reflective endorsement. Hume, as we saw earlier, reverses the realist ordering of things and argues that vice is bad because we disapprove of it. In a similar way, Williams thinks that ethical value is projected onto the world by our ethical beliefs. Both would deny that it is coherent to ask whether our values are true independently of our own moral or ethical sentiments. The only question left to ask is whether it is good for us to have those sentiments, and that question must be answered from the perspective of the other practical claims our nature makes on us. Where Hume establishes normativity by showing that morality is congruent with self-interest, Williams asserts that it would have to be established by congruence with human flourishing.

Like Hume, Williams entertains the possibility that this will not be the result. But the prospect is in one way a more alarming one for Hume. Hume believes that he is talking about a set of evaluative concepts that are deeply grounded in human nature and human psychology. He supposes that, if reflection yielded the re-

[40] Williams, *Ethics and the Limits of Philosophy*, p. 154.

sult that morality is bad for the individual, the truth would have to be sunk in "eternal silence and oblivion" in the interests of social order. Williams, by contrast, supposes that different cultures provide us with different sets of values. He sees the reflective test more as a method for choosing among them. When cultures come into what he calls "real confrontation," their members, forced by that confrontation to reflect on the value of their values, may lose confidence in them and come to the conclusion that some other values would lead to a better way of life.[41] The result will not be that they will decide that their old beliefs were false, or even that after all they did not know what, say, sin or honor was. It will be that they will stop using those concepts altogether.

In one case, a case of our own, this description of changing values rings true. Consider the uneasy fate of the evaluative concepts "masculine" and "feminine." People who have fallen into doubt about the values embodied in these concepts and the way of life to which they once led us do not argue about whether they track the ethical truth. People who have already decided against these values do not run around telling us that masculinity and femininity are false or wrong. If someone says that aggressiveness is not feminine the response will not be that aggressiveness *is* feminine or that aggressiveness is great. The response is "Let's not talk that way." The complaint that has been launched against these values is not that they were false or misleading but that they were straitjackets, stunting everybody's growth. It is that people who hold themselves and others to these ideals do not flourish. They must therefore be abandoned or revised.

There is also an element of *reflexivity* in Williams's view. Williams borrows the idea that morality is a projection of human dispositions from Aristotle rather than from Hume. Now Aristotle believed that an ethically good life must be good for the person whose life it is. And Aristotle, again like Hume, has been accused of harboring some form of egoism under this assumption. In de-

[41] Ibid., pp. 160ff.

fending Aristotle against this charge, Williams points out that the Aristotelian agent will reflect on his ethical dispositions from an *ethical* point of view. Or, if he does try to reflect on his ethical dispositions from a point of view outside of those dispositions, from the point of view of his other needs and capacities, the important question will be whether there is any conflict between the demands of those needs and capacities and the demands of his ethical nature.[42] Aristotle argued that there would not be such a conflict. Again, the conclusion is that our ethical dispositions are judged good from every point of view that makes practical claims on us, including their own point of view. And in this way normativity is established.

The Reflective Agent

Reflection, Williams tells us, can destroy knowledge.[43] History illustrates the point, for when Bentham reflected on Hume's theory of the virtues, he became a utilitarian.[44] Unfortunately, it looks as if there is a clear route from Hume to Bentham. And it is a route that leads through reflection — in particular, through the reflection of *agents*.

We have seen that in Hume's theory just actions are done from the motive of obligation. Sympathy with the public interest inspires us with a sentiment of disapproval when we think of injustice, and this motivates us to avoid it ourselves. Now let us consider a slightly more attractive version of Hume's sensible knave. Our knave is the lawyer for a rich client who has recently died, leaving his money to medical research. In going through the client's papers the lawyer discovers a will of more recent date,

---

[42] Ibid., pp. 51–52.

[43] Ibid., p. 148.

[44] This is by Bentham's own report. In a well-known footnote in *A Fragment on Government* (1776), Bentham reports that when he read Humes's *Treatise*, "I felt as if the scales had fallen from my eyes" (p. 50n). What he learned from Hume was "that *utility* was the test and measure of all virtue; . . . and that the obligation to minister to general happiness, was an obligation paramount to and inclusive of every other" (p. 51n).

made without the lawyer's help but in due form, leaving the money instead to the client's worthless nephew, who will spend it all on beer and comic books. The lawyer could easily suppress this new will, and she is tempted to do so. She is also a student of Hume and believes the theory of the virtues that we find in *A Treatise of Human Nature*. So what does she say to herself?

Well, she says to herself that she would disapprove of herself if she did this. She hates unjust actions and the people who perform them. But since the lawyer knows Hume's theory she also knows *why* she would disapprove of herself. She would disapprove of herself because unjust actions have a general tendency to bring down the system of justice. But she also knows that her distaste for such actions is caused by their general tendency, not their actual effects. As Hume has shown, our moral sentiments are influenced by "general rules." And our lawyer knows that this particular unjust action will have no actual effects but good ones. It will not bring down the system of justice, and it will bring much-needed money to medical research.

The lawyer believes that her disapproval of this action depends on the fact that actions of this kind usually have bad effects that this one does not have. It is almost inconceivable that believing this will have no effect on her disapproval itself. Her own feeling of disapproval may seem to her to be, in this case, poorly grounded and therefore in a sense irrational. And this may lead her to set it aside or, if she can't, to resist its motivational force. She may say to herself: since I approve of just actions because they are, generally speaking, useful, why not simply do what will be useful? And then of course she is not a Humean anymore; she is a utilitarian.[45]

Hume has a defense against this point, but it is a defense of the wrong kind. Consider once more the original sensible knave.

---

[45] There might be arguments of a familiar rule-utilitarian kind against the action she is considering, but if she is moved by those arguments she is still now a utilitarian and not a Humean, at least not in the sense of the *Treatise*.

What does he lose by his knavery? According to Hume, he loses his character with himself, his pleasing sense of self-worth. As I argued earlier, this does not depend on his moral beliefs or on whether he endorses the claims of morality. Since sympathy makes him see himself through the eyes of others, who would disapprove of him for his injustice, it will happen anyway. But that is exactly the problem. If Hume is right, the lawyer may find that she cannot destroy a valid will without intense feelings of humility or self-hatred. These may or may not be strong enough to cause her to desist. But even if they are there will have been normative failure. The lawyer does not believe that the claims her moral feelings make on her in this case are well-grounded. If she could cure herself of them then that is what she would do.

The difficulty in this case is not, strictly speaking, a difficulty with the reflective endorsement strategy. It arises most immediately from something particular to Hume's view: the fact that the moral sentiments are supposed to be influenced by "general rules," rules that do not hold in every case. Such rules cause us to disapprove of certain dispositions or character traits, which are themselves tendencies of a general kind. But that disapproval will be transferred to each and every exercise of the disposition in question only if we forget that the rules that cause it are merely general.

But the difficulty does show us something important about the reflective endorsement method. Consider again the knavish lawyer. She has asked herself whether her feeling of disapproval is really a *reason* — and now I mean a normative reason — not to do the action, and in this case she has found that it is not. She only disapproves of injustice because it is usually counterproductive. But this act, isolated and secret, will be useful in every way. So now she thinks she has a reason to do it.

Or does she? Why should her reflection stop there? We said that she was a convinced Humean, so she rejects realism. She therefore does not think the fact that an action is useful is in and of itself a reason for doing it — that is, she does not think that utility is an intrinsically normative consideration. So why should she be moved by utility, any more than by disapproval? Perhaps she now finds that she is *inclined* to be moved by the thought of utility, but that is no more a reason than the fact that she was *inclined* to be moved by disapproval before. She can also ask whether this new inclination is really a reason for action. What is to stop her from continuing to ask that question, from pushing reflection as far as it will go?

If the reflective endorsement of our dispositions is what establishes the normativity of those dispositions, then what we need to establish the normativity of more particular motives and inclinations is the reflective endorsement of those. That after all is the whole point of using the reflective endorsement method to justify morality: we are supposing that, when we reflect on the things that we find ourselves inclined to do, we can then accept or reject the authority those inclinations claim over our conduct and act accordingly.

But what I have just described is exactly the process of thought that, according to Kant, characterizes the deliberations of the autonomous moral agent. According to Kant, as each impulse to action presents itself to us, we should subject it to the test of reflection, to see whether it really is a *reason* to act. Since a reason is supposed to be intrinsically normative, we test a motive to see whether it is a reason by determining whether we should allow it to be a *law* to us. And we do that by asking whether the maxim of acting on it can be willed as a law.

Hume and Williams see the test of reflective endorsement as a philosophical exercise, used to establish the normativity of our moral dispositions and sentiments. But according to Kant, it is not merely that. The test of reflective endorsement is the test used by actual moral agents to establish the normativity of all their particular motives and inclinations. So the reflective endorsement test is not merely a way of justifying morality. *It is morality itself.* In the next lecture, I will elaborate this view.

LECTURE III: THE AUTHORITY OF REFLECTION

Introduction

Over the course of the last two lectures I have sketched the way in which the normative question took shape in the debates of modern moral philosophy. Voluntarism tries to explain normativity in what is in some sense the most natural way: we are subject to laws, including the laws of morality, because we are subject to lawgivers. But when we ask why we should be subject to those lawgivers, an infinite regress threatens. Realism tries to block that regress by postulating the existence of entities — objective values, reasons, or obligations — whose intrinsic normativity forbids further questioning. But why should we believe in these entities? In the end, it seems we will be prepared to assert that such entities exist only because — and only if — we are already confident that the claims of morality are justified.

The reflective endorsement theorist tries a new tack. Morality is grounded in human nature. Obligations and values are projections of our own moral sentiments and dispositions. To say that these sentiments and dispositions are justified is not to say that they track the truth, but rather to say that they are good. We are the better for having them, for they perfect our social nature and promote our self-interest.

But the normative question is one that arises in the heat of action. So it is not just our dispositions, but rather the particular motives and impulses that spring from them, that must seem to us to be normative. It is this line of thought that presses us toward Kant. Kant, like the realist, thinks we must show that particular actions are right and particular ends are good. Each impulse as it offers itself to the will must pass a kind of test for normativity before we can adopt it as a reason for action. But the test that it must pass is not the test of knowledge or truth. For Kant, like Hume and Williams, thinks that morality is grounded in human nature and that moral properties are projections of human dispositions. So the test is one of reflective endorsement.

In what follows I will lay out the elements of a theory of normativity. This theory derives its main inspiration from Kant, but with some modifications that I have come to think are needed. What I say will necessarily be sketchy, and sketchily argued. My attention here will be focused on four points: first, that autonomy is the source of obligation, and in particular of our ability to obligate ourselves; second, that we have *moral* obligations, by which I mean obligations to humanity as such; third, that since we can obligate ourselves, we can also be obligated by other people; and fourth, that we have obligations to other living things. I will have little to say about the content of any of these obligations. And it will be no part of my argument to suggest either that all obligations are moral or that obligations can never conflict. My aim is to show you where obligation comes from. Exactly which obligations we have and how to negotiate among them is a topic for another day.

The Problem

The human mind is self-conscious. Some philosophers have supposed that this means that our minds are internally luminous, that their contents are completely accessible to us, that we always can be certain what we are thinking and feeling and wanting, and so that introspection yields certain knowledge of the self. Like Kant, and many philosophers nowadays, I do not think that this is true. Our knowledge of our own mental states and activities is no more certain than anything else.

But the human mind *is* self-conscious in the sense that it is essentially reflective. I'm not talking about being *thoughtful*, which of course is an individual property, but about the structure of our minds that makes thoughtfulness possible. A lower animal's attention is fixed on the world. Its perceptions are its beliefs and its desires are its will. It is engaged in conscious activities, but it is not conscious *of* them. That is, they are not the objects of its attention. But we human animals turn our attention on to our perceptions and desires themselves, and we are conscious *of* them. That is why we can think *about* them.

And this sets us a problem no other animal has. It is the problem of the normative. For our capacity to turn our attention onto our own mental activities is also a capacity to distance ourselves from them and to call them into question. I perceive, and I find myself with a powerful impulse to believe. But I back up and bring that impulse into view and then I have a certain distance. Now the impulse doesn't dominate me and now I have a problem. Shall I believe? Is this perception really a *reason* to believe? I desire and I find myself with a powerful impulse to act. But I back up and bring that impulse into view and then I have a certain distance. Now the impulse doesn't dominate me and now I have a problem. Shall I act? Is this desire really a *reason* to act? The reflective mind cannot settle for perception and desire, not just as such. It needs a *reason*. Otherwise, at least as long as it reflects, it cannot commit itself or go forward.

If the problem springs from reflection then the solution must do so as well. If the problem is that our perceptions and desires might not withstand reflective scrutiny, then the solution is that they might. We need reasons because our impulses must be able to withstand reflective scrutiny. We have reasons if they do. The normative word "reason" refers to a kind of reflective success. If "good" and "right" are also taken to be intrinsically normative words then they too must refer to reflective success. And they do. Think of what they mean when we use them as *exclamations*: "Good!" "Right!" There they mean: I'm satisfied, I'm happy, I'm committed, you've convinced me, let's go. They mean the work of reflection is done.

"Reason" then means reflective success. So if I decide that my desire is a reason to act, I must decide that on reflection I endorse that desire. And here we find the problem. For how do I decide that? Is the claim that I look at the desire and see that it is intrinsically normative or that its object is? Then all of the arguments against realism await us. Does the desire or its object inherit its normativity from something else? Then we must ask what makes that other thing normative, what makes it the source of a reason. And now of course the usual regress threatens. So what brings reflection to an end?

Kant described this same problem in terms of freedom. It is because of the reflective structure of the mind that we must act, as he puts it, under the idea of freedom. He says, "We cannot conceive of a reason which consciously responds to a bidding from the outside with respect to its judgments."[1] If the bidding from outside is desire, then his point is that the reflective mind must endorse the desire before it can act on it — it must say to itself that the desire is a reason. We must, as he puts it, *make it our maxim* to act on the desire. And this is something we must do of our own free will.

Kant defines a free will as a rational causality that is effective without being determined by any alien cause. Anything outside of the will counts as an alien cause, including the desires and inclinations of the person. The free will must be entirely self-determining. Yet, because the will is a causality, it must act according to some law or other. Kant says, "Since the concept of a causality entails that of laws . . . it follows that freedom is by no means lawless . . ."[2] Alternatively, we may say that since the will is practical reason, it cannot be conceived as acting and choosing for no reason. Since reasons are derived from principles, the free will must have a principle. But because the will is free, no law or principle can be imposed on it from outside. Kant concludes that the will must be autonomous: that is, it must have its *own* law or principle. And here again we arrive at the problem. For where is this law to come from? If it is imposed on the will from outside then the will is not free. So the will must adopt the law

---

[1] Kant, *Foundations of the Metaphysics of Morals*, p. 448; in Beck's translation, p. 66.

[2] Ibid., p. 446; in Beck's translation, p. 65.

for itself. But until the will has a law or principle, there is nothing from which it can derive a reason. So how can it have any reason for adopting one law rather than another?

Well, here is Kant's answer. The categorical imperative tells us to act only on a maxim that we could will to be a law. And *this*, according to Kant, *is* the law of a free will. To see why, we need only compare the problem faced by the free will with the content of the categorical imperative. The problem faced by the free will is this: the will must have a law, but because the will is free, it must be its own law. And nothing determines what that law must be. *All that it has to be is a law.* Now consider the content of the categorical imperative. The categorical imperative simply tells us to choose a law. Its only constraint on our choice is that it have the form of a law. And nothing determines what that law must be. *All that it has to be is a law.*

Therefore the categorical imperative is the law of a free will. It does not impose any external constraint on the free will's activities, but simply arises from the nature of the will. It describes what a free will must do in order to be what it is. It must choose a maxim it can regard as a law.[3]

Now I'm going to make a distinction that Kant doesn't make. I am going to call the law of acting only on maxims you can will to be laws "the categorical imperative." And I am going to distinguish it from what I will call "the moral law." The moral law, in the Kantian system, is the law of what Kant calls the Kingdom of Ends, the republic of all rational beings. The moral law tells us to act only on maxims that all rational beings could agree to act on together in a workable cooperative system. Now the Kantian argument that I have just described establishes that *the categorical imperative* is the law of a free will. But it does not establish that *the moral law* is the law of a free will. Any law is universal, but

---

[3] This is a reading of the argument Kant gives in ibid., pp. 446–48; in Beck's translation, pp. 64–67; and in *The Critique of Practical Reason* under the heading "Problem II," p. 29; in Beck's translation, pp. 28–29. It is explained in greater detail in my "Morality as Freedom."

the argument doesn't settle the question of the *domain* over which the law of the free will must range. And there are various possibilities here. If the law is the law of acting on the desire of the moment, then the agent will treat each desire as it arises as a reason, and her conduct will be that of a wanton.[4] If the law ranges over the interests of an agent's whole life, then the agent will be some sort of egoist. It is only if the law ranges over every rational being that the resulting law will be the moral law, the law of the Kingdom of Ends.

Because of this, it has sometimes been claimed that the categorical imperative is an empty formalism. And this in turn has been conflated with another claim, that the moral law is an empty formalism. Now that second claim is false.[5] But it is true that the argument that shows that we are bound by the categorical imperative does not show that we are bound by the moral law. For that we need another step. The agent must think of *herself* as a Citizen of the Kingdom of Ends.

The Solution

Those who think that the human mind is internally luminous and transparent to itself think that the term "self-consciousness" is appropriate because what we get in human consciousness is a direct encounter with the self. Those who think that the human mind

---

[4] I have a reason for saying that her behavior will be that of a wanton rather than simply saying that she will be a wanton. Harry Frankfurt, from whom I am borrowing the term, defines a wanton as someone who has no second-order volitions. An animal, whose desire is its will, is a wanton. I am arguing here that a person cannot be like that, because of the reflective structure of human consciousness. A person must act on a reason, and so the person who acts like a wanton must be treating the desire of the moment as a reason. That commits her to the principle that the desire of the moment is a reason, and her commitment to that principle counts as a second-order volition. See Frankfurt, "Freedom of the Will and the Concept of a Person," especially the discussion on pp. 16–19. The affinity of my account with Frankfurt's will be evident.

[5] Bradley and others understood Hegel's famous objection this way, and if it is taken this way it is a mistake. I argue for this in my paper "Kant's Formula of Universal Law." In that paper, however, I do not distinguish the categorical imperative from the moral law, and my arguments there actually only show that the moral law has content.

has a reflective structure use the term too, but for a different reason. The reflective structure of the mind is a source of "self-consciousness" because it forces us to have a *conception* of ourselves. As Kant argues, this is a fact about what it is *like* to be reflectively conscious and it does not prove the existence of a metaphysical self. From a third person point of view, outside of the deliberative standpoint, it may look as if what happens when someone makes a choice is that the strongest of his conflicting desires wins. But that isn't the way it is *for you* when you deliberate. When you deliberate, it is as if there were something over and above all of your desires, something that is *you*, and that *chooses* which desire to act on. This means that the principle or law by which you determine your actions is one that you regard as being expressive of *yourself*. To identify with such a principle or law is to be, in St. Paul's famous phrase, a law to yourself.[6]

An agent might think of herself as a Citizen in the Kingdom of Ends. Or she might think of herself as a member of a family or an ethnic group or a nation. She might think of herself as the steward of her own interests, and then she will be an egoist. Or she might think of herself as the slave of her passions, and then she will be a wanton. And how she thinks of herself will determine whether it is the law of the Kingdom of Ends, or the law of some smaller group, or the law of the egoist, or the law of the wanton that is the law that she is to herself.

The conception of one's identity in question here is not a theoretical one, a view about what as a matter of inescapable scientific fact you are. It is better understood as a description under which you value yourself, a description under which you find your life to be worth living and your actions to be worth undertaking. So I will call this a conception of your practical identity. Practical identity is a complex matter and for the average person there will be a jumble of such conceptions. You are a human being, a woman or a man, an adherent of a certain religion, a member of an ethnic

[6] Romans II:14.

group, someone's friend, and so on. And all of these identities give rise to reasons and obligations. Your reasons express your identity, your nature; your obligations spring from what that identity forbids.

Our ordinary ways of talking about obligation reflect this connection to identity. A century ago a European could admonish another to civilized behavior by telling him to act like a Christian. It is still true in many quarters that courage is urged on males by the injunction "Be a man!" Duties more obviously connected with social roles are of course enforced in this way. "A psychiatrist doesn't violate the confidence of her patients." No "ought" is needed here because the normativity is built right into the role. But it isn't only in the case of social roles that the idea of obligation invokes the conception of practical identity. Consider the astonishing but familiar "I couldn't live with myself if I did that." Clearly there are two selves here, me and the one I must live with and so must not fail. Or consider the protest against obligation ignored: "Just who do you think you are?"

The connection is also present in the concept of integrity. Etymologically, integrity is oneness, integration is what makes something one. To be a thing, one thing, a unity, an entity; to be anything at all: in the metaphysical sense, that is what it means to have integrity. But we use the term for someone who lives up to his own standards. And that is because we think that living up to them is what makes him one, and so what makes him a person at all.

It is the conceptions of ourselves that are most important to us that give rise to unconditional obligations. For to violate them is to lose your integrity and so your identity, and no longer to be who you are. That is, it is no longer to be able to think of yourself under the description under which you value yourself and find your life worth living and your actions worth undertaking. That is to be for all practical purposes dead or worse than dead. When an action cannot be performed without loss of some fundamental part of one's identity, and an agent would rather be dead, then the obligation not to do it is unconditional and complete. If reasons arise from reflective endorsement, then obligation arises from reflective *rejection*.

But the question how exactly an agent *should* conceive her practical identity, the question which law she should be to herself, is not settled by the arguments I have given. So moral obligation is not yet on the table. To that extent the argument is formal, and in one sense empty.

But in another sense it is not empty at all. What we have established is this. The reflective structure of human consciousness requires that you identify yourself with some law or principle that will govern your choices. It requires you to be a law to yourself. And that is the source of normativity. So the argument shows just what Kant said that it did: that our autonomy is the source of obligation.

It will help to put the point in Joseph Butler's terms, in terms of the distinction between power and authority. We do not always do what upon reflection we would do or even what upon reflection we have already decided to do. Reflection does not have irresistible power over us. But when we do reflect we cannot but think that we ought to do what on reflection we conclude we have reason to do. And when we don't do that we punish ourselves, by guilt and regret and repentance and remorse. We might say that the acting self concedes to the thinking self its right to government. And the thinking self, in turn, tries to govern as well as it can. So the reflective structure of human consciousness establishes a relation here, a relation that we have to ourselves. And it is a relation not of mere power but rather of *authority*. And *that* is the authority that is the source of obligation.

Notice that this means that voluntarism is true after all. The source of obligation is a legislator, one whose authority is beyond question and does not need to be established. But there is only one such authority and it is the authority of your own mind and will.⁷ So Pufendorf and Hobbes were right. It is not the bare fact that it would be a good idea to perform a certain action that obligates us to perform it. It is the fact that we *command ourselves* to do what we find it would be a good idea to do.

One more step is necessary. The acting self concedes to the thinking self its right to govern. But the thinking self in turn must try to govern well. It is its job to make what is in any case a good idea into law. How do we know what is a good idea or what should be a law? Kant proposes that we can tell whether our maxims should be laws by attending not to their matter but to their form.

To understand this idea, we need to return to its origins, which are in Aristotle. According to Aristotle, a thing is composed of a form and a matter. The matter is the material, the parts, from which it is made. The form of a thing is its functional arrangement. That is, it is the arrangement of the matter or of the parts that enables the thing to serve its purpose, to do whatever it does. For example, the purpose of a house is to be a shelter, so the form of a house is the way the arrangement of the parts — the walls and the roof — enables it to serve as a shelter. "Join the walls at the corner, put the roof on top, and that's how we keep the weather out." That is the form of a house.⁸

Next consider the maxim of an action. Since every human action is done for an end, a maxim has two parts, the act and the end. The form of the maxim is the arrangement of its parts. Take, for instance, Plato's famous example of the three maxims.⁹

1. I will keep my weapon, because I want it for myself.

---

[7] This remark needs a qualification, which springs from the fact that we can unite our wills with the wills of others. In Kant's theory, this happens when we are citizens who together form a general will or when we make friends or get married. In those cases it is sometimes the united will that has authority over our conduct. For further discussion, see my "Creating the Kingdom of Ends: Reciprocity and Responsibility in Personal Relations."

[8] These views are found throughout Aristotle's writings, but centrally discussed in books VII–IX of the *Metaphysics* and in *On the Soul*.

[9] Plato, *Republic*, I, 331c., p. 580.

2. I will refuse to return your weapon, because I want it for myself.
3. I will refuse to return your weapon, because you have gone mad and may hurt someone.

Maxims 1 and 3 are good; maxim 2 is bad. What makes them so? Not the actions, for maxims 2 and 3 have the same actions; not the purposes, for maxims 1 and 2 have the same purposes. The goodness does not rest in the parts; but rather in the way the parts are combined and related; so the goodness does not rest in the matter, but rather in the form of the maxim. But form is not merely the arrangement of the parts; it is the *functional* arrangement — the arrangement that enables the thing to do what it does. If the walls are joined and roof placed on top *so that* the building can keep the weather out, then the building has the form of a house. So: if the action and the purpose are related to one another *so that* the maxim can be willed as a law, then the maxim is good.

Notice what this establishes. A good maxim is good in virtue of its internal structure. Its internal structure, its form, makes it fit to be willed as a law. A good maxim is therefore an *intrinsically normative entity*. So realism is true after all, and Nagel, in particular, was right. When an impulse presents itself to us, as a kind of candidate for being a reason, we look to see whether it really is a reason, whether its claim to normativity is true.

But this isn't an exercise of intuition or a discovery about what is out there in the world. The test for determining whether an impulse is a reason is whether *we* can will the maxim of acting on that impulse as law. So the test is a test of endorsement.

This completes the first part of my argument, so let me sum up what I've said. What I have shown so far is why there is such a thing as obligation. The reflective structure of human consciousness forces us to act for reasons. At the same time, and relatedly, it forces us to have a conception of our own identity, a conception that identifies us with the source of our reasons. In this way, it makes us laws to ourselves. When an impulse presents itself to us we ask whether it could be a reason. We answer that question by seeing whether the maxim of acting on it can be willed as a law by a being with the identity in question. If it can be willed as a law, it is a reason, for it has an intrinsically normative structure. If it cannot be willed as a law, we must reject it, and in that case we get obligation.

A moment ago I said that realism is true after all. But that could be misleading. That we obligate ourselves is simply a fact about human nature. But whether a maxim can serve as a law still depends upon the way that we think of our identities. So there is still an element of relativism in the system. In order to establish that there are *moral* obligations we will need another step.

Moral Obligation

There is another way to make the points I have been making, and in approaching the problem of relativism it will be helpful to employ it. We can take as our model the way Rawls employs the concept/conception distinction in *A Theory of Justice*. There, the *concept* of justice refers to a problem, the problem of how the benefits of social cooperation are to be distributed. A *conception* of justice is a principle that is proposed as a solution to that problem.[10]

In the same way, the most general normative concepts, the right and the good, are names for problems — for the normative problems that spring from our reflective nature. "Good" names the problem of what we are to strive for, aim for, and care about in our lives. "Right" names the more specific problem of what we are to do. The "thinness" of these terms, to use Bernard Williams's language, comes from the fact that they are only concepts, names for whatever it is that solves the problems in question.

How do we get from concepts to conceptions? What mediates is a conception of practical identity. In Rawls's argument, we move from concept to conception by taking up the standpoint of

[10] Rawls, *A Theory of Justice*, p. 5.

the pure citizen and asking what principles such a citizen would have reason to adopt. In Kant's argument, we move from concept to conception by taking up the standpoint of a Citizen in the Kingdom of Ends and asking what principles that citizen would have reason to adopt.

Because they are normative, thick ethical concepts stand to thin ones as conceptions to concepts. They represent solutions, or at least reasons that will be weighed in arriving at solutions, to the problems that are set by reflection. And that means that they embody a view about what is right or good. If this is right, then Williams is wrong to say that reflection is not inherent in, or already implied by, thick ethical concepts.[11] As normative concepts, they are essentially reflective.

Furthermore, our thin ethical concepts, although not necessarily our thick ones, will be shared with those alien scientific investigators.[12] For the fact that they are scientific investigators means that they have asked themselves what they ought to believe and that they have decided that the question is worth pursuing. And that in turn means that they are rational and social beings, who face normative problems like our own and sometimes solve them. The exact shape of their problems may be different from ours, and so they may have different conceptions. But if we can see their conceptions as solutions to the normative problems that *they* face, there will even be a kind of convergence.

But this does not eliminate the element of relativism that Williams has sought to preserve. The mediation between concepts and conceptions comes by way of practical identity. And human identity has been differently constituted in different social worlds. Sin, dishonor, and moral wrongness all represent conceptions of what one cannot do without being diminished or disfigured, without loss of identity, and therefore conceptions of what one must not do. But they belong to different worlds in which human beings thought

---

[11] See "Bernard Williams" in Lecture II.
[12] See "Bernard Williams" in Lecture II.

of themselves and of what made them themselves in very different ways. Where sin is the conception, my identity is my soul and it exists in the eyes of my God. Where dishonor is the conception, my identity is my reputation, my position in some small and knowable social world. The conception of *moral* wrongness as we now understand it belongs to the world *we* live in, the one brought about by the Enlightenment, where one's identity is one's relation to humanity itself. Hume said at the height of the Enlightenment that to be virtuous is to think of yourself as a member of the "party of humankind, against vice or disorder, its common enemy."[13] And that is now true. But we coherently can grant that it was not always so.

But this is not to say that there is nothing to be said in favor of the Enlightenment conception. This sort of relativism has its limits, and they come from two different but related lines of thought.

We have already seen one of them set forward by Bernard Williams. We could, with the resources of a knowledge of human nature, rank different sets of values according to their tendency to promote human flourishing. If values are associated with ways of thinking of what we most fundamentally are, then the point will be that some ways of conceiving one's identity are healthier and better for us than others.

But it is also important to remember that no argument can preserve any form of relativism without on another level eradicating it. This is one of the main faults with one well-known criticism of liberalism, that the conception of the person that is employed in its arguments is an "empty self."[14] It is urged by communitarians that people need to conceive themselves as members of smaller communities, essentially tied to particular others and traditions. This is an argument about how human beings need to constitute our practical identities, and if it is successful what it

---

[13] Hume, *Enquiry concerning the Principles of Morals*, p. 275.
[14] See, for instance, Michael Sandel, *Liberalism and the Limits of Justice*.

establishes is a *universal* fact, namely that our practical identities must be constituted in part by particular ties and commitments. And the communitarian who has reflected and reached this conclusion now has a conception of his own identity that is universal: he is an animal that needs to live in community.

And there is a further implication of this that is important. Once the communitarian sees himself this way, his particular ties and commitments will remain normative for him only if this more fundamental conception of his identity is one that he can see as normative as well. A further stretch of reflection requires a further stretch of endorsement. So he must endorse this new view of his identity. He is an animal that needs to live in community, and he now takes *this* to be a normative identity. He treats it as a source of reasons, for he argues that it matters that he gets what he needs. And this further stretch of endorsement is exactly what occurs. Someone who is moved to urge the value of *having* particular ties and commitments has discovered that part of their normativity comes from the fact that human beings need to have them. He urges that our lives are meaningless without them. That is not a reason that *springs from* one of his own particular ties and commitments. It is a plea on behalf of all human beings. And that means that he is no longer immersed in a normative world of particular ties and commitments. Philosophical reflection does not leave everything just where it was.

This is just a fancy new model of an argument that first appeared in a much simpler form, Kant's argument for his Formula of Humanity. The form of relativism with which Kant began was the most elementary one we encounter — the relativity of value to human desires and interests. He started from the fact that when we make a choice we must regard its object as good. His point is the one I have been making — that being human we must endorse our impulses before we can act on them. Kant asked what it is that makes these objects good, and, rejecting one form of realism, he decided that the goodness was not in the objects themselves.

Were it not for our desires and inclinations, we would not find their objects good. Kant saw that we take things to be important because they are important to us — and he concluded that we must therefore take ourselves to be important. In this way, the value of humanity itself is implicit in every human choice.[15] If normative skepticism is to be avoided — if there is any such thing as a reason for action — then humanity as the source of all reasons and values must be valued for its own sake.[16]

The point I want to make now is the same. In this lecture I have offered an account of the source of normativity. I have argued that a human being is an animal who needs a practical conception of her own identity, a conception of who she is that is normative for her. Otherwise she could have no reasons to act, and since she is reflective she needs reasons to act. But you are a human being and so if you believe my argument you can now see that *this* is your identity. You are an animal of the sort I have just described. And that is not merely a contingent conception of your identity, which you have constructed or chosen for yourself or could conceivably reject. It is simply the truth. Now that you see that your need to have a normative conception of yourself comes from the sort of animal you are, you can ask whether it really matters whether animals of this kind conform to their normative practical identities. Does it really matter what human beings do? And here you have no option but to say yes. Since you are human you *must* take something to be normative, that is, some conception of practical identity must be normative for you. If you had no normative conception of your identity, you could have no reasons for action,

---

[15] Kant, *Foundations of the Metaphysics of Morals*, pp. 427–28; in Beck's translation, pp. 45–47. I am here summarizing the interpretation of this argument I give in "Kant's Formula of Humanity."

[16] This implies that you must accept the laws that arise from this more fundamental view of your identity, the laws of morality. But it does not imply that the less fundamental laws no longer exist or that the more fundamental ones always trump them. The view I have as I have spelled it out so far leaves room for conflict. Some account of how such conflicts might be negotiated is desirable, but I do not mean to be giving or implying any such account here.

and because your consciousness is reflective, you could then not act at all. Since you cannot act without reasons and your humanity is the source of your reasons, you must endorse your own humanity if you are to act at all.

It follows from this argument that human beings are valuable. Enlightenment morality is true.

Obligating One Another

So far I have argued that the reflective structure of human consciousness gives us legislative authority over ourselves. That is why we are able to obligate ourselves. And just now I argued that once we understand how all of this works, we must concede that our humanity is an end in itself, that human nature as the source of our values is itself a value. This, I should add, is what gives rise to *moral* obligation.

You might suppose that I am claiming that this settles the question of our obligations to others. Since I regard my humanity as a source of value, I must in the name of consistency regard your humanity that way as well. So I must value the things that you value. Or, to put it another way, since I think my humanity is what makes my desires into normative reasons, I must suppose that the humanity of others makes their desires into normative reasons as well.

This is a familiar form of argument. Versions of it appear in Thomas Nagel's book *The Possibility of Altruism*, and in Alan Gewirth's book *Reason and Morality*. And the criticism of this form of argument is always the same. Consistency can force me to grant that your humanity is normative for you just as mine is normative for me. It can force me to acknowledge that your desires have the status of reasons for you, in exactly the same way that mine do for me. But it does not force me to share in your reasons or make *your* humanity normative for me.[17] It could still be true

---

[17] See for instance Williams's criticism of Gewirth in chapter 4 of *Ethics and the Limits of Philosophy*.

that I have my reasons and you have yours, and indeed that they leave us eternally at odds.[18] Human beings might be egoistic, not in the sense of being concerned only about themselves, but in the sense defined by Nagel in *The Possibility of Altruism*. The egoist thinks that reasons are a kind of private property. We each act on our own private reasons, and we need some special reason, like friendship or contract, for taking the reasons of others into account.

In one sense this objection is correct. Consistency is not what forces us to share our reasons. And even if these arguments did work, they would work in the wrong way. They would show that I have an obligation *to myself* to treat you in ways that respect the value that I place on you. But they would not show that I have obligations *to you*. So we need something more.

As we have seen, I can obligate myself because I am conscious of myself. So if you are going to obligate me I must be conscious of you. You must be able to intrude on my reflections — you must be able to get under my skin. People suppose that practical reasons are private because they suppose that reflection is a private activity. And they suppose that, in turn, because they believe in the privacy of consciousness. So what we need at this point is some help from Wittgenstein.

Consider the private language argument. As Wittgenstein defines it, a private language would be a language that referred to something essentially private and incommunicable, say for instance a sensation that is yours alone, and cannot be described in any other way than by a name that you give to it. You can't even call it a tickle or an itch, for then it would be communicable. So you just call it 'S.' And whenever you experience it, you say to yourself, "That was S." [19]

Wittgenstein argues that there couldn't be any such language. One way to understand his argument goes like this: Meaning is

---

[18] In contemporary jargon, the objection is that the reasons the argument reveals are "agent-relative" rather than "agent-neutral."

[19] See Wittgenstein, *Philosophical Investigations*, §§243ff., pp. 88ff.

relational because it is a *normative* notion: to say that X means Y is to say that one ought to take X for Y; and this requires two, a legislator to lay it down that one ought to take X for Y and a citizen to obey. And the relation between these two is not merely causal because the citizen can disobey: there must be a possibility of misunderstanding or mistake. Since it is a relation in which one gives a law to another, it takes two to make a meaning. So you cannot peer inwardly at an essentially private and incommunicable sensation and say, "That is what I mean by S" and so in that way mean something. For if that is what you mean by S, then when you call something S it must be *that*, and if you call something else S you must be wrong. But if what you call S is just that sensation that makes you feel like saying "S," and it cannot be identified in any other way, then you cannot be wrong.[20] The idea of a private language is inconsistent with the normativity of meaning.

If we read Wittgenstein that way, there is an obvious similarity between the kind of normativity that he thinks characterizes language and the kind of normativity that I have been attributing to practical reasons. We could make a parallel argument against private reasons: Reasons are relational because reason is a normative notion: to say that R is a reason for A is to say that one should do A because of R; and this requires two, a legislator to lay it down and a citizen to obey. And the relation between them is not just causal because the citizen can disobey: there must be a possibility of irrationality or wrongdoing. Since it is a relation in which one gives a law to another, it takes two to make a reason. And here the two are the two elements of reflective consciousness, the thinking self and the active self: what I have been talking about all along is how you can make laws and reasons for your self.[21]

[20] See especially ibid., §258, p. 92: "But 'I impress it on myself' can only mean: this process brings it about that I remember the connection *right* in the future. But in the present case I have no criterion of correctness. One would like to say: whatever is going to seem right to me is right. And that only means that here we cannot talk about 'right.' "

[21] It may look as if there is a disanalogy here. The private language argument shows that you cannot mean a certain sensation by 'S' just now and never again,

There are two important points here. The first point is that the mistake involved in thinking that a meaning is a mental entity is exactly like that involved in thinking that a reason or a value is a mental entity. To talk about reasons and meanings is not to talk about entities, but to talk in a shorthand way about relations we have with ourselves and one another. The normative demands of meaning and reason are not demands that are made on us by objects, but are demands that we make on ourselves and each other.

The second point concerns privacy. The private language argument does not show that I could not have my own personal language. It shows that I could not have a language that is in principle incommunicable to anybody else. When I make a language, I make its meanings normative for me. As Wittgenstein puts it, I *undertake* to use words in certain ways.[22] And however I go about binding myself to those meanings, it must be possible for me to bind another in exactly the same way.

If I say to you, "Picture a yellow spot!" you will. What exactly is happening? Are you simply cooperating with me? No, because at least without a certain active resistance you will not be able to help it. Is it a causal connection then? No, or at least not merely that, for if you picture a *pink* spot you will be mistaken, wrong. Causal connections cannot be wrong. What kind of necessity is this, both normative and compulsive? It is *obligation*.

Philosophers have been concerned for a long time about how we understand the meanings of words, but we have not paid enough attention to the fact that it is so hard not to. It is nearly impossible to hear the words of a language you know as mere noise. And this has implications for the supposed privacy of human consciousness. For it means that I can always intrude myself

---

because then you could not be wrong. The remark I just made makes it look as if you could have a reason just now and never again — the thinking self could bind the acting self to act a certain way just now. Actually, however, I do not think that is a possibility, since the acting self cannot coherently be taken to exist just at a particular moment. See my "Personal Identity and the Unity of Agency: A Kantian Response to Parfit," pp. 113–14.

[22] Wittgenstein, *Philosophical Investigations*, §262, p. 93.

into your consciousness. All I have to do is talk to you in the words of a language you know, and in this way I can force you to think. The space of linguistic consciousness is essentially public, like a town square. You might happen to be alone in yours, but I can get in anytime. Wittgenstein says, "Think in this connection how singular is the use of a person's name to *call* him." [23]

If I call out your name, I make you stop in your tracks. (If you love me, I make you come running.) Now you cannot proceed as you did before. Oh, you can proceed, all right, but not just as you did before. For now if you walk on, you will be ignoring me and slighting me. It will probably be difficult for you, and you will have to muster a certain active resistance, a sense of rebellion. But why should you have to rebel against me? It is because I am a law to you. By calling out your name, I have obligated you. I have given you a reason to stop.[24]

Of course you might not stop. You have reasons of your own, and you might decide, rightly or wrongly, that they outweigh the one I have given you. But that I have given you a reason is clear from the fact that, in ordinary circumstances, you will feel like giving me one back. "Sorry, I must run, I'm late for an appointment." We all know that reasons must be met with reasons, and that is why we are always exchanging them.

We do not seem to need a reason to take the reasons of others into account. We seem to need a reason not to. Certainly we do things because others want us to, ask us to, tell us to, all the time. We give each other the time and directions, open doors and step aside, warn each other of imminent perils large and small. We respond with the alacrity of obedient soldiers to telephones and doorbells and cries for help. You could say that it is because we want to be cooperative, but that is like saying that you understand

---

[23] Ibid., §27, p. 13.

[24] More strictly speaking, the needs and demands of others present us with what Kant calls "incentives," just as our own inclinations do. Incentives come up for automatic consideration as candidates for being reasons. I thank Ulrike Heuer for prompting me to be clearer on this point.

my words because you want to be cooperative. It ignores the same essential point, which is that it is so hard not to.

Now the egoist may reply that this does not establish that other people's reasons are reasons for me. He'll say that I am merely describing a deep psychological fact — that human beings are very susceptible to one another's pressure. We tend to cave in to the demands of others. But nothing I have said so far shows that we have to treat the demands of others as *reasons*. It is at this point that Thomas Nagel's argument, from *The Possibility of Altruism*, comes into its own.

Suppose that we are strangers and that you are tormenting me, and suppose that I call upon you to *stop*. I say, "How would you like it if someone did that to you?" Now you cannot proceed as you did before. Oh, you can proceed all right, but not just as you did before. For I have obligated you to stop.

How does the obligation come about? Just the way that Nagel says that it does. I invite you to consider how you would like it if someone did that to you. You realize that you would not merely dislike it, you would resent it. You would think that the other has a reason to stop — more, that he has an obligation to stop. And that obligation would spring from your own objection to what he does to you. You make yourself an end for others; you make yourself a law to them. But if you are a law to others insofar as you are just a person, just *someone*, then others are also laws to you.[25] By making you think these thoughts, I force you to acknowledge the value of *my* humanity, and I obligate you to act in a way that respects it.

As Nagel observes, the argument does not go through if you fail to see yourself, to identify yourself, as just someone, a person, one person among others who are equally real.[26] The argument invites you to change places with the other, and you cannot do this if you fail to see what you and the other have in common. Suppose you could say, "Someone doing that to *me*, why that would be

[25] See Nagel, *The Possibility of Altruism*, pp. 82–84.
[26] Ibid., chapter 9.

terrible! But then I am *me*, after all." Then the argument would fail of its effect; it would not find a foothold in you. But the argument never really fails in *that* way.

For it to fail in that way, I would have to hear your words as mere noise, not as intelligible speech. And it is impossible to hear the words of a language you know as mere noise. In hearing your words as *words*, I acknowledge that you are *someone*. In acknowledging that I can hear them, I acknowledge that I am *someone*. If I listen to the argument at all, I have already admitted that each of us is *someone*.

Consider an exchange of reasons. A student comes to your office door and says, "I need to talk to you. Are you free now?" You say, "No, I've got to finish this letter right now and then I've got to go home. Could you possibly come around tomorrow, say about three?" And your student says, "Yes, that will be fine. I'll see you tomorrow at three then."

What is happening here? On my view, the two of you are reasoning together, to arrive at a decision, a single shared decision, about what to do. And I take that to be the natural view. But if egoism is true, and reasons cannot be shared, then that is not what is happening. Instead, each of you backs into the privacy of his practical consciousness, reviews his own reasons, comes up with a decision, and then reemerges to announce the result to the other. And the process stops when the results happen to coincide, and the agents know it, because of the announcements they have made to each other.

Now consider an exchange of ideas, rather than an exchange of practical reasons. Here we do not find these two possibilities. If meanings could not be shared, there would be no point in announcing the results of one's private thinking to anybody else. If they can be shared, then it is in principle possible to think the issues through together, and that is what people do when they talk. But if we have to grant that meanings can be shared, why not grant that practical reasons can be shared too?

The egoist may reply that I am leaving out an option. The student/teacher relation is a personal one. People who enter into particular personal relationships have special reasons to take each other's reasons into account. So the exchange I've just described takes place against a background agreement that the parties involved will take each other's reasons into account. The egoist is someone who only acts on his own reasons, not someone who has no concern for others. So you and your student reason together because you have tacitly agreed to, but this does not show that this is what usually happens.

But the objection reemerges within this framework. How are we to understand this personal relationship? If reasons are still private then it goes like this: each of you has a private reason to take the reasons of the other into account. A personal relationship is an interest in one another's interests.[27] This doesn't change the shape of the deliberation — you still back into your private deliberative spaces and then reemerge to announce the results. This only shows why you think there's a point in the exercise at all, why you hope to reach a convergence. But if you are really reasoning together, if you have joined your wills to arrive at a single decision — well, then that can happen, can't it? And why shouldn't it be what usually happens? Why shouldn't language force us to reason practically together, in just the same way that it forces us to think together?

I believe that the myth of egoism will die with the myth of the privacy of consciousness. Now you may object that the way in which I have argued against the privacy of consciousness — by arguing that we can think and reason together — has nothing to do with what philosophers mean when they discuss that privacy. What they mean by privacy is that you don't always know what someone else is thinking or feeling. The way in which you have access to the contents of another person's mind — through words and expressions and other such forms of evidence — doesn't allow

[27] And that's not what a personal relationship is. See note 7 of this lecture.

you to look around in it freely, and make sure that you know what's there and what's not.

But that's not an issue about privacy. If you accept the thesis that consciousness is reflective rather than internally luminous, then you must admit that you don't have access to your *own* mind in *that* way. So that doesn't mark a difference between the kind of relationship you have to yourself and the kind that you have to other people. All we've got here is a matter of degree. You know some people better than others; if you're honest and lucky, you know yourself pretty well.

Human beings are social animals in a deep way. It is not just that we go in for friendship or prefer to live in swarms or packs. The space of linguistic consciousness — the space in which meanings and reasons exist — is a space that we occupy together.

The Origin of Value and the Value of Life

Pain is an objection. Interestingly, it is an objection to several of the views that I have discussed here. First, for many, pain is the biggest stumbling block to accepting Wittgenstein's views about our mental lives. It seems to them that pain is a sensation and that it is in the mind and therefore that what it is to be in pain is to have a sensation in your mind. And it seems to them that there could be a pain that was private in just the sense that Wittgenstein denied. Second, for many, pain is the biggest temptation to some form of naturalistic realism about normativity. One can have doubts about pleasure, for there are pleasures we deplore, but pain seems obviously to be a normative fact. And, third, if that is so, pain is an objection to Kantian ethics, or to any ethics that makes the value of humanity the foundation of value. For the other animals suffer pain, and if pain is intrinsically normative, then it matters that they do. Animals just as such should have moral standing.

The first two objections are related. Wittgenstein's argument against a private language deploys one of the standard objections against any form of normative naturalism — that you cannot be wrong. Hobbes said you could only be obligated by the law if the sovereign is able to punish you. But if you break the law and get away with it, then the sovereign was not after all able to punish you and so you were not wrong. Hume says that your reason is your strongest desire. But if you always act from your strongest desire, then you always do what you have reason to do, and you cannot be wrong. Wittgenstein says that if a word just refers to the very sensation that makes you feel like saying that word, then you cannot be wrong.

But both the opponent of Wittgenstein and the normative realist point to pain, and more generally to sensation, as a case where it seems to be no objection to say that we cannot be wrong. In fact it creates a foundation. The utilitarian claims that pleasure and pain are facts that are also values, a place where the natural and the normative are one, and so where ethics can find a foundation in the world. And this is exactly analogous to the epistemological claim that our sensations are the place where the natural and the normative are one, and so where knowledge can find a foundation in the world. Sensations are seen to be intrinsically normative entities, about which we cannot be wrong.

But can't we? "I cannot be wrong about whether I am seeing red." If you mean that the object before you is red, you can certainly be wrong. "No, I mean that I am having a red sensation." And what is that? It is the sensation that makes you feel like saying that a thing is red. You are not describing a condition that explains what you are inclined to say. You are simply announcing what you are inclined to say. In the same way, someone who says he is in pain is not describing a condition that gives him a reason to change his condition. He is announcing that he has a *very* strong impulse to change his condition.

Now that way of putting it, inspired by Wittgenstein, has a problem. People have thought that Wittgenstein was making a point about *language*, to the effect that when people talk about their own inner states and sensations they must be using language expressively, as if "I am in pain" could only be a cry of pain, and you could not simply be reporting your condition. Of course you can report your condition; once you've mastered the language, you can do anything that you like. His point is rather about mental activities, and whether a way of talking leaves anything for them to *be*. If "I see something red" *means* "I am having a red sensation" then one can never perceive; one can only announce the results of a perception that has already taken place. For what is this "having"? Did the little person in your mind perceive the red sensation? Wittgenstein is attacking a certain picture of what it is like to be conscious, which reduces all mental activity to the contemplation of sensations and ideas. And the language of "having" supports this picture. Does "I am in pain" mean "I am having a horrible sensation"? What here is the form of the "having"? Are you contemplating it? What would be so horrible about that?

But surely, you will reply, a *physical* pain is not just an impulse to change your condition. It *is* a sensation of a certain character. Now I am not denying that when we are in pain part of what is going on is that we are having sensations of a certain character. I am however denying that the painfulness of pain consists entirely in the character of those sensations. The painfulness of pain consists in the fact that these are sensations that we are inclined to fight. You may want to ask: why are we inclined to fight them if they are not horrible in themselves? Well, in some cases we are biologically wired this way; pain could not do its biological job if we were not inclined to fight it. When nature equipped us with pain she was giving us a way of taking care of ourselves, not a *reason* to take care of ourselves. Why do you thrash? Is it as if you were trying to hurl your body away from itself? Why do you say "as if"? Pain really is less horrible if you can curb your inclination to fight it. This is why it helps, in dealing with pain, to take a tranquilizer or to lie down. Ask yourself how, if the painfulness of pain rested just in the character of the sensations, it could help to lie down? The sensations do not change. Pain wouldn't hurt if you could just relax and enjoy it.

If the painfulness of pain rested in the character of the sensations rather than in our tendency to revolt against them, our belief that physical pain has something in common with grief, rage, and disappointment would be inexplicable. For that matter, what physical pains have in common with each other would be inexplicable, for the sensations are of many different kinds. What do nausea, migraine, menstrual cramps, pinpricks, and pinches have in common that makes us call them all pains? What emotional pains have in common with physical ones is that in these cases too we are in the grip of an overwhelming urge to do battle, not now against our sensations, but against the world. Stoics and Buddhists are right in thinking that we could put an end to pain if we could just stop fighting. The person who cared only for his own virtue, if there could *be* such a person, would be happy on the rack.[28] They are wrong if they conclude that we should therefore stop fighting. Many pains are worth having; one may even say that they are true. Pain is not the condition that is a reason to change your condition, the condition in which the natural and the normative are one. It is our *perception* that we have a reason to change our condition.[29] Pain itself is not a reason at all.

---

[28] Of course there could not be such a person, or at least, he could not *have* the virtues that were the only things he cared about. To have the virtues is in part to care about certain external things.

[29] When you feel pity for someone, why does it strike you as a reason to help him? Why don't you just take a tranquilizer? Hutcheson says, "If our sole Intention, in Compassion or Pity, was the Removal of our Pain, we should run away, shut our Eyes, divert our Thoughts from the miserable Object, to avoid the Pain of Compassion, which we seldom do . . ." (this passage is not in Raphael; one may find it in Selby-Bigge, *British Moralists*, p. 93). The point is reiterated by Nagel: "Sympathy is not, in general, just a feeling of discomfort produced by the recognition of distress in others, which in turn motivates one to relieve their distress. Rather, it is the pained awareness of their distress as *something to be relieved*" (*The Possibility of Altruism*, p. 80n). Wittgenstein says, "How am I filled with pity *for this man*? How does it come out what the object of my pity is? (Pity, one may say, is a form of conviction that someone else is in pain)" (*Philosophical Investigations* §287, p. 98). Pity is painful because it is the perception of *another's* pain, and so the perception that there is a reason to change *his* condition.

But pain is the perception of a reason. Since animals have pain, and until now I have seemed to suggest that only human beings have reasons, this will take a moment to explain.

The best account of what an animal is comes from Aristotle. We have already seen that Aristotle thought that the form of a thing is the organization or arrangement of its parts that allows it to be what it is, to do what it does, to do its job. Now Aristotle thought that a *living* thing is a thing with a special kind of form. A living thing is so designed as to maintain and reproduce itself. It has what we might call a self-maintaining form. So it is its own end; its job is just to keep on being what it is. Its business in life is to preserve its own *identity*. And its organs and activities are arranged to that end.[30]

If a living thing is an animal, if it is conscious, then part of the way it preserves its own identity is through its sensations. And this is where pain comes in. When something is a threat to its physical existence, or would be if it went on long enough, the animal perceives that fact and revolts against it. The animal is moved to take action to fix what is wrong. Suppose for instance that the animal needs nourishment. It perceives that by getting hungry. It finds this unpleasant and is moved to get something to eat. Don't be confused here: it is not that the pain is an unpleasant sensation that gives the animal a reason to eat. The animal has a reason to eat, which is that it will die if it does not. It does not know that it has that reason, but it does perceive it. The sensation in question is the sensation of hunger, not of pain. But an animal is designed to perceive and revolt against threats to the preservation of its identity, such as hunger. When it does that, it is in pain.

Now consider this comparison. A human being is an animal whose nature it is to construct a practical identity that is normative for her. She is a law to herself. When some way of acting is a threat to her practical identity and reflection reveals that fact, the

---

[30] This account of the nature of an animal is based primarily on *On the Soul*, book II.

person finds that she must reject that way of acting, and act in another way. In that case, she is obligated.

A living thing is an entity whose nature it is to preserve and maintain its physical identity. It is a law to itself. When something it is doing is a threat to that identity and perception reveals that fact, the animal finds that it must reject what it is doing and do something else instead. In that case, it is in pain.

Obligation is the reflective rejection of a threat to your identity. Pain is the *unreflective* rejection of a threat to your identity. So pain is the *perception* of a reason, and that is why it seems normative.

To say that life is a value is almost a tautology. Since a living thing is a thing for which the preservation of identity is imperative, life is a form of morality. Or to put the point less strangely and in a way that has been made more familiar to us by Aristotle, morality is just the form that *human life* takes.

From here the argument proceeds as it did in the case of other people. I won't spell out the details here. Roughly it will look like this: I first point out to you that your animal nature is a fundamental form of identity on which your human identity depends. A further stretch of reflection requires a further stretch of endorsement. If you don't value your animal nature, you can value nothing. So you must endorse its value. Perhaps that by itself doesn't show us that we have obligations to the other animals, since the value could still be private. To show us that we have obligations, animals must have a way of impressing their value upon us, the way we impress our value on each other when we ask, "How would you like it if someone did that to you?" They must be able to intrude into our consciousness and make us think.

But that isn't a problem, is it? The cries of an animal are no more mere noise than the words of a person. An animal's cries express pain, and they mean that there is a reason to change its condition. Another animal can obligate you in exactly the same way another person can. It is a way of being *someone* that you share. So of course we have obligations to animals.

Conclusion

I hope by now it is clear that all of the accounts of normativity that I have discussed in these lectures are true.

Voluntarists like Pufendorf and Hobbes held that normativity must spring from the commands of a legislator. A good legislator commands us to do only what it is in any case a good idea to do, but the bare fact that an action is a good idea cannot make it a requirement. For that, it must be made law by someone in a position to command us.

As we saw, that view is true. What it describes is the relation in which we stand to ourselves. The fact that we must act in the light of reflection gives us a double nature. The thinking self has the power to command the acting self, and it is only its command that can make action obligatory. A good thinking self commands the acting self only to do what is good, but the acting self must in any case do what it says.

Realists like Nagel think that reasons are intrinsically normative entities and that what we should do when a desire presents itself is to look at it more objectively, to see whether it is such an entity. This view is also true. What it describes is the activity of the thinking self as it assesses the impulses that present themselves to us, the legislative proposals of our nature.

Reflection has the power to compel obedience and to punish us for disobedience. It in turn is bound to govern us by laws that are good. Together these facts yield the conclusion that the relation of the thinking self to the acting self is the relation of legitimate authority. That is to say, the necessity of acting in the light of reflection makes us authorities over ourselves. And insofar as we have authority over ourselves, we can make laws for ourselves, and those laws will be normative. So Kant's view is also true. Autonomy is the source of obligation.

Once we see this, we can see that the reflective endorsement theory is true on another level as well. In the end, nothing can be normative unless we endorse our own nature, unless we place a value upon ourselves. Reflection reveals to us that the normativity of our values springs from the fact that we are animals of a certain kind, autonomous moral animals. That is, in the Aristotelian sense, our human form. If we do not place a value on being such animals, then nothing will be normative at all.

That means realism is true on another level too. To see this, recall once again John Mackie's famous "argument from queerness."[31] According to Mackie, it is fantastic to think that the world contains objective values or intrinsically normative entities. For in order to do what values do, they would have to be entities of a very strange sort, utterly unlike anything else in the universe. The way that we know them would have to be different from the way that we know ordinary facts. Knowledge of them, Mackie says, would have to provide the knower with both a direction and a motive. For when you met an objective value, according to Mackie, it would have to be — and I'm nearly quoting now — able both to tell you what to do and to make you do it. And nothing is like that.

But Mackie is wrong and realism is right. Of course there are entities that meet these criteria. It's true that they are queer sorts of entities and that knowing them isn't like anything else. But that doesn't mean that they don't exist. John Mackie must have been alone in his room with the Scientific World View when he wrote those words. For it is the most familiar fact of human life that the world contains entities that can tell us what to do and make us do it. They are people, and the other animals.[32]

---

[31] See "Realism" in Lecture I.

[32] I would like to thank Charlotte Brown, Peter Hylton, Arthur Kuflik, Andrews Reath, Amélie Rorty, Thomas Scanlon, Jay Schleusener, and my commentators on the occasion of the lectures (listed below) for comments on earlier versions of these lectures. A longer version of the lectures, together with commentary by Gerald Cohen, Raymond Geuss, Thomas Nagel, and Bernard Williams, is forthcoming from Cambridge University Press.

BIBLIOGRAPHY

Aristotle. *The Complete Works of Aristotle.* Edited by Jonathan Barnes. Princeton: Princeton University Press, 1984.

Bentham, Jeremy. *A Fragment on Government; with an Introduction to the Principles of Morals and Legislation* (1776, 1789). Edited by Wilfrid Harrison. Oxford: Basil Blackwell, 1948.

Brink, David O. *Moral Realism and the Foundations of Ethics.* Cambridge: Cambridge University Press, 1989.

Brown, Charlotte. "Hume against the Selfish Schools and the Monkish Virtues." Delivered at the meetings of the Hume Society, 1989.

Butler, Joseph. *Fifteen Sermons Preached at the Rolls Chapel* (1726). The most influential of these are collected in Butler, *Five Sermons Preached at the Rolls Chapel and A Dissertation upon the Nature of Virtue.* Edited by Stephen Darwall. Indianapolis: Hackett, 1983.

Clarke, Samuel. *A Discourse concerning the Unchangeable Obligations of Natural Religion, and the Truth and Certainty of the Christian Revelation: The Boyle Lectures 1705.* (I have quoted from both J. B. Schneewind [ed.], *Moral Philosophy from Montaigne to Kant,* and D. D. Raphael [ed.], *British Moralists 1650–1800.*)

Frankfurt, Harry G. "Freedom of the Will and the Concept of a Person." *Journal of Philosophy* 68 (January 1971). Reprinted in Frankfurt, *The Importance of What We Care About.* Cambridge: Cambridge University Press, 1988.

Freud, Sigmund. *Das Unbehagen in der Kultur* (*Civilization and Its Discontents*, 1930). Translated and edited by James Strachey. New York: W. W. Norton and Company, 1961.

Gewirth, Alan. *Reason and Morality.* Chicago: University of Chicago Press, 1978.

Grotius, Hugo. *De juri belli ac pacis* (*On the Law of War and Peace*, 1625). Translated by Francis W. Kelsey. Oxford: Oxford University Press, 1925. (I have quoted from J. B. Schneewind [ed.], *Moral Philosophy from Montaigne to Kant.*)

Harman, Gilbert. *The Nature of Morality: An Introduction to Ethics.* New York: Oxford University Press, 1977.

Hobbes, Thomas. *Leviathan* (1651). Edited by Richard Tuck. Cambridge: Cambridge University Press, 1991.

Hume, David. *The Dialogues concerning Natural Religion* (1779). Edited by Norman Kemp Smith. New York: Macmillan Library of Liberal Arts, 1947.

———. *Enquiry concerning Human Understanding* (1748) and *Enquiry concerning the Principles of Morals* (1751). In *David Hume: Enquiries concerning Human Understanding and concerning the Principles of Morals*. 3rd ed. Edited by L. A. Selby-Bigge and P. H. Nidditch. Oxford: Clarendon Press, 1975.

———. *A Treatise of Human Nature* (1739–1740). 2nd ed. Edited by L. A. Selby-Bigge and P. H. Nidditch. Oxford: Oxford University Press, 1978.

Hutcheson, Francis. *Illustrations on the Moral Sense* (Part II of *An Essay on the Nature and Conduct of the Passions and Affections with Illustrations on the Moral Sense*, 1728). Edited by Bernard Peach. Cambridge, Mass.: Harvard University Press, 1971.

———. *Inquiry concerning the Original of Our Ideas of Beauty and Virtue* (1725). (I have quoted from D. D. Raphael [ed.], *British Moralists 1650–1800*; except on one occasion when I have quoted a passage not in Raphael from L. A. Selby-Bigge, *The British Moralists* [Oxford: Clarendon Press, 1897; reprinted by the Library of Liberal Arts, 1964].)

Kant, Immanuel. *Grundlegung zur Metaphysik der Sitten* (*Foundations of the Metaphysics of Morals*, 1785). Translated by Lewis White Beck. New York: Macmillan Library of Liberal Arts, 1959.

———. *Kants gesammelte Schriften*. Prussian Academy ed. 28 vols. Berlin: Walter de Gruyter and Company, 1902–. (The page numbers found in the margins of most translations refer to this edition. When I have cited Kant, I have therefore referred to these page numbers. The English translations quoted or cited are listed in separate bibliographical entries for the works in question.)

———. *Kritik der praktischen Vernunft* (*Critique of Practical Reason*, 1788). Translated by Lewis White Beck. New York: Macmillan Library of Liberal Arts, 1956.

Korsgaard, Christine M. "Creating the Kingdom of Ends: Reciprocity and Responsibility in Personal Relations." In *Philosophical Perspectives 6: Ethics*, edited by James Tomberlin. Atascadero, Calif.: Ridgeview Publishing Company, 1992.

———. "Kant's Formula of Humanity." *Kant-Studien* 77 (April 1986), 183–202.

———. "Kant's Formula of Universal Law." *Pacific Philosophical Quarterly* 66 (January/April 1985), 24–47.

———. "Morality as Freedom." In *Kant's Practical Philosophy Reconsidered*, edited by Yirmiyahu Yovel. Dordrecht: Kluwer Academic Publishers, 1989.

———. "Personal Identity and the Unity of Agency: A Kantian Response to Parfit." *Philosophy and Public Affairs* 18 (Spring, 1989), 101–32.

———. "The Reasons We Can Share: An Attack on the Distinction between Agent-Relative and Agent-Neutral Values." *Social Philosophy & Policy* 10 (January 1993), 24–51.

Mackie, J. L. *Ethics: Inventing Right and Wrong.* New York: Penguin Books, 1977.

Mandeville, Bernard. *An Enquiry into the Origin of Honor* (1732). (I have quoted from J. B. Schneewind [ed.], *Moral Philosophy from Montaigne to Kant*.)

———. *The Fable of the Bees: or, Private Vices, Public Benefits* (1714). Edited by F. B. Kaye. Indianapolis: Liberty Classics, 1988; reprint of a 1924 edition published by Oxford University Press.

Mill, John Stuart. *Utilitarianism* (1861). Edited by George Sher. Indianapolis: Hackett, 1979.

Moore, G. E. "The Conception of Intrinsic Value." In Moore, *Philosophical Studies.* London: Kegan Paul, 1922.

———. *Principia Ethica* (1903). Cambridge: Cambridge University Press, 1971.

Nagel, Thomas. *The Possibility of Altruism.* Princeton: Princeton University Press, 1970.

———. *The View from Nowhere.* Oxford: Oxford University Press, 1986.

Plato. *The Collected Dialogues.* Edited by Edith Hamilton and Huntington Cairns. Princeton: Princeton University Press, 1961.

Price, Richard. *A Review of the Principal Questions in Morals* (1758). Edited by D. D. Raphael. Oxford: Clarendon Press, 1948. (I have also cited the selections in J. B. Schneewind [ed.], *Moral Philosophy from Montaigne to Kant*, and D. D. Raphael [ed.], *British Moralists 1650–1800*.)

Prichard, H. A. "Does Moral Philosophy Rest on a Mistake?" (*Mind* 21, 1912) and "Duty and Interest" (Oxford: Clarendon Press, 1929). Reprinted in *Moral Obligation and Duty and Interest. Essays and Lectures by H. A. Prichard.* Edited by W. D. Ross and J. O. Urmson. Oxford: Oxford University Press, 1968.

Pufendorf, Samuel. *On the Duty of Man and Citizen according to Natural Law* (1673). Edited by James Tully and translated by Michael Silverthorne. Cambridge: Cambridge University Press, 1991.

———. *On the Law of Nature and of Nations* (1672). Translated by C. H. Oldfather and W. A. Oldfather. Oxford: Oxford University Press, 1934. (I have quoted from J. B. Schneewind [ed.], *Moral Philosophy from Montaigne to Kant*.)

Railton, Peter. "Moral Realism." *Philosophical Review* 95 (April 1986), 163–207.

Raphael, D. D. (ed.) *British Moralists 1650–1800*. 2 vols. Indianapolis: Hackett Publishing Company, 1991; reprint of a 1969 edition published by Oxford University Press. (Where I have quoted from this anthology rather than original sources I have cited it as Raphael I and Raphael II.)

Rawls, John. "Kantian Constructivism in Moral Theory: The Dewey Lectures 1980." *Journal of Philosophy* 77 (September 1980).

———. *A Theory of Justice*. Cambridge, Mass.: Harvard University Press, 1971.

Ross, W. D. *The Right and the Good*. Oxford: Clarendon Press, 1930.

Sandel, Michael J. *Liberalism and the Limits of Justice*. Cambridge: Cambridge University Press, 1982.

Schneewind, J. B. (ed.). *Moral Philosophy from Montaigne to Kant*. 2 vols. Cambridge: Cambridge University Press, 1990. (Where I have quoted from this anthology rather than original sources I have cited it as Schneewind I and Schneewind II.)

Williams, Bernard. *Ethics and the Limits of Philosophy*. Cambridge, Mass.: Harvard University Press, 1985.

Wittgenstein, Ludwig. *Philosophical Investigations*. Translated by G. E. M. Anscombe. New York: Macmillan, 1953.

Rethinking the Meaning of Genetic Determinism

EVELYN FOX KELLER

THE TANNER LECTURES ON HUMAN VALUES

Delivered at

The University of Utah
February 18, 1993

EVELYN FOX KELLER, who is currently a MacArthur Fellow, is Professor in the Program in Science, Technology, and Society at the Massachusetts Institute of Technology. She was educated at Brandeis University, Radcliffe College, and Harvard University, where she received her Ph.D. degree in physics in 1963. She has taught at Cornell, Northeastern, Northwestern, and New York universities, and at the University of Maryland and the University of California at Berkeley, among others, and was a member of Princeton's Institute for Advanced Study. In addition to her numerous published articles in the fields of mathematical biology, theoretical physics, and molecular biology, she has written widely on psychological, philosophical, historical, and feminist perspectives on the nature of scientific thought. Her books include *Secrets of Life, Secrets of Death* (1992), *Reflections on Gender and Science* (1985), and *A Feeling for the Organism* (1983), and she is the coeditor of *Keywords in Evolutionary Discourse* (in press), *Body/Politics: Women and the Discourses of Science* (1990), and *Conflicts in Feminism* (1990).

ABSTRACT: The term "genetic determinism" refers to a belief system that locates the cause of all biological development in an organism's genes: if we only knew enough about genes (about what they are and how they "act"), we could understand all of biology. Such beliefs — codified in what I call the "discourse of gene action" — have been of great importance to the history of genetics and, most recently, to the launching of the Human Genome Initiative. But what does it mean to attribute — or, for that matter, to deny — causal power to genes? Without question, this way of talking has been immensely productive to research in genetics, but it has also impeded the formulation of a conceptual framework adequate to the study of developmental phenomena. Today, with the dramatic resurgence of Developmental Biology as an independent discipline, the need for such a framework has become urgent.

Historians of biology routinely note that, for nineteenth-century biologists, the term "heredity" referred to both the "transmission of potentialities during reproduction *and* [the] development of these potentialities into specific adult traits." [1] The question that compelled their interests above all others was, as August Weismann put it in 1883, "How is a single germ cell capable of reproducing the entire body with all its details?" [2] However, a crucial change occurred in the early part of this century. With the rise of the new discipline of genetics, the two aspects of heredity (transmission and development) grew apart, and the term

[1] Gar Allen, "T. H. Morgan and the Split between Embryology and Genetics, 1910–1926," in T. J. Horder, I. A. Witkowski, and C. C. Wylie (eds.), *A History of Embryology*, p. 114.

[2] Quoted by Klaus Sander, "The Role of Genes in Ontogenesis — Evolving Concepts from 1883 to 1983 as Perceived by an Insect Embryologist," in Horder et al. (eds.), *History of Embryology*, p. 363.

"heredity" was redefined to refer exclusively to transmission. Henceforth, the study of transmission would become the province of genetics, while that of development remained the province of embryology.

These were two separate disciplines, with two different sets of concerns. In a passage from his 1926 book, *The Theory of the Gene*, T. H. Morgan described their relation as follows:

> Between the characters, that furnish the data for the theory and the postulated genes, to which the characters are referred, lies the whole field of embryonic development. The theory of the gene, as here formulated, states nothing with respect to the way in which the genes are connected with the end-product or character. The absence of information relating to this interval does not mean that the process of embryonic development is not of interest for genetics . . . but the fact remains that the sorting out of the characters in successive generations can be explained at present without reference to the way in which the gene affects the developmental process.[3]

Elsewhere the same year he cautioned that

> the confusion that is met with sometimes in the literature has resulted from a failure to keep apart the phenomenon of heredity, that deals with the transmission of the hereditary units, and the phenomena of embryonic development that take place almost exclusively by changes in the cytoplasm.[4]

Genetics provided a power methodology for tracking the transmission of differences among existing organisms, but it couldn't answer the question of how a single germ cell might produce an organism — that remained the province of embryology. Yet, even in the early days of genetics, when the gene was still merely an abstract concept, and the necessity of nuclear-cytoplasmic interactions clearly understood, geneticists took it for granted that these hypothetical particles, the genes, must somehow lie at the root of

---

[3] T. H. Morgan, *The Theory of the Gene*, p. 26.
[4] Ibid., p. 490.

development. If in some of his writings Morgan gave the impression of being ecumenical, granting to embryology a separate but equal disciplinary status, and a separate but equal object of study (the cytoplasm), at other times he was quite clear about the proper epistemological ordering of the two disciplines. Though he well recognized that geneticists could say nothing about what genes are, or how they were subsequently connected to the formulation of adult characters or traits, and little about how they interacted with the cytoplasm of the fertilized egg (the specifically maternal contribution), he nonetheless wrote in 1924, "it is clear that whatever the cytoplasm contributes to development is almost entirely under the influence of the genes carried by the chromosome, and therefore may in a sense be said to be indifferent. . . ." [5]

Others went even further. In an attempt to clarify Morgan's position, the geneticist R. A. Brink explained:

> The Mendelian theory postulates discrete, self-perpetuating, stable bodies — the genes — resident in the chromosomes, as the hereditary materials. *This means, of course, that the genes are the primary internal agents controlling development.* (my italics)

Brink described the great advantage of genetics over other approaches as follows:

> with the primary internal mechanism resolved into definite units which may be combined in various groups. . . . The hereditary complex need no longer serve merely as the passive object in physiological experimentation but may itself be varied in a precise fashion. . . . We are now in a favorable position to get at the dynamic properties of the hereditary mechanism by means of an analysis of the action of its separate elements. This, it seems to us, is the signal contribution which genetics makes to our outlook upon the problems of developmental physiology.[6]

[5] T. H. Morgan, "Mendelian Heredity in Relation to Cytology."

[6] R. A. Brink, "Genetics and the Problems of Development," *American Naturalist* 61, no. 574 (1927), 280–83.

To Morgan's student, H. J. Muller, the most remarkable characteristic of the gene was that it possesses the property he called "specific autocatalysis" (by which he meant self-replication). "Still more remarkable," he wrote, "the gene can mutate without losing its specific autocatalytic power." Largely for this reason, he entitled his own 1926 paper "The Gene as the Basis of Life" (it is said that he refused to change his title to "The Gene as *a* Basis for Life"). There he concluded:

> the great bulk . . . of the protoplasm [is], after all, only a by-product of the action of the gene material; its "function" (its survival-value) lies only in its fostering the genes, and the primary secrets common to all life lie further back, in the gene material itself."[7]

I do not know when the term "genetic determinism" first came into use — it is not a term used by geneticists themselves — but the concept of genes as primary and self-sufficient cause, the notion that it is our genes that determine our biological fate, is clearly already evident here in these writings.

Today it is hard to see what might be controversial in such claims. The attribution of agency, autonomy, and causal primacy to genes has become so familiar as to seem obvious, even self-evident. What I want to do, however, is attempt to dislodge that familiarity — by citing these arguments in their historical context, using the now somewhat quaint language in which they were first posed, to enable you to see them as novel and thereby to see something of the process by which they acquired their familiarity and ring of truth.

In 1926 genetics was still a relatively new discipline, struggling to establish itself against the established hegemony of embryology and physiology. Earlier in the country the rediscovery of Mendel and the identification of chromosomes as the carrier of genetic

---

[7] H. J. Muller, "The Gene as the Basis of Life," *Proceedings of the International Congress of Plant Sciences* 1 (Ithaca, 1926), 897–921.

material had marked the start of this new discipline; and by the mid-1920s the taming of *Drosophila* and corn as model organisms for tracking the transmission of hereditary traits lent it a rigor and productivity that other disciplines could scarcely match. But the first generation of geneticists — Morgan and his school — did more than develop the techniques and practice of genetics as a rival of embryology; they also forged a way of talking about genes — about their role and meaning in reproduction, growth, and development. When Muller identified the gene as *the* basis of life, he was claiming for it both ontological and temporal priority. First the gene, then the remaining protoplasm (i.e., the cytoplasm), appearing as a "by-product" whose only function is that of facilitating environment, to "foster" the gene. First the gene, then life — or rather, with the gene comes life. The concept of gene invoked here is Janus-faced: it is part physicist's atom and part Platonic soul; at one and the same time, fundamental building block and animating force. Only the "action" of genes can initiate the complex manifold of processes constituting a living organism.

But what exactly is it that genes *do*? This of course Muller, Brink, and Morgan could not say. The notion of "gene action" may even have been facilitated by the very absence of knowledge of what a gene is (in the sense that not knowing what a gene is may have made it easier to attribute to it any, even miraculous, properties). But even though these early geneticists could tell us nothing about the nature of the presumed source of all subsequent growth and development, could give no scientific account of "gene action," they offered future generations of geneticists something equally valuable.

Scientists usually assume that only their data and theories matter for scientific progress, that how they talk about these data and theories is irrelevant to their actual work, but here, in introducing this particular way of talking, the first generation of American geneticists provided a conceptual framework that was of critical importance for the future course of biological research. To capture both its rhetorical and conceptual force, I will call this way of talking the "discourse of gene action" — a discourse that was, for genetics, undeniably productive. It enabled geneticists to get on with their work without worrying about their lack of information about the nature of such "action" — to a considerable degree, it even obscured the need for such information. (Throughout the interwar period American geneticists routinely invoked the notion of "gene action" as if its meaning was self-evident.) At the same time, the attribution of agency, autonomy, and causal responsibility to genes lent primacy both to the object of geneticists' concern and to the discipline of genetics — in their own eyes and in the eyes of others. They were dealing with *the* basis of life. If, as Brink wrote, the hereditary complex is elevated from a "passive object" to a locus of primary activity, the student of that hereditary complex is, by the same move, also elevated to primary activity.

Indeed, I suggest that the discourse of gene action provides the specific hallmark (or trademark) of the American school of Morganian genetics, especially of its approach to development. If its first use was to bracket the question of development, later, in the mid-1930s, when a number of American geneticists did turn their attention to development, it helped define the approach they then took: it framed the questions that could or could not be meaningfully asked, the organisms they chose to study, the experiments that did or did not make sense to do, the explanations that were or were not acceptable. In this sense, it served cognitive as well as political functions. Ian Hacking has suggested that every scientific discipline has its own "style of reasoning," which constitutes the epistemological context of that science. In other words, it creates the very possibility for truth or falsehood and therefore determines what counts as objective.[8] My notion of "discourse" is close to Hacking's notion of "style."

---

[8] Ian Hacking, "Language, Truth, and Reason," in M. Hollis and S. Lukes (eds.), *Rationality and Relativism*, pp. 48–66.

Needless to say, this way of talking about the relation between genes and development — a way that recasts the dynamics of development as a consequence of "gene action" — was markedly less congenial to most embryologists. It offered the student of development not a separate domain of inquiry (as Morgan's remarks implied), but rather a promissory note for inclusion or, more accurately, for incorporation. As early as 1924 the German embryologist Hans Spemann, Morgan's most important counterpart, wrote:

> The previous progress [of genetics] has been amazing, and it is not from a feeling of futile labours but rather from being aware of their paramount powers of appropriation that geneticists now are on the look-out for new connexions. They have cast their eye on us, on *Entwicklungsmechanik* . . .[9]

And a decade later, in his presidential address to the AAAS, Ross Harrison sounded a similar warning:

> Now that . . . the "Wanderlust" of geneticists is beginning to urge them in our direction, it may not be inappropriate to point out a danger in this threatened invasion.
> The prestige of success enjoyed by the gene theory might easily become a hindrance to the understanding of development by directing our attention solely to the genome. . . . Already we have theories that refer the processes of development to genic action and regard the whole performance as no more than the realization of the potencies of the genes. Such theories are altogether too one-sided . . .[10]

Embryologists had good grounds for concern. Not only was the status of their discipline under threat; so too was the status of their question: How *does* a germ cell develop into a multicellular organism? If the genetic content of all cells in an organism is the same, then how is one to make sense of the emergence of the mani-

---

[9] Hans Spemann, "Vererbung und Entwicklungsmechanik," *Z. Indukt. Abstammungs- und Vererbungslehre* 33 (1924), 293.

[10] Ross Harrison, "Embryology and Its Relations," *Science* 85 (1937), 369–74.

fest differences among all the cells that make up a complex organism? To them, it seemed self-evident that this problem of differentiation, so deeply at the heart of their own concerns, was simply incompatible with the notion that the gene was the exclusive locus of action.[11] As Morgan himself subsequently admitted (speaking now as an embryologist):

> The implication in most genetic interpretation is that all the genes are acting all the time in the same way. This would leave unexplained why some cells of the embryo develop in one way, some in another, if the genes are the only agents in the results.[12]

Few if any geneticists heeded Morgan's warning. (Even Morgan did not heed his own warning.) Instead, those interested in the relation between genes and development found another route: they changed the subject — or, more precisely, they transformed the embryologist's question into a different one. Alfred H. Sturtevant spelled out how to do this. Sturtevant opened his paper on "the developmental effects of genes" at the 1932 International Congress of Genetics by observing:

> One of the central problems of biology is that of differentiation — how does an egg develop into a complex many-celled organism? That is, of course, the traditional major problem of embryology; but it also appears in genetics in the form of the question, "How do genes produce their effects?"

Between "the direct activity of a gene and the end product," he argued, "is a chain of reaction." And the task of the geneticist is to analyze these "chains of reaction into their individual links."[13]

---

[11] Geneticists, after all, could only study variations in already existing organisms; the question of how organisms come to be formed in the first place was thus beyond their ken.

[12] T. H. Morgan, *Embryology and Genetics*, p. 9.

[13] Alfred H. Sturtevant, "The Use of Mosaics in the Study of the Developmental Effects of Genes," *Proceedings of the Sixth International Congress of Genetics* (1932), 304.

What does this rephrasing accomplish? Actually, quite a lot. Once the problem of development is translated into the question of "how genes produce their effects," the task is immediately — and almost miraculously — simplified. No longer need one get bogged down in the complex dynamics of eggs and multicellular organisms; it ought to suffice to study single-celled organisms, where one should have a better chance of analyzing "chains of reaction." George Beadle and Edward Tatum chose *Neurospora*, a single-celled organism that can be cultured *in vitro*, and their choice paid off handsomely. In 1940 they proposed their famous "one gene–one enzyme" hypothesis as an explanation of how genes produce their effects. At last, the mysterious notion of "gene action" seemed to have real content. Beadle and Tatum provided a particular kind of answer to the question of how a gene produces its effects, namely, "It makes an enzyme." Accordingly, developmental genetics could henceforth be understood as the biochemistry of gene action.

Together, the turn to *Neurospora* and the "one gene–one enzyme" hypothesis proved to be of decisive importance to the future development of genetics. It provided critical encouragement for the development of bacterial genetics and, eventually, of molecular biology. The rest of the story you all know. In 1953, with the definitive identification of DNA as the genetic material, Watson and Crick struck gold. Simple hydrogen bonding turned out to provide the secret of how genes reproduce themselves, and nucleic acid sequences, of how they make enzymes. As they discreetly wrote, "In a long molecule, many different permutations are possible, and it therefore seems likely that the precise sequence of the bases is the code which carries the genetical information." [14] All one needed to know was the code, and soon that was forthcoming as well.

[14] J. D. Watson and F. Crick, "Genetical Implications of the Structure of DNA," *Nature* 171 (1953), 964–67.

There it is: what *must* be the answer! DNA carries the genetical information (or program), and genes "produce their effects" by providing the "instructions" for protein synthesis. DNA makes RNA, RNA makes proteins, and proteins make us — without doubt, one of the greatest milestones in the history of science. But in what sense is it the answer? What in fact do "information," "program," "instruction," or even the verb "makes," actually mean?

Watson and Crick have gotten a lot of credit for their work, and deservedly so, but one contribution has, I fear, been overlooked: the introduction of the "information" metaphor into the repertoire of biological discourse was a stroke of genius. The story of this metaphor — its uses and implications — is an immensely rich one, but perhaps a few brief comments might nonetheless be in order. Just a few years earlier the mathematician Claude Shannon had proposed a precise quantitative measure of the complexity of linear codes. He called this measure "information" — by design independent of meaning or function — and by the early fifties "information theory" had become a very hot subject in the world of communications systems. It seemed to hold enormous promise for the analysis of all sorts of complex systems, even of biological systems. And the fact that DNA seemed to function as a linear code made the use of this notion of information for genetics appear natural. But as early as 1952 it was recognized that the technical definition of information simply could not serve for biological information. (It would, for example, assign the same amount of "information" to the DNA of a functioning organism as to a mutant form, however disabling that mutation was.) The notion of "genetical information" that Watson and Crick invoked was thus not literal, but metaphoric. But it was an extremely powerful metaphor. Even though it permitted no quantitative measure, it authorized the expectation, anticipated in the notion of "gene action," that biological information does not increase in the course of development: it is already fully contained in the genome. By this move, and even more, by the subsequent collapse of "information" with "program" and "instruction," the concept of gene action was vastly fortified. Just as Erwin Schrödinger had anticipated, the "chromosome structures are law-code and executive power — or, to use another simile, they are architect's plan and builder's craft — in one." [15]

Classical embryologists would surely not have been happy with this turn of events — their questions, their organisms (even the lowly *Drosophila* had come to be seen as too complex, too messy), and they themselves had been left behind — but a new generation of biologists had little cause to look back. The first generation of molecular biologists could not answer the question of how an egg turns into an organism (could say nothing, e.g., about how a gene comes to make the particular enzymes that are needed for the development of a many-celled organism, in the right amounts, at the right time and in the right place), but they had a powerful new rhetorical resource for managing such questions. They could talk instead about "development" in the abstract, and the genetic programs or instructions that are needed to guide it. In his presidential address to the BAAS in 1965, Sir Peter Medawar offered something of a retrospective eulogy to embryology:

> Wise after the event, we can now see that embryology simply did not have, and could not have created, the background of genetical reasoning which would have made it possible to formulate a theory of development. . . . Embryonic development . . . [must] be an unfolding of pre-existing capabilities, an acting-out of genetically encoded instructions.[16]

The progression from Watson and Crick to the Human Genome Initiative, as Watson himself has so often reminded us, appears straightforward and logical. If all development is merely an un-

---

[15] Erwin Schrödinger, *What Is Life?*, p. 23.

[16] Sir Peter Medawar, "A Biological Retrospect," *Nature* 207, no. 5004 (1965), 1328–29.

folding of preexisting instructions encoded in the nucleotide sequences of DNA — if our genes make us what we are — then it makes perfect sense to set the identification of these sequences as the primary, and indeed ultimate, goal of biology.

What, then, do I mean when I say that the discourse of gene action — now augmented with metaphors of information and instruction — exerted a critical force on the course of biological research? Can words have force in and of themselves? Of course not. They acquire force only through their influence on human actors. Through their influence on scientists, administrators, and funding agencies, they provide powerful rationales and incentives for the mobilization of resources, for the identification of particular research agendas, for focusing our scientific energies and attention in particular directions. The discourse of gene action has worked in just these ways. And it would be foolhardy to pretend it has not worked well. The history of twentieth-century biology is a history of extraordinary success; genetics — first classical, then molecular — has yielded some of the greatest triumphs of modern science. Indeed, this way of talking has proven so powerful that now, after all these years, it seems to be finally on the verge of making good the promissory note that Morgan and his school extended in the early part of the century — and not just rhetorically, but in actual scientific practice. Over the last few years molecular biology has made extraordinary progress in elucidating just how it is that (as they say) "genes control development."

But a funny thing happened on the way to the holy grail. That extraordinary progress has become less and less describable within the discourse that enabled it. The dogmatic focus on gene action called forth a dazzling armamentarium of new techniques for analyzing the behavior of distinct gene segments; and the information yielded by those techniques is now radically subverting the doctrine of the gene as sole (or even primary) agent. It has also become conspicuously evident that there were all along serious problems with the discourse of gene action — besides its productive blindness to questions of development and cell differentiation. As Richard Lewontin reminds us:

> DNA is a dead molecule, among the most nonreactive, chemically inert molecules in the world. . . . [It] has no power to reproduce itself. Rather it is produced out of elementary materials by a complex cellular machinery of proteins. While it is often said that DNA produces proteins, in fact proteins (enzymes) produce DNA. The newly manufactured DNA is certainly a *copy* of the old, . . . but we do not describe the Eastman Kodak factory as a place of self-reproduction [of photographs] . . .

He continues:

> Not only is DNA incapable of making copies of itself, . . . but it is incapable of "making" anything else. The linear sequence of nucleotides in DNA is used by the machinery of the cell to determine what sequences of amino acids is to be built into a protein, and to determine when and where the protein is to be made. But the proteins of the cell are made by other proteins, and without that protein-forming machinery *nothing* can be made. There is an appearance here of infinite regress . . . , but this appearance is an artifact of another error of vulgar biology, that it is only the genes that are passed from parent to offspring. In fact, an egg, before fertilization, contains a complete apparatus of production deposited there in the course of its cellular development. We inherit not only genes made of DNA but an intricate structure of cellular machinery made up of proteins.[17]

Of course, you may say. We knew this all along. Well, yes and no. Yes in the sense that, apart from the reference to DNA, it is the sort of observation embryologists used to make all the time. But no in the sense that, except for an occasional aside (like

---

[17] Richard Lewontin, "The Dream of the Human Genome," *N.Y. Review of Books*, May 28, 1992, p. 33.

Morgan's), geneticists did not; Lewontin, interestingly, is a geneticist, not an embryologist. The simple fact is that for many years geneticists had little reason to refer to eggs and their cytoplasmic structure, and even less reason to talk about events prior to fertilization. The discourse of gene action had established a spatial map that lent the cytoplasm scientific invisibility to geneticists ("indifferent" was how Morgan described the cytoplasm) and a temporal map that defined the moment of fertilization as origin, with no meaningful time before fertilization. In this schema, there was neither time nor place in which to conceive of the egg's cytoplasm exerting *its* effects.

With the emergence of molecular biology in the 1950s and 1960s, and its powerful metaphors of information and programs, the significance of the cytoplasm eroded even further. And once the bacterium *E. coli* came to serve as the model organism (recall Jacques Monod's famous remark, "What's true for *E. coli* is true for the elephant"), questions about eggs and fertilization ceased to be applicable. What is new is that Lewontin's commonplace observations can now not only be articulated, but actually heard. They have once again come to make sound biological sense, even in genetics. Current research — drawing on the phenomenal technical successes of molecular biology, and even on the sequence information emerging from the Human Genome Initiative — invites (ever more insistently) a shift in locution in which the cytoplasm is just as likely as the genome to be cast as the locus of control. What has happened?

Part of the precondition of this transformation has been the return of higher organisms to center stage. With that return, the study of embryogenesis has become fashionable, indeed a site of intense activity for geneticists. And *that*, it turns out, has made an important difference.

As recently as 1984 David Baltimore was still invoking the more familiar language of molecular biology to explain the distinction between modern genetics and classical physiology (or embryology):

> The approach of genetics ... is to ask about blueprints, not machines; about decisions, not mechanics; about information and history. In the factory analogy, genetics leaves the greasy machines and goes to the executive suite, where it analyzes the planners, the decision makers, the computers, the historic records. ... Biologists needed to find the cell's brain.[18]

But today he writes of the extent to which differentiation is governed by "active control" mechanisms, in which "the expression state of each gene [is] determined by the dynamic interaction of regulatory proteins present in the cell at any given time."[19]

Indeed, even as Baltimore spoke of the need to find the cell's brain in "the executive suite" (i.e., the DNA), the "cell's brain" was already in the process of moving out of the executive suite and into the factory. In 1984 Sidney Brenner, himself one of the major architects of molecular biology, confessed:

> At the beginning it was said that the answer to the understanding of development was going to come from a knowledge of molecular mechanisms of gene control. ... I don't know if anyone believes that anymore. The molecular mechanisms look boringly simple, and they don't tell us what we want to know. We have to try to discover the principles of organization, how lots of things are put together in the same place. I don't think these principles will be embodied in a simple chemical device, as it is for the genetic code.[20]

Today the really "smart genes" are seen as those that have the capacity to respond to a complex of signals encoded in cytoplasmic proteins. Genes may be "smart," but the "brain of the smart gene"

[18] David Baltimore, "The Brain of a Cell," *Science* 84 (November 1984), 150.

[19] Helen M. Blau and David Baltimore, "Differentiation Requires Continuous Regulation," *Journal of Cell Biology* 112, no. 5 (1991), 781–83.

[20] Quoted in Roger Lewin, "Why Is Development So Illogical?" *Science* 224 (1984), 1327–29.

is not to be found in the genes themselves: as Eric Davidson puts it, it is a "complicated assemblage of proteins known as a transcription complex."[21] The point is that, as we learn more about how genes actually work in complex organisms, talk about "gene action" subtly transmutes into talk about gene "activation," with the locus of control shifting from genes themselves to the complex biochemical dynamics (protein-protein and protein-nucleic acid interactions) of cells in constant communication with each other. *Scientific American* glosses this shift as the "news" that "organisms control most of their genes."

New metaphors abound. Marking the long-overlooked distinction between program and data, Henri Atlan and Moshe Koppel suggest "an alternative metaphor of DNA as data to a parallel computing network embedded in the global geometrical and biochemical structure of the cell."[22] A yet more radical inversion is proposed by H. F. Nijhout. In lieu of the metaphors of "control" and "programs" that have so pervaded modern thinking in molecular, developmental, and evolutionary biology and that, he says, "have shaped priorities in research," Nijhout suggests that "a more balanced, and useful, view of the role of genes in development is that they act as suppliers of the material needs of development and . . . as context-dependent catalysts of cellular changes . . ."[23] "Genes," he concludes,

> are passive sources of materials upon which a cell can draw, and are part of an evolved mechanism that allows organisms, their tissues and their cells to be independent of their environment by providing the means of synthesizing, importing, or structuring the substances (not just gene products, but all substances) required for metabolism, growth and differentiation.

[21] Quoted in Tim Beardsley, "Smart Genes," *Scientific American* (August 1991), 87.

[22] Henri Atlan and Moshe Koppel, "The Cellular Computer DNA: Program or Data," *Bulletin of Mathematical Biology* 53, no. 3 (1990), 335–48.

[23] H. F. Nijhout, "Metaphors and the Role of Genes in Development," *Bioessays* 12, no. 9 (1990), 441.

> The function of regulatory genes is ultimately no different from that of structural genes, in that they simply provide efficient ways of ensuring that the required materials are supplied at the right time and place.[24]

Nijhout's proposal may be extreme. But there is no question that a new way of talking is in the air, in keeping with the emergence of a new biology: molecular biologists have discovered the organism. The new developmental biology brings with it a resurgence of interest in many of the problems of "organization" and morphogenesis that had occupied an earlier generation of embryologists, and even a resurrection of a number of the same experimental protocols. The findings that result point neither to cytoplasmic nor to nuclear determination, but rather to a complex but highly coordinated system of regulatory dynamics that operates simultaneously at all levels: at the level of transcription activation, of translation, of protein activation, and of intercellular communication — in the nucleus, in the cytoplasm, indeed, in the organism as a whole.

So what is it that I, and I hope by now you too, find so interesting about this story? For a scientist (even a semilapsed scientist), what compels the greatest interest must surely be the specific content of the conceptual revolution now under way. The shift in discourse we are now seeing in the literature marks a conceptual shift of startling magnitude; it will require us to learn how to think in radically new ways. Sixty years ago men like Joseph Needham, C. H. Waddington, and J. H. Woodger sought a language for the complex dynamics relating nuclear and cytoplasmic elements in the process philosophy of Alfred North Whitehead. Today Whitehead's language is too foreign to us to be of use. But we have other resources to compensate — especially in mathematics and computers. For some time now a number of workers — Stuart Kauffman and René Thomas, among others — have been

---

[24] Ibid., 444.

developing models for genetic networks that represent a great advance over more simplistic notions of gene action. These models illustrate how networks of genes in interaction can give rise to stable, self-perpetuating patterns of biochemical dynamics of a kind radically different from anything autonomously acting genes could ever yield. In so doing, they give substance to Waddington's earlier notions of epigenetic pathways and, at the same time, automatically and irrevocably undermine traditional divisions between genetic and epigenetic. But as interesting as they are, such models are only a beginning. In keeping with the new talk of cytoplasmic control, it would also be useful to develop models of somatic networks of interacting proteins, in which genes would be the covert intermediaries of protein interaction, rather than proteins being the intermediaries of gene interaction (as they are in gene network models). Ultimately, of course, one needs full-scale models of genes and proteins in interaction — of a kind that large-scale computers are now making possible. In the end, I think that the most important function of all these models will be to stimulate the growth of just those intuitions about interactive and emergent phenomena that past discourses have so helped to stymie. I have no doubt that the effect will be a transformation in the way we think about biological systems that will make the changes we have already begun to witness look like mere harbingers.

For an observer of scientific change, however, this story provokes other questions. Put simply, they are twofold. First, what lent the discourse of gene action such persuasiveness for so many years? Second, why is it now giving way? (Or relatedly we might ask, why did embryology languish for so many years, and what has permitted its return today?) These are different versions of the same questions just because of the extent to which the fate of embryology has been so intimately linked historically to talk of gene action. Posed either way, they are far more difficult to answer than naive empiricism might suggest. The simplistic answers might go like this: embryology languished because it was bad and unproductive science; we talked about gene action because we didn't know better; indeed, developmental phenomena are so difficult to study that real progress was impossible until the advent of the techniques of recombinant DNA that molecular biology has brought. All of these claims might be true — and still only part of the story. What they leave out is the entire issue of motivation.

Relatedly, they also ignore the awkward fact that the first experimental studies to spark the interest of molecular biologists in the early development of higher organisms relied solely on classical techniques that were labor intensive to be sure, but that had long been available. I think especially of the studies of "maternal (or cytoplasmic) effect" mutants and of cytoplasmic rescue in *Drosophila* first undertaken by Alan Garen and others in the early 1970s and carried to such dramatic fruition a few years later by Christianne Nusslein-Volhard and her colleagues. What these studies did was to establish the critical role played by the cytoplasmic structure of the egg *prior to fertilization, before* time zero. The most conspicuous question is, why were these efforts undertaken in the 1970s, and not before? I do not have time to go into the details of these studies, but they reveal, as Garen and others confirm, that no technical impasse prevented their being done years, if not decades, earlier. Maternal effect mutants — even in *Drosophila* — had been accumulating since the early part of the century; and the most crucial technical instrument, the micromanipulator, had been developed and used in the 1930s. Of course, it is well known that *Drosophila* was an exceedingly difficult organism to study embryologically, but even this ostensible impasse had been largely overcome by the early 1950s — again, by the application of long-available techniques. What was missing — both for the study of *Drosophila* embryology and for the more specific examination of maternal effects — was the motivation to invest the necessary effort. The very term geneticists invoked for "maternal effects" worked to discourage interest — since 1930 they had argued for the term "delayed inheritance" as a more accurate description of these mutants. More generally, the belief — prevalent among geneticists at least since the mid-1920s — that the genetic message of the zygote "produces" the organism, that the cytoplasm is merely a passive substrate, could not but sap the motivation needed to undertake such undeniably difficult experiments. The question therefore becomes, what overcame that assumption?

If, as I have been arguing, the ways in which we talk about scientific objects are not simply determined by empirical evidence, but, rather, actively influence the kind of evidence we seek (and hence are more likely to find), then other factors must be considered if we are to understand the strength and persistence of the discourse of gene action. Let me, in my remaining minutes, very schematically indicate what some of these other factors were, at least as they operated between the two world wars.

In the 1930s the Swiss embryologist Oscar Schotté liked to illustrate the relations between embryology and genetics with a sketch of two views of the cell: as perceived by the embryologist, the nucleus is very small; but as perceived by the geneticist, it virtually fills the entire cell.[25] In this sketch, the nucleus and cytoplasm are employed as tropes for the two disciplines — both lend to their object of study a size in direct proportion to their perceived self-importance. In like fashion, the two disciplines lent to each object, nucleus and cytoplasm, their own self-attributes of agency, autonomy, and power. As L. C. Dunn put it, "Genetics had to be a bit pushy in order to get itself established."[26] In addition, however, the nucleus and cytoplasm also came to stand as tropes for national importance, agency, and power, with the former, as the domain in which American genetics had come to stake its unique strengths, associated with American interests (and prowess) and the latter, with European, and especially German, interests and prowess. German biologists were often explicit about what

[25] Sander, "The Role of Genes."

[26] L. C. Dunn, Oral History Transcript, Columbia University Oral History Project (1959), p. 319.

they saw as the attempt by American geneticists to appropriate the entire field. In 1927, for example, V. Haecker described the field between genetics and development as the "no-man's land" of somatogenesis — "a border field which by us has been tilled for quite some time. . . . The Americans have taken no notice of this." [27] This tension persisted throughout the interwar years and was resolved only with the resounding defeat of Germany (and the destruction of German biology) in World War II.

But the most conspicuous metaphoric reference of nucleus and cytoplasm is surely to be sought in sexual reproduction. By tradition as well as by biological experience, at least until World War II, nucleus and cytoplasm are also tropes for male and female. Until the emergence of bacterial genetics in the mid-1940s, all research in genetics and embryology, in both Europe and the United States, focused on organisms that pass through embryonic stages of development; and for these organisms, a persistent asymmetry is evident in male and female contributions to fertilization: the female gamete, the egg, is vastly larger than the male gamete, the sperm. The difference is the cytoplasm, deriving from the maternal parent (a no-man's land indeed); by contrast, the sperm cell is almost pure nucleus. It is thus hardly surprising to find that, in the conventional discourse about nucleus and cytoplasm, cytoplasm is routinely taken to be synonymous with egg. Furthermore — by an all too familiar twist of logic — the nucleus was

---

[27] V. Haecker, "Phänogenetisch gerichtete Bestrebungen in Amerika," *Z. indukt. Abstammungs- und Vererbungslehre* 41 (1926), 232–38. Richard Goldschmidt, the leading figure in Germany in physiological genetics, registered a similar complaint, attributing American indifference to "the rise of a school of geneticists to whom biological knowledge apart from Mendelism did not seem necessary, whereby they were entirely content with knowing the work of the schools most closely akin to their own approach" (trans. by Sander, "The Role of Genes," p. 389). And elsewhere he commented, "It is really too bad that Morgan and his students . . . have got stuck in such a narrow interpretation of genetic phenomena and oppose at all costs any new idea, especially a physiological one. . . . I have discussed this at length with my dear friend Morgan, but he insists that a thing [phenotype] has been explained once one has mapped a corresponding Mendelian factor" (quoted in Jonathan Harwood, *Styles of Scientific Thought: The German Genetics Community, 1900–1933,* p. 50).

often taken as a stand-in for sperm. Theodore Boveri, for example, argued for the need to recognize at least some function for the cytoplasm on the grounds of "the absurdity of the idea that it would be possible to bring a sperm to develop by means of an artificial culture medium" (published posthumously in 1918 and translated in Fritz Baltzer, *Theodor Boveri*, pp. 83–84).[28]

Many of the debates about the relative importance of nucleus and cytoplasm in inheritance thus inevitably reflect older debates about the relative importance (or activity) of maternal and paternal contributions to reproduction, where the overwhelming historical tendency has been to attribute activity and motive force to the male contribution, while relegating the female contribution to the role of passive, facilitating environment. In Platonic terms, the egg represented the body, and the nucleus, the activating soul. (In a related vein, E. B. Wilson's remarks about Morgan's early passion for embryology may also be worth noting: "It is an open secret that even now he sometimes escapes from the austere heights where Drosophila has its home in order to indulge in the illicit pleasures of the egg and its development.")[29] In these associations surely lies part of the background for both the force of the assumption of gene action and for its gradual fading away from the status of self-evident truth.

Change, of course, did not come overnight. While embryology was no longer a thriving research enterprise after the war, the memory of that disciplinary struggle took time to abate. It also took time — roughly two decades — for German biology to rebuild. Lastly, it took the women's movement to change our ideas about gender, and perhaps the hiatus of bacterial genetics (where no one had to think about male and female contributions) for these changes to creep into biology. By the time that the study of higher organisms began to reemerge in the 1970s, the entire

---

[28] See also E. B. Wilson, *The Cell in Development and Heredity*, p. 262.

[29] E. B. Wilson, "Opening Address," *Proceedings of the Sixth International Congress of Genetics* (1932), 82.

world had changed, and so had the ways that seemed natural to talk. Embryology was no longer a rival, Germany had become a friend, and gender equity was all the rage. There were of course also other changes, which I have not talked about — most notably, perhaps, the emergence of a discourse of feedback and of bodies as cyborgs, both associated with the extraordinary developments in systems analysis and computer science. And last but hardly least were the equally extraordinary developments internal to molecular biology, especially the techniques of recombinant DNA. Concurrent with the changes in the way we talked, and thought, these developments soon effected dramatic changes in what could be done in the lab. Over the last decade the world of technical feasibility has changed beyond recognition. These very different kinds of changes — in how we talk and in what can be done in the lab — have worked in concert and in mutual reinforcement, the one creating the opportunity and the other the need to radically rethink the meaning of genetic determinism.

Acting in synch (as it always does), the social, cognitive, and technical history of twentieth-century biology has once again brought us to a dramatic and critical juncture. Now all that is needed is for scientists to take advantage of the opportunity that has been created and respond to the need that has been uncovered. But if there is a moral to this story, it is this: lest we be too quick to congratulate ourselves for our newfound enlightenment, we should remember that our predilections — grounded though they must be in our particular social and political realities — are all we have to guide us. Thus there is no guarantee that the opportunity now before us will not be seized by new doctrinaires; indeed, there is every reason to expect that it will. After all, how else can science proceed? Still, I retain the hope that, as scientists, we may become more aware of the weight and force of the language that we have no choice but to borrow from the larger culture of which we, inescapably, are part.

BIBLIOGRAPHY

Allen, Gar. "T. H. Morgan and the Split between Embryology and Genetics, 1910–1926." In T. J. Horder, I. A. Witkowski, and C. C. Wylie (eds.), *A History of Embryology*, pp. 113–46. Cambridge: Cambridge University Press, 1986.

Atlan, Henri, and Moshe Koppel. "The Cellular Computer DNA: Program or Data." *Bulletin of Mathematical Biology* 52, no. 3 (1990), 335–48.

Baltimore, David. "The Brain of a Cell." *Science* 84 (November 1984), 150.

Baltzer, Fritz. *Theodor Boveri*. Translated by Dorthea Rudnick. Berkeley: University of California Press, 1967.

Beardsley, Tim. "Smart Genes." *Scientific American* (August 1991), 87–95.

Blau, Helen M., and David Baltimore, "Differentiation Requires Continuous Regulation," *Journal of Cell Biology* 112, no. 5 (1991), 781–83.

Brink, R. A. "Genetics and the Problems of Development." *American Naturalist* 61, no. 574 (1927), 280–83.

Hacking, Ian. "Language, Truth, and Reason." In M. Hollis and S. Lukes (eds.), *Rationality and Relativism*, pp. 48–66. Cambridge, Mass.: MIT Press, 1986.

Haecker, V. (1926) "Phänogenetisch gerichtete Bestrebungen in Amerika." *Z. indukt. Abstammungs- und Vererbungslehre* 41 (1926), 232–38.

Harrison, Ross, "Embryology and Its Relations." *Science* 85 (1937), 369–74.

Harwood, Jonathan, *Styles of Scientific Thought: The German Genetics Community, 1900–1933*. Chicago: University of Chicago Press, 1993.

Horder, T. J., J. A. Witkowsky, and C. C. Wylie (eds.). *A History of Embryology*. Cambridge: Cambridge University Press, 1986.

Lewin, Roger. "Why Is Development So Illogical?" *Science* 224 (1984), 1327–29.

Lewontin, Richard. "The Dream of the Human Genome." *N.Y. Review of Books*, May 28, 1992.

Medawar, Sir Peter. "A Biological Retrospect." *Nature* 207, no. 5004 (1965), 1327–30.

Morgan, T. H. "Mendelian Heredity in Relation to Cytology." In E. V. Cowdry, *General Cytology*, pp. 691–734. Chicago: University of Chicago Press, 1924.

———. "Genetics and the Physiology of Development." *American Naturalist* 60, no. 671 (1926), 489–515.

———. *The Theory of the Gene*. New Haven: Yale University Press, 1926.

———. *Embryology and Genetics*. New York: Columbia University Press, 1934.

Muller, H. J. "The Gene as the Basis of Life." *Proceedings of the International Congress of Plant Sciences* 1 (Ithaca, 1926), 897–921.

Nijhout, H. F. "Metaphors and the Role of Genes in Development." *Bioessays* 12, no. 9 (1990), 441–46.

Sander, Klaus. "The Role of Genes in Ontogenesis — Evolving Concepts from 1883 to 1983 as Perceived by an Insect Embryologist." In Horder et al. (eds.), *History of Embryology*, pp. 363–95.

Sapp, Jan. *Beyond the Gene*. Oxford: Oxford University Press, 1987.

Schrödinger, Erwin. *What Is Life?* Cambridge: Cambridge University Press, 1944.

Spemann, Hans. "Vererbung und Entwicklungsmechanik." *Z. Indukt. Abstammungs- und Vererbungslehre* 33 (1924), 272–94.

Sturtevant, Alfred H. "The Use of Mosaics in the Study of the Developmental Effects of Genes." *Proceedings of the Sixth International Congress of Genetics* (1932), 304.

Watson, J. D., and F. Crick. "Genetical Implications of the Structure of DNA." *Nature* 171 (1953), 964–67.

Wilson, E. B. *The Cell in Development and Heredity*. New York: Macmillan, 1896.

———. "Opening Address." *Proceedings of the Sixth International Congress of Genetics* (1932), 82.

I

Mendacity Enforced: Europe, 1914–1989

II

Freedom and Its Discontents: Postunification Germany

FRITZ STERN

The Tanner Lectures on Human Values

Delivered at

Yale University
March 1 and 2, 1993

FRITZ STERN, currently University Professor and formerly Seth Low Professor of History at Columbia University, received his Ph.D. degree from this institution in 1953. He has taught at the Free University of Berlin and Yale University, and been visiting professor at the University of Konstanz (FRG) and the Fondation Nationale des Sciences Politiques (Paris). He is a member of the American Philosophical Society and a fellow of the American Academy of Arts and Sciences, and received the Officer's Cross of the Order of Merit from the Federal Republic of Germany in 1976. He has been a consultant for the U.S. Department of State, and is currently a member of Helsinki Watch and on the advisory board of the Einstein Forum (Potsdam). He is editor of *The Varieties of History* (1956), and author of numerous books and articles, including *Dreams and Delusions* (1987), *The Failure of Illiberalism* (1972), and *The Politics of Cultural Despair* (1961). His book *Gold and Iron* (1977) received the Lionel Trilling Book Award and was nominated for the National Book Award in 1978.

I

That the peaceful revolutions of 1989 were glorious and momentous was instantly recognized. Four years later the euphoria has dissipated, as nations confront the immense difficulties of building new institutions and of fighting economic hardships. It was marvelously inspiring to tame or topple Communist regimes; it is painful to create and adapt to market economies and liberal polities. For East Europeans — to say nothing of the peoples of the former Soviet Union — the daily struggles and privations, the new conflicts and corruptions, are dispiriting. The Western nations seem mired in the gloom of recession and political apathy; these same nations, the United States included, have been lavish in praise of the East but reticent in aid. And still: what happened in Poland, Hungary, and Czechoslovakia (and quite differently in East Germany) had grandeur; despite all the uncertainties, we know that the process of self-liberation from Communism is irreversible.

I believe that, seen in a longer historical perspective, the events of 1989 will assume a still greater magnitude: they were dramatic then, they are historic now. I consider 1989 as important in the history of Europe as 1914 — for it ended the epoch that began then. The Great War, which legitimated ever-escalating violence, was the beginning of a chain of horrors committed by national states that was carried to the ultimate extreme when two great ideological movements, born of war, captured the state and established our century's characteristic form of tyranny, totalitarianism. The war machines created ever new means of maiming and killing people — and inevitably the slaughter raised the most elemental questions and by a thousand means inhibited answers. Governments needed to deceive their people — and their people, at least most of them, wanted to be deceived. Hate-filled untruths were concocted to rally or comfort the much-tested, grieving peoples of Europe; they confounded them still further. But brutal killing demanded a brutal or at least an anesthetized mind.

In 1917 the Bolsheviks seized power in Russia, determined that the war of nations had to be transformed into the historically prescribed conflict, a war of classes; put differently, the national war, according to Bolshevik doctrine, had sprung from and yet concealed the real subterranean war; an end to the imperialist war would signal the beginning of the real civil war. In the same year, provoked by German power, the United States entered the war and Wilson and Lenin began a duel for Europe's mind and soul. After 1945 the two powers confronted each other directly over a prostrate Europe — and for all the brief periods of détente and peaceful coexistence, the struggle on both sides was Manichean. In 1989 Communism collapsed — by now it is all but buried — and America, seemingly strong and victorious, having accumulated its own huge deficits that go far beyond the material, found its power, influence, and interest, even its role in Europe, diminished. After 1989 the rise of a new, autonomous Europe — at last spanning all of the historic Europe — seemed possible. It still does, though Europe's dismal failure to act in the civil war that is destroying the former Yugoslavia is tantamount to a declaration of temporary bankruptcy.

How did the peoples of Eastern Europe liberate themselves from structures and controls that had for so long been considered unassailable? As in all great historic upheavals, historians will come to recognize the confluence of many factors — for one, Communist rule in Eastern Europe never acquired true legitimacy, and a faltering economy gave added strength to a spirit of opposition that was never wholly quashed. The decline of Soviet authority began in the Brezhnev era: the irrepressible voices of dissidents, the presence of a Polish pope, the immense costs of the war in Afghanistan and the arms race with a technologically superior United States, Gorbachev's realization that *glasnost'* was a prerequisite for economic recovery, and the magnet of the much-heralded Europe '92 — these are some of the factors that future historians will have to assess.

For my purposes I want to emphasize what I think was the principal theme of the leaders of the revolution: Václav Havel's defiant insistence that men and women must have the right to "live in the truth." This, I believe, was the common inspiration of East European opponents of Soviet tyranny, and all of them sensed that liberation had to be peaceful — to protect lives and to prevent still further rounds of violence and untruth.

Allow me a personal aside: I was thrilled by the self-liberations of 1989; I saw them as the first peaceful, glorious revolution in our dark century. The round table, the civic forum, the disciplined thousands in the streets — all of these were spontaneous claims to emancipation, the desire for freedom and dignity. These velvet revolutions of poets and intellectuals gave voice to the millions who sustained them. The voice that struck me most forcefully was Havel's. He was a chronicler of what was spiritually intolerable. Hearing his defiant insistence that people must "live in the truth" I was suddenly struck that this was the very thing that had been denied to so many people in the decades after the Great War; that repression was the hallmark of the era — and I had experienced it in my own childhood and early adolescence. Havel's words struck me because they evoked memories of living under the enforced mendacity of National Socialism, of the double life: silence in a school in which classmates and teachers were joyfully National Socialist, with all the doctrinal and symbolic trappings that implied. And at home, the hushed — and no doubt partial and distorted — truth or corrective, a truth tempered by prudence. I had lived that kind of endangered double life: how could one not empathize with people who wanted to shake off its shackles — and do so at home rather than in exile abroad? Havel's words offered a key by which to understand and explicate what I thought was true: the continuities that marked those years.

The intellectual leaders of 1989, many of them former dissidents who had been imprisoned for their words more often than for their deeds (in those days, words were deeds), rebelled against the enforced mendacities, the dogmatic untruths and distortions. They demanded truth, sought truth, saw it as essential for any political and moral reconstruction. Havel, Bronislaw Geremek, Adam Michnik, and others wrote what many people *felt* and what propelled them to take risks, to go out on the street: they knew that their lives were being traduced by officially imposed lies, by a corrupt and decaying party claiming a monopoly of truth. Of course, people also rebelled against the unrelenting drabness of everyday life, against the imprisonment within the Soviet bloc, but they acted out of a deep revulsion against the daily lies of the enforced orthodoxy, against what George Orwell had recognized long ago as the party's corruption of the language, against what Havel called "evasive thinking." The daily compromises became unbearable, as did the sense that one's children were being indoctrinated in a travesty of truth.[1]

It was this declared hunger for truth and commitment to nonviolence that allows us to say that 1989 marks the end of an era in European history of unparalleled violence and untruth. The Great War saw the perfection of mendacious propaganda and created the conditions by which the totalitarian regimes could establish themselves, could use all the instrumentalities of power to control

---

[1] Attacking any economic interpretation of the Puritan Revolution, Thomas Carlyle imagined a Puritan's response to the tax-gatherer: " 'Take my money, since you *can*, and it is so desirable to you; take it, — and take yourself away with it; and leave me alone to my work here. *I* am still here, can still work, after all the money you have taken from me!' but if they come to him, and say, 'Acknowledge a lie; pretend to say you are worshipping God, when you are not doing it; believe not the thing *you* find true, but the thing I find, or pretend to find true!' He will answer: 'No, by God's help, no! You may take my purse; but I cannot have my moral Self annihilated. The purse is any Highwayman's who might meet me with a loaded pistol: but the Self is mine and God my maker's; it is not yours; and I will resist you to the death, and revolt against you, and, on the whole, front all manner of extremities, accusations and confusions, in defense of that!' " "On Heroes, Hero-Worship, and the Heroic in History," quoted in Fritz Stern (ed.), *The Varieties of History* (New York, 1973), p. 105.

and distort truth, to preach violence in order to practice it. I believe this chain of violence and untruth was broken in 1989.

A caveat must be entered at once: of course, untruthful dogma and subversive heresy have always existed. Dissimulation is to be found in nature and is even considered part of the evolutionary process.[2] Lying is part of life, despite the moral and pragmatic censure of it. But there have been times throughout history when dissimulation has become a collective, hence historical, phenomenon. Religious orthodoxy enforced by instruments such as the Inquisition has commanded conformity — and driven rival faiths to death or denial, and to dissimulation as a means of staying alive.[3] That lying is part of statecraft is enshrined in the modern idea of *raison d'état* — the link between mendacity and murder was one of Shakespeare's dominant themes.

Most of us believe in some untruths or half-truths, whether we inherit or acquire them, whether they are communal or deeply personal. We may even sense that some half-truths are what Edmund Burke called "pleasing illusions." The repression of truth as an individual act can be life-sustaining or life-destroying, but a coercive state power enforcing orthodoxy is always deadly for the heterodox. Of course many Bolsheviks and Nazis believed in their truths; they believed in them so much or so little that they banished all other truths. The fear of contamination by a different version of the truth is the trigger for instituting terror. I know that "truth" is a philosophical conundrum, but public truths traduced or suppressed are easily recognized, especially since they involve the falsification or expunging of the past. In the Communist countries the daily circumlocutions and euphemisms of the party were experienced as grating lies.

---

[2] See Randolph M. Nesse, "The Evolutionary Functions of Repression and the Ego Defenses," *Journal of the American Academy of Psychoanalysis* 18, no. 2 (Summer 1990), 260–85.

[3] A major work on this theme is Perez Zagorin, *Ways of Lying: Dissimulation, Persecution, and Conformity in Early Modern Europe* (Cambridge, Mass., 1990), which examines the historic texts justifying dissimulation.

It was in Enlightenment Europe as an idea, and in early-nineteenth-century liberal Europe as an approximation of reality, that there arose a presumption for liberty — by which at the time was meant free speech, free expressions, tolerance, heterodoxy, and a rule of law that would protect these. Scientific progress, based on rational experiment, strengthened and justified this faith in truth. I do not mean to suggest that in that period political leaders or ruling classes or historians did not bend truths, insist on nationalist dogmas and shibboleths, but in most advanced countries minority views enjoyed some protection. John Stuart Mill not only prescribed but reflected these liberal attitudes. The great liberal achievement, never unchallenged, was to have the state accept the legitimacy of lawful opposition and of a free press. These rights, enshrined in the American Bill of Rights, were approximated in parts of Europe as well. The liberal presumption was that to oppose orthodoxy no longer required martyrdom.

But the liberal-rational world was also, in Max Weber's words, a "disenchanted world." In a world, moreover, in which God Is Dead there is psychological-intellectual room for new pseudo-religious myths, and the "disenchanted" world before 1914 was full of myths and fabrications.[4] There were repeated attempts at throttling the truth, the most notorious being the Dreyfus Affair, which ended with the vindication of truth by determined individuals using the instruments of a liberal society, a free press. The very arrogance of the Europeans at the height of their world power involved delusions: the assumption of Europe's racial superiority, for example, or the image of the ignoble savage. Imperial Ger-

---

[4] At the end of his life, Weber also warned against the intellectual's self-deception, an altogether common affliction, and he chose an extremely important instance: "the honesty of a contemporary *Gelehrte*, and above all of a contemporary philosopher, can be measured by how he confronts Nietzsche and Marx. Whoever does not acknowledge that major parts of his own work could not have been achieved without the work which those two did, deceives himself and others. The world in which we ourselves exist intellectually is to a large extent a world marked by Marx and Nietzsche." Quoted in Wilhelm Hennis, *Max Weber's Fragestellung: Studien zur Biographie des Werks* (Tübingen, 1987), p. 167.

many, the most powerful country in Europe, was beset by willfully self-deceiving rulers, with a vastly exaggerated fear of enemies at home and abroad. They believed that — reformist — Socialists were revolutionaries, and that foreign powers were encircling Germany. But against the forces of repression and mendacity were ranged corrective, reformist opponents. As but one example, as long as Jean Jaurès was alive, no political repression would go unchallenged. He was killed hours before the Great War broke out.

The Great War was the great denial of Europe. The state mobilized men and women "for the duration," regulated the economic life of nations, and sought to capture or control the minds of people, perhaps nowhere more than in Germany. The high pitch of hatred and of released aggression did not and could not end on November 11, 1918. There was no spiritual armistice, no intellectual peace after Versailles. An enfeebled and still enraged Europe created the conditions for totalitarianism, for extremist traditions in Russia and Germany to dominate.

Both Bolshevism and National Socialism had deep roots in opposing strands of nineteenth-century thought. Once in power, these movements preached and practiced ideological bellicosity; mortal enemies deserved to be eliminated, they believed, so that a utopian vision could be realized. Both regimes instituted state terror. This terror was public in order to intimidate, but also concealed; the National Socialists often killed "in night and fog." The proximity of the two regimes — for so long and by so many denied — has now become a kind of conventional truth that may, in turn, blind us to the differences that did exist.

I speak of the organized lie, and I will try to recall the many different manifestations of the suppression or distortion of truth. I will focus on Germany, the central power of Europe, which, beginning with the Great War, was subjected to a succession of lies; I will discuss the decision of the democratic German government in 1919 *not* to publish diplomatic documents that would have proven Imperial Germany's particular responsibility for the outbreak of the war, a suppression that allowed the myth of Germany's total innocence to flourish. The Bolsheviks, also, were duplicitous from the beginning, claiming that duplicity was a weapon of "truth" against their implacable enemies. They *did* publish secret treaties that incriminated their immediate predecessors, but they had no use for truth, class-bound as they believed it to be; truth became what the party decided — hence it was infinitely malleable though at each turn the absolute canon. The National Socialists used different language but they too believed in "unmasking" their enemies — Jews, liberals, Socialists — as exploiters and despoilers. The political use of "unmasking" can be seen as a perverted tribute to "truth." (For the Soviets, "unmasking" often became a prelude to execution and hence acquired a desperately cynical note.) The Soviet-German Pact of 1939 was a triumph of reciprocal mendacity; for both powers it was a total repudiation of their ideological *raison d'être* and neither believed in it.

In the Soviet Union the show trials of the mid-1930s were a diabolical travesty of truth, facilitating the mass murders that accompanied them. Or consider the massacre at Katyn Forest; the Poles have always known that the Soviets killed their officers, but after the triumph of the Red Army, the Soviet lie holding Germans culpable had to be obeyed in every school and on every public occasion. As Lionel Trilling wrote in 1958, referring to Katyn: "These were the facts, all clear to the view. But it is characteristic of well-developed ideology that it can diminish or destroy the primitive potency of fact." [5]

After 1945 the dazed and exhausted Europeans did not want to confront the past. At first the Germans lived in willed amnesia: they could not mourn the collapse of a regime that so many had believed in; they could not focus on their own complicity. Silence and denial were the earliest reactions, as they were in some of the

---

[5] Lionel Trilling, "Introduction," in *The Broken Mirror: A Collection of Writings from Contemporary Poland* (1958), reprinted in *Speaking of Literature and Society* (New York, 1982), p. 302.

countries Germany had briefly conquered. Myths and alibis veiled the divisive truth about past crimes and culpability. And historians — as so often before and after — served rather than confronted the national myths.

There are many different modes of suppressing the truth, and lies engender lies. For all those terrible years of 1914 to 1989 men wielding power sought to rely on mendacity and violence, each demanding the other, in order preemptorily to destroy any challenge to their power. They never fully succeeded: that, too, is part of the story, part of our memory.

The terror began with the Great War. August 1914 was a moment of unprecedented exaltation, especially in Germany, where the war was greeted as a liberation from all kinds of anxiety and boredom. Germans felt the thrill of unity, the more so as even the Socialists supported the war as being a defensive effort against tsarist Russia, bulwark of reaction. But in every country at the beginning, there was a spontaneous sense of the sanctity of service. The servants of God, among others, intoned the nobility of sacrifice and thus blessed the carnage.[6]

Governments of national unity, as they were called, recognized that people's minds — as well as goods and services — had to be mobilized. All manner of propaganda and censorship were put in place: truth — always the first casualty of war — was suppressed. The war saw the birth of modern political propaganda, of telling simplicities to manipulate people's minds. The injunction "Love your country and defend it" in time became "Hate your enemy and kill him."

---

[6] Churches had not been immune to bellicose chauvinism even before the war. Consider one example of how churches adapted themselves to the nationalist ethos of the time: during the second Morocco crisis in 1911, the chief German Protestant paper, *Allgemeine evangelisch-lutherische Kirchenzeitung*, wrote, "Better war than giving in! . . . [Nations require] for their healthy education that occasionally the Almighty calls them to task." Quoted in *Die Zeit*, July 19, 1991. See also A. J. Hoover, *God, Germany, and Britain in the Great War: A Study in Clerical Nationalism* (New York, 1989).

There was of course a beleaguered minority who from the beginning believed that the war was a tragedy for European civilization. As the war continued with ever greater losses and no apparent cause but greed and hatred, the dissent gradually became louder: workers struck and soldiers mutinied. The styles of suppression differed from country to country, but everywhere the spontaneity of patriotism yielded to ever greater regimentation.

The Allies railed against the harshness of the Germans' occupation and fabricated atrocity stories about them. Germans did not hack off the hands of Belgian children, though they did shoot hostages and deported hundreds of thousands of Belgian workers to the Reich.[7] For the British, in particular, the much-esteemed German of the prewar period became the hated Hun. The British government installed a Press Bureau, which clever people quickly dubbed the "Suppress Bureau" — it might have served as a name for European censorship in general.[8]

German censorship, easily organized, served concealment. The people were not to know that the battle of the Marne had thwarted Germany's plans for victory. The Reichsbank concealed its disastrous inflationary policy; in 1915 a respected bank director, Ludwig Bendixen, wrote an article against a government policy of which "the result is that one simply does not believe us anymore. Thus we discredit our integrity and the healthy position of the Reichsbank with a hateful trick that we could easily do without." The article could not be published until 1919.[9]

The government could not articulate its grandiose war aims; it lacked a universal principle to justify the sacrifices it was asking

---

[7] For a brilliant — and surprising — comparison of the two German occupations during the two world wars, see Richard Cobb, *French and Germans, Germans and French: A Personal Interpretation of France under Two Occupations 1914–1918/ 1914–1944* (Hanover and London, 1983).

[8] M. L. Sanders and Philip M. Taylor, *British Propaganda during the First World War, 1914–1918* (London, 1982), p. 20.

[9] Gerald D. Feldman was kind enough to send me proofs of his forthcoming work on the German inflation: *The Great Disorder: Politics, Economics, and Society in the German Inflation* (New York, 1993), p. 36.

of its citizens, and the leaders thought that only the promise of a *Siegfrieden* could preserve German morale. What unacknowledged contempt they had for their people! These masters of the military-industrial-agrarian complex also believed that only a total victory, establishing Germany as the unassailable hegemonial power in Europe, could preserve their preeminence, preserve the constitutional provisions on which their power rested. So the leaders fought a double war: against a ring of enemies abroad *and* against political opponents at home who wanted to alter the Constitution in order to rid it of its most blatantly undemocratic features. Meanwhile the facts about the war had to be censored, enemies pilloried, imperialist war aims concealed.

In the summer of 1917 moderate leaders in the Reichstag successfully pushed for a resolution urging a "peace of reconciliation." Amidst the sudden political crisis this created, Walther Rathenau, a self-conscious Jew who in 1914 had persuaded the military that German raw materials had to be husbanded and who had been put in charge of the allocation of these resources, told Ludendorff that he, too, had his doubts about a *Siegfrieden*. Ludendorff insisted that he was not opposed to a negotiated peace but that the mood of the country was against it. Rathenau replied that the mood had been carefully cultivated: the "English way . . . of constantly pointing out to the nation the seriousness of the situation [was better]. We had emasculated opinion by three years of deception, at least thirty illusions had come into being during that time and were completely believed." [10]

The Reichstag's resolution enraged the right-wing diehards, who instantly organized a new party — pan-German, wildly annexationist, violently antisemitic. This Fatherland party quickly gained a million members and exulted in attacks on "weaklings of the Left." Army censorship shielded them to some extent, but

---

[10] Hartmut Pogge von Strandmann (ed.), *Walther Rathenau: Industrialist, Banker, Intellectual and Politician, Notes and Diaries 1907–1922* (Oxford, 1985), p. 229.

Max Weber warned against these "swaggering braggarts" for whose wild program the soldiers at the front would be shedding their blood. Soldiers returning to Germany should not have to face a future in which "war profiteers had exclusive power."[11] The Fatherland party, with its support from the German elites, was a foretaste of that embittered hatred that came to characterize the defeated Germany.

In the spring of 1918, and largely as a result of the Bolshevik Revolution, the Germans seemed once more close to victory. At Brest-Litovsk they dictated a Carthaginian peace to the Bolsheviks and took control over vast areas of Eastern Europe, including the Ukraine. Its armies, freed from fighting in the East, launched one more offensive in the West — and nearly succeeded in reaching Paris. By July the offensive had stalled; by August the German armies had suffered their "black day"; in September Ludendorff panicked, demanding the immediate installation of a democratic government to appeal instantly to President Wilson for an armistice. When Ludendorff's representative informed the Reichstag deputies in secret session that the war was lost, that at any moment the armies might disintegrate, the deputies were stunned, incredulous — and many wept. Deception and willed self-deception had done their work; most Germans were estranged from reality. A people had been misled — in all senses of the word.

The disbelieving Germans surrendered to a new illusion: they believed that President Wilson would become the guarantor of a mild peace. Wilson demanded that Germany form a reliable democratic regime. As the fighting continued, the old order finally collapsed; the Kaiser fled to Holland, but the old, now frightened, cadres remained intact. The Socialists assumed power, but to what end? As patriotic receivers of a bankrupt country or as revolutionaries who would fashion a new order? On November 11, on the last day of universal rejoicing, no one knew the answer.

[11] Max Weber, *Gesammelte politische Schriften* (Munich, 1921), pp. 143–45.

Germany's new leaders, ominously (for the bourgeois) called the Council of People's Commissars, inherited chaos and hatred: how could they establish a new republican order amidst such unprecedented collapse, with millions of people in the streets? Most German Socialists — stolid patriots — were desperately afraid that the political upheaval could end in a social revolution. We now know that there was no real danger of a Bolshevik coup, but fear of it then inhibited radical reform. The new rulers also faced the inevitable question in such a situation: how should they deal with the failures and deceptions of the old regime? What about German leadership before and during the war? Defeat was hard enough for Germans to grasp. There was spontaneous anger at the old rulers, and officers had their epaulettes torn from their uniforms. A true reckoning with the past might push anger into revolution — or so some of the new rulers thought.

In November 1918 Kurt Eisner, an Independent Socialist who had become minister-president of Bavaria, published in abbreviated form some diplomatic reports from the Bavarian minister in Berlin of July 1914. They showed a Jingoist, irresponsible Kaiser and an aggressive German policy. There was an outcry against what people thought was Eisner's treason. Eisner was a Socialist — and a Jew. German Jews had a habit of disturbing the taboos of sentimental Germans: thus Marx in regard to economic interests, Freud in regard to the unconscious power of sexual impulses, and now Eisner in regard to the origins of the war. But the issue was central — and the Council of Commissars in Berlin had to deal with it. It commissioned Karl Kautsky, the leading prewar Socialist theorist and by now, like Eisner, an Independent Socialist, to study and collect the documents relating to German policy before the outbreak of the war. In March 1919 Kautsky submitted to the government a selection of documents making clear that in the weeks after Francis Ferdinand's assassination in 1914 German policy had been anything but peaceful. The Kaiser's marginalia were an embarrassment of bellicose bombast. These documents disproved all German assertions of innocence. The old regime had deceived its own people.

Even as the Allies were hammering out the peace terms in Paris, a newly elected German government, a coalition of Socialists, Centrists, and Democrats, met on March 22, 1919, to debate whether to publish these documents. President Ebert participated, an uncommon occurrence, and surprisingly — given his conservative leanings — urged publication: "Condemn in sharpest terms the sins of the old regime. Define the position of the new government." A fellow-Socialist, Eduard David, who had supported the war, seconded him: "The old system cannot be defended anymore. Principal content of our announcement in Paris must be that we are not responsible for decisions over which we had no influence. Moral guilt [*Schuld*] rests to a large extent with the German side." Eugen Schiffer, a Democrat, argued against publication, fearing the domestic repercussions — and for the moment, his side won. Two weeks later the issue was raised again and David again demanded publication, arguing that the Allies knew the substance of these documents already; under the circumstances "only complete clarity and truth" could help. But the spirit of the old system lingered on, and the new government decided against discrediting it, against publishing the incriminating documents.

In August the first postwar Congress of the Majority Socialists debated the war guilt question. Most speakers congratulated the party on its Socialist patriotism and argued against national self-incrimination. Only the old irenic revisionist Eduard Bernstein, who out of anger at the war had joined the Independent Socialists, called for disclosure and warned his party against remaining prisoners of its original decision supporting the war: "Let us liberate ourselves from the bourgeois concepts of honor; only the truth, the full truth can help us." It was not to be.[12]

---

[12] I was first alerted to this issue by the historian Heinrich August Winkler's article "Die verdrängte Schuld," *Die Zeit*, March 17, 1989. See also Hagen Schulze

The consequences of this concealment are staggering, while counterfactual arguments about what might have happened if the government had acknowledged German responsibility are necessarily speculative. But it is clear that silence allowed the entire nationalist Right in Germany to propagate what was later dubbed the *Kriegsunschuldlüge* or the lie of German innocence. Article 231 of the Versailles Peace Treaty, the so-called war-guilt clause, enraged Germans of all classes. They believed that if the Allies were claiming that Germany was responsible for the war, then the opposite must be true. The notorious article — so it seems — was drafted by a young member of the American delegation, John Foster Dulles; it was an early example of the misplaced moralistic streak in his work. In fact, the article was not intended to determine war guilt; but when the Germans challenged Article 231, Wilson himself, to their distress, agreed that the Germans were responsible for starting the war and that the article could not be deleted. There was no alternative but to sign the treaty — or face the resumption of hostilities.

The German Right now possessed an inestimable capital of mendacious arguments against the Weimar (or the "Jew") Republic that had signed the infamous article, besmirched the fatherland, and acknowledged a guilt that allegedly did not exist. To such Germans, the very harshness of the treaty proved that already in 1914 the Allies had been plotting against Germany. Now the full indictment against Weimar could be drawn up: Socialists, pacifists, and Jews had not only stabbed an undefeated German army in the back but had betrayed the honor of the nation as well.

No single allegation was so damaging to the Republic as these untruths and none so widely disseminated. Hitler's endless attacks against "the November traitors" was his most successful, most widely accepted nationalist argument. How prescient is Bernstein's

---

(ed.), *Das Kabinett Scheidemann, 13 February to 20 June 1919* (Boppard am Rhein, 1971), pp. 87–88, 146–47; and Ulrich Heineman, *Die verdrängte Niederlage: Politische Öffentlichkeit und Kriegsschuldfrage in der Weimarer Republic* (Göttingen, 1983).

letter of 1924 to his old ideological foe Karl Kautsky: the nationalists' claims of innocence taught the people that " 'the Jew-Republic' and its fulfillment policy was responsible for all the evil that Germany suffers from today. We are moving toward the nationalists' coup d'état. . . . Those who would emerge on top this time are unscrupulous brutal thugs." Bernstein died six weeks before the thugs assumed power in 1933 — not by a coup d'état but by beguiling or deceiving a third of the German electorate and a large part of the German elites. Four years later Hitler declared the signature of Article 231 invalid, and two years later he began the *revanchiste* war.

This is a rare instance where we can reconstruct how so portentous a decision was reached. We know the Cabinet majority in March 1919 acted out of what they believed to be patriotism and prudence. They feared that if they did not suppress the truth Allied vengeance and right-wing nationalist fury at home would increase.

But one must ask: could the nationalist reaction against the Republic have been any worse than it was? Could it have done more than it did — trying to overthrow it in 1920, assassinating its leaders, beginning with Eisner, denouncing its "fulfillment policy," and drawing strength from the mendacious notion of German innocence?

Ebert and his partisans believed that telling the truth about the myopic egoism and recklessness of the old regime could have enhanced the embattled legitimacy of the new Republic. I agree, and I believe the documented truth — though it would not have converted the Right, aggrieved by the country's defeat and the decline of its own power — would have been a brake on its self-righteousness. The government's silence encouraged others to remain silent as well and allowed for a kind of national conspiracy to believe in a fatal falsehood.

Historians were not exempt from this conspiracy of silence — even when they knew better. Thus, in a private letter in late

October 1918, Friedrich Meinecke wrote that in the face of defeat he, like everyone else, would wish for an honorable death, adding, "A frightful, dark existence awaits us under all circumstances! And as much as my hatred for the bestial greed of our enemies smolders in me, equally hot is my anger and outrage about the German power politicians, who through their arrogance and stupidity have driven us into this abyss."[13]

Such thoughts were kept to private correspondence. With a few exceptions, German historians continued to deny major responsibility for 1914 until well after the Second World War. They were outraged in 1962, when Fritz Fischer, on the basis of new documents, established that Germany had pursued an aggressive forward policy in July 1914.[14]

The Great War had brutalized, weakened, and radicalized Europe, but there was nothing inevitable about its further descent into totalitarian violence and mendacity. Indeed, in the immediate aftermath of the war, there was cause for hope: the Treaty of Versailles, however flawed, had established a new order in record time. Czechs, Slovaks, Poles, and Balts could feel that the Wilsonian principle of national self-determination had liberated them. The League of Nations theoretically provided the machinery for peaceful change and for collective action against aggressors. The early 1920s were in many ways a high watermark for European democracy, and later in the decade the names of Aristide Briand and Gustav Stresemann evoked the hope that the historic conflict between France and Germany might be overcome.

Still, the war had bred such deep resentments, fears, and intransigence and had so weakened Europe's material and moral con-

---

[13] Hans-Georg Drescher, *Ernst Troeltsch: Leben und Werk* (Göttingen, 1991), p. 453.

[14] On the Fischer debate and the outrageous attempt by older German historians to silence him, see my "German Historians and the War: Fischer and His Critics," as well as "Bethmann Hollweg and the War: The Bounds of Responsibility," in *The Failure of Illiberalism: Essays on the Political Culture of Modern Germany* (New York, reissue, 1992), pp. 147–58 and 77–118.

ditions that efforts at pacification, often proffered late and grudgingly, failed. The economic consequences of the peace (to evoke John Maynard Keynes's legendary denunciation of Versailles) manifested the inextricable mixture of economic, political, and psychological factors. Again the German experience was central — with effects still felt today: no event so dramatized the manifold insecurities of the time as the hyperinflation in Weimar Germany. A bourgeois government expropriated its own middle class, mendaciously blaming Allied reparation claims for the disaster. A major work on the hyperinflation concludes that it introduced "elements of barbarism into the political culture of Germany" that help to explain "that peculiarly hideous combination of indifference and careerism that characterized the behavior of so many intellectual workers in the Third Reich." [15]

During the war minds had been poisoned by nationalist simplicities; wars rarely offer lessons in complexity. Opponents of the war became militant pacifists or antimilitarists and had their own cast of villains. George Grosz and Otto Dix carried on a merciless, brilliant campaign against Europe's ancient warrior caste, especially venerated in Germany. This friend-foe thinking was hardly conducive to the development of democratic polities.

Bolshevism, Fascism, and National Socialism were ideologies claiming a monopoly of truth: part of their appeal was the promise of absolute authority. These apparently radically different systems — Bolshevism was rational and scientific, National Socialism intuitive-mystical — dispelled uncertainties by "unmasking" conspiratorial groups of "wreckers" and "wirepullers" that caused evil. They all offered visions of redemption, of the "new Soviet man" or of the "Aryan superman" in a new *Volksgemeinschaft*. Totalitarians glorified decisiveness and swept away parties and parliaments. As servants of providence or of the historic process, their leaders identified their own demand for power with the dictates of their aggressive ideology. They became ruthless warriors

[15] Feldman, *The Great Disorder*, p. 858.

on behalf of their utopian visions: they killed out of a composite of hatred, dogma, and a desperate, paranoid will to power.

The greatest delusion that these totalitarian movements spawned was the belief in their radical opposition to each other. Fascists or National Socialists were anti-Communist, Communists were anti-Fascist, and they did kill each other, as in the Spanish Civil War. But this sworn enmity concealed a common nature and a common hatred for bourgeois life and bourgeois values. Their common enemy was liberal Europe and human rights. The certainty of their unalterable opposition was a major source of their strength: they lived off each other.

To see how this dynamic worked, we must go back to 1917, Europe's year of desperation. It was also in that year that Germany — too weak to achieve a victorious peace and too strong to accept a negotiated one — expanded the war. By resorting to unrestricted submarine warfare, Germany's divided leaders thought they could starve Britain into submission, even if the United States entered the war. So it was German power that brought the United States to Europe, just as its stratagem to return Lenin to Russia enabled Bolshevism to triumph in Russia.

One gamble came terrifyingly close to success: the submarines did nearly destroy British shipping. The other gamble, the transport of Lenin, succeeded, in the short run. The Germans were playing with fire — only to suffer from the conflagration. By these decisions they unwittingly introduced a new ideological fervor to the war: both Wilson and Lenin believed in visions transcending the nationalist passions that had thus far informed the war. Our century — so proud in so many ways of its rational capacity for planning, for calculating results — has seen a daunting succession of historic decisions recklessly taken.

Lenin: a dominant figure who will remain controversial even after his empire has vanished. His brother was killed by tsarist thugs; in him, personal venom and Marxist doctrine at its most bellicose coincided. He had no doubt that he and his little band of fellow-revolutionaries were the executors of a historic process and that his enemies would end in the dustbin of history.

From 1914 to 1917 Lenin opposed all Socialist pleas for ending the war, believing that utter exhaustion would signal the moment for a proletarian revolution. His call for "revolutionary defeatism" had no compassion for those still to be slaughtered. The war was the locomotive of history that should run to its appointed end, the destruction of the capitalist-imperialist world — not for him the "sentimental" desire for peace.

No sooner back in Russia, then, Lenin and his comrades plotted the overthrow of the Kerensky government. But he—and *a fortiori* Leon Trotsky and Grigory Zinoviev — did not believe in a merely Russian revolution; when a tiny minority seized power in October, they thought that their fragile victory would be the prelude to a world revolution. At the very least, it would be followed by a revolution in Germany, where a large, disciplined proletariat would eventually tire of being sacrificed in an imperialist war. Bolshevism was a speculation in Europe's bankruptcy.

The prospects for a revolutionary regime in Russia were dismal; the prospects for a European conflagration seemed better, and the Bolsheviks saw the latter as the only means of saving the former. Within hours of seizing power, they issued a "Declaration of Peace," addressed — characteristically — both to the warring governments *and* to the international proletariat. They demanded an immediate armistice, then a universal peace without annexations or indemnities. To the Allies, this bid for world salvation was rank treason. To the German government, it signaled the sudden prospect of a German victory. To the war-weary peoples of Europe, and to some disillusioned Socialists and intellectuals, it sounded a new note of hope.

In that first hour the Soviet appeal or temptation was born. Here was more than an alternative to tsarist autocracy, to an obscurantist empire that was, in Lenin's words, "a prisonhouse of nationalities." [16] Here was an alternative to a class-ridden, imperialist order that had turned all Europe into a slaughterhouse. Here were heirs of the French Revolution promising the next stage of historical development: socialism, egalitarianism, peace. Was not Lenin, in his simple suit and simple style, the living antithesis of the bemedaled general and the purse-proud magnate? To those hungry for belief, Lenin appeared as the emancipator, the liberator of talent, the proletarian (which he was not) in power. Those who knew him best — such as Rosa Luxemburg — apprehended the truth; her response to the October Revolution, however sympathetic, included the early warning that "freedom is always freedom for the one who disagrees with you." The image of the idealistic revolutionary was of course at odds with Lenin at home. He never doubted that the Bolshevik party would have to establish a dictatorship that would act for the proletariat.[17]

From the very first day and first decree, Bolshevism was the great divider of, the great deceiver in, Europe. Its enemies fastened only on its atrocities, only on its terror, which began almost at once. Its sympathizers clung to the rhetoric about its final aims and egalitarian promise — they blamed "reactionaries" for what was in fact the Bolsheviks' inherent ruthlessness.

The Bolsheviks' demand for universal peace fell on deaf ears; they had to sue for peace, but the Germans dictated a peace that robbed the new regime of some of the richest parts of old Russia. For Lenin, there was no alternative but to submit to this, and in his hardest dispute with his fellow-revolutionaries he carried the day. To him, even the most appalling peace was a condition for sur-

[16] Adam Ulam, *The Bolsheviks* (New York, 1965), p. 391.

[17] In 1904, when Trotsky attacked Lenin's "orthodox theocracy," he also warned against "substitutism": "the party organization [the caucus] at first substitutes itself for the party as a whole; then the central committee substitutes itself for the organization; and finally a single 'dictator' substitutes himself for the Central Committee." Quoted in Isaac Deutscher, *The Prophet Armed: Trotsky: 1879–1921* (Oxford and London, 1954), p. 90. A decade and a half later Trotsky became Lenin's lieutenant in establishing just such a system of substitution.

vival. His policy already prefigured Stalin's later call for "socialism in one country."

For a brief moment in 1919 the Soviet hope for a chain of revolutions seemed realizable: in Hungary and Bavaria short-lived Communist regimes were established; in Germany there were Communist uprisings. Within weeks these attempts were crushed, and their only lasting effect was to add to capitalist fright.

Indeed, the capitalist world took the Bolshevik threat with desperate seriousness, with contempt, and with fear. Western statesmen vacillated between a hope for accommodation and a wish to strangle, while the Bolsheviks simultaneously sought recognition as a normal state and as a revolutionary power tried to subvert other states. British and French workers had little use for Bolshevism at home, but they were unwilling to support yet another military venture, this time against weak but militant Socialists. Still, France, Britain, and the United States did intervene in Russia, with risible means and forces far too weak to overthrow the Soviets. Their very presence, however, confirmed Soviet assumptions that a state of war necessarily (objectively, to use that dreadful term) had to exist — and also gave the Bolsheviks a pretext to appear as the hapless victims of capitalist aggression.

Lenin was to discover, as he put it, that in no country was it so easy to gain power and so difficult to maintain it as in Russia. Inside Russia, the Bolsheviks faced civil war and chaos. They themselves enhanced the chaos by their efforts to destroy the bastions of capitalism and the existing property relations, all the coercive measures known as war communism. And weeks after the Revolution the Bolsheviks organized a new secret police known as Cheka, their own instrument of terror. Even among the small urban proletariat (as compared to the mass of the peasantry) there were few Bolsheviks, and former allies (Social Revolutionaries and Anarchists) were gradually hounded and eliminated.

Terror and mendacity became instruments of Soviet administration: Russia had become a dictatorship — not of any class, but of the party, which became the final, the only authority in the Soviet state, the sole repository of truth. Lenin warned against diluting its cadre: "careerists and charlatans, who deserved only to be shot, inevitably strive to attach themselves to the ruling party."[18] By definition those who were shot deserved to be shot. The mutineering sailors at the Kronstadt naval base in 1921, murdered for their insistence that pledges of proletarian democracy be honored — the very group Lenin had called "the pride and beauty of the Revolution" — were now slandered as petty bourgeois, anarchists, or counterrevolutionaries.[19]

The eventual triumph of the Bolsheviks in Russia had a decisive and divisive effect everywhere in the world and brought on a latent civil war in most other countries. When the Bolsheviks founded the Third Internationale, the Comintern, the very name identified their principal foe: the Second Internationale of Democratic Socialists. In time Moscow wiped out all vestiges of independence in the Communist parties elsewhere in the world; in democratic countries, these parties operated openly and competed in national elections; everywhere they also operated covertly through intricate networks of agents and infiltrators.

Equally determinative were the sworn enemies of Bolshevism: the *bien pensants* of every country and every church inveighed against Soviet atrocities, against the godless bandits who threatened all values, all traditions, everything that was sacrosanct, including private property. In the beginning the Entente powers depicted the Bolsheviks as German-Jewish agents; Churchill's assessment that the Bolsheviks were but "the rabble from the East European ghettos" was quite representative. So the anti-Bolshevik campaign began early and took immensely ugly forms; thereafter, the anti-Bolsheviks were just as free in their calumnies as their enemies.

[18] V. I. Lenin, *"Left-Wing" Communism, an Infantile Disorder* (Moscow, 1952), p. 51.

[19] Ulam, *The Bolsheviks*, p. 472.

Fascism throve on the perceived Bolshevik dangers. How these sworn enemies approximated each other and even served each other very few people in that time understood. Oddly enough, it was a Bolshevik, N. I. Bukharin, "the darling of the party," who acknowledged similarities in April 1923 at the Twelfth Congress of the Russian Communist Party. A bourgeoisie unable to govern the economic life of its country, he explained, resorts to these Fascist parties. Bukharin referred specifically to Mussolini as well as to Hitler's movement as the most important German Fascist organization. Fascism represents "a peculiar form of legalizing civil war. . . . It is characteristic of the methods of the Fascist struggle that to a greater degree than all other parties they have appropriated the experience of the Russian Revolution and apply it practically. They have used Bolshevik tactics for their own purposes." [20] I know of no other acknowledgment of affinity from an authoritative Soviet source.

The appeals of Communism continued for decades. The Communist parties outside Russia attracted millions of the most aggrieved members of the proletariat — as well as some intellectuals. (The working class was thus split between Communists and Socialists.) The Bolsheviks could also count on a large band of sympathizers of varying degree of loyalty, fellow-travelers, as they were called. These saw in the Bolsheviks some kind of potential hope, saw them perhaps as barbarians of promise, and fastened on Soviet successes, of which there seemed to be many. This was the spirit that animated Sidney and Beatrice Webb's Fabian tract *Russia: A New Civilization?* The psychology of fellow-traveling included the yearning for the new faith, the wish to be thought "progressive" and at one with the working class. As Czeslaw Milosz put it in 1951: "To belong to the masses is the great longing of the 'alienated' intellectual." [21]

[20] I owe this reference to my colleague Peter Krupnikov of the University of Riga.

[21] Czeslaw Milosz, *The Captive Mind* (New York, 1955), p. 8.

Fellow-traveling with the Communist party almost always involved some kind of emotional or intellectual alienation from the bourgeois world, some deep-seated antagonism to capitalist life. In the 1930s the anti-Fascist impulse proved very powerful: Fascism was the immediate aggressor. Almost always, fellow-traveling involved a measure of self-deception, a wish not to see what was all too apparent, not to believe what seemed incontrovertible.[22]

But sympathizers found it desperately hard to break with the party or abandon the hope. To believe in the truth about Soviet atrocities and betrayals, to see Leninism and later Stalinism for

---

[22] In the moral-intellectual history of our century, the phenomenon of "the God That Failed" — even the ironic invocation of a deity is suggestive — is central and it may take a long time to understand it. Rather than appear pharisaic in my judgments, I would want to recount my own experiences, however trivial or commonplace they were. Between the ages of seven and twelve — that is, until 1938 — I lived under National Socialism; I remember the early victims of the regime as well as the awesome choreography of Nazi will and power. But I also remember the thrill of surreptitiously listening to Radio Moscow, the *frisson* of hearing the forbidden text in German "proletarians of the world, unite," followed by the Internationale. The twelve-year-old believed in the anti-Fascism of the Communists and my passions were all on the side of the Spanish Loyalists. I remember the secret delight at the shamefaced German announcement of the Fascist defeat at Guadalajara.

The news of the German-Soviet pact shattered that world and I shed my first political tears. How fortunate the lesson! I was appalled at teachers who insisted that America should stay out of "the imperialist war" — until on June 22, 1941, the war became the great anti-Fascist crusade. Soviet resistance revived earlier hopes, but a protective skepticism had been added. In 1943, after Stalin's murder of two Polish-Jewish labor leaders, Henryk Erlich and Victor Alter, I went to a protest meeting, at which brave union leaders denounced the murder; at some point New York's irrepressible mayor, Fiorello La Guardia, appeared, jumped on the platform, mourned the dead, and warned: "And I say to Uncle Joe: Don't do it again." Even then I was struck by the cheerfully naive response.

I was reluctant to accept the truth about slave labor camps and gulags: were these perhaps fabrications or exaggerations of the extreme Right? By 1948, after the Czech coup and the death or murder of Jan Masaryk, any hopes born, say, of Stalingrad vanished. In 1954, teaching at the Free University of Berlin, I became visually aware of the resemblance between the two totalitarian regimes. At the same time I watched apprehensively the giant marshaling of anti-Communism in America during the McCarthy era and at home experienced the insolent intolerance of some professional anti-Communist intellectuals. My passion came to be with the dissidents in Eastern Europe, with the Poles and Hungarians in 1956, with the Czechs a decade later, with the Soviet dissidents I came to know in Russia in 1979, and above all with the Polish opposition I first encountered in Poland in 1979, with Bronislaw Geremek and Adam Michnik. I give this summary to orient the reader: I have had a smattering of the Soviet appeal — at a safe distance.

what it was — that was to play into the hands of Fascists or reactionaries. George Orwell, a Socialist, a foe of imperialism and of Fascism, put it clearly: "Everyone who has ever had anything to do with publicity or propaganda can think of occasions when he was urged to tell lies about some vitally important matter, because to tell the truth would give ammunition to the enemy." [23]

The strength of Communism's earlier appeal must not be forgotten today, with the crumbling of the Soviet Union. Its appeal had deep psychological-political meaning. It will take tact and empathy to understand why for so many Communism seemed different from what it was: a most terrible union of utopian dreams, bellicose dogma, paranoid terror, and the brutal suppression of all opposition, real and imagined. Will future generations remember how easily people became "unpersons" and had their lives posthumously expunged? Orwell invented nothing; he dramatized the truth and transposed history to fiction — so that people could grasp the truth more easily.

And what of the appeal of Fascism? The Great War gave Bolshevism its chance — and the same is true of Fascism and National Socialism. Prewar Europe had known a longing for Fascism before Fascism itself. Writers and intellectuals spoke of their yearning for a new authority, for community, for national discipline and greatness. They hated the liberal, bourgeois world. In France and Austria, for example, mass movements vaguely expressed these feelings. The war offered community and meaning to those people whose previous lives had been materially and spiritually impoverished; after the war many of these people felt adrift, alienated, rootless, unwilling to return to an anonymous

---

[23] *As I Please 1943–1945: Collected Essays, Journalism and Letters of George Orwell*, ed. Sonia Orwell and Ian Angus (New York, 1968), vol. 3, p. 170. Orwell also knew about the great reluctance of publishers to accept anti-Soviet writings. In June 1944 he reported to T. S. Eliot, then an editor with a British publisher, that some authority or other had urged that in *Animal Farm* "some other animal than pigs might be made to represent the Bolsheviks" (ibid., p. 176).

humdrum life in a bourgeois world. For some, adventure and violence had become addictive.

Benito Mussolini, a brutal if literate misfit, knew how to exploit the thirst for action experienced by the discharged but not emotionally demobilized soldiers. At the same time he played on the immense fears of the propertied classes in the face of "red" dangers, aroused especially by the sit-down strikes of 1919. As a prominent ex-Socialist, he knew how explosive the idea and reality of class war could be; he sought to transcend or deny it in a brilliantly orchestrated invocation of national grandeur. At the same time the Fascists before 1922 were marauding thugs; the brutal *squadristi* resorted to torture, a practice that a liberal Europe had foresworn.

The specter of Bolshevism haunted Italy, though there was no possibility of a Bolshevik coup. Landless peasants and underpaid workers had a vague notion that life was better in "the workers' paradise." More importantly, the propertied lost all faith in parliamentary solutions; the emergence of mass parties, the Socialists and the Catholic Popolari, made them realize their own political vulnerability. In Mussolini they saw their protector, and many of them supported him.

Yet the march on Rome in 1922 was a sham — a proper beginning for what came to be dazzling choreography, deceit and terror, and very little substance. Mussolini in power proceeded slowly: at first he collaborated with other parties, tolerated opposition newspapers, and tried to ameliorate economic conditions. The break came in 1925, after the Fascist murder of Giacomo Matteotti, a courageous Socialist who had exposed Fascist complicity in crime. Mussolini's opponents were outraged, but took no effective action; after some hesitation Mussolini acknowledged responsibility for the crime and swiftly established a dictatorship. Now he suppressed, imprisoned, or exiled his opponents; all opposition was stamped out and conformity imposed; there was to be no cultural or intellectual life outside Fascist control. The willing subservience of intellectuals — born of some mixture of enthusiasm, careerism, and fear — helped the regime; some intellectuals tried to accommodate *and* criticize. The much-vaunted Fascist corporatism represented some veiled collusion between the party and the propertied classes, with incidental benefits to workers. The Duce sought to reduce politics to intimidating pageantry — with terror as the ultimate weapon.

Strident nationalism marked Mussolini's foreign policy, aggressive in form and cautious in substance. With the help of foreign loans, the economy recovered; with the Vatican's imprimatur in the form of the Lateran Treaty of 1929, the regime acquired new respectability, even exuded political glamour. Some Westerners, including Churchill and G. B. Shaw, thought of the Duce, the dictator, as the incarnation of the strong man, a new authority, who made trains run on time, drained swamps, restored national pride. The world had yet to learn that the brutality Mussolini had unleashed against Italians could — under the right international circumstances — also be unleashed against foreigners, against Ethiopians and against Republican Spaniards. What Bolshevism was for the left, Fascism came to be for the Right: a vision of an efficient and exciting alternative to the dull routine of "bourgeois" democracy. It had many admirers. Even after its demise there has remained a condescendingly benevolent memory of Fascism, as if all that was remembered was the theatricality and not the terror.[24]

The vilest form of Fascism developed in Germany, where the Great War had brought incalculable losses: the bereavement of millions, the presence everywhere of multilated veterans, disrupted and disoriented lives even among the physically unaffected — and all this suffering after the gigantic exertions of the war. Humiliated and with a deep sense of instability, many Germans clung to the notion that all misery had its ultimate cause in the *Dolch-*

---

[24] A splendid analysis of the difference in practice between Germans and Italians during the Second World War may be found in Jonathan Steinberg's *All or Nothing: The Axis and the Holocaust 1941–1943* (New York, 1990).

stoss — a Wagnerian term that the translation "stab-in-the-back" only inadequately conveys — a legend that traduced the truth and engendered the deepest discord. Resentments fed German intransigence, a self-destructive *Trotzigkeit*. Germany had become a country in which the legacy of the war exacerbated every intellectual and material conflict — of which there were many.

Is it odd that our century, in which the power of individuals to shape history has been so terrifyingly demonstrated, should also be the century in which historians have mocked the notion that individuals matter. If Hitler had been killed in the Great War, the world would have been different. It has often been said that Hitler's success depended on his being underestimated — a statement both true and explicable. Rational people assumed that the rage and violence he spewed forth were vulgarities with which to attract a crowd; pure evil — his nihilism — they could not understand. Marxists were doctrinally incapable of understanding the movement he inspired, which by its pseudo-religious, paramilitary appearance satisfied psychological, not material, needs. They thought of Hitler as the paid agent of capitalism, a doctrinal misjudgment that was later enshrined as orthodoxy in the German Democratic Republic.

The astounding thing is that Hitler was quite candid about his ideas. *Mein Kampf* was an explicit account of them. The war and subsequent defeat had confirmed the misfit's experience: war was a communal escape from loneliness, defeat was the work of traitors and racial enemies. Providence had chosen him as the redeemer of his people. He sought absolute power to fulfill that destiny and to escape the empty self. His chief weapon was directly born of his wartime experience: he had imbibed a fanatical faith in the power of propaganda, as practiced, he thought, by the British. *Mein Kampf* was a manual on how to mobilize the German public so that it would rally to his vision of violence and deliverance. Propaganda had to be simple and endlessly repetitive; simple slogans would identify enemies and promise greatness.

The masses with their "feminine" mentality would respond to emotions, never to reason or nuanced judgments. Truth — always complex — was utterly irrelevant; what mattered was igniting people's passions. As orator (and the spoken word, according to Hitler, was the most successful instrument of propaganda) needed to reach people's instincts.

Hitler and his immediate underlings were masters of propaganda, amazing choreographers of hate. Their message was simple: all suffering came from the November criminals, from Marxists and Jews who had stabbed a victorious army in the back; the greatest danger to Germandom was Jewry, the mortal racial enemy. The promises of the Third Reich were also simple: absolute authority; the regeneration of the Reich and the extrusion of the Jews; a genuine national community that would break the fetters of Versailles, find new *Lebensraum*, and forever destroy Jewish Bolshevism. Hitler's violence was manifest in the party's provocative parades of uniformed men with flags, daggers, and truncheons, singing inflammatory songs and shouting murderous threats.

Once in power, National Socialism was incredibly swift in establishing totalitarian rule. *Gleichschaltung* (coordination) implied conformity and the organized elimination of all opposition, but it also dramatized the achievements of the regime: economic recovery, order and discipline, and an aggressive foreign policy (aggressive in style *and* substance) that successfully defied the existing order. *Gleichschaltung* also demanded acceptance of a mendacious orthodoxy, and most members of the German elites found forms of accommodation with it. Tacitly they accepted the extrusion of Jews, tacitly they accepted the "legal" suspension of all law — and hence the SA cellars of torture and the carefully erected concentration camps, the existence of which was proclaimed in March 1933 — to intimidate.

The initial victims were Germans themselves — Communists and Socialists, and Jews if they happened to fall into these categories. If Germans could torture and murder Germans, would they show restraint in dealing with non-Germans? And yet the National Socialists also maintained a deceptive normality, at least until *Kristallnacht* in 1938. Success that seduced and mendacity that was shielded by terror help to explain why Hitler's regime in the prewar years was probably the most popular in modern German history.

The National Socialists had their foreign sympathizers, though interestingly they had no label to identify them, no analogue to "fellow-travelers." But many people outside Germany were as vulnerable to Hitler's promises and successes as Germans were, and they too admired the man of destiny, the strong and triumphant leader. Some foreigners were more vulnerable than others: the propertied, those of the Right, technocrats, people disillusioned with democracy and anxiously struggling with a worldwide depression.

What mattered most in the 1930s was the response of Europe's political elites to Hitler. With diabolical cunning and dizzying speed he defied the restrictions of Versailles and built up a new German army; at every moment of unilateral aggrandizement, he promised them that this was his last demand. The feeble efforts of gullible foreign leaders at defending the status quo only increased his contempt. As he grew stronger, as his demands multiplied, the British adopted a policy they called appeasement, a policy made easier by their willed blindness about the nature of Hitler's regime, by a pervasive fear of war, by their deep-seated anti-Communism. In early September 1938 the British ambassador in Berlin, an arch-appeaser, urged that the British press should "write up Hitler as the apostle of Peace. It would be terribly shortsighted if this is not done." [25]

In the end appeasement deluded Hitler himself: he assumed that appeasement had become the permanent stance of the British and French, decadent as he thought them to be. In 1940 he briefly hesitated in pushing his campaign against Britain, hoping that the

---

[25] Quoted in A. J. P. Taylor, *Europe: Grandeur and Decline* (Hammersworth, 1967), p. 240.

old appeasers would become defeatists (as many did) and come to terms with him. He misjudged the embattled hold that Churchhill, that magnificent antiappeaser, had on his nation.

The Second World War was the climax of what I call the Second Thirty Years' War, a climax of unimaginable horror. This time the war began with the ideological fanaticism that had been spawned by the First World War. This time noncombatants suffered at least as much as soldiers; it was a total war almost from the start.

In one year Hitler's *Wehrmacht* — adjudged the best fighting force of the century — conquered most of continental Europe. But even in conquest, the Germans implicitly acknowledged the tragic difference between East and West Europe. In the West, after the Germans routed the French in a matter of weeks, the conquerors behaved with confident correctness — for a while. In the East, the German ideology dictated a different conduct. The Germans had been told that Poles and Russians were *Untermenschen* and should be treated accordingly. Just before the invasion of the Soviet Union, the High Command's infamous Commissar Decree ordered instant brutality, demanding that the army carry out a murderous occupation. Hatred and the fear that such aggression visits upon itself turned Germany's occupation in the East to such horror that Russians and Ukrainians who had initially greeted the Germans as liberators turned into fierce defenders of the Russian motherland. The war broke all restraints.

The greatest injury of all was the systematic extermination of six million Jews — an act of such fanatical hatred so systematically organized that even now we cannot grasp it. Thousands upon thousands took an active part in the Holocaust; even more were passively complicitous. And yet there were those who risked their lives rescuing individual Jews. This was a German crime with countless European accomplices. It was the ultimate measure of terror and mendacity. The victims should be mourned and remembered: their memory should be sacrosanct; it should never be exploited.

As the Wehrmacht conquered Europe and until its aura of invincibility was shattered at Stalingrad in 1943, a fair number of Europeans — in Western Europe and in a few places in Eastern Europe — believed in Hitler's New Order. I am thinking not solely of active collaborators or those who enlisted in Hitler's legions, but also of people who accepted the skillful propaganda for the New Europe and who succumbed to the appeal of power, order, and violence that Germans had succumbed to earlier. They, too, listened to their rationalizations and made their gestures of accommodation. We forget how deeply split the conquered countries were, how deeply even a neutral country like Switzerland was split. German atrocities and deportations disabused some of the sympathizers; German defeats disabused most. In the end, I suspect, most people forgot their earlier aberrations.

The war ended when Americans and Russians met at the Elbe, when the Allies finally crushed Nazism. In that era of 1914–1945 the number of people killed was greater than the total population of Europe had been two centuries earlier. With the end of Nazism, the Western world — or most of it — embraced another hope that turned to illusion; this time it was the hope that the Grand Alliance would survive the defeat of the common enemy, that the celebrated comradeship in war (never easy, never trusting) would endure in some kind of partnership in peace. But before long an old conflict reemerged and decades of violence and untruth had yet to be endured.

I want to be brief about Europe in the post-1945 period, because in some ways that age is better known and also because we lack distance from that epoch, lying as it does somewhere between memory and history. I hope that historians, freed from orthodoxy, with access to hitherto closed archives, will gradually gain a more nuanced sense of the last decades. In time the links between the post-1945 and the pre-1914 periods should become clearer, as, I hope, will the links between the visible changes in the international scene and the subterranean changes, especially in Eastern Europe.

In the postwar Europe of 1945–1948, devastated as it was, with many millions hungry, homeless, and on some desperate trek for shelter, there was hope nevertheless — hope that after the horrors of war and Fascism there would be peace and reconstruction, that the Grand Alliance would hold, that the United Nations would strengthen the world order. Many people hoped that some kind of moral compatibility between the Western powers and the Soviet Union — as hinted at by the Nuremberg trials — could become a political reality. For that hope, much truth was sacrificed: for example, we did not want to know the full extent of Soviet barbarism in their liberation of Germany—something that Lev Kopelev witnessed and for speaking the truth about it suffered years of torment. Only recently have we come to know that the Western powers delivered thousands of Russians against their will into the hands of the Soviet Union. As an aside, let me add that American intelligence, vastly expanded during the Second World War, inherited a legacy of stealth that in subsequent decades brought about frequent battles to protect constitutional rights against the presumed requirements of national security.

The origins of the cold war, controversial from the beginning, may become clearer with the opening of Soviet archives. But I doubt that we will need to abandon our sense that reciprocal fears about military security were conflated with ideological and paranoid fears going back to 1917. Russia and America emerged from the war as — unequal — superpowers, and this fact necessarily intensified their old conflict. Stalin, fearful and ambitious, wished to augment his power by expanding his empire. In the United States the indisputable facts of Soviet espionage and expansionism strengthened the old "red scare" and allowed for politically exploitable fears of "un-American activities" at home. It took a long time to combat the mendacities of a Joseph McCarthy; in that harmful conflict as in subsequent ones, courageous individuals protecting the rights of free expression demonstrated how vulnerable as well as indispensable a free press is.

In France and Italy, Communists, by virtue of their leading role in the Resistance, had won for themselves a kind of moral rehabilitation. Americans did not understand how a quarter or a third of French and Italian voters could support the Communist parties, which prescribed a line that rarely and then only minimally deviated from Moscow's orthodoxy. Among intellectuals a significant, if gradually shrinking, band of sympathizers remained: Jean-Paul Sartre can serve as the best exemplar of that group. They would criticize particular acts of horror — the Czech coup in 1948, the subsequent show trials, the crushing of the Hungarian revolt in 1956 — but they would shut their minds to the notion that the "excesses" were also the essence of the regime, and thus they continued the willed self-deception that had favored Bolshevism from the beginning. (The full horror of indigenous Communist torture in the satellite countries is only now being fully, gruesomely documented. In the first two decades after the war the Communist regimes set out to crush whatever resistance, real or potential, they encountered, resorting to the most inhuman forms of degradation.) A growing American presence in Western Europe — as witness the Marshall Plan — added to the ideological conflict; Communists and left-wing intellectuals tried to exploit the ever-present anti-Americanism, the antagonism against what was called the "Coca-Colonization" of Europe. In his recent book, *Past Imperfect*, Tony Judt has given a devastating analysis of "the political irresponsibility" of so many French intellectuals.[26]

But during and after the fratricidal wars the idea of "Europe" was born or reborn. In the underground papers and manifestos of the French and Italian Resistance, hopes for a unified democratic Europe were first expressed. Altiero Spinelli, in Italian captivity, envisioned a new Europe; the great architects of the postwar order in Western Europe, Jean Monnet and Robert Schuman, did not

[26] Tony Judt, *Past Imperfect: French Intellectuals, 1944–1946* (Berkeley, 1992).

want the fatality of a divided and nationalistic Europe to reappear. The cornerstone of the Europe they foresaw rested on the reconciliation between France and Germany, slowly achieved, and finally crowned in the great symbolic (and religious) moment when Charles de Gaulle and Konrad Adenauer celebrated mass together at the Cathedral of Rheims in 1962.

This Europe of hope, of spiritual regeneration, enjoyed a period of unprecedented economic growth and social transformation. It was a time of rising standards of living, of a democratic consumerism that survived all manner of setbacks and oil shocks. The French call them the thirty glorious years — and in them the class divisions were much attenuated. The European Community, subject to all kinds of vicissitudes, facilitated Western Europe's march to prosperity and to a measure of political cooperation. As the Europe of Brussels grew beyond its original six members and sought to give greater meaning to "Community," it began to think of itself as Europe *tout court*, presumptuous in its self-assessment, comfortably parochial, and in some measure oblivious of the fact that it was but a part of Europe. There were, of course, important exceptions: the practitioners of *Ostpolitik* acted out of a combination of genuine fraternal concern and *raison d'état*. The many people in France and elsewhere who kept up contacts with East European intellectuals and artists contributed in ways that have yet to be honored fully to the eventual reunification of Europe. The myth of Europe was a powerful magnet to the nations in search of freedom: I am thinking of Spaniards and Portuguese who overthrew their dictatorships; and Europe '92 contributed importantly to the self-liberation of Eastern Europe.

The enthusiasm for "Europe" was genuine, but the building of a Western European collectivity, beginning with the Schuman Plan in the late 1940s, was cumbersome, and the vision of a European future may have served as a temporary cover for the European past. It was not so much that West European states sought to deny or hide the truth as that the people shared a willed amnesia. The Germans talked of the "Stunde Null," of a total caesura; but despite many courageous voices, people were profoundly reluctant to face the past, to grapple with massive complicity, or to acknowledge the deep continuities in German history that had led to National Socialism. In France we find a similar reluctance, again a kind of taboo, to face the truth about Vichy, to acknowledge the continuities between prewar rightist and antisemitic views and movements and their triumph under Vichy. The Fifth Republic's effort to ban Max Ophul's dramatic film about collaboration and resistance, *Le chagrin et la pitié*, was a clumsy, symbolic effort — in a democracy — to banish a true confrontation with the past.[27] Perhaps the stark division between "resisters" and "collaborators" — categories that applied in all the occupied countries of Europe — obstructs a clearer sense of the past, blurs the subtle and terrible ambiguities of the real situation: how only a few were fully committed to one cause or the other, how doubts and misgivings crept in, how people lived and acted in several worlds simultaneously or successively: people alternated, changed with time. In 1940 Hitler's New Order seemed attractive to some and irresistible to many; after Stalingrad "the wave of the future" receded — and people's minds adjusted to new realities.

How different the world of Eastern Europe! For decades, the Soviet Union had been isolated and insulated; its borders were sealed, and technology facilitated the insulation — governments could jam foreign broadcasts, for example — even as more recent technology has made such insulation all but impossible.[28] The German invasion of the Soviet Union in 1941 had shown the extraordinary disaffections that existed there, especially among peoples who had a sense of their own ethnic identity, such as the

---

[27] On this, see Henry Rousso, *The Vichy Syndrome: History and Memory in France since 1944* (Cambridge, Mass., 1991).

[28] The connection between technology and terror has undergone many changes. Access to communications has helped dissidents. Brutal repression can rarely be hidden today; the means of underground publications have also changed.

Ukrainians. I now ask myself whether the Great Patriotic War, as it was dubbed by Stalin and glorified for decades thereafter, did not prolong the life of the Soviet Union: it was the one common memory that legitimized the dictatorship and gave some belated justification for the regime's ruthless drive to industrialize at all costs.

Whatever hopes or illusions existed in the first three years after the end of the war, by 1948 it had become clear that Stalin was determined to consolidate his totalitarian grip over the countries of Eastern Europe. In the wake of the Red Army, Communist regimes were installed, loyal to Stalin and imbued with Stalinist fears of foreign and internal enemies. Huge Communist parties evolved everywhere, as did an all-controlling, privileged *apparat* and eventually the rule of the *nomenklatura*. The nightmare of totalitarian rule now extended from Vladivostok to the Elbe, and the Soviets needed still greater repression to rule over nations that treasured their historic independence. Stalin unleashed yet more terror: the show trials against Rudolf Slansky and Anna Pauker, the doctors' plot, the persecution of bourgeois remnants — the endless lies, the perpetual rewriting of history.

Stalin's death in 1953 marked a caesura in the history of Bolshevism: for the first time in thirty years there was a moment of controlled truth. Nikita Khrushchev's secret speech in 1956 — instantly published in the foreign press, but, as the property of the party, kept from the people — accused Stalin of having instituted a reign of terror, of murdering innocent people. "De-Stalinization" indicted the "cult of personality," thus suggesting that Stalin and not the system was responsible for the horrors hitherto concealed. For all the zigzags of Soviet policy thereafter, and despite the ruthless crushing of the Hungarian and Czech revolts, the full force of Stalinist totalitarianism was not resurrected. "Thaws" would alternate with freezes, but the most brutal forms of systematic, sadistic torture began to give way, though the gulags and psychiatric wards continued. Torture as a habitual instrument of power began to disappear; deposed rulers, like Khrushchev, were no longer executed.

A kind of degrading, repressive drabness descended over much of the Soviet empire. The regime still claimed that the party had an absolute monopoly on the truth, silencing all criticism and crushing all opposition. A new life, however, sprang up in the underground: it was in bondage that the hunger for freedom was nurtured; it was the ever-present lie that inspired that hunger for truth, the determination "to live in the truth," to face down the oppressor, to make no compromise. All of this has been told in many stirring accounts; consider as but one poignant example Adam Michnik's *Letters from Prison*. In the cellars of the Resistance in occupied Europe, a dream of a Europe purged of hate had been born; in the underground of repressive Communist regimes, courageous and incorruptible men and women depicted the ambiguities of life under declining totalitarianism — with an astounding compassion. To recall but a few names — Václav Havel and Adam Michnik, Efim Etkind and Czeslaw Milosz, Jury Afanassjew and Andrei Sakharov — is to remember this deep outcry against untruth, this revulsion against the lying society with its rewards for compliance and its demands for soul-destroying compromises. This was still a time when the two parts of Europe were divided and estranged from one another, but I think it was also a time when the poorer half developed a richer sense of what Europe meant or could mean than did the prosperous part.

Gandhi's philosophy of nonviolence may have been a beacon for some, but many, many people developed a stoic, defiant awareness, in Havel's words, "of the power of the powerless." I believe that it was in the countries of Eastern Europe that a new idea of Europe was born, that in the leaders of KOR (Committee for Defense of Workers' Rights) and of Solidarity, the members of Charter '77, and the thousands and later the tens of thousands who with incomparable spirit and discipline defied regimes and somehow conquered them morally there was something more deeply European, more self-consciously European than in voices in Western Europe. At the heart of their lives and doings lies a humane vision that wants to end and yet understand the chain of horrors that began with the terror of 1914.

In conclusion I wish to repeat what I said at the beginning: in 1989 this chain of horrors was broken. I do not believe that we have reached the end of history or a surcease of conflicts; the passions of primordial untruth and violence, hatreds, and nationalist intolerance are dangers that have already overwhelmed some of the recent achievements. But I do believe we have reached the end of an era when Europe was wracked by hegemonial wars, made worse by new means of destruction, when these wars exacerbated the social and national conflicts that bred or shaped them, when the utopian visions of totalitarian regimes enthralled and enslaved millions, and when these totalitarian states amassed a monopoly of power that also controlled a monopoly of truth.

The terrible era behind us — and the astounding four years since 1989 — have once again taught us the unpredictability of events. Still, I would venture to say that in Europe today there is — perhaps for the first time in its modern history — a presumption for peace. Perhaps there is even a presumption against soldiers shooting their fellow-citizens — despite the horrors in what used to be Yugoslavia.

The leaders of self-liberation of Eastern Europe had to fight specific, local enemies and ensconced *apparatchiki*; they rejected violence and untruth. Once in power, they started a new and different chain: on behalf of their nations, they offered formal apologies for injuries done to other nationalities or countries; hands have been stretched out in reconciliation. Skeptics may scoff that these were mere words — as if the whole preceding era had not proven the power of words and symbols. But even skeptics must acknowledge that the gestures of reconciliation were followed by definitive treaties; the German-Polish Treaty, for example, aimed at ending centuries of brutal conflict. Treaties have been supplemented or complemented by unprecedented, if still insufficient, efforts at regional cooperation.

The process of reconciliation has its entrenched opponents, including powerful remnants of the old *apparat*. Nationalism — which has always had its emancipatory and its brutal, aggressive sides — may be moving in the latter direction. Patriotism inspired the liberators, but xenophobia and violence are ever-present.

I believe historians have a particular responsibility at this point — and I say this knowing full well that our collective impact has diminished. We are at the threshold of a new era in which "the white spots of history," as they are called in Russia, have a chance of being filled. As archives are opened, as historians become unfettered, there are immense opportunities, yet what obstacles. Powerful interests will want to prevent disclosures that would document their complicity or the falseness of so much that went under the name of history.[29] We need to remember that the revolutions of 1989 marked the victory of those who believed in the rule of law, in free speech, in representative government, in the open society. As party orthodoxies and lies about the past are destroyed, old myths might newly emerge: to topple Lenin in order to celebrate Nicholas II is but an alternation in myth-making. The same would be true if Bolshevik ideology were replaced by Russian nationalism or Ukrainian antisemitism; a world controlled by the Stasi must not be replaced by a society intimidated by roaming skinheads.

This is not a time of triumphalism for capitalism; true, the free market has proven its far greater efficiency than the controlled economy, but it has its own deficiencies. Despite reforms, there is little evidence that a free or unregulated capitalist system can satisfy human needs for security or justice. Men and women have died for truth, freedom, and dignity — but have they died for capitalism? As Communism collapsed, the United States offered a

[29] On this, see the moving essay by Juri Afanassjew, "Das beschädigte Gedächtnis," *Transit: Europäische Revue* (Summer 1991), 110–20.

distressing example of what harm unleashed greed can create. The immense human, moral, and material costs of Reaganite free-market euphoria have only just been acknowledged. The balance between the needs of the free market and the claims of social justice are always in dispute, always in need of political adjustment. For some people it has proven ideologically profitable to declare the identity of Bolshevism and Socialism. But Bolshevism was a perversion of Socialism, and Democratic Socialism has helped to humanize capitalism, to keep it alive. The Socialist impulse has been a useful irritant to capitalist insouciance.

For all the risks and dangers ahead, for all the reminders of how vulnerable people are to myths and illiberal promises, we should recognize the magnitude of the changes that have come to Europe with the revolutions of 1989. Truth has been vindicated. The value of liberal institutions and of a liberal spirit have reappeared, not with any kind of fanfare, but perhaps "as self-evident truths," as they first appeared to the framers of the American Declaration of Independence. Perhaps we are returning to some of the values of the eighteenth century, of the Enlightenment, of a moment in Europe that has been called the "Discovery of Liberty." The Defense of Liberty is our next task.

II

My second lecture deals with a short and very recent period, focusing on postunification Germany. I suppose I could justify this effort simply by saying that German developments are at once unique and symptomatic of developments in Eastern Europe and that Germany's place in Europe is central. But I take additional comfort from what two colleagues from this distinguished university have said. As Hajo Holborn wrote, "There can be no question that history must be interpreted as an evolution, of which our present age is a mere part. If so, we should make every effort to relate the history of the past to our present vital concerns and try in particular to recover the knowledge about the day before yesterday that has slipped from living memory and not been caught by the professional historian."[1] And as C. Vann Woodward has said — and exemplifies in his life — "since the historian lives in the present he has obligations to the present as well as to the past he studies."[2] What happened the day before yesterday does touch on our present vital concerns — hence my effort to put that period in some historical perspective.

We all remember the euphoria that the breaching of the Berlin wall created: the world saw an event — an improvised event — that had the deepest symbolic and dramatic meaning: on November 9, 1989, in Berlin a people were let out of some kind of prison in a scene reminiscent of the prisoners coming out into sunlight at the end of *Fidelio*, and it was altogether appropriate that a few weeks later Leonard Bernstein conducted an orchestra of East and West German musicians performing Beethoven's Ninth Symphony

---

[1] Hajo Holborn, *The Political Collapse of Europe* (New York, 1951), p. vi.

[2] C. Vann Woodward, *Thinking Back: The Perils of Writing History* (Baton Rouge and London, 1986), p. 98.

to celebrate. He substituted the word "freedom" (*Freiheit*) for "joy" (*Freude*) in the Schiller poem sung in the last movement, and for a fleeting moment the two were paired. It is the rupture of that union that has become my text for today.

In an immediate sense, the breach of the wall was an accident: in the confused turmoil of early November 1989 during which the Communist leaders of East Germany realized that they were confronting uncontrollable developments, a Cabinet minister read an ambiguous announcement to the press that suggested a forthcoming relaxation of travel restrictions. Within minutes, a few demoralized guards along the wall allowed a trickle of people to pass into West Berlin, an early trickle that in the next days became a human flood. It was an accident that was validated by the sweep of history.

We should realize a further ironic, ominous accident: in the Germany of our century no other day of the year has seen such momentous events as November 9. In 1918, on that day, masses of Germans, hungry, war-weary, and enraged, took to the streets and overthrew their imperial and imperialist rulers. That revolution, however incomplete, frightened the old elites, but essentially it left them intact, and most of them came to feel a sullen homelessness in the new Weimar Republic. In subsequent disasters, some of these elites saw Hitler as a possible redeemer, the same Hitler who on November 9, 1923, attempted to overthrow the democratic Weimar Republic — the failed putsch that first gave him national notoriety. Some nine years later he became chancellor of Germany and embarked on a course of measured violence; on November 9, 1938, *Kristallnacht*, Hitler unleashed his fury against the Jews — in full view of his people. Why liberation on so ambiguous a day?

No one had predicted the drama of that summer and fall of 1989 in Central Europe, and few people anticipated that the euphoria would soon yield to disillusion. (An American social scientist has been quoted as saying, "None of us predicted these events, and all of us could explain why they were inevitable.") In discussing the aftermath of that euphoria, I would cite as an epigraph something that Heinrich Heine wrote in 1831 in his exile in Paris: "It is a peculiar matter with patriotism, with the real love for the fatherland. One can love one's fatherland and get to be 80 years old and never have known that love; but then one would have had to remain at home. The nature of spring one recognizes only in winter, and it is behind the oven that one writes the best spring poems. The love for freedom is a dungeon's flower and only in jail does one feel the value of freedom. Thus love for the German fatherland begins only at the German border, but principally when seeing German misfortune from abroad." ³

The opening of the Berlin wall was a climax of processes that had begun elsewhere in Europe, that found indispensable support in Mikhail Gorbachev's Soviet Union, and that finally brought East Germany close to a revolutionary situation. In October 1989, on the fortieth birthday of the DDR, Gorbachev had warned, "Life punishes those who come too late." He hoped that in East Germany as elsewhere in the crumbling Soviet imperium, party leaders would move to a liberalized Communism, would stage "a revolution from above," marked by *glasnost'* and *perestroika*. But he also made it clear that if the East German regime were to use violence against its people, Soviet troops would stay in their barracks.

In the early fall of 1898 the East German state was in danger of withering away, as thousands of its citizens found their way to West Germany, as millions had done before the wall had been built in 1961. They reached West Germany — where by law they instantly received citizenship — via the accommodating corridor of Hungary's opened borders and by crowding into the West German embassy in Prague, whence they were taken through DDR territory to the Federal Republic. At the same time, an ever growing number of their compatriots took to the streets demanding

³ Heinrich Heine, "Vorrede zum ersten Bande des 'Salon'" (1833), in *Sammtliche Werke* (Hamburg, 1876), vol. 14, pp. 44–45.

greater freedom and a more humane existence under the memorable slogan "We are the people" — as against the lie of forty years that the party represented the people. These marches showed admirably planned restraint — and still required great courage. After all, the thugs in the Politburo who had practiced repression for decades still had the means of emulating the butchery of Tiananmen Square, which but a short time before they had officially welcomed. They had the means but, at the decisive moment, no longer the will. We now know that the regime was in fact readying new internment camps, that, anticipating violence, it had sent extra blood supplies to local hospitals on the day of the greatest demonstration in Leipzig, October 9. At the last moment bold local leaders, including Kurt Masur, persuaded the powers to parley and not to shoot. After that, the people of East Germany dictated the pace, the streets decreed the agenda, and the Communist leaders hobbled behind.

At the same time oppositional groups emerged, such as the Civic Forum, demanding free elections and an end to Communist rule. I doubt that most of the leading dissidents or their followers had the unification of Germany in mind. In the beginning they hoped that the DDR could be turned into a social-democratic state, could find the fabled third way between Communism and capitalism, in some union with the bigger brother. Belatedly the regime lurched toward compromise, pressed from below. Honecker was replaced by a younger but no less compromised leader, Egon Krenz, who much too late was replaced by Hans Modrow, at the time a politician with the reputation of a true reformer. All the while the exodus to the West continued — and the specter of East Germany becoming a kind of prison house for the aged began to haunt Germans of both East and West.

The DDR regime agreed to hold free elections — and instantly the major West German parties sent money and experienced organizers to the East. They found indigenous leaders, of course — but relatively few; much of whatever reservoir of political talent might have existed in East Germany had chosen at an earlier time to emigrate to the West. For multiple reasons — to which I shall return — the potential for East German leadership was feeble, certainly feeble as compared to that in Poland or Czechoslovakia, and it was easily overwhelmed by the well-schooled and well-financed influx of West German politicians. It gradually became clear that even the most attractive of the East German leaders had complicated, in some instances compromised, pasts. In the election held in March 1990, a replica of the CDU triumphed, and the appealing Lothar de Mazière became the first non-Communist minister-president of the DDR, destined as well to be the last. As the Communist state disintegrated, his task was to negotiate the demise of the DDR.

With the disappearance of the wall and the threat of a mass exodus from East Germany, it was clear that a German solution had to be found speedily. The East German proletariat demanded capitalism — and at once. Kohl seized the moment and with somnambulistic skill exploited a favorable international constellation. Backed by the United States, the one ally cheerfully distant from Germany, Kohl began the 2+4 negotiations that resulted in the United States, France, Britain, and the Soviet Union agreeing to a unified Germany that would be free to remain in NATO and remain integrated in the West. Kohl paid heavy ransom to the Soviets to make the unpalatable at least swallowable. He defied his own Bundesbank, decreeing a 1:1 exchange rate with the much weaker East Mark. And he negotiated a treaty with de Mazière, whereby the reconstituted *Länder* of the DDR would join the Federal Republic—alongside the old *Länder*, and with the same rights.

This near miracle was achieved on October 3, 1990, the formal sanctioning of what Willy Brandt had celebrated a year earlier: "What belongs together grows together." This was not a moment of German triumphalism; it was not even a victory of German nationalism. Economic aspirations dictated the pace, not ideological fervor. That unification would bring immense challenges was clear of course; in June 1990 I remarked to de Mazière that I thought that the economic problems of unification, though huge, would turn out to be manageable, but that the moral-psychological problems would be far greater and their resolution take much longer. He agreed, saying, "Yes, we do not want 16 million psychological cripples." Many West Germans, especially Oskar Lafontaine and some of his Social Democratic colleagues, warned about the likely costs of unification, but Chancellor Kohl exuded insouciance, a profitable stance in an election year. Thus he missed the chance to ask of West Germans sacrifices for their long-lost brothers and sisters — who had really paid for Hitler's war. Had he done so there would have been a willing response; but Churchillian "blood and sweat" demands come hard to German leaders; they are afraid of their own people — they don't trust them.

Such has been the pace of events that much has already been forgotten or distorted about the events of 1989–1990. While the two states existed, Germans could believe in the unity of their nation, of a people with a common language and a common past, in Honecker's phrase, a people with a community of fate. Now, within one state, the deep divisions among Germans are more visible. No doubt there is truth in Freud's words about "the narcissism of small differences" that divides neighbors and family members,[4] yet in 1989 there was an expectation that Germans would understand Germans. In the first flush of enthusiasm people forgot the estrangements that had grown so strong over forty years, as West Germans came to regard the French or the Tuscans or the Dutch as closer, and perhaps more attractive, to them than the East Germans. For their part, the East Germans lived with a prescribed if gradually attenuated hostility to the Federal Republic, and with a nonprescribed envy and resentment of its freedom and prosperity, which they witnessed nightly on their television screens. Visitors to East Germany could sense this estrangement;

[4] Sigmund Freud, *Gesammelte Werke, Werke aus den Jahren 1917–1920* (London, 1947), vol. 12, p. 169.

I sensed it myself when I visited both Germanies in 1954 and very frequently after that. And in the Federal Republic, for all the ritualistic invocations of German solidarity, for all the many individuals who did genuinely care about their fellow-Germans in the East, one sensed an enormous, unacknowledged indifference to them. Sudden commonality, sudden huge demands, did not instantly transform indifference to open-hearted solicitude.

In a general way, some of the turbulence was predictable; as the process of unification was under way and not only Iron Ladies worried about a new hegemonial Germany, I repeatedly asserted my confidence that even a unified Germany would not pose a threat to peace or stability, always adding that "the first test of the new Germany would be how Germans treat Germans" — and I said that in part out of the recollection that the first victims of Hitler's regime had been Germans — Socialists, Communists, and other political enemies. Once Germans had tortured and murdered fellow-Germans in the cellars of the SA, would one expect that they would treat their avowed enemies — whether Jews or, later, Slavs — with any humanity?

Second, the new Germany was facing an enormous economic challenge: the rebuilding of a devastated third of the country. For years we had been told that the East German economy was the eighth or tenth largest in the world; it looked as if Germans could make even Communism work. But the DDR's putative success was a case of the one-eyed leading the blind; by the 1980s its entire economy was in a free fall; even the regime had lost hope, and the country came to depend on ever greater subsidies, both hidden and open, from the Federal Republic. The regime was consuming its own stock, living off its antiquated, minimal accumulation. With the revolutions in Eastern Europe, the DDR's ready market in the Comecon countries disappeared; East German industry could not compete with the superior industrial and consumer goods produced in West Germany, perhaps the world's most efficient economy. None of the other liberated countries of the former Soviet bloc faced such competition within their own borders, and none had a big brother who in the process of helping out took charge. The Germans had to dismantle a bankrupt system that had maintained full employment by sanctioning low productivity, and this meant instant dislocations, harsh measures, and inevitably resentments and recriminations. Add to these dislocations the claims of West Germans — and of former Germans now living in the United States and elsewhere — who claimed restitution of property that had been expropriated by the Nazi or DDR regime. Almost at once East Germans felt endangered — and exploited, forgetting the old adage that if there is one thing worse than being exploited it is *not* being exploited.

Marc Bloch, the great historian of socioeconomic life, once remarked that all historical facts are psychological, and I invoke his words to justify my particular focus on the psychology of this process.[5] I believe that both Germanies gained greater, if sharply different, kinds of freedom after unification — and with that freedom came new uncertainties and discontents. In the East it was the freedom from the knock at the door, freedom to travel, release from a regimented, intimidating, false existence, freedom to examine one's life. But almost immediately 17 million East Germans discovered that freedom also meant freedom to face an uncertain future, freedom to lose a job, to lose support nets, however inadequate they may have been. For forty years most East Germans had accommodated themselves to life in a world of public lies and private doubts. Totalitarian regimes mobilize people into passive participation in politics. After twelve years of Nazi rule and forty years of Communist rule they may have survived psychologically by practicing denial, by wishing not to see. Friedrich Nietzsche, in one of his most extravagant attacks on Germans, held them responsible for all manner of crimes against European culture "and always for the same reason, out of their innermost *cowardice* before reality, which is also their cowardice before truth, out of their

---

[5] Marc Bloch, *The Historian's Craft* (New York, 1953), p. 194.

untruthfulness which has become instinctual with them, out of 'Idealism.' " [6]

After 1989 avoiding reality became impossible, given the economic dislocations of transforming a dysfunctional, decaying command economy into a market economy — as if there was but one type of market economy. The closing of state-run enterprises led to mounting unemployment. Consider the magic word "privatization" — the term in its strict sense signifying the process whereby state property is placed in multiple private hands; in the East German case, this often enough meant Western hands. But economic affairs were only part of what had been prescribed under the earlier command economy; so much of life had been lived in the public realm, ordered from above or by inherited routine. That kind of society left little room for choice, for private initiative, for any kind of voluntary *civisme*. Suddenly the East Germans were released from this nonage, from public control, and had to learn to make their own choices, think their own thoughts, find their own truths. They were indeed "privatized" at a time when the associational life of a civil society was being but slowly introduced.

Market economies presuppose legal structures, a system of private and public law — a legal code that has to be taught, learned, and gradually assimilated. The art of evasion is also practiced in market economies — as the 1980s so vividly illustrate. Western enthusiasts for the free market in the former DDR often ignored the social costs of the transformation. Worse, the abrupt introduction of new forms of economic life also created what sociologists (and Marxists) have long identified with modern capitalism: alienation, *anomie*, insecurity. For the East Germans, the move from the rigid world of Communist rule to the demands of a mobile society was hard. The very notion of "planning" for a market economy had an ironic ring to it. A new dependency developed: much of life in the eastern *Länder* came to be organized

---

[6] Friedrich Nietzsche, *Werke in drei Bänden, Ecce Homo*, ed. by Karl Schlechta (Munich: 1955), vol. 2, p. 1147.

by Westerners, who were practiced in making decisions, in making things work, in assessing the risks of the market, and who had the skills and the funds to take charge. East Germans had been taught to live and work by plans that bore little relation to reality; they had learned to suffer and endure but not to take responsibility or to live by trial and error.

East Germans hoped that the end of Communism would bring instant rehabilitation as well as instant improvement in their living standard. But soon they began to think they were being "colonized" — a word used commonly that was infuriating to Western ears. (Even before formal unification, I thought of the analogy to Northern carpetbaggers after the Civil War: were the East Germans going to endure something similar to the experience of the defeated South in the era of Reconstruction? In his history of Reconstruction, Eric Foner writes, "Most carpetbaggers probably combined the desire for personal gain with a commitment to reforming the "unprogressive" South . . ." [7]) Defeated, humiliated, more object than subject, many East Germans expressed their disappointment in terms of self-pity and resentment. Was there no end to their being victimized? In the early years of occupation the Russians had dismantled and taken what had been left of German industrial plants in their zone; a current scholarly estimate is that the Russians extracted some 54 billion D-Marks in reparations — all this while the western zones and later the FRG received Marshall Plan aid.[8] Of course the balance sheet is far more complicated: on the one hand, the West Germans also benefited from the huge influx of refugees from the Soviet zone and of Germans expelled by Poles and Czechs; on the other hand, Bonn did make restitution payments to Israel and gradually gave support to East Germany. But East Germans believed, with some justification, that they had paid disproportionately for Hitler's war.

[7] Eric Foner, *A Short History of Reconstruction* (New York, 1988), p. 130.

[8] Jörg Fisch, *Reparationen nach dem Zweiten Weltkrieg* (Munich, 1992), as quoted in *Die Zeit*, January 8, 1993.

After 1990 both East and West Germans had to consider their separate and joint pasts. Former DDR citizens had to address questions that have beset other countries at other times in our century: questions of collaboration and collusion, of culpability and trustworthiness. Which of them were so compromised that they could no longer be teachers or judges, civil servants or plant managers, professors or members of renowned academies? Who was to make these judgments — and on what basis?

West Germans, hardly at peace with their own past, were ready to make their judgments about Easterners. From the moment of unification I was concerned that the West Germans would be far more cheerfully, self-righteously assiduous in punishing suspected collaborators with the Communist regime than their forbears had been in dealing with servants of the Nazi regime. The very popularity of that regime had made de-Nazification difficult. Even now West Germans with an undetected compromised past continue to flourish; a prominent West German physician recently was forced to resign from a major post in an international organization because it was revealed that he had participated in the Nazis' euthanasia program. The Nazi past divides West Germans still, as shown by the controversy surrounding President Reagan's visit to Bitburg in 1985, by the *Historikerstreit*, and by the decades it has taken to document the complicity of the German army in atrocities on the Eastern front. To this day many Germans, in and out of uniform, choose to believe in the *Wehrmacht*'s innocence. We should remember that National Socialism never needed a wall; there was never a threat of a mass exodus. By comparison, millions of East Germans voted with their feet. Under the Nazis an indeterminate number of Germans had gone into "inner emigration," tried to remain insulated, to purchase peace at the price of silence. West Germans who were confounded by this past — and divided among themselves about it — were now called upon to judge fellow-Germans who had lived for a further forty years under a totalitarian regime initially held in place by foreign bayonets.

Most East Germans knew that their leaders, piously mouthing peace, had believed in violence and had no mercy. What they could not have known (because the tape was released only in February 1993) was that in February 1982 Erich Mielke, head of the Stasi, had told his closest colleagues that to save the lives of millions one might have to kill a bandit: "All this drivel about not executing and no death sentences, all crap, comrades."[9] The tone does remind one of Nazi evil. In the post-Stalinist era East Germans leaders, like leaders throughout the Soviet bloc, sought to replace torture with other kinds of intimidation, including the abomination of psychiatric wards. Party leaders ordered monstrous crimes: they ordered alleged enemies of the regime to be tortured, incarcerated, or shot; they organized espionage and initiated or facilitated international terrorism. But these same leaders after 1970 and especially in the 1980s garnered official recognition by other states: Chancellor Kohl received them in Bonn; Franz Joseph Strauss visited them and arranged for the DDR to receive a 1 billion DM credit. West German Social Democrats collaborated with functionaries of the East German Communist Party to hammer out a joint paper defining areas of agreement and disagreement. Today Honecker is free in Chile and only a few frontier guards are in prison, while tens of thousands of teachers and other East German civil servants have been suspended or dismissed.

As the Communist regime crumbled, East Germans, left in their crowded, drab, decaying dwellings, ill-lit and ill-equipped, saw pictures of how the *nomenklatura* had lived in insulated comfort, and they read about the perquisites that ranged from special medical care to Swiss bank accounts. Had they really not noticed before that the much-touted egalitarianism of the first German Socialist state had been traduced daily, visibly and invisibly? The *apparatchiki* had their own Volvos, their children had privileged

---

[9] Quoted in announcement of Der Bundesbeauftragte für die Unterlagen des Staatssicherheitsdienstes der ehemaligen Deutschen Demokratischen Republik, February 16, 1993.

access to education, and all of them could shop in the Intershops where Western goods could be bought for Western currency. The revelations of the extent of these special benefits — petty by Western standards — enraged many East Germans: they felt betrayed. They remembered the leaders' endless invocations that, unlike the rapacious capitalist West, the DDR was an egalitarian society where austerity and sacrifice provided a psychological guarantee of a better future. But they must have had at least an inkling that their leaders had not practiced the virtues of delayed gratification that they had preached.

The resultant outburst sprang from what I think was the East Germans' ambivalence about deprivation. They minded it, of course, but they may have felt that austerity was virtuous — in old Germanic terms, ennobling. To have stark proof that their leaders had mocked this notion was offensive. In this largely Lutheran country, was this a distant echo of Martin Luther's attacks on a Roman hierarchy that preached poverty but lived in corrupt luxury?

The East Germans were made to realize something far worse: their insidious, malevolent regime had managed to entrap vast numbers of them in collusion and corruption. The state security police had organized an unprecedented web of surveillance. In its final days the Stasi consisted of 97,000 full-time employees — with perhaps as many as 140,000 IMs (unofficial collaborators), most of whom had acknowledged their commitment in writing. Only the "higher" ranks of society, such as professors or members of elite academies, were allowed to register their agreement orally. In addition, membership in the Communist Party rose to 2 million people, who were particularly vulnerable to Stasi demands. All this machinery for 17 million Germans — while the Gestapo, helped by countless voluntary informers, at the end of the Nazi regime had only 32,000 members for 80 million Germans.[10] The

[10] Interview with Pastor Joachim Gauck, special chairman of the organization listed in note 9, May 6, 1993. On the Gestapo, see Robert Gellately, *The Gestapo and German Society: Enforcing Racial Policy 1933–1945* (Oxford, 1990), pp. 44–46, 253–61.

Stasi files — 150 kilometers of them — offered poisonous proof of a poisoned society.

The Stasi were the eyes and ears of a regime deeply distrustful of its own people. Born of distrust, the Stasi became an agent of distrust. An earlier Tanner lecturer, Annette Baier, talked of the centrality of trust.[11] In a repressive society like the DDR, the desire for trust was great; reaching out for it, fraught with danger. In a world without laws or enforceable rights, a person searches for the like-minded, for another person to talk to, if need be in some outside place where surveillance is more difficult. West German observers thought that East Germans had managed to have closer, more trusting relationships in what they called a niche society. Some East Germans probably did have a particular affinity for trust and friendship; they invested in them as rare human goods at a time of moral scarcity. Imagine, then, the shock, the retroactive dissolution of trust, when one discovered that one's friend had been an informer, that husbands informed on their wives, wives on husbands, parents on children, friends on friends. Even now, as more information is divulged, the web of suspicion spreads ever wider.

During the 1970s, when the East German regime gradually replaced physical terror with calculated intimidation, the Stasi, like other secret police, learned to play with fiendish aptitude on people's vulnerabilities, operating an ever more elaborate system of carrots and sticks. The rewards for being an unofficial collaborator varied: career advancement, travel to the West; the sticks were more formidable, often involving the punishment of children for the alleged sins of their parents. The Stasi also resorted to more lethal methods, such as efforts to bring about "personal destabilization," including undermining marriages — a whole array of Iago-like villainies aimed at destroying trust among friends and potential critics.

---

[11] Annette C. Baier, "Trust," in *The Tanner Lectures on Human Values*, vol. 13, ed. Grethe B. Peterson (Salt Lake City, 1992).

Opposition to the DDR regime was feeble compared to that elsewhere in the Soviet bloc. After the one great outburst of June 17, 1953, when East German workers took to the streets to defy their ever more demanding and repressive regime and were crushed by Soviet tanks, there was apparent conformity. There was no East German equivalent of the repeated uprisings or of the great alliance of workers and intellectuals in Poland's Solidarnosč, or of the Hungarian rebellion of 1956, or of the Czech spring of 1968 and later Charter 77. It has often been said that Germans are somewhat untutored in civic courage; they have the word but not the all-essential practice. Albert Hirschman once wrote of moral resources, including civic spirit and trust, "These are resources whose supply may well increase rather than decrease through use; . . . [they] do not remain intact if they stay unused — like the ability to speak a foreign language or to play the piano, these moral resources are likely to become depleted and to atrophy if not used.[12]

Stasi revelations have threatened some of the most promising political careers in the new *Länder* of the united Germany. Two examples may suffice: Lothar de Mazière, the first vice-chancellor of the unified Germany, resigned when it was said that he had Stasi contacts; and insinuations continue to be made against the only Socialist minister-president in the new *Länder*, Manfred Stolpe of Brandenburg. Stolpe had worked in and with the Protestant churches and had helped them to help victims of the regime. He had regular contacts with the Stasi — how else could he help people entrapped by them? Knowledgeable defenders of Stolpe and others similarly accused insist that any responsible person who tried to help people who had fallen afoul of the regime had to deal with the Stasi. But critics claim that even talking to Stasi officials was the first step on a slippery slope. Others, myself included, might argue that in a tyrannical system only absolute im-

---

[12] Albert O. Hirschman, *Rival Views of Market Society and Other Recent Essays* (New York, 1986), p. 155.

mobility can protect one from the dangers of that slope. Once upon a time the Stasi oppressed a people; its legacy has been to demoralize them, perhaps to deprive them of the few good political leaders they might have had.

The Ulbricht-Honecker regime, mixing German traditions with Soviet models, had promoted a separate cultural life in the DDR. It had wanted to create athletes of the spirit, writers and artists who could dazzle the outside world and satisfy some aspirations of their own people. As the East German molecular biologist and admirable citizen-thinker Jens Reich makes clear in a new book, the regime sought to implicate the entire *Intelligenz* — technicians as well as poets — and to a devastating degree it was successful.[13] For many reasons the *samizdat* literature that flourished in Poland, Czechoslovakia, and Russia did not exist in the DDR. In the early years of the regime writers like Robert Havemann were imprisoned and gifted irritants like Wolf Biermann were expelled. This last decision prompted East German writers to protest for the first time. But by and large the limits of state tolerance for dissent were rarely if ever tested.

Gradually the demands for socialist realism were relaxed; other kinds of art were allowed. The novelist Christa Wolf was able to depict life in the DDR with some degree of candor. Writers jousted with censors, parodists ventured the occasional mischief, as when the writer Heiner Muller said, "We are the most progressive state ever: 95 percent of the people are against it — such a thing has never happened before," or when he sang, "The Stasi is my Eckermann."[14] Now come the revelations that these writers, too, were once part of the Stasi net. In the late 1950s and early 1960s Christa Wolf was an unofficial informant, unbeknownst even to her husband. Decades later she described at length how she too came under Stasi surveillance. As the most

---

[13] Jens Reich, *Abschied von den Lebenslügen: Die Intelligenz und die Macht* (Berlin, 1992).

[14] Quoted in *Frankfurter Allgemeine Zeitung*, June 27, 1992.

prominent and promising of East German writers, she has been denounced and defended. For my purposes, she illustrates how easy it was under that regime to move from being accomplice and perpetrator to victim, how difficult it is for us to judge the conduct of people enmeshed in a system with all these visible and invisible tentacles.

There is at present a great controversy about the conduct of DDR authors and *Intelligenz*. Some West German critics express outrage, and there is a danger that in time the work of these writers might be altogether forgotten. This would be a distortion and a loss: some of them were guarded witnesses to life under dreadful conditions — conditions that did not exist in the old Federal Republic. Now, in the unified Germany, West Germans have assumed a leading role in decision-making, in dismissals and recruitments throughout the eastern *Länder*. Their work is officially subsumed under the term *Abwicklung*. This sanitized bureaucratic term, once used by the Nazis, suggests legal procedures or business liquidations; it bespeaks distance and condescension; it is unattuned to tact or compassion.

The question of judgment is inherently difficult. In the case of many of the accusations against former DDR citizens one must ask: how reliable are the files of the Stasi, and how often were they slanted by inferiors trying to curry favor with their superiors? Finally, as Jens Reich has implicitly warned, the Stasi could easily become a scapegoat for the DDR regime. The greater villains were the party and state functionaries; the Stasi were not autonomous villains, and some of their collaborators may have had mixed or honorable motives. Only the clearest picture of life in the DDR can help to render humane judgments. There may be good reason to sympathize with those West Germans of an impeccable past who say of all these leaks and revelations "Enough" — a reaction that has been much heard in the countries of Eastern Europe.

In the years to come Germans of both East and West will continue to find it difficult to deal with the history of their divided forty years, of the DDR and the Federal Republic, two entities that lasted almost as long as the Bismarckian Reich. Polemical, divisive arguments have already begun about who supported whom and when, who really promoted unification and who opposed it. Right-wing Germans or newborn nationalists are already accusing the Left of the old Federal Republic of national neglect, of having slighted the goal of national unity, of having collaborated with the SED or of having been "soft" on East German criminals or collaborators. In time, after the calumnies and the memories are extinguished or transformed, later generations may "bracket out" the history of the DDR, as Germans call such a deletion, while finding that it remains hard to expunge the Nazi past, efforts to "relativize" the crimes notwithstanding. As President von Weizsäcker has said, the DDR neither started a war nor committed genocide. It may gradually fade from historical consciousness, be dismissed as a Soviet satellite, an alien excrescence of something called the cold war. The West Germans' earlier indifference to the DDR would facilitate so convenient a lapse of memory. But the DDR in all its ambiguity needs to be remembered and in some way integrated into the history of Germany and Europe in our century.

The beginnings of the DDR are most likely to be forgotten, the time immediately after the war when in the Soviet zone of occupation a so-called Socialist state was gradually established, expropriating the large estate owners and nationalizing what was left of German industry there. In the baggage train of the conquering Red Army arrived Moscow-trained German Communists — many of whom had earlier been tortured in Nazi camps — determined to forge a union between Socialists and Communists in order to present what they called a great anti-Fascist bloc, a bulwark against what people then thought a plausible contingency: a revived German Fascist-type nationalism. True Socialists, remembering how at the end of the Weimar Republic Communists had in fact facilitated the rise of Nazism, defied Communist pleas and demands; men like Gustav Dahrendorf and Kurt Schumacher never had any doubts about the true nature of Communism. A few Socialists in the Soviet zone believed that the Communist party was genuinely anti-Fascist, that it would radically purge all former Nazis and would recruit its own cadre, mostly young, untrained people from the unpropertied classes. The claim that the German Democratic Republic, formally established in 1949, would become the first Socialist state in German history, that by its extrusion of Nazis and its dismantling of capitalism it was cleansing German soil of Nazi poison, that out of devastation it was building an egalitarian society — all this had a certain appeal, particularly for writers and intellectuals. Bertolt Brecht, long the lyricist of a proletarian culture, happily left his American exile, with its capitalist culture and McCarthyite hysteria, in order to win honors and his own theater in East Berlin. Lesser writers followed. Thomas Mann accepted an honor from the new state — though he decided to settle in Switzerland, spiritually equidistant from both Germanies. In the DDR as elsewhere at the time, Communists had the inestimable advantage of claiming to be the vanguard of a new culture; judge us by some distant future, they said, and not by the bleak present. Intellectuals, once committed to the faith, found it hard to break with it, to confess their error to themselves.

In the last few months an old German word with no English or French analogue has reappeared over and over again in books and articles. *Lebenslüge* roughly means the lie that is life-giving, the lie that is essential to a particular life, the lie that a person or a people may know to be false but without which the person or state would perish. The DDR was saddled with one *Lebenslüge* from the start: the fundamental insistence that the Soviet Union was at once liberator and fraternal master and model. The East Germans sensed the travesty of truth: they knew that the Red Army had raped and looted, they knew that the Soviets had despoiled their country, and they sensed as well that their rulers, at least in the beginning, were servile instruments of Soviet masters.

One of the many East German witticisms — the one commodity in which they outperformed the West Germans — insisted that the Russians were indeed brothers with whom one had indissoluble fraternal bonds: friends one chooses, brothers are unalterably inflicted. Gradually the anti-Fascist principle, the sole threadbare claim to legitimacy, lost its credibility as well: to call the Berlin Wall the great anti-Fascist wall was too grim an absurdity.

The Soviets and the DDR's rulers needed each other. For the former, East Germany was the frontier state, the most important defense post with the greatest arsenal of weapons; for the rulers of the DDR, the Soviet presence was the ultimate reserve army against their own people. The Federal Republic, its own legitimacy accepted by its citizens, had tied itself to the West, but these attachments enhanced security and prosperity and corresponded to the wishes of most of its people. In the 1980s the DDR regime, encouraged by the Federal Republic's ever more enterprising *Ostpolitik*, sought to gain some greater room for maneuver, some independence from Moscow. Characteristically, Honecker's greatest moment of independence came at the end, when he banned Soviet publications carrying Gorbachev's liberalizing message. To the end, Honecker remained a German Leninist — German because there was a tinge of sentimentality to his inhumanity. He and his closest advisers, most of them ardent believers in the powers of repression, ignored the younger members of the *nomenklatura* who understood the need for reform in East Germany. Their day came too late. The DDR was founded on deception, on various *Lebenslügen*, and its end was hastened by the self-deception of its aged leaders.

As I have said, the end of the DDR will inevitably affect the interpretation of its history and of the entire period when there were two Germanies. At this point I want to ask myself: how is my comprehension of the DDR a function of private experiences? Let me put these experiences before you — for what they might say about the DDR and about me as an interpreter. My first contact came in June 1950 in Munich, when I spent an evening with a young German writer, Peter Hacks, a contemporary, the son of close friends of my parents. The Hackses were so-called Aryans, radical Socialists under Weimar, who had behaved with exemplary decency under the Nazis.

Peter was about to emigrate to the newly established DDR, to the anti-Fascist bastion, hoping to work with Brecht. For hours that night we argued, I trying to dissuade him from subjecting himself to yet another dictatorship, he certain that socialism with whatever distortions offered a freer atmosphere than cold-war capitalism. I failed and he went; eventually his plays were performed in both parts of Germany. At times he fell into disfavor, but he retained his faith to the very end.

In the summer of 1954 I taught at the Free University in West Berlin; in those days it was relatively easy to cross into East Berlin, with its extraordinary theaters and inexpensive bookstores. But much of what I saw and felt in East Berlin reminded me of my childhood under National Socialism: the omnipresent police, the grimness of the border guards, the sea of flags and banners. Each visit was a trial—despite the protection of an American passport.[15]

Then in 1961 — just before the wall went up — and in 1962, roughly a year later, I was allowed (via the help of French colleagues) to work in the great archives that the DDR had inherited from Prussia and the Reich at the end of the war. For two weeks each time I stayed in Merseburg, a small town in the ecologically destroyed heartland of East German industry. There was pervasive smog and the smell of brown coal; the few stores had almost nothing to sell: canned cherries from Bulgaria were the great luxury. It was all so drab and shabby. I was the first American scholar, or one of the first, in the archives and the young archivists wanted to talk to me. They had become archivists by choice; in-

---

[15] On this, see my "Germany Revisited. Berlin 1954," in *The Failure of Illiberalism, Essays on the Political Culture of Modern Germany* (New York, reissue, 1992), pp. 210–33.

terested in the past, they had shied away from becoming historians because that would have subjected them to the most rigorous ideological dogmas. They wanted to tell me how much they disliked the regime and what their reasons had been to stay in the DDR — mostly concern for parents. I sensed that they were living in a gray zone of outward obedience and inner dissent. They yearned for "more light," for greater freedom and a better life — yet for all their misgivings they had a certain pride in their society, if not in their state. I wandered into a Lutheran church that bore the bold placard *Museumsreif? Nein, lebensfähig!* (Ripe for a Museum? No, very much alive!) and the fervent choir struck me as performing an act of unacknowledged defiance. I found the people I met sympathetic and suffering; I also experienced the peculiar pleasure of mocking the regime with impunity or talking to people who in some ways defied it — with far less impunity. Back in West Germany, enjoying creature comforts and yet aware that I missed some kind of healthy pain, I was astounded that my West German friends and colleagues had so little interest in the East Germans.

I tried to keep in touch, to keep informed about an abhorrent regime and its confused, ambivalent people. Then in the late 1970s I sensed that life in and between the two Germanies had begun to change. In 1979 I wrote of the Federal Republic "as the strongest state between the United States and the USSR, and the state with the greatest national grievance."[16] I argued that *Ostpolitik* was clearly successful in mitigating this grievance: the ties between the two Germanies were becoming closer. The DDR's efforts at claiming the Prussian heritage — its reinstallation of the famous statue of Frederick the Great was an example — pointed to change, as did much more significantly the joint East-West celebration in 1983 of the 500th anniversary of Luther's birth. On June 17, 1987, in a speech I gave before the Bundestag on the day of national unity, commemorating the uprising of June 1953, I

[16] See my *Dreams and Delusions: The Drama of German History* (New York, reissue, 1989), p. 209.

said, "On this day we should honor the clear, courageous voices from the other German state that demand human dignity and human rights. These voices often come from the church, for which the teachings and the example of Dietrich Bonhoeffer are still very much alive." On the same occasion I mentioned Weizsäcker's speech of May 8, 1985, being hailed abroad as the "authentic voice of the Federal Republic, perhaps even of the silent suprastate nation." [17]

Shortly before and then after the destruction of the Berlin wall in 1989, I met many of the leaders of East German dissent. In 1991, at the meeting of the West German Academy for Poetry in Weimar, I heard a well-known West German professor denounce the DDR's abuse of the German language — it was his own form of *Abwicklung*. I objected that he had not mentioned that the language had already been abused under an earlier dictatorship. He seemed baffled by my comment. An East German pastor who had been active in the oppositional movement was listening to the same speech and said, "I used to feel like a liberator [*Befreier*] and now I feel like someone vanquished [*Besiegter*]." In 1992, when at the University of Halle, I met an opposition leader who was now in charge of the commission to review members of the university. Herself young and always uncompromising, she had no patience with those who wanted to forgive their colleagues for ambiguous behavior because of extenuating circumstances.

In short, having had the good fortune of seeing something of the DDR and having had a sympathetic interest in its people, I continue to have concerns about their life now. The history of the DDR — from its beginning to its dissolution — is very much a part of the drama of German history.

The DDR leaves an ambiguous legacy, as does the Federal Republic; the difference is that the institutions of the old FRG have not ended but are in the process of having to adapt to different conditions. The old political culture of the Federal Republic

[17] Ibid., pp. 304, 294.

is being tested and, in part, measured by Eastern ideals. In the historic rivalry between Communism and Social Democracy, the former by its very collapse has scored a major triumph. Many people, especially on the political Right, rejoice in confounding Communism and Socialism, interpreting the dismal failure of the one as irredeemably discrediting the other as well. The historic task of Democratic Socialism has been to correct the most grievous, ruthless qualities of what Jacques Delors once called "capitalisme sauvage." It is doubtful that this task will ever be totally completed.

The DDR is dead, and some East Germans already have their nostalgic moments. Disappointed in the present, prompted by a selective memory, they ask: "Was everything wrong in the last forty years?" And they tend to erase from memory the hopelessness of the old regime and remember that at some level of subsistence, even if drab and uniform, ordinary citizens could count on the essentials of life: housing however wretched, food however meager, medical care however inferior and indifferent. They remember that in the old DDR there was no crime, no drugs, no pornography. The Communist rulers of the DDR could have echoed President Nixon's boast: "We have taken crime off the streets." The government had assumed a monopoly of crime.

Citizens remember the much vaunted *Kinderkrippen*, a grandiose term for child care centers to which working parents could send their children. The memory of the *Kinderkrippen* evokes the DDR's traditional concern for family life, for women's rights, including the nontraditional right of abortion, for social welfare — all this in contrast to the cold life in unified Germany, where the cash nexus rules all. These *Kinderkrippen* have become a kind of talisman for the better part of DDR life, and people forget that these benefits were palliatives to cover deeper pain. The *Kinderkrippen* were the decorous part of a controlled society that violated at will the health of the home it pretended to protect.

On some deep psychological level the unified Germany is more divided than before; the physical wall has been internalized.

Where once was the untroubled hope that at some future date the division of the country, unnaturally maintained, would be healed, there are now painful inequalities of power, wealth, experience, and assertiveness. The living standard of East Germans is still very much lower than that of West Germans; wages are lower and unemployment at least three times higher. Economic inequalities heighten psychic discontent: Ossies are given to self-pity, Wessies to arrogance and exasperation. Some West Germans themselves complain of Western self-righteousness. The country is rent by a psychological dissonance. Both sides deserve understanding, and there are many Germans who demand solidarity not in words but in deeds. But their pleas are lost on pusillanimous politicians who in confusion think mostly of the next election.

In March 1993 the Bonn Parliament voted a Solidarity Pact that has brought some predictability into the economic picture. It provides for new taxes to fund specified payments to the new *Länder*. Approximately 7 percent of GNP will be transferred to the East over the next decade — roughly 1 trillion D-Marks. Four months later even the European Community agreed, reluctantly, to provide 27.5 billion D-Marks over six years to the same *Länder* out of its regional assistance funds. The strains are clear: Germany as a whole is in a deep economic recession, with continued negative growth; according to many observers, it is the most serious recession since the founding of the Federal Republic. Hence the great unease pervading both parts of Germany. Still, the Solidarity Pact affords real chances for the new *Länder*, as Kurt Biedenkopf, minister-president of Saxony, made clear in a speech to his Diet — a candid speech that exemplified the possibilities of democratic leadership.

The old Federal Republic has also gained greater freedom in 1989, but a very different kind of freedom from the East Germans'. Unification has fulfilled the old national dream and has attenuated, on some level even removed, Germany's dependency on its Western allies. From the beginning of the Federal Republic, it needed Allied protection, most clearly in the ever vulnerable city of Berlin. For forty years this dependency set the parameters of choice. Now questions about German national interest and purpose reemerge in full force. In the ongoing debate there are some who demand greater German assertiveness, who are tired of being held hostage to the memory of the Nazi past. That sentiment is so strong that Jürgen Habermas has warned against yet another *Lebenslüge* for Germany, the *Lebenslüge*, as he puts it, "of us being a normal nation." [18] How understandable the wish of so many Germans to be liberated of the burden of the past, to "relativize" Nazi crimes, to seek a retrospective moral equality — how understandable, and probably how unattainable!

It is one of the tragic ironies of the revolutions of hope of 1989 that they coincided with deepening crises in the West. The newly liberated countries reached out for a market economy at a time of worldwide recession; they sought to embrace democracy when the democratic countries had plunged into scandals of corruption and a general paralysis of leadership. They looked to Europe just as the hopes of Europe 1992 faded in the post-Maastricht malaise, and when the term "democratic deficit" seemed to have resonance beyond the internal arrangements of the European Community.

Germany's unanticipated unification, with its staggering demands, came at a time when the old Federal Republic was already experiencing mutually reinforcing pressures. The West German economy — in the past the guarantor of West German democracy — was slowing down. The capitalist world was not at its most dynamic, or at what Joseph Schumpeter defined as its most destructively creative, when East Germans clamored for a free market and the many gurus of the market economy urged instant transformation. Nor had West Germany and its leaders been immune to the greed and corruption of the Reaganite 1980s. Faith in the political system was shaken. Put differently, the twin miracles of

---

[18] Jürgen Habermas, "Die zweite Lebenslüge der Bundesrepublik: Wir sind wieder normal geworden," *Die Zeit*, December 11, 1992.

Bonn's beginnings, the economic miracle and the political miracle — that is, the emergence after the devastation of the Nazi years of unprecedented political leadership in Germany — had come to an end. Germany now faces its gravest crisis since the end of the war.

A new ultra-right-wing party, the Republicans, has scored impressive victories. I doubt that the massive increase in asylum seekers between 1987 and 1992 (some 800 percent) is solely or even primarily responsible for the dissatisfaction that this party exploits. Various instances of corruption have tainted the political system — and had done so even before President von Weizsäcker in 1991 delivered his severe strictures on the German party system, which, he believed, had come to diminish the democratic element in Germany's political process.[19] These very strictures on democracy may have exceeded the limits of his constitutional prerogatives.

People in all parts of Germany feel an imbalance between the economic and moral requirements of their new situation and their political response. There has hardly been a time in which the political classes were held in such low esteem — as is true in the rest of Europe. The uncertainties prompted Marion Countess Dönhoff, Helmut Schmidt, and a few like-minded citizens to issue a manifesto in November 1992 under the title "Because the Country Must Change."[20] The message is that consumerism in the *Raufgesellschaft*, in competitive greed, is not enough. Or consider Jens Reich's fears of future unrest "when I observe our dance around the golden calf, called property, prosperity, consumerism, . . . which we hold sacrosanct. Even now I see the coming disgust and the helpless failure of the putative victors. Late socialism clung to the illusion of eternal growth and progress. We should not succumb to it under different guise."[21]

[19] *Richard von Weizsäcker: Im Gespräch mit Gunter Hoffmann und Werner A. Perger* (Frankfurt am Main, 1992).

[20] Marion Dönhoff et al., *Ein Manifest: Weil das Land sich Ändern muss* (Reinbeck bei Hamburg, 1992).

[21] Reich, *Abschied*, p. 165.

The eruption of xenophobic violence, the killing of Turkish children, has horrified the world. Hundreds of skinheads are supported by thousands of nationalist, perhaps even neo-Nazi sympathizers, while millions of Germans organize silent marches to protest this ugliness, a demonstrative solidarity never before seen in Germany. To some, the very silence of these marches, however impressive in themselves, is disturbing. Germans need speech, thought, and moral authority; the charged questions about asylum seekers and the solidarity pacts proposed to deal with needed transfer payments to the East need public argument. Over and over again Chancellor Kohl has been admonished to "tell the truth."

Freedom has brought its own discontents, and Germans, with their terrible pasts, have to live in the knowledge that there is no acceptable alternative to freedom; for them, as for all of us, the great task is to ground freedom in the exercise of citizenship. They too need leadership that heeds the wisdom of Thucydides: "Now a man may have a policy which he cannot clearly expound, and then he might as well have none at all." [22]

In both parts of Germany there is a palpable deficit of trust — trust in leaders, trust in almost all aspects of life. The English philosopher John Dunn has spoken of trust as the core element of democracy, and this truth is confirmed empirically in Robert Putnam's study of Italian politics, just published.[23] While trust is in short supply in all our countries, its steady decline in Germany is alarming. Degrees of trust cannot be quantified, unlike the interest rates of the Bundesbank — yet the two are linked. The D-Mark remains the symbol and the instrument of Germany's economic stability and the unarticulated incantation could be "In the D-Mark we trust." While that same D-Mark will — by the painful transfer

---

[22] Thucydides, *The Peloponnesian War*, book II, chapter 60.

[23] Robert D. Putnam, *Making Democracy Work: Civic Traditions in Modern Italy* (Princeton, 1993). See, as one example John Dunn, "Trust and Political Agency," in Diego Gambetta (ed.), *Trust, Making and Breaking Cooperative Relations* (Oxford, 1988), pp. 73–93. I owe this last reference to Russell Hardin.

of some trillion DM in the next decade — transform the new *Länder*, especially Saxony, into the most modern region of Europe, the moral-psychological recovery and unity will take much longer.

I say this with a certain sadness, sadness that the promise of 1989, or what I thought of as Germany's second chance in this century, has been mired in pain and disappointment. Once again Germany's history did not have to be like this; there was nothing inevitable about it. More truth, better leadership, and greater tolerance would have made a difference. Even now pessimists see a political system without leadership — and see a repeat of Weimar; optimists see the possibility of rejuvenation and reciprocal learning, of which so far there has been too little.

But let me end on a different note. My friend Leonard Krieger, for so many years at home in Yale, wrote a great work, *The German Idea of Freedom*, an analysis of how in German thought and politics the idea of freedom has always been linked to the authority of the state.[24] To seek freedom in the defiance of the state is not part of the German political tradition, as it is of the English, Dutch, French, and American traditions. Yet twice in the last half century Germans defied a tyrannical state: on July 20, 1944, a few Germans tried to overthrow Hitler — they failed, and the two Germanies have had a difficult time assimilating or celebrating their memory; and in the fall of 1989 hundreds of thousands of East Germans successfully defied their regime, admittedly at a time when neighboring countries had already thrown off the Communist yoke, but nonetheless it was a momentous achievement in German history. Their leaders have already sunk into oblivion, and the memory of those great days has faded. People refer to these events as *die Wende*, the turn, thus transforming what had been dramatic and heroic into something prosaic and bureaucratic. But for all the disappointments that have followed, we should celebrate not merely the collapse of the wall, but the men and women

---

[24] Leonard Krieger, *The German Idea of Freedom: History of a Political Tradition* (Boston, 1957).

who by their demand for a better and freer life made that collapse one of the great moments in their history and ours.

The revolutions of 1989 — however darkened in the meantime by the return of barbarism in many parts of the world — have given us an opportunity to live in trust and truth, to validate the hopes of Václav Havel. It is not only great universities that depend on *lux et veritas* for life.

*The Nation, Nationalism, and After:
The Case of France*

STANLEY HOFFMANN

THE TANNER LECTURES ON HUMAN VALUES

Delivered at

Princeton University
March 3 and 4, 1993

STANLEY HOFFMANN, currently Douglas Dillon Professor of the Civilization of France at Harvard University, has also been the Chairman of the Center for European Studies there since its creation in 1969. Born in Vienna, he graduated from the Institut d'Études Politiques of Paris; he later taught there and at the École des Hautes Études en Sciences Sociales. His books include *Contemporary Theory in International Relations* (1960), *The State of War* (1965), *Decline or Renewal: France Since the 30s* (1974), *Duties Beyond Borders* (1981), and *Janus and Minerva* (1986), among others, and he is the coauthor of *The Fifth Republic at Twenty* (1981), *Living with Nuclear Weapons* (1983), *The Mitterrand Experiment* (1987), and *The New European Community: Decision-Making and Institutional Change* (1991).

I. From Revolution to Liberation

My purpose in these lectures is not to discuss once again the enormous subject of the modern nation, its aspiration to have a state of its own in order to be independent, or its creation by a preexisting state. Nor do I want to describe the many varieties of nationalism. But at a time when nations multiply and when nationalism seems to be the most widespread and troublesome of the ideologies that survive after the fall of communism — thus guaranteeing that there will be no "end of history" — it may not be without interest to examine one particular case, unique as it may seem; for the tribulations of France may carry lessons for contemporary cases as well. Also, at a time when the sovereign nation state is still the chief actor in world politics, but sovereignty is eroding and other actors both provoke and benefit from that erosion, the case of France today is again instructive. (One of the many paradoxes of that case is that in a country where historical writings are a growth industry, and where nationalism has counted for so much, there is no overall history of French nationalism.)[1]

Let me begin with a few simple definitions. A nation is a group of people who, for what may be a multitude of reasons (a common ethnic origin, a common language, a comon and distinctive past, etc.), feel linked by a bond that transcends kinship and geographical proximity, and see themselves as belonging to a single community. It is a bond across space, as well as through time; it brings together people and groups that are not in physical contact and links the present generations to those of the past.

As for nationalism, it is an ideology that, like other ideologies, is, first, a reaction to a problem: what is the secular community to

---

[1] The best short and partial history remains Raoul Girardet's essay in *Le nationalisme français 1871–1914* (Paris: A. Colin, 1966).

which individuals and groups should owe their highest allegiance and from which they should receive their social identity? Second, it is an answer and an explanation: the nation is the community in which we do more than merely live and work; we are actually constituted as social beings by our membership in it. Third, it offers a program: our duty is, at a minimum, to ensure and protect the cohesion, uniqueness, and independence of our nation and to promote its interests; at a maximum, it is to assure its superiority over all others or to carry out its mission. National consciousness is a sense of solidarity and originality. Patriotism is a sentiment of love and loyalty for one's nation; nationalism is both a sentiment and an ideology. It uses patriotism as the foundation of its program, giving it specific directions. Again like other ideologies, it appears with the weakening or the demise of the religious and monarchic conception of the polity — when the emphasis shifts from the Church and the king to the people, or to individual rights, when the press and the books, the brochures and the academic competitions, "public opinion" and the intellectuals, challenge the established order in all its spiritual, social, and political dimensions.

My purpose in these lectures is to examine how, in the French case, nationalism conceived the nation and its mission, at home and abroad; how, in particular, it reacted to and dealt with the contradictions that appeared both in these conceptions and between its program and the real world; what, if anything, is left of it today, and what problems a nation so deeply marked both by the strength and by the torments of nationalistic ideology faces in the present international system.

For nationalism to succeed and to become a significant or even the dominant ideology, the answer it provides has to make sense. Whatever the strength of other loyalties, religious and secular, a sense of belonging to a single and distinctive nation has to exist — this is why a nation begins by being an "imagined" community,[2]

[2] See Benedict Anderson, *Imagined Communities* (London: Verso, 1983).

and why it is always necessary to distinguish between the "imagined" nation, which may be little more than an aspiration, and the "completed" nation, achieved through the enforcement of a nationalist policy. The reason disparate groups begin to feel connected by national kinship varies; it can be a sense of being oppressed by a foreign conqueror; it can be shaped, as in England,[3] by a sharp and contentious relationship with outsiders: wars against France, a Protestant country confronting Catholic foes. In the case of France, it was spurred by an increasingly widespread opposition to the absolute but inefficient monarchy at the end of the eighteenth century. The word "nation" ceased to have its purely descriptive and vague earlier meanings,[4] and took on its revolutionary one, when both the defenders of privileges who feared a reformist "enlightened despotism" and promoted the *thèse nobiliaire* (which insisted on the privileged orders' ancient right to be consulted and to consent) and the enemies of privilege and feudalism who saw the monarchy as the apex and linchpin of the feudal order used the concept of the nation as a ram against the Old Regime's political system. History was already both used as a weapon and turned into a stake. Supporters of the *thèse nobiliaire* and radical critics of the Old Regime both sought to strengthen their arguments with readings of the past: the former remembered, or invented, the assemblies of Frankish nobles; the latter saw the Franks as the conquerors and oppressors of the Gauls and wanted to recover the latter's "rights."

Nationalism, reduced to the skeletal ideal-type I have presented above, is almost devoid of substance. When the nation conceives itself — which means, in effect, when its leaders and elites conceive it — primarily in opposition to distant foreigners, as in

---

[3] See Linda Colley's admirable book, *Britons* (New Haven: Yale University Press, 1992).

[4] On those meanings, see Liah Greenfeld, *Nationalism* (Cambridge, Mass.: Harvard University Press, 1992); and Pierre Nora, "Nation," in François Furet and Mona Ozouf (eds.), *Dictionnaire critique de la Révolution française* (Paris: Flammarion, 1988), pp. 801–12.

Britain, nationalism can coexist with and complement the ideology or ideologies that have shaped the domestic institutions. (In the American case, it was this ideology — liberalism — that provoked a nationalist rebellion against Britain, accused of violating the colonies' rights.) But when the nation conceives itself in a struggle over political legitimacy against either an established regime (France) or foreign rule (Germany, Italy), then it needs to add flesh and blood to the skeleton; it must give itself a far richer substance, to try to recruit and inspire believers and militants by making explicit its views of what the nation is based on and how it should be governed. This was what happened in France at the end of the eighteenth century.

The nationalism of the revolutionaries of 1789 was turned inward. It attacked the Old Regime on three grounds: for its principle of legitimacy — the divine rule of kings, the sovereignty of the monarch; for its failure to establish a fair society and an efficient administrative and economic organization — considerations of justice and efficiency were always blended by the *philosophes* of the Enlightenment; and for its failure to spread what might be called the culture of Enlightenment widely enough in a still largely illiterate society. In other words, even though nobles joined in the assault, and bourgeois had little enthusiasm for the poor, the nationalism of the revolutionaries was inherently democratic and had a project that covered *both* the state and society; but everything turned around the nature of the *state*, its philosophical basis and its political structure. The "nation" felt it was left out by the preexisting state, and its first mission was the conquest of the state. Once conquered, the new state could destroy the institutions of the Old Regime and build a "national" France. From the start, French nationalism glued together what Tzvetan Todorov calls the cultural nation,[5] made of common memories and customs, and the civic nation, based on common citizenship. It presented itself

---

[5] In *Nous et les autres* (Paris: Seuil, 1989).

as the claim of the cultural nation to the conquest and exercise of citizenship, in order to be able to turn an imagined community into a real one — with new customs, new institutions, and a set of richer memories all the French could be proud of.

When the revolutionaries sought to provide their inward-turned nationalism with the substance they needed, they found two very different models. One was the liberal formula of inalienable individual rights, limited and representative government for the protection of those rights, and divided powers as a guarantee of freedom. It certainly had the potential of destroying the social order of feudalism and of building a new state founded on the consent of citizens. But a second model seemed to provide the same results on a different basis: that of the *Social Contract*. If the key word of the liberal formula is "balance" — between rights retained by individuals and the powers delegated to the state, among the branches of the government — the key word of Rousseau's quasi-mystical formula is "unity": the unity of the general will, the fusion between the individuals who form this will and the state that expresses and enforces it. Here there are no individual rights protected from the state (since *we* are the state): it is up to the state — our general will — to define the content and limits of our rights; and because the sovereign will is *une et indivisible* there can only be a hierarchy of, but not a balance among, the organs of the state; representation is ideally to be avoided since representatives might substitute their (partial) will for the general one. Where liberalism tries to define a common will out of the clashes of and bargains among individual and group interests, Rousseau based his general will on the sense of a common interest he believed inherent — consciously or not — in all members of a civic community. He postulated a hierarchy in each of them, between the (superior) will to the common good and their (inferior) individual or group interests, and he demanded the repression of the latter in the public sphere. Insofar as the ideal community had to live in a predatory world of states, its best foreign policy would be to have none, so as to avoid both the greedy designs of others and the domestic corruption that would result from entanglements abroad.[6] At home and abroad, this was the model of the closed community.

When the Revolution began, its champions tried, for a while, to blend the liberal and the Rousseauistic conceptions. Emmanuel-Joseph Sieyès's *Qu'est-ce que le Tiers Etat*, and even more the *Declaration of the Rights of Man and Citizen*, are the best examples of this attempt. The central concept was the Nation; it was a revolutionary notion precisely because its use was aimed at instituting both liberty and equality. The nation was defined by Sieyès as "a body of associates living under a common law and represented by the same legislature"[7] — a definition acceptable to a liberal *and* to a disciple of Rousseau willing to make adaptations for a country the size of France, where the people could not meet in a single place. Soon, however, contradictions appeared, and choices had to be made.

Let us begin with what the revolutionaries considered their main task: the reconstruction of the domestic political and social order. It must be noted that it was perfectly possible, at first, for the Constituents to combine the idea of a sovereign nation made of all French citizens with a fine distinction between nation and people that allowed them to restrict the suffrage, not merely to males, but to "active" male citizens, those who had a certain amount of wealth (only the Jacobins remained faithful to the democratic content of the *Social Contract*, to Rousseau's notion of popular sovereignty). Thus they could borrow a leaf from the liberal book where it served their interests, and they also tried to devise a representative system with divided powers. But there was a tension between the idea of the king as the servant of the law (i.e., subordinated to the legislature) and the idea of the king as

---

[6] See Stanley Hoffmann and David Fidler, *Rousseau and International Relations* (London: Oxford University Press, 1991).

[7] *Qu'est-ce que le Tiers Etat* (Paris: Presses Universitaires, 1982), p. 69.

the nation's delegate with independent powers alongside the powers delegated by it to the legislature. The king's refusal to act as the former sealed his fate. There was a tension between the liberal formula of sacred individual rights and Rousseau's ideal community. It was the latter that prevailed. Sieyès himself presented the image of a sovereign nation whose powers could not be subordinated to any Constitution: "the national will needs only its reality to be always legal, it is the origin of all legality." It was the nation, not the individual, that had inalienable rights: "it can neither alienate nor ban the right to will . . . it cannot lose the right to change its will when its interest dictates it." [8]

Why the Revolution, as it evolved, made of the nation a mirror image of the old monarchy, with the absolute and indivisible sovereignty of the king transferred to the nation, is perhaps the most fascinating question in the history of modern France. Was it simply the imprint of centuries of monarchic rule justified by *légistes* and preachers? The imprint of another illiberal and authoritarian institution, the Church? Was it — as for Sieyès in 1789 — the fear that a set of liberal institutions, with all their checks and balances, might actually impede the huge task of overhauling all existing barriers to unity, allow the supporters of feudalism to entrench themselves in part of the legislature or to barricade themselves in their unbreachable rights? Was it because of the unwillingness of the court, of many of the nobles, of much of the Church, to accept the rules of the game that liberalism presupposes? In every one of these hypotheses, the stake is the same: the capacity of the revolutionary state to carry out its program of reshaping French social and political institutions. The nation, or rather its spokesmen, condemned the monarchy for having failed to carry out its own program of national unification and homogenization, because of the fundamental handicap constituted by the remnants of feudalism: all Richelieu and Louis XIV could do was build a centralized administrative structure above a maze

[8] Ibid., p. 68.

of social, local, and linguistic particularisms, in a society where many "public" functions (*offices*) were in private hands because of the financial needs of the Crown. The revolutionaries thus wanted an appropriate politico-philosophical basis, a new principle of legitimacy that would allow them to complete unimpeded what the monarchy had barely begun. National sovereignty was the chief weapon. The Rousseauistic insistence on *volonté une*, the relegation of pluralism to the private sphere, the distrust for groups and factions, the refusal to see as legitimate anything except the nation and the "social" part of the individual (i.e., the part that is included in the general will) — all could serve as weapons against resistances and particularisms.

But here a second contradiction appears, or rather a clash with reality. The nationalism of the revolutionaries was aimed at unifying France, at removing all the obstacles to unity. But the obstacles to unity were inside France, and the history of the Revolution involved a supreme paradox that many nationalisms have experienced: exclusion in order to unite. This can be seen on two fronts. The main one was that of the "enemies of the Revolution." Sieyès described the privileged order as being *outside* the nation: "if one removed the privileged order, the nation wouldn't be something less, but something more,"[9] for the Third Estate *is* the nation, albeit "hampered and oppressed." When delegates of the Third Estate, following Sieyès rather than Mirabeau, called themselves the National Assembly (rather than the Assembly of the People's delegates), they prefigured what was going to follow: exclusions and self-exclusions that led to a lasting split in French society and thought, between those who accepted the new dogma of the nation and those who did not and gradually rallied around the counterrevolutionary doctrines of Louis de Bonald and Joseph de Maistre. The long rift between an anti-Catholic Republican Revolution and Catholics faithful to Rome and to the king had thus begun.

[9] Ibid., p. 36.

It wasn't only the problem of the enemies. Sieyès had given a voluntaristic definition of the nation; but it left open the question of who were the "associates": all those who lived under French rule and were not enemies of the new dogma of the nation? Two problems in particular arose. One was that of the Jews. They were already the targets of a traditional Catholic antisemitism, for instance in the statements of the Abbé Grégoire (who supported political and civic rights for Jews), and of a left-wing antisemitism that attacked them as capitalist corrupters (Marat).[10] Here inclusion prevailed, although with the assumption, expressed by Grégoire, that this would lead to complete cultural assimilation of the Jews, to gradual discarding of their language and their ancestral superstitions: once again, a dream from the "old order" — that of the Catholic Church — was being taken over by the nation (it was not by accident that the granting of these rights was especially controversial in the case of the Jews of Alsace, who were less "assimilated" than those of the Southwest). The other problem was that of the Blacks in France's colonies — or rather that of the abolition of slavery and that of the rights of people with mixed blood. The Constitution of 1791 did not extend to the colonies. The debates revealed a mass of arguments for the status quo: a relativism based on climate and a "radical cultural determinism,"[11] which took a particularly rabid form in Honoré de Mirabeau's case. Ultimately, the mulattoes were granted political rights, but the main reason was that they would thereby help the French settlers preserve order against the slaves. Slavery was abolished in February 1794, but mainly in order to prevent a revolt that, according to the *rapporteur*, was being fostered by counterrevolutionaries and foreign agents. Thus, in these two cases, an inclusive definition prevailed, but in conditions and with arguments that showed that the extension of citizenship rights to

---

[10] See Olivier Le Cour Grandmaison, *Les citoyennetés en révolution* (Paris: Presses Universitaires, 1992), pp. 239–71.

[11] Ibid., p. 199.

all who lived under French rule was far from automatic. Since in the revolutionaries' conception citizenship and nationality were indissociable, the question Who is a citizen? immediately became Who is entitled to be called French? Would the varying legal answers given by the Revolution's Constitutions and laws be accepted by all as conclusive and valid?

The program of the Revolution was the forging of national unity at home. What would its policy be abroad? Was Rousseau's isolationism at all practicable? Here the revolutionaries faced two dilemmas. The first was war or peace. The very enormity of the domestic task, a priori, made peace eminently desirable. Indeed, the Constituents proclaimed that the Revolution wanted to be at peace with the world. It was the impossibility of achieving domestic unity without battle and exclusion that actually fueled the debate between "warmongers" and Robespierre. The former called for war because they deemed their domestic enemies encouraged and inspired by "Old Regimes" and enemies of France abroad: they wanted, so to speak, to invade those sanctuaries and to go to the source. Jacques-Pierre Brissot, the Girondin leader who proclaimed that the Revolution needed "great acts of treason,"[12] probably saw in war a means of forcing the king to reveal his true colors; war was also, clearly, a diversion from domestic conflicts, a way of unifying the French behind patriotic duty, as a complement to and substitute for domestic ideological unification around the new principles of government and society. What the idea of the nation could not achieve at home by itself, it could try to achieve by battle abroad. Robespierre replied that only the court and its ministers had an interest in war and that the home front was all that mattered; war would only reduce the vigilance of the people at home. France's "salvation" resided in "public spirit": "if this sacred flame . . . exists in the soul of the French, war is unnecessary; if it doesn't exist, war is a scourge."[13] Even when

[12] See Frank Attar, *La Révolution française déclare la guerre à l'Europe* (Paris: Editions Complexe, 1992), p. 131.

[13] *Textes choisis*, vol. 1 (Paris: Ed. Sociales, 1956), p. 154.

he came to power and had to wage the war the Girondins had started, Robespierre never lost his sense of priority. But the die had been cast; it was a debate that other nationalists and other revolutionaries were often going to repeat.

A second question now arose: war for what? Nationalism, once again, showed its lack of substance when left to itself. Would France at war export revolution and set out to destroy old regimes, to bring about the rule of liberty and equality, all over Europe? This meant, literally, fostering nations — in the modern sense — abroad, and treating foreigners as brothers, if they shared the same ideals as the French nation. Many of the great actors of the Revolution supported both a missionary conception of nationalism and the granting of French nationality to foreign champions of its principles. But another tempting course was a far more traditional one: the nation as (once more) the persistent and, one hoped, successful continuation of the Old Regime, pursuing a policy of "natural borders" (i.e., self-interested expansion). Danton, characteristically, moved from messianism to annexation.[14] Robespierre's hostility to the former remained based on principle — liberty can't be brought by force, nations can't be made happy against their will.[15] But both his defensive nationalism and the more traditional expansionist one resulted in substituting for a transnational cleavage between the good people and the enemies of freedom everywhere (i.e., for a kind of militant internationalism whose secular arm would happen to be "big brother" France) a sharp barrier between France and the French, on the one hand, and all foreigners, on the other, whether abroad (occupied or, as in the case of Belgium, annexed, rather than liberated) or at home, where, under the Terror, foreigners were increasingly suspected, attacked, excluded, and charged with trying to divide the French. "Cosmopolitanism," once celebrated, was now proscribed, both because it seemed to call for a risky crusade abroad and because foreign in-

---

[14] Cf. his *Discours* (Paris: Ed. de l'Aire, 1983), pp. 105, 126.
[15] *Textes choisis*, vol. 2 (Paris: Ed. Sociales, 1957), p. 102.

vasion and fears of collusion between foreign and domestic enemies turned the revolutionaries and many of their provincial supporters into ardent xenophobes.[16] The Declaration of Rights of 1789, by emphasizing the Rights of Man, had seemed to give to foreigners a promise of equal rights. The Rousseauistic construction of the nation equated citizenship and nationality, and thus reserved the former to the French; the xenophobia raised by war threatened the foreigners' other rights.

Ultimately, what caused the failure of the revolutionary program was more than the dilemmas discussed above. They point out the difficulties of the project and certainly contributed to the final fiasco, which resulted from the inability to establish a set of institutions that could function efficiently and enjoy a sufficiently broad support. For a project whose success depended on the state, the failure to provide it with institutions both legitimate and effective was a fundamental flaw.

After the Revolution, nationalism stopped being an overt political program and became a subject for political theorists and historians. To be sure, Napoleon kept many of the trappings of revolutionary ideology, but the work of unification he pursued was centered on his own power, and the main function of Napoleon's nation was waging Napoleon's wars — which were not inspired by the messianism of freedom and promoted national self-determination only when he deemed it to be in France's enlightened self-interest. After Waterloo and the return of the Bourbons, the afterglow of *la gloire*, the memories of *la grande Nation* (a notion that seemed to combine or confuse messianism and power politics in modern garb), and the legend of Napoleon as the exporter of Jacobin ideals showed that nationalism had survived both defeat and Restoration. Even a fervent Catholic monarchist like Chateaubriand longed for the days of French expansion and roundly con-

---

[16] See the excellent study by Virginie Guiraudon, "Cosmopolitism and National Priority," *History of European Ideas* 13, no. 5 (1991), 591–604.

demned cosmopolitanism. But the two regimes that ruled France between 1815 and 1848 were not in the hands of nationalists. The first man to use the word "nationalism," pejoratively, had been an ardent counterrevolutionary, the Abbé Barruel, and French counterrevolutionaries remained firmly attached to a vision of the polity in which family virtues, social hierarchy, and a strong monarch preserved traditions, order, and stability, in which revolutionary notions of universal rights and national sovereignty were banned as nefarious products of the Enlightenment, and in which the pope exerted spiritual power over all Catholic countries. As for the Orléaniste liberals who took over in 1830, their dislike of Rousseauistic and Jacobin notions of absolute sovereignty, their belief in either limited and delegated popular sovereignty or the "sovereignty of reason," their view of parliamentarism as a transnational force of progress, their suspicion of state power, and their preference for the "spirit of commerce" over the atavistic desire for conquest placed them far from the Revolution's nationalism in any of its domestic and external forms.[17] Their two greatest thinkers, Benjamin Constant and François Guizot, were cool admirers of England.

The nationalist tradition was carried on by Republicans, who did not add much to the thought of the revolutionaries. Charles Renouvier, in his *Manuel républicain* — a dialogue between a schoolteacher and a pupil — has the student say: "the Republic makes me French twice": pride in France and national unity have lifted him beyond his village origins ("I lived only in my village, and now I live in France").[18] Once again, nationalism is associated with, and inherent in, a certain form of government and society: it is the Republic that is the beacon for the French inside and for oppressed nations abroad. The most interesting innovations come from historians; for they turned to the history of

[17] Cf. Benjamin Constant, *De l'esprit de conquête*, ed. René-Jean Dupuy (Paris: Imprimerie Nationale, 1992).

[18] *Manuel républicain de l'homme et du citoyen* (Paris: Garnier, 1981), p. 116.

France in order both to find the roots of the nation summoned almost *ex nihilo* by the Revolution and to rekindle revolutionary ardor dormant since the end of the Revolution — the memory of the past was now being asked to play the role that the political philosophies of the eighteenth century had played earlier.

Their investigations of France's origins aim at, or end in, supporting the voluntaristic conception of the nation. In Augustin Thierry's view of France as a "race," there is no biological determinism, only the story of the "conquered" Gauls emancipating themselves from the rule of their conquerors and thus regaining their unity.[19] In Jules Michelet's vision, France is a blend of races; such a blend is essential (once again) for unity and progress: it gradually lifted the French above regional and ethnic particularisms and led to the emergence of France's unique feature and contribution, fraternity. The conception of history that underlies his works, but also those of the brothers Thierry, is one of an ideal archetypical France, which is at first almost a void, an empty circumference (or hexagon), that history gradually fills, both geographically and politically, as if French history had been nothing but the necessary fleshing out of an Idea of France, culminating in the Revolution. Thus the abstract ideal of unity achieved, in Rousseau's *Social Contract*, by the general will, becomes a concrete march toward unity, in which the different elements that went into the final product are praised not for their distinctiveness, but for their contribution to the synthesis. A history of multiple and inexpiable conflicts is thereby provided with a magic thread, held by the writer, who condemns or praises actors and peoples depending on whether they contributed to ultimate unity.

There were, of course, contradictions between this view of French history and reality, which Michelet had to face. He did so in two ways. As for the past, he demonstrated the potential for

[19] On Thierry, see Marcel Gauchet, "Les lettres sur l'histoire de France d'Augustin Thierry," in Pierre Nora (ed.), *Les lieux de mémoires, II: La nation*, 3 vols. (Paris: Gallimard, 1986), vol. 1, pp. 247–316; and Lionel Gossman, *Between History and Literature* (Cambridge, Mass.: Harvard University Press, 1990), ch. 4.

unity around the nation, despite the prevalence of strife, by stressing such moments of national harmony as the Fête de la Fédération of July 14, 1790, and such symbols of national fervor as Joan of Arc. In the present, the contrast between social conflict and the aspiration to unity, or the destiny that is unity, could, he asserted, be overcome by education, a nationalist education for rich and poor alike, all receiving on the same school benches "an ineradicable impression of *la patrie*." [20] It is the great dream of inclusion again — not by juxtaposition of disparate parts, but by fusion into a higher, single whole. In Michelet's account of the people, there are vices and "servitudes," but no internal enemies — Christianity is treated as if it had been superseded by another manifestation of God: nationalism.

One problem, of course, remains: how should the nation behave in the world? Michelet's answer is perfectly schizophrenic. On the one hand, he celebrates "an era of benevolence and fraternity," based on the coexistence of sharply distinctive nations: the more internal differences are eroded, the sharper differences among nations, now transformed into "persons," become. Michelet, who celebrates internal unity, believes in a world of diverse nations: a unified world would be "monotonous and barbarous"; the destiny of each nation is to "fortify its individuality." But, on the other hand, in this "concert" all the instruments are not equal: France alone has a universal mission and significance — "in her we find both the representative of the world's liberties and the country sympathetic above all, the initiation to universal love." There are pages of *Le peuple* that are almost delirious: "France superior, as dogma and as legend," France as the modern "pontiff" of Europe, which owes its superiority to what it has done for others and also to its two unique features: the principle of fraternity (i.e., "the biggest idea") and the most constant tradition. Here a cosmopolitan ideal — fraternity, *l'égalité fraternelle*, a task begun by Rome and Christianity — becomes a source of chauvinism: an

[20] *Le peuple* (Paris: Julliard, 1965), p. 82.

international mission becomes a reason for nationalist celebration. It is the chauvinism of universal service. The peculiar historical model described above serves as its justification: "any other history is mutilated, only ours is complete." England has wealth, Germany has "systems," but both "are foreign to the world's great tradition, roman-christian and democratic." [21]

Nowhere does Michelet repudiate the voluntaristic idea of the nation. Indeed, he presents it as "a great friendship," an association whose members are tied together by mutual sympathy. But despite this, and his repudiation of any racial determinism, elements of determinism creep in. As Todorov has noted,[22] if each nation becomes more and more distinctive — unlike the elements that lose their originality by forming the nation — French citizens will find it difficult, as well as improper, to escape the "determinism of being French." This determinism, which is never spelled out, results from two factors, both of which will have a bright future in French thought. One is, obviously, history: are the French all those who want to be French or those who are themselves the products of French history, the descendants of the French? The other one is the soil: France's backbone is the peasant-proprietor, rooted in the land; "the English, who don't have the same roots in the soil, emigrate to where there are profits. . . . In France, man and earth are inseparable." [23] This allows Michelet to exclude the Jews from the nation: their roots, their *patrie*, are at the London stock exchange. The revolutionary project was ahistorical: indeed, it was a revolt against history and gave France a new calendar. Entrusting the revival of nationalism to historians carried risks.

In 1789 the myth of the nation had created a new state, which was too divided and beleaguered to carry out its mission of turning the myth into a reality — except in a few moments of internal cele-

[21] Ibid., p. 267.
[22] *Nous et les autres*, pp. 243–44.
[23] *Le peuple*, p. 80.

bration (Fête de la Fédération) or victory over invaders (Valmy). The state finally received a lasting (albeit originally tenuous) Republican set of institutions, after a double defeat: that of France in the war against Prussia and that of the Paris Commune; it was now able at last to "nationalize" the country. How this was done has been admirably studied by Eugen Weber,[24] and I will try not to repeat what he has told us.

Let us focus again on the project — on how the Republicans in power conceived their task. Once again, it was turned inward, by choice as well as necessity. It had two main domestic dimensions. The first was the reshaping of the polity. Here one of the tensions that had racked the revolutionaries was overcome: the constitutional laws of 1875 represent a compromise between two traditions. One was the Rousseauistic conception of the nation, which survives in the theory of national sovereignty as the expression of the general will (i.e., the will to the common good, superior to and excluding selfish and group interests), in the persistence of centralization, in profound distrust for an independent executive, and in the refusal to submit the constitutionality of laws (i.e., the delegated will of the sovereign) to any independent judicial body. The other was the liberal conception of representative and limited government, guaranteed rights, and divided powers. This compromise was obviously a political necessity and part of the Gambettiste politics of inclusion. But the contradiction between an official discourse of unity and inclusion and the reality of ideological and political conflict did not disappear: a nationalism of inclusion requires, as in the United States, a consensus on the central political tenets and institutions, and in France this consensus continued to elude the Republicans. They could not convert easily those, on the Right, who remained hostile to the very principles of liberalism and democracy; nor could they count on the

---

[24] *Peasants into Frenchmen* (Stanford: Stanford University Press, 1976). See also Carlton J. Hayes, *France a Nation of Patriots* (New York: Octagon Books, 1974).

support of those, on the Left, who were impatient with a social status quo that seemed bolstered both by the delays, checks, and balances of representative and divided government and by the Republican interpretation of the general will. For it left out of the public agenda everything except "Republican and religious questions," in Léon Gambetta's formula. Anticlericalism and social conservatism on top prevented a full consensus from below.

The second dimension of the Republican project tried to address the problem of political consensus and also to deal with a contradiction inherent in the Rousseauistic limitation of the general will to "what is common to all." The Rousseauistic notion of citizenship was equalitarian (and France, since 1848, had universal suffrage); but French society was not; the "inferior" sphere of the private, in which individuals and groups could operate and worship freely, was a sphere of both ideological conflict — because it included the Church, especially after its formal separation from the state — and social conflict — because it included classes with opposite interests, clashing organizations, and unequal power. The highly articulate politicians of the Republic thought that ideological conflict in society was something the *state* had to deal with, because the principles of organization of the polity itself were at stake. But they also believed that social problems should be resolved primarily by *voluntary* acts: "association" and "solidarity," with very little role for government. Thus, both in order to win the ideological battle and in order to predispose the French to lower social tensions, the Republican nation needed to complement its political institutions with a project that could be called either cultural or ideological, aimed at shaping and unifying — once again — the minds and mores of the French. This was the educational project, which owed a great deal to unfulfilled revolutionary designs and to Michelet's dream. (As Weber and others have shown, another revolutionary imperative — eradicating *patois* and regional languages such as Breton — was a major part of it.)[25]

[25] See the remarks of Pierre Jakez Hélias in *Le cheval d' orgueil* (Paris: Plon, 1975), ch. 4.

In France, the Republicans thought that education was not only a *public* function or interest, but a function of the *state* (the British train their future elites in public schools that are private, the French in schools that are part of the state).

This project entailed a kind of gentle Republican indoctrination, aimed both at uprooting Catholic "obscurantism" (by substituting either Kantian ethics or faith in science for religious dogmas) and at inculcating the principles of Republican citizenship. Here the key was the teaching of history, what might be called the popularization of Michelet by historians such as Ernest Lavisse and Charles Seignobos, and their countless disciples who, like Michelet, interpreted French history as a gradual elevation toward Republican unity and as the gradual realization of a "preexisting nation" or national idea.[26] A history that focused on chronology, events, and great individuals, primarily those of France, was thought to be the best discipline, as well as the approach that would be easiest for the children to learn and remember; it allowed the right kind of lessons to emerge from the data.

What this ambitious and grandiose design could not do was reach all its goals. It could spread and deepen the roots of Republican citizenship; but as long as Catholic schools coexisted with lay schools, ideological harmony was not going to be possible. The interpretations of central events — the Old Regime, the Revolution — remained profoundly different. Also, if the civic values taught were egalitarian and democratic — you are the people, all authority comes from you — the social values stressed were traditional: hard work, thrift, moderation in behavior and ambitions, a vision of society based on the way of life of peasants and artisans; these teachings were less and less persuasive to sons and daughters of industrial workers and/or of the "uprooted."

Abroad, what saved the Republicans from the dilemmas their revolutionary ancestors had encountered was, paradoxically, the

[26] On Lavisse, see Pierre Nora, "Lavisse, instituteur national," in *Les lieux de mémoire, I: La République* (Paris: Gallimard, 1984), pp. 247–90. For a criticism of this whole approach, see Suzanne Citron, *Le mythe national* (Paris: Ed. Ouvrières, 1987).

defeat of 1871 and the loss of Alsace-Lorraine. The latter gave French nationalism abroad both a goal and a limit. The problem of war or peace did not arise, because France no longer had the means to initiate war. If war should come, its goal could no longer be the missionary expansion of freedom — the voluntaristic definition of the nation was now being used defensively, by historians like Numa Denis Fustel de Coulanges and Ernest Renan, against German historians who justified the annexation of Metz and Strasbourg on ethnic and linguistic grounds (but note that their voluntarism includes, in the reasons for the "daily plebiscite" that is a nation's existence, a "community of memories" [Fustel] and the "common possession of a rich legacy of memories ... a legacy of glory and regrets" [Renan]).[27] The Revanche was both a limited mission, the application of universal principles to a single small area, and an undisputed national interest. (Indeed, it is because France needed soldiers for its cause that Republican legislators made a remarkable exception to the voluntaristic definition of the nation: the law of 1889 on French nationality removed the right of foreigners who were born in France and whose fathers were foreigners born in France to reject French nationality.)

However, the idea of Revanche did not suffice in unifying the French, any more than the Republican ideal. There are many reasons for this. The first is that precisely because an immediate Revanche was impossible, a choice quickly arose, between a policy of rebuilding and concentrating strength for the future confrontation with Germany and a policy of colonial expansion, encouraged by Bismarck; the controversy between Georges Clemenceau and Jules Ferry showed once again that the same concern for France's position in the world that had animated those revolutionaries who were not "cosmopolitan" exporters of freedom and equality and reestablished a bond of continuity between the strategy of the kings and that of the Republic did not suffice to define a policy.

[27] See texts in Girardet, *Le nationalisme français*, pp. 62ff.

A second reason is that, once colonial expansion was chosen, it did not arouse great popular enthusiasm. Those who pushed for it were marked by the same internal contradiction that had characterized Michelet's views of France in the world. Was it an altruistic "mission of civilization," in which France would bring the light of justice and humanity to the weak, as a pre-Socialist Jean Jaurès argued?[28] Was it a simple exercise in power politics, aimed at saving defeated France from becoming another Belgium, at finding safe markets for France's goods, and at providing *la patrie* with manpower to compensate for its failure to produce enough children on its own? Ferry used both sets of arguments, but the second set dominated. Nevertheless, just as, almost a hundred years earlier, both the missionaries and the nationalists motivated by power calculations shared to a large extent a view of French superiority (either because of greater power or because France was the carrier of the highest idea), both kinds of arguments assumed a superiority of civilized France over "weak" or "inferior" races. Alexis de Tocqueville, who believed in the equality of races and had no illusions about the civilizing mission, nevertheless defended French colonialism as a useful component of national sentiment, which he considered to be a necessary antidote to democratic individualism; in Todorov's words, "universal morality stops on the threshold of international relations."[29]

Third, France's freedom of maneuver abroad was limited — Britain had the lion's share of colonies, and, as long as Bismarck was chancellor, France remained isolated in Europe. This meant that foreign policy could not be used by the Republicans as a diversion from domestic divisions. Finally, if the main function of the state was to shape a unified nation, if another function of the national state was to protect the nation's interests and security, then nothing was more important for a nationalist Republic than its

[28] Ibid., pp. 94–96.
[29] *Nous et les Autres*, p. 229.

military mission. History taught the schoolchildren the importance of martial values, the virtues of sacrifice, and the crucial role of battles in the fate of peoples and nations. Robespierre, the dark prince of suspicion, had feared war because he distrusted the military and their *esprit de corps*. The Republic made a valiant effort to democratize and control the army. But General Boulanger, one of the generals who seemed closest to the radicalism of Clemenceau — i.e., a Jacobin — bolted in the mid-1880s; ten years later the Dreyfus case obliged the Republicans, pressured by the intellectuals and the press, to make a highly unwelcome choice between the principles of justice on which Republican nationalism was based and the massive refusal of the army's leaders to reopen the "traitor's" case. External nationalism and a strong defense against Germany seemed to require solidarity with the army — and injustice. Fidelity to the domestic project of the Republic — a nation based on respect for individual rights and justice — required a dramatic breach with the military and meant a domestic rift that made the unifying dream of the Republic seem more unachievable than ever.

Boulangisme and the Dreyfus case were important for another reason as well. For the first time, Republican nationalism was confronted with a counternationalism, which actually tried to monopolize the word "nationalism" itself. Its glue — for it was made of diverse elements — was the notion that the Republican project had failed both to unify France at home and to defend its interests abroad. The drive for unity, transmitted from the Old Regime to the revolutionaries, was now picked up by the new nationalist project, as was the traditional concern for status. Both nationalisms invoked French history.

What, then, was original? First, the motivations of the new nationalists: men like Edouard Drumont, Maurice Barrès, and Charles Maurras were above all obsessed with the idea of French decadence, the fear of a disintegration of French society through the effects of class conflict, social change destroying traditional values and ways of life and work, and "foreign" influences — Jews were now seen as "unassimilable" ferments of decay. A whole vocabulary of health and sickness, diseases and cures, virility and impotence, replaced the romantic and moralistic vocabulary of the Republicans.[30] It is, almost, a nationalism of despair replacing the nationalism of hope, a nationalism of defense replacing the conquering one. One can say that it was, unlike the Revolution's and the Republicans', turned both inward and outward; its main concern was about France's survival, but this required both external strength (in a strictly "realistic" way) and drastic internal regeneration.

A second novelty was the repudiation of the voluntaristic definition of the nation. Barrès moved from his Boulangiste cult of energy and Jacobin support for the principle of national self-determination to a gloomy determinism of *la terre et les morts*, a belief in the primacy of the unconscious, a conviction that "there is no such thing as freedom of thought: I can only live according to my dead." [31] Maurras shared Michelet's "religion of the divinity France," and Michelet's view of France as the only "completed" nation, but he denounced in the romantic Michelet the "chronicler of a decapitated France," [32] and saw in the nation not a voluntary association but a "natural" or "historical" society whose preservation was the duty of every individual, who would be naked without the nation. This is not an ethnic nationalism — Barrès explained that France, alas, was not a race — but it embodies history, the soil, and the dead with the defining, determining, and excluding power of an ethnic conception. And like ethnic conceptions,

---

[30] Girardet, *Le nationalisme français*, parts 3 and 4. See also Zeev Sternhell, *Maurice Barrès et le nationalisme français* (Paris: A. Colin, 1972); Yves-Marie Hilaire, "L'ancrage des idéologies," in Jean-François Sirinelli (ed.), *Histoire des droites,* 3 vols. (Paris: Gallimard, 1992), vol. 1, pp. 519–66.

[31] Girardet, *Le nationalisme français*, p. 189.

[32] *Oeuvres capitales: Essais politiques* (Paris: Flammarion, 1954), p. 74.

Maurras's divided the world's nations into superior and inferior ones.

Third, what was new about this right-wing nationalism was that it was a blend of two very different components. One was a group of Republican nationalists disappointed by what they saw as the fiasco of the Republican project: at home, the school lessons of Kantian ethics and the references to the general will had not succeeded either in integrating the workers into the nation or in diverting them from the cosmopolitan, antinationalist ideology of socialism (already denounced by Michelet); abroad, the regime had behaved weakly when bullied by Bismarck. Disappointment and the fear of decadence led Paul Déroulède and Barrès out of the Republican camp, into a revolt not only against parliamentarism — a revolt Jacobins would have understood — but against the whole cultural project of the regime, toward a defense not only of authority but of social authorities such as the Church and the army: Barrès, haunted by decline and *déclassement*, took refuge in traditionalism and elitism. Never before had defectors from the Republican version of nationalism built their own counterideology.

The second element was provided by Maurras. Before him, counterrevolution had been ultramontane and had denounced in nationalism, correctly, a manifestation of the hated democratic spirit. By the end of the nineteenth century, and especially after the official *ralliement* recommended by the pope to the French Church, the intellectual capital of the ultras seemed depleted. Maurras's only real intellectual contribution was to graft nationalism onto old counterrevolutionary verities and hatreds, to justify antisemitism, antiprotestantism, and antimasonic feelings in nationalist terms, to add foreigners to the list of enemies, and to present a Catholic monarchy based on a traditional social hierarchy and on a repudiation of liberalism, representative government, and universal suffrage not as a dictate of God or providence but as a "positive" empirical law of political science, defined as the science of the preservation of nations.

In the short run, the new right-wing nationalism, despite its attempt to feed on the turmoil of the Dreyfus case and on the separation of Church and state, made little headway — partly because it focused so heavily on the internal enemies of the French nation that it seemed to promise even more disunity and political strife than the regime provided, partly because its two elements never blended enough to agree on a positive internal project. Barrès counted the Revolution and the Republic among France's traditions and worried about the lack of popular support for Maurras's system; Maurras, of course, deemed such support irrelevant and made the history of true France stop in 1789. Moreover, the external program of the new nationalists — vigilance against Germany and a deliberate preparation of the Revanche — did not differ all that much from the policies of Théophile Delcassé and Raymond Poincaré. The "nationalist revival" that Eugen Weber has described[33] represented, in the years before World War I, a convergence of Republican nationalism (which had rediscovered the cult of the military — Alexandre Millerrand, in December 1912, stated that the army was France) and the new nationalism of the Right.

Charles Péguy's unique and unclassifiable philosophy, which mixed populism, Catholicism, antiparliamentarism, militarism, a call for the Revanche in terms of the universal Rights of Man, and a defense of colonialism in terms both of France's mission and of France's energy and power, shows the strength of nationalist feelings partly rooted in and partly extending far beyond the nationalism of the regime itself.[34] Péguy's France is much closer to Michelet's than to Maurras's, although the cosmopolitanism of Jaurès and the flabbiness of parliamentarians are Maurras's and Péguy's common enemies. But the celebration of the Convention,

[33] *The Nationalist Revival in France 1905–1914* (Berkeley: University of California Press, 1968).

[34] See in particular *Notre patrie* and *L'argent suite*; also Géraldi Leroy, *Péguy entre l'ordre et la révolution* (Paris: Presses de la Fondation Nationale des Sciences Politiques, 1981).

and even the cult of Joan of Arc, brought close together the austere politician Poincaré and the passionate poet for whom, "in times of war, there is only the State; and it is *Vive la Nation*." [35]

It is both significant and sad that the nationalist rapprochement could occur only around war, and that the most effective, indeed often heroic, demonstration of the unifying function of nationalism was provided by French behavior in World War I. Péguy, who had demanded both unity and war, was vindicated — but killed. Since the main charge of the new nationalism had been aimed at the Republic's alleged lack of national spirit in facing the German threat, its champions had to proclaim a truce and to join their foes for national defense. The circumstances of the war — Austria's attempt to humiliate Serbia, Germany's invasion of Belgium — legitimized a Republican nationalism that could express itself both in elementary terms of survival and in the lofty terms of France's role as a defender of the right of the weak to national independence.

The victors produced a peace that was an unstable and somewhat unsavory mishmash of old-fashioned liberal nationalism (with the spread of the principle of national self-determination and the creation of a League of Nations aimed at furthering the cooperation and at resolving the conflicts of nation-states) and power bargains among greedy states. An exhausted France became, for a while, the preponderant power on the continent and the guardian of the new status quo. But even the sharp nationalism of Clemenceau could not obtain from France's allies the borders and guarantees that his strong drive for security and his "national egoism" — anything but missionary — had demanded. The nationalist Right could use this failure as a weapon against both the regime and France's unreliable allies. But the stage on which French history was being played had changed so drastically as to make past dogmas and policies irrelevant.

[35] Girardet, *Le nationalisme français*, p. 258.

At home, the Republicans, represented above all by the Radical party, had, it appeared, exhausted their program. The legitimacy of the democratic and representative system was challenged only by dwindling traditionalists and by admirers of Italian fascism, altogether not much of a threat. If the central problem was no longer the basis of political legitimacy, however, the Republic's efficiency soon became the main issue — and in the eyes of many, inefficiency and protracted social strife could not fail to reopen the question of Republican legitimacy. The cultural project of ideological harmonization through schooling was undermined by the "desertion" of the "footsoldiers," or missionary branch, of Republican nationalism: the schoolteachers, who were increasingly concerned with issues of class and class conflict, rather than national unity, and whose inclination toward a pacifist internationalism, already apparent before 1914, had received a decisive boost from the horrors of the war.[36] Abroad, a wide gap between France's status and France's actual resources incited its leaders to a retreat from what might be called great power chauvinism, especially after the fiasco of Poincaré's occupation of the Ruhr.

What changed the scene and introduced into French affairs what I once called the tyranny of the outside was not only a victory that had bled France white and left it exposed in turn to German revanchism. It was also the effect, both on France's position abroad and on France's polity, of two new ideologies that had emerged in Europe.

The Bolshevik Revolution, while it quickly moved from a missionary universalism reminiscent of that of 1792 France to "socialism in one country," deprived France of an ally against Germany and above all established a party of radical sympathizers with Moscow within France. It evolved just as quickly from being a party of Socialists radicalized by war and eager to repudiate the Socialist wartime policy of class collaboration and national unity

---

[36] See Jacques Ozouf and Mona Ozouf, *La République des instituteurs* (Paris: Gallimard, 1990).

that had led to no significant advances for the workers to a highly centralized and undemocratic party led by tough Moscow-trained militants who defined the interests of the French working class in terms of the Soviet Union's needs and ambitions. In August 1914 the defensive nature of the war, the assassination of the "cosmopolitan" Jaurès, the relative success of Republican ideology in persuading workers that the regime that had protected their right to vote was their regime (even if, and while, syndicalism taught them to distrust the state and its politics), Jaurès's interpretation of socialism as the simple extension of the Republicans' internal national program from political, religious, and educational issues to economic and social ones — all these factors had pushed the leaderless Socialists into joining *l'union sacrée*. With the appearance of the Communist party, a very different kind of actor had reached the stage: one that could occasionally promote a familiar-sounding Jacobin nationalism of unity at home and of national defense abroad, but only insofar as this was required by the interests and security of the USSR. It was a flickering and conditional nationalism, which could alternatively whip up and freeze the national sentiment or patriotism of its electorate.

As for fascism, it provided right-wing critics of the regime — especially those who remained obsessed by decadence and who saw in social conflict, particularly in the emergence of "Moscow's party," a deathly threat to the established social order — with foreign models that had been missing before; and it thus led people whose doctrine was the absolute primacy of the national interest to define it in such a way as to minimize any possible conflict with the new "regimes of order" or to seek an alliance with Italian fascism as a way of containing the potential German threat.

In the 1930s, after Hitler's advent to power and the formation of the Popular Front in France, the nation, which had often suffered from the contradictions and inadequacies of its nationalisms, now suffered grievously from their collapse. For there really was something extraordinary about a situation in which the old Jacobin message of internal unity around 'les petits" and external resistance to the forces of oppression — now fascism and Nazism — was carried only by the Communists, a handful of Socialists, and Radicals (and some more conservative Republicans in the Poincaré tradition, but only insofar as foreign policy was concerned). As the Communists moved from "defeatist" internationalism to Republican nationalism, and not by coincidence, many of the other Republicans retreated. At home, the resistance of the "big ones' made long overdue social reforms both deeply divisive and impossible to sustain (partly because of the Popular Front government's economic mistakes); abroad, the corrosive effects of pacifism (a hybrid product of revulsion against another war and of awareness of France's declining birthrate and economic stagnation) — reinforced by distrust of the Communists — led half of the Socialist party, most of the Radicals, and many of the trade union leaders into appeasement.

As for the ex-nationalist Right, its "nationalism" was preserved in words, but in completely perverted form. Before 1914, the Republic had been presented as the enemy largely — although by no means only — because of its alleged failure to protect the nation in the world. Now the internal vices of a Republic equated with a Left in which Communist "antinationals" and Kerensky-like Socialists dominated, a Republic corrupted by Jews and invaded by foreigners, were seen as so threatening for France's survival that they had to be addressed and removed *before* any resistance to foreign threats could be mounted — indeed the greatest threat, because it came from inside as well as from abroad, was communism. And so the champions of Maurras's "integral nationalism" turned their wrath on those who wanted to fight Germany before the French house had been put in order, while some of fascism's admirers stepped into the shoes of "defeatist internationalism," abandoned by the Communists.

In this lamentable debacle, in which right-wing nationalism seemed to gird itself for civil war — as in Spain — and the heirs of Republican nationalism dropped their principles, lost their faith, and sometimes embraced a pacifism that could not have flourished at a worse moment, the only common bond of nationalism that connected the Right (Maurras or the Fascist Jacques Doriot) with the Republican Center (Edouard Daladier) was a defensive colonialism, a chauvinistic celebration of the French Empire as a testimony to and remnant of French grandeur — but also as a compensation for the shame of retreat in Europe. Nothing could have been more symbolic of the flight from a Michelet-like nationalism than the cult of the defensive into which the regime locked itself and than the failure of its last governments, after the war began in September 1939, to call either on the ideological arsenal of liberalism and democracy or for a new *union sacrée* in order to galvanize the public.[37]

What happened after the fall of France is too familiar to deserve a long treatment. After another rare moment of quasi-unanimity around Marshal Pétain, the traumatized French were torn by the kind of crisis of loyalty that had not occurred since the Revolution, Napoleon, and the Restoration. Among the collaborationists, some were no longer patriots at all. Most French split over the very meaning of patriotism: two conceptions of political legitimacy, of the national interest — indeed two conceptions of what and where the nation was — were at war and placed the servants of the state (soldiers and civil servants) in a particularly painful dilemma, which many, alas, resolved by continuing to serve the "legal" authorities, despite what they were doing, rather than the rebel of June 18, 1940, and his fellow rebels of the Resistance. The Vichy regime represented the temporary victory of a bizarre "national revolution" that combined the reactionary and exclusionary nationalism of Maurras with a foreign policy that oscillated from a sullen acceptance of defeat (accompanied by a foolish hope of being able to limit further German encroachments

---

[37] See my introduction to Marc Bloch's *L'étrange défaite* (Paris: Gallimard, 1990).

and a determination to resist fiercely what were seen as the encroachments of ex-allies) to enthusiastic collaboration; in the eyes of Republican nationalists, the latter was treason, the former a tragic absurdity. Indeed, even if the National Revolution's program had been less elitist and *passéiste*, how could it have been carried out in a country two-thirds occupied and with more than a million prisoners of war? Vichy propaganda could try, grotesquely, to enlist Péguy, who had been no admirer of the "tough little minds" around Maurras. But all Vichy could do was exclude and repress: a Maurrassian definition of Frenchness produced denaturalizations, the persecution of Freemasons and democrats, and the scandalous policy that deprived French Jews of their rights and many foreign and also French Jews of their lives. A certain kind of nationalist perversion was thus discredited for a long time.

What was rehabilitated was a new version of Republican nationalism, which emerged gradually under the influence of Charles de Gaulle and in the Resistance. Its foreign program was simple: the recovery of French status (which entailed a *crispation* on the preservation of the empire) after the defeat of the enemy. Its domestic program was a kind of neo-revolutionary policy: the establishment of a more democratic regime of national sovereignty (but each component of the coalition had its own idea of democracy) and a program of national regeneration and unification that required both (as usual) the exclusion of the wicked — those who had supported Vichy—and a policy of unification, not through educational indoctrination, whose limits had become obvious (common values and myths are no substitute for social reforms), but through economic and social change — that is, through a more interventionist and extended state. Communists, Socialists, Christian Democrats, and de Gaulle could all rally behind this project. The lesson of the "dark years" seemed to be that France's renewal required a new nationalism — broader in scope as well as in the basis of its support. The collapse of the Right, the nationalist and Jacobin turn of the Communists, and the experience of defeat, occupation, and quasi–civil war all appeared to make the effort worthwhile and likely to succeed. But it did not: neither the French nor the world turned out to be right for it. The great, brief moment of national unity, at the Liberation, the first exalted one since World War I, soon became a bitter memory.

At home, the new nationalism did succeed in expanding the scope of the state and in launching thereby a *dirigiste* policy of modernization and industrialization. It aimed at deriving lessons from Keynesian experiences abroad just as the French after 1871 had sought lessons in the victorious Germans' practices. The new policy substituted planning for laissez-faire at home, a measure of openness for protectionism at the border. It accelerated the "rural exodus," the decline of France's traditional peasantry, and thus changed (but did not destroy) the celebrated special relationship of the French to the soil. It created a system of social security — which undoubtedly raised solidarity and welfare. But the new institutions of the Fourth Republic could be set up only against the wrath of de Gaulle, who found them too weak and similar to those of the Third Republic, and with grudging support from the Communists, who were soon thrown into opposition by another manifestation of the tyranny of the outside: the cold war. De Gaulle's Rally, the Rassemblement du Peuple Français, launched a nationalist barrage against the "Republic of parties," comparable to Barrès's Boulangiste assault: in both cases, the regime was deemed too weak to defend the nation's interests abroad. Once again the regime was confronted with an ardent nationalist critique on its Right; but its own nationalism had been much battered and dampened since the breakup of the coalition that had gone from Maurice Thorez to de Gaulle; moreover, de Gaulle's conception of the nation was not deterministic — it was Michelet's — and the ferments of decay he denounced were not Jews and foreigners, but pusillanimous politicians insufficiently concerned with France's honor and independence and the "separatists": the Communists faithful to Moscow. The presence of the latter as a countersociety in the midst of French society prevented the social program of national unity through integration of the working class from succeeding fully — and anyhow the parties of the governing "Third Force" had no coherent idea about how to achieve full integration.

Abroad, even though de Gaulle reproached the leaders who had emerged from the Resistance for showing more concern for domestic issues than for the defense of the nation's interests in the world, and more inclination to accommodate powerful allies than to resist their transgressions, the political class that he left to its own devices when he resigned in January 1946 tried at first to pursue his nationalist program. It was certainly not a messianic or cosmopolitan one; it was strictly the protection of French security, the defense of France's positions, the recovery of status. The latter was, thanks to de Gaulle, largely successful — but it was also more symbolic than real. On two fronts, the new realities of the international system rebuffed French aspirations. In Europe, de Gaulle tried to revive the hard policy of German division and dismemberment that had failed in 1919. His successors pursued the effort for a while; as after World War I, France alone was unable to impose its views; its allies proceeded without it. The French tried to adjust their policy by switching from repression and occupation to cooperation and the construction of a common European entity. It was a remarkable attempt at blending a traditional concern for security and control over the German neighbor, the new Federal Republic (this was the calculation of a nationalist Quai d'Orsay), with the utterly antinationalist functional Federalism of Jean Monnet, latter-day disciple of Saint Simon. But the fact that the attempt entailed transfers of national sovereignty enraged the Gaullists. When the policy was extended from coal and steel to armies, a coalition of Gaullists, Communists opposed to the Atlantic alliance, and Third Force politicians hostile to German rearmament defeated the scheme for a European Defense Community. A kind of traditional (and situational) nationalism had prevailed. However, it was a Pyrrhic victory: the Federal Republic was allowed to rearm anyhow, and the Fourth Republic returned in 1957 to a policy of West European integration that entailed more pooling of sovereign powers over atomic energy policy and for a common market. France seemed to have discovered that it could no longer act alone in Europe — that the interests of the nation might even require restrictions on its independence.

It was on the colonial front that the experience was most bitter. The nationalist revolts in Indochina and in North Africa not only challenged French positions and power, they turned against France the very ideology of national self-determination and the principles of national sovereignty that France had once been so proud to incarnate and to export.[38] French universalism did not yield without a last stand: the Socialist leader Guy Mollet asserted that the kind of national community France wanted others to develop was a community of enlightened and responsible individuals: a *Gesellschaft* of free wills, not a *Gemeinschaft* based on ethnic identity. In his eyes, neither Communist nationalism nor that of the Algerian Muslims met the requirements: both were of the obscurantist variety, imposed on confused and ignorant individuals. But whose fault was it if they were confused and ignorant? The colonial army mounted an effort to develop first a theory of revolutionary war to win hearts and minds and later a theory of Algerian "integration" that contradicted more than a century of discrimination between natives and citizens — for in the colonies nationality and citizenship were dissociated — as well as denied the natives any right of self-determination. Nevertheless, France lost the war in Indochina, and the prospect of losing Algeria brought down a regime that a combination of desperate clinging to "French Algeria" and disagreements on how far to go, or not to go, in introducing cosmetic reforms had doomed to paralysis and exposed to a revolt of settlers and soldiers in Algiers.

[38] Cf. the remarks of Benjamin Stora, *La gangrène et l'oubli* (Paris: La Découverte, 1991), ch. 22.

The new nationalism forged in the Resistance had paled and failed. The nation's capacity to act as well as its standing in the world seemed impaired, domestic unity imperiled by external defeats. But the story was far from over. The drama of French nationalism had been the clash between a Sisyphean effort at unifying the French behind a certain idea of France and realities that always kept them divided. And yet never had these splits been more murderous at home and fateful abroad than when nationalism had been abandoned and perverted. Would there be a way out of this dilemma?[39]

II. FRANCE BETWEEN DE GAULLE AND EUROPE

The second coming of Charles de Gaulle is the latest, most singular, and perhaps ultimate peak in the mountain range of French nationalism. For he was the first French leader and thinker for whom the independence and greatness of France were the alpha and omega, the entire substance of nationalism. As we have seen, the revolutionaries and the Third Republic's Republicans had domestic imperatives and gave to their nationalism the substance of a democratic ideology; the nationalists of the Right at the end of the last century were locked in a static and defensive view of France at home and abroad. Michelet's mystical celebration of the "Christ of nations" taught his listeners and readers that the mass could only be sung again if the people came to power and

[39] I agree neither with Liah Greenfeld's (*Nationalism*) nor with Louis Dumont's interpretations of French nationalism (see his *L'idéologie allemande* [Paris: Gallimard, 1991]). Her view of the French conception as imported from Britain, but turned into a "super-human collective person" instead of an association of free, rational individuals (p. 167), is a misreading of Rousseau. The "collective person" is the product of an association of free, rational individuals, the expression of their rational and moral common will. But Dumont's belief that the individualism of French culture makes the French consider themselves human beings first, and French only accidentally, his simple contrast between individualism and holism, and his conviction that holism can be found only on the Right are just as unsatisfactory. Maybe one should define the Rousseauistic conception as a holism resting on an individualistic basis, as opposed to ethnic holism; individualism has coexisted with nationalism in much of French history.

perfected what the Revolution had begun. De Gaulle was far more ecumenical.[1] First, "there is only one French history" and he endorsed all of it, judging leaders and regimes only with the yardstick of national grandeur. This was definitely not Maurrassian; it could have been Barrèsian, had the shivering Barrès not found warmth only in the soil and amidst the dead. De Gaulle was turned toward the future; he shared both Michelet's view that France was an incessant blending of peoples and his idea of a distinctive personality formed by and imposed upon this blend,[2] but Michelet looked at France as a historian, de Gaulle as both an avid reader of history (son of a teacher of history) and a man of action: what mattered most to him was the mark France could still leave, the *grandes entreprises* it could still undertake — if well led. The dead provided an inspiration, not a mold; the soil was an essential feature, but not the soul of France. The call of June 1940 had come from "the depths of History," but aimed at reclaiming France's future, and it came from London: it was Pétain who celebrated the cult of the soil.

In behalf of his mission, he was the supreme pragmatist. This is why his domestic program was so flexible, except for one essential imperative — the precondition for action abroad was a strong state, "in charge of France." But even on this point — how to build such a state — he took what he needed from a variety of conflicting traditions. The strong executive from which all other powers flow he borrowed from the monarchy and Bonapartism; from these and from the Jacobins, the centralized administrative structure (until the day, in 1968, before the "events," when he found it had become stifling); from the Republican and revolutionary tradition that had built modern France and to which the

---

[1] As Jean Touchard put it, in *Le gaullisme 1940–69* (Paris: Seuil, 1968), p. 301, "The nationalism of the General was diachronically *unitaire* . . . it was also synchronically *unitaire*."

[2] Cf. the *Mémoires d'espoir*, 2 vols. (Paris: Plon, 1970), vol. 1, p. 7 — an opening paragraph as revealing as the more famous opening paragraph of the *Mémoires de guerre*.

French were attached, the principle of national sovereignty, and — despite his ferocity against the *régime d'Assemblée* and the rule of parties in the previous two Republics — the trappings of representative and parliamentary government. Indeed, what he added went further in the democratic direction: the direct popular election of the president, which had only been tried (disastrously) in the quite special circumstances of 1848, and the referendum. It was, deliberately or not, an ingenious synthesis of all French regimes. As Jean Charlot has noted, this was a means, not an end.[3] But it was perhaps here that de Gaulle succeeded most: gradually, around the institutions of the Fifth Republic, a consensus formed. Was the old dream of unity finally realized? — only in a very limited way. On the one hand, the rest of the domestic program — modernization — succeeded neither in finding the "third way" de Gaulle had successively called association and participation, which was supposed to reconcile the workers and the bourgeois somewhere in between socialism and capitalism (but closer to the latter), nor in avoiding the explosion of student malaise and worker discontent in May 1968. On the other hand, what all of these efforts, constitutional and economic, were geared to — bold activism abroad — while also enjoying very broad support from the public, never managed to overcome the rather hostile skepticism of a sizable part of the elite, which was not nationalist (cf. Raymond Aron) and the somewhat more friendly and admiring skepticism of the people (I think of the nuclear force).

The heart of the mission, then, was in foreign policy. Without great external enterprises, the French would divide and quarrel. But these endeavors were not just means to unity, they were a duty by themselves. Here too, de Gaulle determined the substance of his program by combining a few simple principles with what mattered above all, "realities" or "circumstances." The imperatives were to preserve French independence, "free hands," from

[3] In "Le gaullisme," in J.-F. Sirinelli (ed.), *Histoire des droites en France*, 3 vols. (Paris: Gallimard, 1992), vol. 1, p. 661.

foreign domination or "supranational" control and to maximize French power and influence in a world where two superpowers left little leeway for allies, clients, and neutrals. How de Gaulle tried to loosen their grip I have told elsewhere.[4] Two things stand out. The first is that, far more than in 1944–46, he succeeded in combining the two orientations of French nationalism. The politics of power and interest he had practiced before with prickly virtuosity, during the war. His policy of military emancipation from NATO, his costly and persistent construction of a nuclear force, his determination to get the Common Market to serve France's agricultural interests while diluting the supranational aspects of the Community, and his buildup of financial reserves are the main examples of this side of his policy. What is striking is that so many of his efforts were aimed at defending or recovering *external* sovereignty. The revolutionaries and the Republicans had planted French nationalism on the ground of national sovereignty as a principle of *domestic* legitimacy; right-wing nationalism before World War I had, like de Gaulle, been anxious about French power and freedom of action abroad. But this time, it was sovereignty itself, the source of freedom of action, that was at stake, because of the entangling institutions de Gaulle had inherited from the Fourth Republic: NATO and the EEC.

At the same time, he also tried to recapture the tradition of French universalism, the missionary or exemplary role of France, in singularly changed conditions. He may have been helped by the fact (which has rarely been pointed out) that, unlike Michelet, he did not simultaneously believe in "friendship" among true nations and in the superiority of France: on the one hand, for him, nations may have feelings and souls, but states have only interests; on the other hand, while the world, as always, listens to and waits for France, other nations are owed respect even when there are

---

[4] See the chapters on de Gaulle in *Decline or Renewal: France since the 1930s* (New York: Viking, 1974) and my chapter on de Gaulle's diplomacy in the forthcoming volume on the post-war diplomats, edited by Gordon Craig.

clashes of power with France. The mission of France was — once again — to champion the right of other nations to self-determination and independence. Now this meant decolonization: exemplary retreat, rather than missionary expansion. De Gaulle's tortuous policy in Algeria was anchored, as of 1959, in the principle of self-determination, and the rest of the former empire followed. This obliged de Gaulle to confront head-on the exacerbated and violent nationalism of those, on the Right, who confused France's possessions with France's heritage, mistook its past for its destiny, saw in retreat the latest form of decadence, and therefore tried to present their rebellion against him as comparable to his own rebellion against the armistice of June 1940. But it allowed him to pose and parade as the champion of the new and smaller states against the "two hegemonies" of Moscow and Washington: a message he carried around the world, from Latin America to Poland, from Cambodia to Quebec. His plan for a sort of West European Confederation, the Fouchet plan of 1961–62, was an attempt at combining the French rejection of supranationality and the need for a broad cooperation among West European nations, so as to maximize their combined autonomy at the superpowers' expense. The nationalist of German dismemberment of 1945 became the solemn celebrant of Franco-German reconciliation and collaboration.

This did not proceed without contradictions. Guinea incurred French wrath when it chose independence too swiftly; de Gaulle's rough pursuit of French interests, his concern for rank, his refusal to tie France's hands, and his determination to push his European partners in the only direction he deemed valid — a "European Europe" — instead of settling for ambiguous compromises resulted in the fiasco of the Fouchet plan and the gradual paralysis of the Community. His West European policy failed because it could not bridge the gap between a *French* policy for Europe and a common policy acceptable to partners he deemed — correctly — insufficiently concerned with Europe's independence and too eager to seek America's protection. Another factor explains the failure of his other grand designs: a reunited Europe from the Atlantic to the Urals, the *querelle de l'homme* that was the economic development of the Third World, the abolition of the dollar's privileges. Quite simply, France did not have the power and wealth to reach de Gaulle's objectives, without the support and cooperation of others, which he did not get and which his style did little to provide. Or else France did not have the means to accelerate a history that moved, *grosso modo*, in the direction de Gaulle had foreseen — the end of the cold war, the reunification of Europe and Germany, the fall of the Bretton Woods monetary system — but not necessarily toward the specific alternatives he favored.

By his relentless energy, ambition, and disciplined imagination, he shook up the "tyranny of the exterior" and gave the French the impression, or the illusion, of having regained mastery, of having loosened and held at bay the constraints of the international system. But his words and prophecies had more resonance than his moves had success. He left French power far less burdened and in many ways modernized and increased. But the constraints had not been removed, and the gap between independence and effectiveness, between sovereignty and achievements, meant that grandeur was in the style and the designs more than in the results. Ultimately, his greatest achievements were at home: not merely the political regime, but the restoration of French self-esteem, through a combination of great deeds, at home and abroad, and some myths.

It may be a paradox that France, whose long history has produced no uncontested national heroes comparable to other nations' "founding fathers," finally found one in de Gaulle, at what may have been the end of France's nationalist history; but it is not surprising that this hero should have been both a military man and a powerful writer, who, wisely if not always accurately, put into immortal words the "last chapters" of that history: "since everything always begins again, what I did will, sooner or later, be a source of new ardor after my disappearance." [5] But the question is: can it be?

[5] *Mémoires de guerre*, 3 vols. (Paris: Plon, 1959), vol. 3, p. 289.

We can try to answer it first, obliquely, by examining the forms of French nationalism today. We do not find it at the centers of power, the presidency and the prime minister's office. After the death of de Gaulle's stolid "heir," Georges Pompidou, the French turned first to a liberal technocrat, Valéry Giscard d'Estaing, who did his best to combine the far less nationalist policy he preferred — promoting European integration and calling for "mondialisme" — with the Gaullist legacy he could not afford to renounce. Then came François Mitterrand, whose own balancing act was between a traditional Socialist vision of international cooperation (including further European integration) and, again, the Gaullist legacy, especially in the realm of military independence. The two Gaullist imperatives: the defense *tous azimuts* of sovereignty and the pursuit of grandeur, were, in fact, quietly shelved after 1974.

And yet, one can speak of a new nationalist revival, in parts of the political class, a very small fraction of the intelligentsia, and a sizable portion of the public. But it takes two quite different forms. One is the nationalism of Jean-Marie Le Pen's National Front, on the Right.[6] Here we find a thoroughly degraded version of the right-wing nationalism that had emerged in the late 1880s. Once again, there is the obsession with decadence, now equated with the "invasion" of Muslims, the danger of miscegenation (*métissage*). In the words of one right-wing Catholic, "heirs in danger of being the last survivors of the people of cathedrals and crusades, chivalry and mission, we are colonized."[7] Le Pen has revived the determinism of Barrès and Maurras: the nation is defined as a heritage, identified with the family, and therefore endowed with "biological reality." (A sociologist whose theses

---

[6] See in particular the chapter by Pierre Milza in Sirinelli (ed.), *Histoire des droites*, pp. 519–66; and the chapter by Pierre-André Taguieff in Nonna Mayer and Pascal Perrineau (eds.), *Le Front National à découvert* (Paris: Presses de la Fondation Nationale des Sciences Politiques, 1989), pp. 195–227.

[7] Jean Madiran, quoted by Pierre Birnbaum in Gil Delannos and Pierre-André Taguieff (eds.), *Théories du nationalisme* (Paris: Ed. Kimé, 1991), p. 136.

are remarkably close to the Front's has recently tried to defend the use of the word "race.")[8] If the theme of constitutional reform is less present than among its predecessors, it is because the National Front realizes that the present institutions are popular. But like those predecessors, Le Pen's nationalism is turned both inward and outward — arresting France's decline in the world by drastic antiegalitarian yet populist (i.e., anti-"gros") measures inside. Moreover, as in the 1930s, the inner program almost removes the external one from view and exhibits a glaring contradiction between the ritual appeal for unity and the inevitable denunciation of all those culprits who "plot" and foster French decadence (the Left, antinational intellectuals and syndicalists, technocrats, Jews, etc.), who are pilloried in terms that mix sexual metaphors and Darwinian images. It is a nationalism of resentment barely disguised by the call for regeneration. What inspires it is, underneath it all, the bitterness left by the loss of Algeria, the first scene of Le Pen's exploits.[9] It animates both his demand for an end of immigration, accused of destroying French identity, and his "solution" for the Muslims in France: total assimilation or else expulsion. A quest for virility turned toward the past, it exploits deep feelings of physical and patriotic insecurity. It is not surprising that this cramped defense of French identity entails a rejection of European integration: the Maastricht treaty was attacked as a "form of mental AIDS."[10]

The debate on Maastricht brought to light a second kind of nostalgic nationalism: an appeal to the revolutionary and Republican tradition of national sovereignty, to the august myth of *la République* but turned outward (as in de Gaulle's nationalism, but he did not specifically appeal to the Republican model since

---

[8] Paul Yonnet, *Voyage au centre du malaise français* (Paris: Gallimard, 1993), pp. 70ff.

[9] Cf. the comments of Benjamin Stora in *La gangrène et l'oubli* (Paris: La Découverte, 1991), pp. 281ff. and 317ff.

[10] Quoted by Alex Stone in "Ratifying Maastricht," *French Politics and Society* 2, no. 1 (Winter 1993), 83.

the defense of sovereignty abroad had been the mark of both of France's unifying regimes, the Old Regime *and* the Republic). Moreover, it was used defensively (whereas de Gaulle used his call for sovereignty both defensively and as a demand for bold initiatives and actions). In an integrated Europe, France — in the arguments of the Gaullist Philippe Séguin and the nationalist Socialist Jean-Pierre Chevènement — would lose both its independence and the possibility of promoting its universal principles throughout the world. As Séguin put it, the "social contract" that is the foundation of sovereignty, both internal and external, would be transferred abroad and thereby broken.[11] The notion of French exceptionalism — a uniqueness that consists both in the fact that "of the twelve states of the Community, France is the most attached to its identity and national unity"[12] (what about Britain or Holland?) and in the universality of its principles of legitimacy, national sovereignty, and self-determination — thus emerges again in terms that Michelet, who believed that Europe could only be a concert of distinctive nations, would have approved. But what had been a conquering notion has become a deeply "protectionist" one, which explains why the anti-Maastricht coalition brought together champions of the Republican version of nationalism *and* Le Pen: the (respectively) depleted and degraded nationalist traditions, waging battle against all those who acted as if not only nationalism but the nation state itself had become obsolete — even if they carefully avoided saying it too crudely and preferred to defend the treaty in terms of France's national interests (which include, above all, they said, the containment of a reunited Germany).

The size of the anti-Maastricht vote in the referendum of September 1992 has many "contingent" reasons: unhappiness with an economic downturn for which Brussels was made partly respon-

[11] Ibid., p. 76.
[12] Quoted by Stone (from a petition of mainly Gaullist senators to the Constitutional Council), ibid., p. 82.

sible, distrust of a president who has overstayed his welcome, and so forth. But there were two deeper reasons as well, and they take us from the study of French nationalism's ideas and tribulations to a look at the modern nation that two centuries of efforts, from the Revolution to the present, have built — consciously and conscientiously — around the *idea* of the nation. In the self-image of the French as in the rhetoric of nationalism, there are two components: an internal one, which can be called national identity or specificity, and an external one: the nation-state.

The revolutionaries and the Republicans tried to define France's national identity in political terms. What constitutes the nation *is* the social contract that set up a national, democratic polity; it was around those principles, transmitted by the school and the army, that foreigners were not merely "naturalized" but "nationalized" (i.e., assimilated). But, as we have seen, the initial voluntarism was enriched and modified by an increasing emphasis on historical continuity, on *l'héritage*: the weight of the past, a Burkean notion, was providing roots and substance to the abstract and somewhat formalistic notions derived from Rousseau. It is the combination of historical identity and political specificity that provided the formula of the French melting pot. As in the United States, the absorption of immigrants has been a constant (it is Germany that today remains reluctant to conceive of itself as a "country of immigration").[13] In both the United States and France — in this country, because of the liberal tradition, in France, because this is one point on which liberalism and Rousseauism converge, yet without merging — the distinction between the public and the private spheres means that the foreigner who becomes a national, and thereby a citizen, is supposed, in receiving all the rights of citizenship, also to accept the principles of legitimacy and government as well as the laws of his or her adopted country (explicitly in

---

[13] See Gérard Noiriel, "Difficulties in French Historical Research on Immigration," in Daniel L. Horowitz and Gérard Noiriel (eds.), *Immigrants in Two Democracies* (New York: New York University Press, 1992), pp. 66–79.

the United States, where these principles are not in dispute, implicitly in France), but can, in private life, remain faithful to his or her customs and religion. The public person must speak English or French; the private one can keep speaking his or her language of origin. In both countries, the naturalization of foreigners was made easy (in France, through the use of *jus soli* as well as through voluntarism — requests for French nationality after a few years of residence).

But the French melting pot has never been quite like the American one. The United States *is* "a nation of immigrants"; France is a nation that attracts and incorporates immigrants: this is a major difference. It accounts not only for waves of xenophobia that French historians are beginning to study[14] — against Italians and Belgians in the 1880s and 1890s, against Poles and refugees from Germany and Central Europe in the 1930s — after all, there were comparable waves in the United States. It accounts also for two distinctive features. First, because French nationality is not merely, so to speak, contractual — signing on to the principles of the Constitution, as in the United States — but has a heavy historical component, the "public" dimension is *both* political and cultural: it entails the assimilation of French culture, which the school system is supposed to produce. Moreover, the political principles were, so to speak, more pointed or militant, as the result of long struggles; thus, the notion of citizenship entailed not merely the separation of Church and state, but *la laïcité*, an aggressive *rejection* of the Catholic Church, precisely because of its old connections with and public role in prerevolutionary France and its determination to have a say in public affairs. Second, whereas the French idea that the Republic integrates only individuals, not "communities," and does not "recognize" communities as public actors is one that Americans would share, the private sphere is

---

[14] See especially Gérard Noiriel, *Le creuset français* (Paris: Seuil, 1988), ch. 5, and his *La tyrannie du national* (Paris: Calmann-Lévy, 1991). See also Rogers Brubaker, *Citizenship and Nationhood in France and Germany* (Cambridge, Mass.: Harvard University Press, 1992).

regarded, in France, with far greater suspicion than in America. It is the combination of these two differences that explains why the idea of "multiculturalism" remains repugnant to the French, in their great majority: there is only *one* French culture, and "separate" subcultures are not welcome insofar as they impede assimilation to French culture.

To be sure, there are occasional similarities between American debates about, and resistance to, the demands of Black militants who insist on group identity and group rights and reject the model of individual integration and French debates about the integration of Muslims. But America has a special and weighty problem with the Blacks: they are Americans and descendants of slaves forcibly brought to this country long ago. Claiming group rights is a way of obtaining at last the full range of individual civic and social rights they were denied for so long. The Muslims are immigrants. And while the arguments about their "unassimilability," their ineradicable "difference," are no different from earlier anti-Italian or anti-Polish arguments, there is a novelty: Islam, as Fernand Braudel duly noted.[15] Islam is not only an "alien" religion (unlike Catholicism, Protestantism, and Judaism), it is a powerful culture (which, unlike Catholicism, has not been a major part of French culture), indeed "a way of life," and (like Catholicism in this respect) a code that includes the private *and* the public.

Hence the intensity of the debate about immigration. This time, French national identity is felt to be at stake by many more people than those who ranted about what the "invasion" from the East in the 1930s was doing to the French race (I am thinking of Jean Giraudoux). There are two sources of worry. One is that many of the Muslims, particularly those who are deeply religious (*a fortiori* the Fundamentalists) will be "unassimilable": either French identity will be deeply transformed if they become French or they will be "a danger to the nation" if they are not assimilated.[16] The other worry is that the mechanisms that succeeded in

---

[15] *L'identité de la France*, vol. 1 (Paris: Arthaud-Flammarion, 1986), p. 195.
[16] Noiriel, "Difficulties in French Historical Research," p. 74.

assimilating men and women whose "cultural distance" from the French was often wide are no longer as effective. The directives of the Ministry of Education about the civic and social values children must be taught may well be unchanged since Jules Ferry.[17] It is the capacity of schools to transmit them that is questioned, partly because the content of French education has become less "cultural" and parochial and more technical (mathematics and science count for more, history and the French classics for less), partly because many primary schools are now predominantly frequented by the sons and daughters of immigrants in districts — urban and suburban — where they are most numerous and from whose schools the French have fled. There are other aspects of the "weakening of the French melting pot"; as an important report has pointed out,[18] spatial segregation, the loss of influence of the Catholic Church on the Muslims, the flabbiness of French voluntary associations such as unions and parties (remarks that acknowledge the role the Church and the Communists, two organizations seen as "antinational" by many French, had played in the process of assimilation), the decline of the army as an integrative body, because of shorter military service and, here also, because of the preponderance of technical expertise over civic training — all these factors make the Republican model of individual assimilation far more dubious. Thus many foreigners want to become French but without assimilating, and the process that turned foreigners into French is faltering. The nature of the "demand" has changed: it is tougher; so has the supply (i.e., the melting pot): it has softened.

The paradox is that the most common reaction, among intellectuals and politicians, from the conservative Catholic historian

[17] Quoted in Danielle Boyzon-Fradet, "The French Education System: Springboard or Obstacle to Integration," in Horowitz and Noiriel (eds.), *Immigrants*, p. 149.

[18] Rapport de la Commission de la Nationalité, *Etre français aujourd'hui et demain* (Paris: Documentation française, 1988), vol. 2, pp. 82ff. See also François Bourricaud, "1945–1992: La crise des référents," in Sirinelli (ed.), *Histoire des droites*, pp. 567–99.

Pierre Chaunu, to the Socialist leader Michel Rocard, via the Jewish sociologist Dominique Schnapper, is an act of faith in the very process that, all agree, no longer performs as it once did. "Integration will be easiest if the consciousness of French identity is strongest," [19] and such a reinforcement of national consciousness cannot be left to "the free play of the spontaneous forces of social life" (the old distrust of private forces left to themselves is obvious here).[20] A deliberate policy is needed, and it sounds most familiar: on the one hand, the goal of full integration is preserved — hence the rejection of the suggestion, made by Giscard among others, to make the *jus sanguinis* the exclusive mode of acquisition of French nationality — as well as the "voluntaristic" approach to the acquisition of French citizenship (but when there was a contradiction between the two, the former used to prevail, as in the laws that granted French nationality automatically to certain categories of foreigners living in France). On the other hand, a reinvigoration of the school and the army, as vehicles of civic training, is being demanded; little is said about how this is to be done. Around the need for full assimilation, the Republican and the far Right traditions curiously converge. It is true that the former wants to facilitate integration, the latter, which fears it, wants to make it more arduous; one stresses the political component of the melting pot, the other the cultural one. But there is a common enemy: the pluralism of multiculturalism. Jews who have become fully and proudly assimilated are, occasionally, the strange bedfellows of Catholic *intégristes*.[21]

The episode of the *foulards islamiques* in 1988 — the national debate about the insistence of three young Muslim girls on wearing a veil over their heads at school — showed both the French

[19] Rapport, *Etre français*, vol. 2, p. 82.

[20] Ibid., p. 86.

[21] The book of Paul Yonnet (*Voyage au centre*) requires particular attention. Rather than defending racism, he attacks antiracism; he charges foreign historians with having destroyed "le roman national français," along with French critics such as Bernard-Henri Lévy, who has a "sick fear of French identity" (pp. 277, 281).

penchant for turning small incidents into grand symbolic issues and the depth of the anxiety about Muslim distinctiveness. The defenders of the traditional mechanism of assimilation thought that such a demand was intolerable, because it challenged *la laïcité* in the very heart of the process of homogenization: the school system. American quarrels over multiculturalism, especially in schools and universities, have been followed with a certain amount of *Schadenfreude*.[22] What will happen to American national identity if Hispanics, Blacks, Native Americans, and others request a right to their separate cultures in the public realm (remember: this includes education for the French)? All these comments and warnings seem to suggest that, whereas each wave of American immigrants contributes to and shapes American identity, French ones are asked to adopt a firmly preestablished French identity. Indeed, Gérard Noiriel boldly asserts that whereas the American melting pot began with the Revolution, the French one ended with it.[23]

And yet . . . There are genuine grounds for believing that France's capacity to assimilate immigrants has not been seriously impaired. Most of them speak French — part of the labor of integration is therefore unnecessary. Many of them, especially Algerians, appear to want integration, while preserving cultural and family links with their country of origin — neither an unreasonable demand nor an original one and not a fatal obstacle to assimilation; events in Algeria contribute to this. The power of French culture, even in a "weaker" school system, remains enormous, and many elements of that culture get transmitted in the working place and through the media and entertainment industries. Finally, for all the ideological resistance to the taboo of multiculturalism, all the Rousseauistic suspicion of pluralism as a threat to *la volonté une*, a *de facto* pluralism has spread. It was always there in the private sphere, which is where people mostly live. But what is

[22] See *Le Débat* 69 (March–April 1992).
[23] In Horowitz and Noiriel (eds.), *Immigrants*, p. 73.

significant is the loosening of the Jacobin corset in the public sphere and the lowering of the barrier between public and private. Regional government is gaining strength. The legislator's will can be declared unconstitutional by unelected judges. The French state encourages the building of mosques. The "private" (i.e., Catholic) school system has, for many years now, been subsidized by the state and treated as part of the public service of education. When Mitterrand tried to tighten state control over it, millions of French marched, not in defense of the Church, but for the right of families to choose their children's schools. In *l'affaire des foulards*, many Catholics and Jews — the former because the whole Republican model was built to *expel* the Church from the public domain, the latter because of their own new restlessness about a model of *inclusion* that required assimilation but did not, in the horrible crunch of 1940–44, protect them from discrimination and death — supported the girls' request.

There is, thus, an increasing distance between the old Jacobin model, or straitjacket, and the modern French society and polity, but this distance does not doom the French melting pot. A certain amount of friendly tolerance for diversity might turn out to be as good a force for integration as the old Republican indoctrination. What is needed to keep the melting pot busy and effective is, in the first place, the prevalence of values of decency, sympathy, and universality in French society; this is why the refusal of right-wing parties to make deals with Le Pen, even though much of his electorate comes from theirs, is essential: the values common to liberalism and to the French version of democracy are more important than the narrow model produced by the latter. In the second place, the success of the melting pot may be helped by the strength of French cultural identity, which remains as well established and (despite an apparent lack of public confidence in its force of attraction — i.e., a lack of self-confidence) as solid as ever. It may be that the doubts about its strength are nothing other than pure and simple xenophobia, pure and simple rejection of the others not because they cannot or don't want to become "like us" but because we don't want them to. In this respect, it cannot be said that the champions of the old model have always done their duty by combating repugnance for the "invader." Their timidity in fighting xenophobia provides one reason why one cannot end this analysis on an unqualified hopeful note. The other reason is the new legislation the predominantly right-wing Parliament passed in the spring of 1993: the new provisions on naturalization and on the treatment of foreigners, even as softened by the Constitutional Council, are, to put it mildly, ungenerous and often mean. Much will depend on how they are enforced.

Fears about not the substance but the potency of French national identity are also fed by questions about the European enterprise. It was, as we have seen, initiated by the Fourth Republic both as the best way to defend French interests now that France had slipped in rank and power *and* as a bold endeavor in reconciliation (with Germany) and cooperation worthy of French ideals. The sacrifices of sovereignty entailed by supranationality had been, after the debacle of the European Defense Community, both reduced (insofar as the Common Market's Commission, unlike that of the Coal and Steel Community, was not a decision-making body) and postponed (majority rule in the Council). De Gaulle's *Blitzkrieg* against the EEC's Commission 1965, when the latter tried to increase its powers, led to the Luxembourg compromise, which eliminated the "threat" of majority rule in matters deemed of essential importance by a member. Under those conditions, the preservation of French independence seemed quite compatible with the construction of a West European entity in economic and monetary matters: the Community helped French modernization, French civil servants dominated its bureaucracy, and France was *prima inter pares*, the only nuclear power of the entity and a fully sovereign state next to a divided Germany with restrictions on its sovereignty. Moreover, in a world dominated by the cold war,

French military autonomy was widely seen as a great asset, offsetting whatever constraints the Community's rules might impose on French economic and financial freedom of maneuver. France was, in the eyes of many French leaders, still a great power: through Europe, by its presence outside Europe, especially in Africa, and by virtue of its nuclear nuisance power.[24]

A certain complacent pride began to evaporate in the 1980s. The Socialist government's attempt to pursue a *dirigiste* policy of nationalizations and massive public spending disrupted France's balance of payments and trade and jeopardized France's ability to remain within the limits of the European Monetary System established in 1978. The sudden awareness of the costs that would have been imposed by the pursuit of such a policy in the midst of a recession, when most of France's European partners were tightening belts and fighting inflation — a huge loss of competitiveness and the need to insulate France from the EMS and the EEC's rules — revealed how much modernization and the abandonment of traditional industrial protectionism had made France dependent on the world market and especially the West European one and the impossibility of pursuing an economic and financial policy that would be both independent and beneficial. Having, so to speak, finally chosen Europe and austerity — the latter because of the former — Mitterrand needed a new political initiative and turned to a *relance* of Europe. It was, once more, presented as essential for French power and welfare. The switch to majority vote entailed by the Single Act of 1987 was accepted by Parliament with little turmoil: it was presented as a logical and necessary effect of the decision, unanimously made by the governments of the twelve members, to establish a single market by 1992. But clouds formed soon enough. The inevitable clash between sovereignty and integration, avoided

---

[24] See my chapter on "French Dilemmas and Strategies in the New Europe," in Robert Keohane, Joseph Nye, and Stanley Hoffmann (eds.), *After the Cold War* (Cambridge, Mass.: Harvard University Press, 1993).

since 1965 when the latter had been set back, could not be postponed anymore.

First, there was the problem of agriculture. The Common Agricultural Policy imposed by de Gaulle had been a tremendous engine of modernization and expansion for French agriculture, just as the size of the rural population was falling to a new low. But the cost to consumers was high, and the accumulation of surpluses exorbitant. When Brussels, partly because of this and partly under GATT pressure, began demanding a reform of the CAP, French farmers ceased seeing in the Community their savior and instrument and turned their anger against its new policies. The "transfer of competence" that had made Brussels, not Paris, the locus of France's agricultural policy was now seen as a fatal giveaway.

Second, it became gradually clear that the European Court of Justice was quietly but relentlessly giving a "Federalist" interpretation of Community competences and establishing the superiority of Community over national legislation. The French Conseil d'Etat was the last to accept this, but it finally did. Effectiveness within the Community clearly required the enforceability of its norms, regulations, and directives in the courts of the members. But French sovereignty, again, was being eroded.

Third, the reunification of Germany transformed the political context. The economic and monetary giant of the EC (however hampered, temporarily, by a hasty policy of absorption of former East Germany that was supposed to be painless) was now a full "sovereign" state with enormous political weight. In the absence of the Soviet threat, France's exclusive card—the *force de frappe*—was devalued, and France's nuclear preference meant that Paris lacked military freedom of action where it mattered: in the conventional domain (it was no consolation that Germany had voluntarily shackled its own freedom in this realm, since the addition of two *impuissances* left Western Europe still utterly dependent on the United States).

Fourth, the Maastricht treaty on European Union, despite its "essential conservatism," seemed to assault French sovereignty sufficiently on three points to oblige the government to ask the Constitutional Council for a judgment on its compatibility with the French Constitution. The Union was receiving the power to regulate the entry of non-EC nationals into the Community, possibly by majority rule in the future. The Monetary Union meant that France would have to give up both the franc and the theoretical autonomy of its financial policy, symbolized by the existence of a Bank of France submitted to government orientation, in exchange for a dubious share in the control of a European Central Bank that would be fully independent of governments and a carbon copy of the Bundesbank. Indeed, in order to reach the nirvana of Monetary Union, France would have to meet the highly constraining "convergence criteria" that Germany had demanded concerning inflation, interest rates, deficits, and public debts. The treaty also gave to EC nationals the right to vote in local elections and for the European Parliament in whatever country of the Community they were living: a breach in the historic French association of nationality and citizenship, in behalf of foreigners, whereas the only past dissociation — in colonies — had been at the expense of foreigners.

The Constitutional Council and the French Parliament, which had to revise the Constitution so as to make it compatible with the treaty, focused on these points (the new title XVI reduces the right of non-French EC nationals to vote and be elected to a possibility and keeps them from becoming mayors or assistant mayors). The public debate, opened by Mitterrand's decision to submit the treaty itself to the public, and not merely to Parliament, as we have seen, went far beyond this. What emerged from the sound and fury were two central issues. The first was the need to choose between two radically different conceptions of sovereignty — this trickiest of all concepts. An "absolutist" one, which happened to be deeply engraved in French culture, from the days of the Old Regime *and* the proclamation of national sovereignty, logically led to a rejection of all the *abandons* and entrapments entailed by the infernal machine of the Community, with its treaties, its technocrats, and its judges. But the cost of keeping "free hands" risked being the lack of any hands at all: monetary sovereignty had already, *de facto*, been given up, and the champions of French independence were sufficiently lucid to realize that its recovery entailed jettisoning the EMS and weakening the single market altogether. The alternative economic policy they advocated, however, by imperiling French competitiveness and the franc through inflation and deficits, was no more attractive than in 1983 and no more likely to reduce unemployment than the official course.

A pragmatic and relative notion of sovereignty looked at it not as an indivisible substance but as a bundle of competences that could be gradually pooled or transferred to common bodies, so as to substitute the efficiency of the whole for the relative inefficiency of the members. But this raised as many questions as it answered. As Gaullist senators put it in a request to the Constitutional Council,[25] which had adopted the pragmatic version in its ruling in April, "if sovereignty is no longer anything but an addition of competences, if one can successively remove them as one would the leaves of an artichoke, at what point, or at what degree, do we arrive at the heart?" — a metaphor I had used many years ago![26] (The Council declined to answer.) Also, who was collecting these leaves? A classical "international organization . . . invested with powers of decision by virtue of transfers of competences consented to it by the member-states,"[27] as the Council put it, or, as many "European" jurists see it (and contrary to the Council's opinion), a supranational entity with a "distinct juridical order" of its own both superior to and part of the juridical order of the members? When the French Parliament, before the public debate on the treaty, amended the Constitution, it carefully avoided taking sides,

[25] See footnote 12.
[26] See "Obstinate or Obsolete," in *Decline or Renewal*, p. 379.
[27] Stone, "Ratifying Maastricht," p. 74.

but it just as carefully limited the "transfer of competences" to the establishment of economic and monetary union and to the setting of rules of entry into the Community.

The second issue that dominated the public debate was the famous democratic deficit. Here again, the Rousseauistic, revolutionary, and Republican tradition weighed heavily. It attributes legitimacy only to decisions either taken by representatives of the nation, who have full legislative power, or controlled by these representatives. There is, so far, no European nation. The structure of the Community is such that decisions are taken either by "irresponsible" bureaucrats (the supranational Commission) or by ministers of the various member-states who exert jointly the Community's legislative power; even after Maastricht, which increases the European Parliament's powers, the Council will remain the main legislator and the Parliament a body that can more easily plead and remonstrate than decide and control.

Here the defenders of the treaty were at a disadvantage. They could try to argue that a "transfer of competences" was a better choice for France than a jealous defense of sovereignty because a strong collective hand is better than a weak and empty national one. But there was no way they could argue that this transfer was to a fully democratic system. If the EC was just an international organization, the question of democracy was secondary, but the effectiveness of such an entity would continue to be impaired (the French government had to reassure Parliament that the Luxembourg compromise was still valid). If the new Union was going to become what its name implied, the absence of democratic institutions was a major handicap (the two countries most responsible for this were Britain and France — logically in the former case, since Britain is now the most ardent champion of national sovereignty or rather, in Thatcherian words, the sovereignty of the British Parliament; but illogically in the French case, since it is the French government that wants the Union to have the broadest possible jurisdiction). The treaty's opponents were able to use the "democratic deficit" as a major part of their case: France, they said, was caught in an *engrenage* in which more and more decisions affecting its future were going to be taken by faceless figures operating on their own, and in which the representatives of the French people were being doubly dispossessed: by an executive that defined the European policy of France all by itself (it is true that the French Parliament has debated European policy only rarely, but it is also true that these debates were remarkably ill-attended) and by European institutions that eat up, one by one, the leaves of the national artichoke.

The debate on Maastricht also raised two broader issues, one directly, the other indirectly. The first is the relation of the French nation-state to the European Community or Union. The Community, so far, is not a classical confederation — it goes far beyond — or a federal union — it falls far short — or an ordinary international (i.e., intergovernmental) organization. The more it evolves, the more *sui generis* it becomes: its range expands, but its "supranationality" gets diluted (except insofar as the European Parliament's powers are grudgingly increased); its institutional structure becomes more byzantine, its legal homogeneity more cracked. Pooled sovereignty means, in practice, that agents of the members behave both as guardians of national interests and as European trustees. To present the Community enterprise as a zero sum game for the members is wrong: what the states "give up" is not necessarily lost, and much of what is "transferred" does not go to Brussels but to the private actors of the new European economy. Each of the members — by which I mean their governing elites — believes that, left to itself, the European small or medium-size nation-state is doomed to being less prosperous at home and less effective abroad than if it pursues the complex course of European integration.

But this is not the whole answer. What is this course leading to? It has kept advancing, despite periods of stagnation and setbacks, partly for the reason just given and partly because it has kept its ultimate configuration in the dark. Ambiguity, which preserves most alternatives, has been both the condition and the price of progress. But there is something about the French mind that resists ambiguity: the pragmatism and open-endedness of the "Monnet method" appeals more to businesspeople, and often to bureaucrats, than to lawyers, political thinkers, and intellectual politicians. De Gaulle's insistence on setting goals, on eliminating alternatives, and on prescribing policies, while it always left room for pragmatic adaptation to *les circonstances*, aimed at ruling out shackles on French hands; and the formal anxiety about being governed from Brussels barely conceals a real anguish about being dictated by Bonn (or Berlin), entrapped in a Community that would be an extension of German might rather than, as was hoped originally, French power. For even though all the European nation-states are, in dozens of ways, dependent on each other, on the world economy, and on the country that still appears to have the greatest influence in shaping the world economy — the United States — some European states have greater means of affecting their milieu than others, and the new Germany is seen as potentially the most able to do so. There exists, at present, a gnawing fear of being caught in an enterprise that either will lead to a Federation in which the nation will lose its identity as a political unit (with its political powers going both upward, to the new central institutions of the Union, and downward, to the regions) or else will result in a Baroque or Gaudiesque construction, multileveled and multispeed, manipulated above all by Germany. There is a fear that the Community is beginning to resemble much more the German model of federalism and "social market economy" than the French model of the unitary and regulatory state.

The second large issue is the relation of the French nation-state to the new global system that is now emerging. The French conception of political rule is heavily territorial: the soil and the hexagon are inseparable from French conceptions of authority. But in the new system, as many observers have noted, what one of them has, somewhat inelegantly, called "nonterritorial functional space" is developing:[28] systems of regulation that are collective and apply to specific activities across geographical space. This "unbundling of territoriality" also takes the form of unregulated transnational economic and financial transactions. Both kinds affect all nations and states, but hardest hit, of course, are those that participate least or carry least weight in the regulatory institutions or in the "transnationalized microeconomic links" and economic and financial flows and those that find it hardest to conceptualize a system not based on sharp territorial demarcation. Nations such as the United States, Japan, potentially China, perhaps Germany, although their capabilities are obviously uneven (among countries and among sectors) may be able to control the nonterritorial flows and institutions more than France. There is little solace to be found, for French men and women attached to the nation-state, in the emergence of so many new ones on the ruins of the former Soviet internal and external empire and of Yugoslavia: these are either eager to join the Community or else degenerating into economic mess and violent conflict.

However, the French predicament is one that all nation-states will face (worse is that of states that have not succeeded in becoming nations, either because, like Russia, they are still multinational, or because, like many African countries, they have failed to integrate their disparate and feuding elements). The nation-state has been a blend of cultural unity (often compatible, as in Britain, with the survival of regional cultures) and political unity; as Ernest Gellner has put it,[29] culture became the access card to citizenship and dignity. How far can these two elements be dissociated? What will happen to cultural identity if they are separated?

---

[28] John Gerard Ruggie, "Territoriality and Beyond: Problematizing Modernity in International Relations," *International Organization* 47, no. 1 (Winter 1993), 171.

[29] In *Culture, Identity and Politics* (Cambridge: Cambridge University Press, 1987), pp. 6–28.

And where should, or will, the political component of nationhood go, in this divorce?

To this last question, different countries may give different answers. Some, in Western Europe, for instance, may be quite ready for a leap into Federation, others (Switzerland, it appears) not at all. If Auguste Comte's old principle still applies — that one can only destroy what one can replace — then the nation-state, including in its political dimension, still has a bright future: there is, so far, no higher allegiance, nothing that replaces the nation as a legitimate source of social identity — even though, as Judith Shklar has pointed out,[30] the modern nation-state has so often been nothing but a war machine and a source of oppression for minorities and deviants. International institutions, although increasingly endowed with powers, remain utilitarian enterprises — they are not objects of loyalty. An entity such as the European Community is still, when it comes to allegiance, primarily a collection of cooperating national loyalties, with loyalty to "Europe" superimposed on national loyalty (just as allegiance to Britain is over, say, loyalty to Scotland) only in the rare cases of devoted Eurocrats.

It may well be that my judgment of 1965 still stands: the nation will survive, with diminished political powers, and those powers that it will keep losing or has already lost will not go to a single, concentrated higher source. The model of modern state-building out of dispersed and overlapping earlier units may not tell us anything about the future. There may well be no European Federation, at least in the foreseeable future and unless all the members of such a potential Federation are willing to begin by establishing both a genuine European electorate and an effective European Parliament; and there will be no world state. But the surviving nation-state will bear little resemblance to the Rousseauistic sovereign community, or even to the liberal, Mazzinian, or Millian, or Wilsonian model of cooperating, homogeneous nation-states. It will no longer be possible to write a purely,

[30] Unpublished remarks on nationalism.

fiercely, proudly "hexagonal" history. A world of "pooled" and "unbundled" sovereignties, in which states collectively decide on the attribution and on the use of the powers that they put in common and that they are no longer strong enough to apply effectively all by themselves — even in the military realm: this may well be the immediate future of the nation-state, the natural result of an evolution marked both by increasing interpenetration and by the continuing elusiveness of that general society of humankind whose absence Rousseau has noted — with, Todorov notwithstanding, more complacency than regret.[31]

As for French cultural identity, it has never been detachable from French political institutions and programs — it has always been tied to the state. The abandonment by the French state of many of its powers over the French economy, the "Europeanization" or "globalization" of that economy, cannot therefore fail to affect French cultural identity. The French have in the past been proud of their unique economic "balance": this was a significant component of their sense of social distinctiveness, as well as a major component of Michelet's nationalism, vis-à-vis England, and later of right-wing nationalism, especially in its anti-American incarnation. This singularity began to fade with post–World War II industrialization, urbanization, and the lowering of trade barriers. It is bound to vanish with the creation of a single European market open to the world. The very dispossession to which the state has thus consented will produce sharp reactions of national sentiment and resistance, as in the case of French farmers, and renewed demands for greater state management and control of whatever can still be managed and controlled from Paris. But insofar as the strategic, high-tech sectors of the industry are concerned, regulation will make sense only at the European level. It may be true that the more European and global economic integration intensify, the greater will be the temptation to defend and to mythologize all the remaining components, social and political, of French national

[31] Cf. T. Todorov, *Nous et les autres* (Paris: Seuil, 1989), pp. 206ff.

identity (just as global economic integration feeds the tendency of the "Eurocrats" to insist on Europe's distinctiveness — not always obvious — vis-à-vis the United States and Japan). But the nationalist reactions are more likely to be recurrent bouts of fever than returns to the dominant ideologies, policies, and practices of the self-contained past.

French national consciousness will therefore have to concentrate increasingly on such components of identity as, in the public sphere, virtues of France's constitutional system — which, despite the consensus around it, are far from uncontroversial — as well as those of France's system of social protection, and the many elements of cultural distinctiveness still provided by French education, the French intellectual tradition, whatever persists in the French style of authority, the sometimes frivolous, but permanent belief in the importance of high culture (which state policies have strengthened since André Malraux) as well as a certain art of life and leisure, a unique rapport with nature, an "agreement of earth and foot" (to quote from a character in Albert Camus's *Caligula*) — that is, what the French have done and will continue to do with the imprint of their history and of geography. What may, therefore, occur is something that would be most welcome: the end of the need Rousseau had posited: to choose between being a human being and being a citizen. The French revolutionary and Republican nationalism tried, heroically but falteringly, to bridge the gap by making of France the universal carrier of the citizen model. If the operational content of citizenship and sovereignty continues to shrink, then the emotional charge of a national feeling all too ready to veer into chauvinistic nationalism may shrink as well, despite occasional surges, and cosmopolitanism will no longer have to be either a chosen nation's "mission" or a term of insult.

It may turn out that French national identity will actually be reinforced by current churning about immigrants and about Europe and that this renewed vigor will make a more self-confident nation less hesitant to accept the transfers, losses, poolings, and dilutions that currently affect the political dimension of nationality, as well as more willing to let foreigners — and not only the nationals of other Community members — share some of the rights of citizenship.[32] This would mean a nation without the claws of nationalism — expansive or defensive — without the powerful impetus of external threat and external loss as a goad to internal conformity, without the trappings of full international sovereignty to buttress the assertion of the supremacy of the nation's claims and values.[33]

Nationalism, in French history, *has* served as a catalyst of unity, but only at certain times: in the heady confusion of a Revolution that seemed, in July 1790, to have won almost too easily — an illusion that quickly dissolved in blood — and, much more usually, in moments of war fervor. At least as often, it has been divisive. If grave external threats were to appear again — and this cannot be ruled out: the great Kantian idea of universal pacification through commerce and the evident horror of modern war remains a seductive but unrealized dream — nationalist ardor will be necessary again. The trouble is that it feeds fears of imaginary threats and magnifies existing dangers.

There are signs that the present-day French are, more or less prosaically, ready to give up the inspiring myths of universalist exceptionalism and the mythical views of their past. This is suggested, not by a turning away from their history, but by a new look at it, which is far more critical *and* objective. The dark story of Vichy, of its French roots and of its crimes, has come out of the closet; foreign historians such as Robert Paxton, who was first vilified for having opened the door, are now honored as pioneers —

---

[32] See Pierre Rosanvallon, *Le sacre du citoyen* (Paris: Gallimard, 1992), pp. 436ff.

[33] See the cogent and powerful analysis of Isaiah Berlin in his *Against the Current* (New York: Viking, 1980), pp. 327–55.

except of course on the far Right.³⁴ The dignified debate over France's responsibility for the persecution of Jews in 1940–44 — with the Resisters, understandably, denying with indignation that Vichy was France, and those who disagree pointing out that the civil servants and police who gave and carried out the evil orders had been the functionaries of the Republic — is a sign not of continuing "Franco-French warfare," but of strength. The Algerian war is also beginning to come out of the closet; it is no longer a war without a name; and this, again, is the way to overcome "the black violence of family secrets." ³⁵ A huge mass of historical publications — competing histories of France as well as fragmented examinations of all the facets of national consciousness and sensibility — shows the industry of the French historical profession, always the bellwether of French national feelings, in looking for all that may have remained hidden under unturned stones, the thirst of the public for a scrutiny of France's rich past that comforts a bruised sense of national identity without encouraging illusions, and the possibility of finding a middle course between debunking and mystifying.

The rage of commemorations noted by Pierre Nora gives a similar indication.³⁶ It isn't simply that "the emptier they are the more they succeed." It is the fact that almost every part of France's multicolored past can now be publicly remembered, including some of the shameful episodes (from the revocation of the *édit de Nantes* that threw the Protestants out of the French community to the deportation of the Jews in July 1942). The "commemoration" of 1789 was a particularly bizarre and remarkable affair. The authorities — Socialist, and therefore heirs of a tradition that sees the Revolution as a single bloc and, like Renouvier, attributes its

---

³⁴ See for instance Jean-Pierre Azéma and François Bédarida (eds.), *Vichy et les Français* (Paris: Fayard, 1992).

³⁵ Stora, *La gangrène*, p. 11. See also Jean-Pierre Rioux, *La guerre d'Algérie et les Français* (Paris: Fayard, 1990).

³⁶ In *Le Point*, February 14–21, 1993.

cruelties to the need to save France from its enemies[37]—were careful to select for celebration only the uncontroversial aspects of the Revolution (the Rights of Man), and to give show business precedence over intellectual argument. The historians, especially those who had once been Communist or *gauchisants* and had now discovered the virtues of liberal moderation, basically explained that there was nothing to celebrate: either because the Revolution was a thing of the past and it was time for the French to put it behind them or because of its "totalitarian" deviation (*dérapage*) of 1793. Only in France, perhaps, would the idea that the Revolution ended circa 1880 (an idea I don't share) cause an ideological quarrel, but what was remarkable was not the fact of the dispute, but its coolness. After the terrible, real, and recurrent "Franco-French" wars (the Revolution, the June days of 1848, the Commune, Vichy vs. the Resistance, Algeria) and the intellectual and political "wars" (such as the Dreyfus case, the Popular Front, and the battle over EDC in 1952–54 or even over Maastricht) — when the French had to decide each time what national loyalty meant and to whom or to what allegiance was due — perhaps battle fatigue will bring appeasement or a modicum of serenity. When national feeling is at a fever pitch, it usually means war, foreign or civil.

There can only be a partial, and temporary, and tentative conclusion to this interrogation, which has been both protracted and condensed. As of now, I would say that Isaiah Berlin was right when he wrote that "no political movement today . . . seems likely to succeed unless it allies itself to national sentiment" [38] — including those in the Western world. But that sentiment need not be so red-hot as to follow nationalist ideology; it may be reasonable and realize that openness, tolerance, and the acceptance of limitations of external sovereignty are both right morally and in the nation's

---

[37] *Manuel républicain de l'homme et du citoyen* (Paris: Garnier, 1981), p. 117.

[38] *Against the Current*, p. 355.

interest. A lively national sentiment remains necessary to give a people self-confidence and self-esteem; but other loyalties need not be distrusted or downgraded; in the world of the twenty-first century, cosmopolitan practices, indeed a cosmopolitan ethics that accommodates national sentiment, will be the only answer to mounting problems. In the case of France, its national identity is strong, and the French national consciousness is also vigorous, although less confident than it ought to be. French nationalism is down, if not out, and only nostalgic manifestations of it, some honorable, some ugly, are left. As for the French nation-state, if, like nostalgia, it isn't what it used to be, it is still a significant actor on the scene, whatever the constraints and the shackles, and a worthy object of interest and study. It is fitting to end with de Gaulle: France lives — "elle vit." [39]

---

[39] *Mémoires d'espoir*, p. 7.

The Archaeology of Identity

COLIN RENFREW

THE TANNER LECTURES ON HUMAN VALUES

Delivered at

Stanford University
March 31 and April 1, 1993

COLIN RENFREW was educated at St. Albans School and St. John's College, Cambridge. He was taught at the University of Sheffield between 1965 and 1972, and from 1972 to 1981 he was Professor of Archaeology and Head of the Department at the University of Southampton. In 1981 he became the Disney Professor of Archaeology and Head of the Department of Archaeology at Cambridge, and in 1986 became Master, Jesus College, Cambridge. Since 1990 he has been the Director of the McDonald Institute for Archaeological Research. His many publications include *The Emergence of Civilisation* (1972), *Problems of European Prehistory* (1979), *The Archaeology of Cult: The Sanctuary at Phylakopi* (1985), *Archaeology and Language: The Puzzle of the Indo-European Origins* (1987), and *The Cycladic Spirit* (1992). He was made a life peer in 1991 with the title Lord Renfrew of Kaimsthorn.

I. Archaeology, Language, and Genetics:
The Ingredients of Human Diversity

Allow me first to say what a great honour I consider it to be invited to deliver the Tanner Lectures for 1993 in Stanford under the general rubric "On Human Values" and to join the highly distiguished series of Tanner lecturers who have spoken under this head. You might at first be tempted to ask what the deep past, as represented by archaeology, has to do with the field of present-day human values. As usual Shakespeare had a phrase for it, in *Hamlet*, where Hamlet asks of the player, lamenting with such passion the sorrows of Hecuba, long-dead Queen of Troy:

> "What's Hecuba to him or he to Hecuba
> That he should weep for her?"

In these two lectures I shall try to remind us that the past, or at least our perception of it, does indeed shape the present, and that we all have much to weep over.

The theme of my Tanner lectures is identity. Who are we? The question can apply at the most general level: who are we as human beings? Where do we come from? What are our origins? What factors determine the human condition? Archaeology can give answers to some of these conundrums.

Comparable questions can apply at the most individual and personal level. Each of us may ask: who am I? What is particular to me, that I differ from my neighbour? What factors in our own society govern the way in which the self is determined or established? Such questions may appear at first to belong to the realm of psychology, and so they do. But when set along a time dimension of several million years they take us into the realm of cognitive archaeology. The self, or Ego, can be defined in terms of kin relationships, as social anthropologists have shown by very sophisticated studies. Or it may be determined partly in terms of ownership, wealth, and prestige. But the archaeological record shows us that wealth too has a prehistory; that in the early days of human societies there was no such thing as wealth, that there were indeed no commodities[1] — no goods recognised as of high value — by which wealth could be measured or transferred. So the answer that one gives to the question "Who am I?" — even in the most personal sense — is very much time-dependent. The archaeologist can seek to show how the various landmarks by which each of us judges our own individuality, our status, our abilities, and our potential have themselves come into being and become established over the centuries and over the generations.

But in entitling these lectures "The Archaeology of Identity" I am not seeking either on the one hand to undertake a general examination of the human condition as a universal feature of our species or on the other to focus on the role of the individual and to examine how the notion of the self has come to be constituted in modern western society. I want rather to look at human diversity and at human groups, real or imagined.

For it is a reality of our species that we divide ourselves into groups. The modern world is divided into nation-states: you cannot travel very far today without a passport, which allows you to cross the border from one state to another and which proclaims you to be the citizen of one (and usually only one) such state. But as my colleague Ernest Gellner showed in his *Nations and Nationalism*,[2] the nation-state of this kind is only about a century old, and other kinds of group division go very much earlier than this.

For many people their identity is also bound up with their religious persuasion: for many to be a Christian, or a Muslim, or a Hindu is one of the most important factors of their collective iden-

---

[1] See A. Appadurai (ed.), *The Social Life of Things* (Cambridge: Cambridge University Press, 1986).

[2] E. Gellner, *Nations and Nationalism* (Oxford: Blackwell, 1983).

tity. For many, indeed, the distinction is *within* these categories: to be a Sunni or a Shia Muslim; to be a member of the Church of England or a Branch Davidian.

Traditionally the range of human diversity has been tackled under the three rubrics of language, race, and culture, and it is certainly possible to begin the task with a review of linguistic diversity, of genetic diversity, and of cultural diversity. Indeed, these are perhaps the most important ingredients that come together to shape the whole range of communities and of collective identities that we see in the world today. In this first lecture I plan to concentrate upon these ingredients and to offer some suggestions as to how the present diversity in the world came to be as it is.

In my second lecture I shall turn towards the question of ethnicity — how specific groups of people come to be defined or to define themselves so that their collective identity becomes for them an intense reality so pressing as to become sometimes a cause, in whose name they are willing to fight, to die, and to kill.

For, if we are speaking of human values, is it not remarkable that from the raw ingredients of human diversity there emerges a widespread tendency to divide the world into Them and Us? And is it not even more remarkable that a large part of the history of most nations or communities is taken up with accounts of the hostilities, the warfare, that have taken place between Us (or our ancestors) and Them?

Nothing has saddened me more, over the past couple of years, than to see how this remains true, even in the modern world, even with developments in international law, in the emergence of the United Nations. But when we look today at what used to be Yugoslavia, we seen the hostility among Serbs, Croats, and Bosnians, former citizens of that unhappy state who should have so much in common, and we see the resurgence of that terrible doctrine that a nation (or a people) is itself a worthy cause. When the Serbs announce and implement a campaign of "ethnic cleansing" they are repeating the terrible fallacy — and it is a fallacy in the name of identity — that was perpetrated by the National Socialists of Germany during the Second World War with their own particular doctrine of Aryan supremacy.

Most wars — and certainly those wars — are in large measure about "identity," about what we may regard as misconceptions about collective identities. These misconceptions often go deep into the past, just as the real diversity among humans that they seek to categorise does indeed go deep into the past. That is the reason I believe we should all think carefully about human diversity. And then we should try to think, as a separate exercise, about the relationships between human diversity and appropriate human values. Are we justified in esteeming the group that we place ourselves in — that is to say the group called "Us" — more highly than the others, the groups called "Them"?

The question of values will appear more directly in my second lecture, when I try to consider the question of group definition, of ethnicity, with particular reference to the ancient Greeks.

Today I shall try to move away from the more directly political issues of self-identity and to look more scientifically — if one may still use that term in the "postmodern" era — at the ingredients of global diversity.

On Human Diversity

Recent work in the fields of archaeology, linguistics, and genetics suggests that a new and more coherent view, a new synthesis of the origins of human diversity, may soon emerge and that the outlines of this new synthesis may already tentatively be suggested.

Central to this new perspective will be the more sophisticated view of the nature of genetic diversity that has emerged in recent decades, strongly supported by the great flow of data that developments in molecular genetics are making available. For it is clear now that the simple and direct concept of "race" — in the sense that humankind may simply be divided into half a dozen or more discrete races — is no longer an adequate one. Maps showing gene frequency distributions across the world indicate that the patterns of variation and diversity are more complex than had earlier been realised.[3] Such maps do indeed contain much information that is relevant to the historical reconstruction of the demographic events and processes that underlie their present nature. But the story in most cases will be a more complex one than the simple narrative of a small sequence of migrations such as writers in the last century may have imagined.

New perspectives in archaeology, as well as in genetics, have an important part to play in this synthesis. For some decades now archaeologists have realised that the study of culture process involves models of thought (and the construction of theories and models) that again are considerably more complex than those of an earlier period of research, when simple migrationist explanations could be used to cover every contingency. The social and demographic processes underlying culture change have to be much more clearly and explicitly analysed. And it has to be appreciated that to correlate cultural changes with changes in the genetic composition of a population or with changes in language is no simple undertaking.

The third pillar of the new perspective comes from the field of historical linguistics. For many years it had seemed that the pattern of linguistic diversity across the world is just too complicated to permit of any meaningful analysis or explanation framed in historical terms. Of course in the early years of the nineteenth century and earlier several very simple, indeed simplistic, explanations were offered, again in migrationist terms, for the existing pattern of world languages. But these were long ago rejected by most scholars as misleading and inadequate, and rightly rejected on those grounds. It is only in the past couple of decades that the possibility has emerged of an approach that will permit the classification of the world's languages into larger groups or families that may indeed be of some historical significance.

[3] L. L. Cavalli-Sforza, A. Piazza, and P. Menozzi, *The History and Geography of Human Genes* (Princeton: Princeton University Press, in press).

The notion of classification is an important one for the new synthesis. For in most cases, historical interpretations can be shown to depend upon what are in fact classifications — that is to say, groupings that recognise and organise variability in the world in terms of similarities and differences. So the procedures of taxonomy — the science or discipline of classification — are crucial to the undertaking. And the important point soon emerges that often there is no single, obvious, "natural" classification to which we may aspire. In almost every field it is the researcher who has to take responsibility for the proposed classification. Moreover, different classifications of the same body of material are possible. In general it is not feasible to say that one is straightforwardly better than another without specifying the purpose for which the classification is to be used.

Of the three areas or dimensions of variability that we are considering — genetic, cultural, and linguistic — it is in fact the third that at the outset seems to offer itself most readily for classification. But, as we shall see, beyond the initial stage major problems soon emerge. At least, in the field of linguistics, there is some measure of agreement about the definition of the "natural" units of study — namely, languages. For whereas the separation or subdivision of population on genetic grounds into discrete units (such as "races" is now seen as a hazardous undertaking, and similar reservations are held about any "natural" division of archaeological cultures,[4] there is a good measure of agreement among linguists that individual languages may indeed be recognised, studied, and defined. Of course there is variation within languages, internal variation often being discussed in terms of "dialects." And as in any classificatory exercise, there can be discussion about the independent status of individual units and about the proper fixing of boundaries and divisions. But it is nonetheless fair to say that the division of the world's populations into perhaps 5,000 lan-

[4] C. Renfrew, *Approaches to Social Archaeology* (Edinburgh: Edinburgh University Press, 1984), p. 36.

guages is in terms of methodology less hazardous than any analogous division in overall genetic or cultural terms. The disagreement can come, as we shall see, when individual languages are classified together into language "families," especially when higher levels of classification into "macrofamilies" are attempted.

Underlying the global variability in these three fields is the emerging picture of human evolution itself. There is a general agreement that the earliest hominids, designated the genus *Australopithecus*, emerged in Africa some 4 million years ago and that it was there that the evolution of *Homo erectus* occurred some 1.6 million years ago, with a subsequent dispersal of that species out of Africa and also into Europe and Asia. Our own species, *Homo sapiens sapiens*, undoubtedly evolved from our *Homo erectus* ancestor more than 100,000 years ago. Probably the majority of archaeologists see that crucial transition as taking place within Africa,[5] followed by the dispersal, out of Africa, of our own species to Western Asia, to Europe, to central and eastern Asia, to Australia, and (across the Bering Strait) to the Americas. But there is at present an alternative view that sees the evolution from *Homo erectus* to *Homo sapiens sapiens* taking place over a much wider area, not just in Africa but in southeast and eastern Asia and perhaps elsewhere.[6] This is relevant to our story, for while all current human genetic diversity can undoubtedly be traced back to African populations of *Homo erectus*, the same may not be true for African populations of *Homo sapiens sapiens* as universal ancestor.

Language Families and Their Origins

In the year 1786 Sir William Jones, then serving as a judge at the High Court in Calcutta and a student of the ancient languages

[5] C. B. Stringer and P. Andrews, "Genetic and Fossil Evidence for the Origin of Modern Humans," *Science* 239 (1988), 1263–68.

[6] M. H. Wolpoff, "Multiregional Evolution: The Fossil Alternative to Eden," in P. Mellars and C. B. Stringer (eds.), *The Human Revolution: Behavioural and Biological Perspectives of the Origins of Modern Humans*, vol. 1 (Edinburgh: Edinburgh University Press, 1989), pp. 62–108.

of India, made an interesting observation. He noticed that the Sanskrit language, in which the earliest literary and religious texts of India are written, could be compared with many of the early languages of Europe, notably Greek and Latin, as well as old Persian. These resemblances were not only in the field of vocabulary, the lexicon (where there were resemblances between the forms of words in different languages that held the same meaning), but also in the morphology (such as the conjugation of verbs) and in other ways. And he made his famous pronouncement that the Sanskrit language had a stronger affinity to Greek and Latin,

> both in the roots of verbs and in the forms of grammar, than could possibly have been produced by accident; so strong indeed that no philologer could examine them all three, without believing them to have sprung from some common source.[7]

In making this observation, Jones accomplished a number of advances. First, he began to define the ways in which relationships between different languages might systematically be studied. Second, he indicated that it was possible to group such related languages together into what we would today call a language family. Third, he gave a very good outline of what subsequently came to be called the Indo-European family. And fourth, he indicated the likely explanation for the family resemblances: that each member of the language family was the descendant of a hypothetical ancestral language or proto-language.

Each of these ideas was highly influential, and many other language families have now been recognised, although the most thoroughly studied remains Indo-European. As Jones saw, this includes most of the languages of present-day Europe (with the notable exceptions of Hungarian, Estonian, and Basque) as well as those of Iran and much of north India and Pakistan. The Indo-

---

[7] Sir William Jones, Third Anniversary discourse, "On the Hindus," reprinted in *The Collected Works of Sir William Jones III* (London: John Stockdale, 1807), pp. 23–46.

European language family is thus spoken over very wide areas, even before one takes into account its spread to the Americas, to Australia, and to other regions during the European colonial expansion since the fifteenth century A.D. In some other parts of the world, however, several language families together occupy a much smaller area. New Guinea, for instance, is the home of no fewer than twelve families.

For Jones, and for most of those who followed him, it seemed clear that the living languages constituting a family were all the descendants of the proto-language, which must have been spoken at some earlier time in some specific homeland area. Obviously, the determination of that area would be a problematic matter once one started to inquire into periods before the origins of writing systems, the earliest of which emerged in the Near East shortly before 3000 B.C. But successive generations of Indo-European linguists have developed the comparative method, by which the affinities and resemblances in the existing (daughter) languages are systematically studied, so that the ancestral proto-language may be reconstructed and the various rules for sound changes and for other systematic patternings established by which the evolution of the descendant languages could be understood. The underlying principle here is one of divergence: groups of language speakers who become physically separated come to differ progressively in their speech, so that over time distinct languages emerge where previously there had been only dialectal variation. This process of linguistic divergence may be compared with the phenomenon of genetic drift in genetics.[8]

This pattern of descent from a common ancestor can readily be arranged in "family tree" form, in much the same way that the followers of Darwin arranged the evolution of the various animals and plants of the world. But it should be noted that other kinds of explanation would theoretically be conceivable. It would, for

[8] M. Slatkin, "Gene Flow and the Geographic Structure of Natural Populations," *Science* 236 (1987), 787–92.

instance, be possible to emphasise "convergence" processes, which are perhaps more common in linguistic than in genetic evolution. The borrowing of words between adjacent but not otherwise related languages is a well-understood phenomenon, as are "area effects" by which grammatical and phonological features come to be shared. The Russian linguist N. S. Trubetzkoy went so far as to propose (in a paper that very few linguists acknowledge today as plausible) that the family resemblances might be explained as the product of convergence among previously unrelated languages, rather than divergence from a common ancestor.[9] But most linguists have followed Sir William Jones's insight that they "have sprung from some common source."

The field of linguistic classification is, however, a difficult one, if one proceeds beyond the initial recognition of individual languages and then their classification into families on the basis of very strong resemblances. For, as noted above, some language families (like Indo-European) are spoken over very wide areas, while in some more restricted regions, such as New Guinea or the Caucasus, languages belonging to several families are spoken. The American linguist Johanna Nichols has recently written suggestively of "spread zones" and "residual zones" for these two cases with the clear implication that different historical processes have been at work in each,[10] a suggestion to which we shall soon turn. But it is worth emphasising that if one looks at any world map of languages one will see areas assigned to language families — like Indo-European or Afroasiatic — about which there is very wide consensus among linguists. Other areas have classifications — such as "Indo-Pacific" for many of the languages of New Guinea — that do not indicate a single language family, but rather a whole series of juxtaposed families that do not necessarily share a common ancestor.

[9] N. S. Trubetzkoy, "Gedanken über das Indogermanenproblem," *Acta Linguistica* 1 (1939), 81–89.

[10] J. Nichols, *Linguistic Diversity in Time and Space* (Chicago: Chicago University Press, 1992), pp. 13–24.

At this point it is necessary to refer to the vexed question of the possibility of achieving larger and more inclusive groupings, whereby entire language families themselves may be grouped together and recognised as "macrofamilies." One pioneer of this approach was the Russian scholar Illich Svitych, who made a systematic study of what has been termed the Nostratic family (or macrofamily), in which he included the Indo-European family, the Afroasiatic family, the Dravidian languages of India, the Altaic language family, the Kartvelian (South-Caucasian) languages, and the Uralic-Yukaghir language family.[11] His work has been carried forward by Aharon Dolgopolsky.[12] In their studies they follow the comparative method of the Indo-European linguists in reconstructing the proto-language (Nostratic) and in formulating the various rules for sound change for the descent of the daughter families. Despite this, their work has been criticised by many scholars as speculative.[13]

The American linguist Joseph Greenberg has been the most ambitious advocate of the macrofamily approach. In 1963 he produced a major new classification of the languages of Africa,[14] which he was able to assign to just four major language families (or macrofamilies). It should be noted, however, that he did not attempt in each case to reconstruct the ancestral proto-language, but operated rather on a basis of "multilateral comparison," by which he compared words in several languages at a time, rather than proceeding to consider two languages at a time as most of his predecessors have done. Today his African classification is very

[11] V. M. Illich Svitych, *A Comparison of Nostratic Languages* (Moscow: n.p., 1976–84).

[12] A. B. Dolgopolsky, "Boreische-Ursprache Eurasiens?" *Ideen des Exacten Wissenschaft und Technik in der Sovietunion* 73 (1973), 19–30; idem, "The Indo-European Homeland and Other Lexical Contacts of Proto-Indo-European with Other Languages," *Mediterranean Language Review* 3 (1987), 7–31.

[13] A. Morpurgo Davies, "Comments on C. Renfrew, Models of Change in Language and Archaeology," *Transactions of the Philological Society* 87 (1989), 156–71.

[14] J. H. Greenberg, *The Languages of Africa* (Bloomington: Indiana University Press, 1963).

FIGURE 1. World linguistic diversity: the distribution of the world's major language families as classified by Merritt Ruhlen. 1: Khoisan, 2: Niger-Kordofanian, 3: Nilo-Saharan, 4: Afroasiatic, 5: Caucasian, 6: Indo-European, 7: Uralic-Yukaghir, 8: Altaic, 9: Chukchi-Kamchatkan, 10: Eskimo-Aleut, 11: Elamo-Dravidian, 12: Sino-Tibetan, 13: Austric, 14: "Indo-Pacific," 15: Australian, 16: Na-Dene, 17: "Amerind."

widely used, and there is little doubt that the Afroasiatic language family and the Niger-Kordofanian language family are valid classificatory units. It is possible, however, that the Khoisan family may not represent languages that are all descended from a common ancestor, but that, as has been suggested for the Indo-Pacific languages, the relationship is geographical (involving elements of convergence) rather than historical. More recently Greenberg has applied his multilateral approach to the language of the Americas,[15] producing three major groupings. The first two, Eskimo-Aleut and Na-Dene, have won widespread acceptance, but the third, "Amerind," which includes all the languages of South and Central America as well as many in North America, has been much criticised by many American linguists.[16] Yet the case that he has set out is, at least to the nonspecialist, an impressive one, even if it has not yet won general acceptance.

The map (fig. 1) illustrating the world's major language families is by Merritt Ruhlen, from his very systematic study,[17] which draws heavily upon the work of Greenberg. In view of the controversy over the status of "Amerind" as a valid category, as well as that of "Indo-Pacific," I have chosen to put those terms in quotation marks in the caption. Like all such maps this is a composite, showing a number of generally accepted families (e.g., Indo-European, Afroasiatic), others that are still open to discussion (like those of southeast Asia or Uralic-Yukaghir), and others that are, as just indicated, widely disputed. In the discussion that follows this classification is not accepted uncritically. But it is a useful starting point for a consideration of world linguistic diversity. For, as we shall see, it allows us to go on, using the lessons of

[15] J. H. Greenberg, *Language in the Americas* (Stanford: Stanford University Press, 1987).

[16] L. Campbell, review of J. H. Greenberg, *Language in the Americas*, *Language* 64 (1988), 591–615.

[17] M. Ruhlen, *A Guide to the World's Languages, 1* (Stanford: Stanford University Press, 1987); idem, *A Guide to the World's Languages, 1, Classification*, with postscript (Stanford: Stanford University Press, 1991).

recent archaeological research and of molecular genetics, to consider how that diversity might have come about.

Culture Process and Human Diversity

Until the beginning of the present century, and indeed for some time after, the prevailing view of prehistoric change — whether in the genetic, the cultural, or the linguistic field — was essentially a migrationist one. The explanation for new features in any early context was generally taken to be the arrival of new groups of people — in other words, a prehistoric migration. This view appeared sanctioned by biblical accounts of many historical events, not least the departure of the sons of Noah and their followers in different directions after the Flood, establishing, as later scholars argued, the Semitic, the Hamitic, and the Japhetic language families, respectively. The scholarly task then seemed to be the recognition of some material indicators — characteristic artefact forms or types of pottery decoration — by which the paths of these migrations might be recognised, and the migrants traced back to their original homeland.

The now conventional view of Indo-European origins took shape, essentially along these lines, in the nineteenth century and was elaborated systematically by Gordon Childe in the 1920s.[18] Ingenious and plausible arguments based on the vocabulary of the reconstructed proto-Indo-European language, insofar as it related to the natural environment, suggested a possible origin in the steppe lands of South Russia and the Ukraine, immediately north of the Black Sea. It was suggested that migrations took place out of this homeland area at about the beginning of the bronze age and that mounted nomad warriors moved westwards, bringing with them proto-Indo-European speech to Europe. The artefacts most characteristic of these groups were pottery vessels made of corded ware, along with battle axes, and further west drinking

[18] V. G. Childe, *The Aryans, A Study of Indo-European Origins* (London: Kegan Paul, Trench and Trubner, 1926).

vessels known as beakers. These objects were often found in characteristic circular burial mounds or barrows, of the kind known in the Russian steppe lands as kurgans. Very much this view has been advocated and elaborated over the past thirty years by Marija Gimbutas,[19] and the case for linking the supposed kurgan migrations with Indo-European language origins has been ably summarised by J. P. Mallory.[20]

Unfortunately, there are several arguments against this rather simplistic migrationist view. The most obvious is that there is no good archaeological evidence for such migrations taking place, although some local movements are perfectly possible, and it is indeed likely that nomad pastoral economies, following their development in the Pontic steppe lands, did indeed become more influential in parts of eastern Europe for a while around this time. There is, moreover, good evidence that the horse was first domesticated in the steppe lands prior to the beginning of the bronze age. But most European archaeologists see the development of the beakers, with their prominent burials and accompanying prestige goods, as the result of local social developments within western Europe and as a product of the establishment of new communication networks, rather than as a result of the advent of new populations.

The second counterargument is that there is no clear reason why there should have been a sudden surge of migrations out of this region. Certainly the newly developed pastoral economy was an effective one for the steppe lands, but there is no reason why it should have supplanted the already well-established farming economy in the arable lands to the west. The emphasis in the kurgan

---

[19] M. Gimbutas, "Proto-Indo-European Culture: The Kurgan Culture during the 5th to the 3rd Millennium B.C.," in G. Cardona, H. M. Hoenigswald, and A. Senn (eds.), *Indo-European and Indo-Europeans* (Philadelphia: University of Pennsylvania Press, 1970), pp. 155–98; *idem*, "The Three Waves of the Kurgan Peoples into Old Europe," in *Archives suisses d'anthropologie générale* 43 (1979), 113–17.

[20] J. P. Mallory, *In Search of the Indo-Europeans* (London: Thames and Hudson, 1989).

theory upon warrior horsemen is entirely misplaced, since there is no evidence for the use of horses in warfare until about a thousand years later — and then they were first used to pull chariots and only subsequently to support mounted warriors.

Archaeology today tends to use what has been called a "processual" approach, with the emphasis upon economic, social, and demographic processes in society, rather than on dramatic historical events, such as migrations. The old equation between particular tribes or ethnic groups and specific artefacts is no longer accepted, and to look instead in the archaeological record for evidence of processes of change that might accompany linguistic change seems much more reasonable.

A systematic consideration of the various processes by which the language spoken in a given territory may come to change suggests that there are four major categories.[21] The first is the evident one of initial colonisation. Obviously, if a given area has not previously supported a human population, the first inhabitants, however small their number, will be responsible for introducing the language spoken. Second, there is divergence as discussed earlier, whereby languages come to grow more unlike each other with the passage of time. Third, there are convergence processes, like those discussed by Trubetzkoy, although these have not been favoured by linguists in their discussion of the origins of language families. And finally there is the important phenomenon of language replacement, whereby the language originally spoken in the area comes to be replaced by another.

The most obvious example of language replacement would indeed be offered by prehistoric migration — for example, the arrival of mounted nomad warriors from the east. But here it is important to note that language replacement can take place in a number of ways that we must consider a little further.

---

[21] C. Renfrew, "Models of Change in Language and Archaeology," *Transactions of the Philological Society* 87 (1989), 103-55.

The first is *elite dominance*, where the incoming elite (sometimes no doubt in the form of mounted warriors) from a nearby region invade the area in question and displace the existing elite, thereby taking over the effective control of power. In some cases the language of the incoming elite may come to dominate and to exclude the preexisting language, even though the incomers are effectively, by definition, a minority group of the total population. But it should be noted that this model assumes the preexistence of an elite group (the invaders) and also of an elite group in the society in question. Both societies therefore must have some kind of ranked or stratified social system, traces of which we can expect to see in the archaeological record.

It should be noted that in Europe it was not really until the iron age (around 1000 B.C.) that powerful chiefdoms or other elite-dominated social groups are widely seen, although certainly there were some ranked societies in the European bronze age, notably in Mycenaean Greece. But it is doubtful if there were already elites of sufficient prominence in Europe (or in the steppes) at the beginning of the bronze age for the elite dominance explanation to be a good one in this case.

The second process by which language displacement can occur is the emergence of a *lingua franca*, generally through the development of intensive trading links. With these links there can come the emergence of a trade language or "pidgin," which serves as a common means of communication all the way along the trade route, in areas that formerly were very linguistically diverse. In favourable circumstances the pidgin can become a creole — that is to say, the inherited first language or mother tongue for many along the trade route. One can imagine how in some circumstances this could come to be a prevailing language over a considerable area.

The third process for linguistic replacement within a given territory is *system collapse*. Here the social and economic changes taking place following the failure and collapse of a state society allow populations at the periphery to move in. With these quite localised movements there can come linguistic change. This is much the scenario generally imagined for the Migration Period in Europe north of the Alps after the collapse of the Roman Empire. But it would hardly be applicable to Europe at an earlier period.

The fourth model for language replacement, and the one that it seems appropriate to stress here, is the *subsistence/demography* model. Here emphasis is laid upon a new technology, or upon some other innovation of adaptive significance, that makes one group of people more effective than another. The most obvious case is that of the inception of farming. In general, farming populations can live in a given environment at a much higher population density than can hunter-gatherers. Where there is a greater productive efficiency, there is often scope for population increase and later and in consequence for local outward movements of people as a result of demographic pressure. As A. J. Ammerman and L. L. Cavalli-Sforza have shown,[22] in these circumstances the gradual propagation of the new adaptive economy can result in a "wave of advance," whereby increase of population leads to a gradual spread. The example they discussed was the spread of farming across Europe at the beginning of the neolithic period. I have suggested that it was this process that was responsible for the spread of the proto-Indo-European language across Europe, since only at this time was there a demographic and economic change, seen right across Europe, that was of sufficient significance to spread a new language (or proto-language) across an entire continent.

These, then, are some of the models that current archaeological thinking suggests may be appropriate for a more systematic consideration in historical terms of the roots of linguistic diversity.

---

[22] A. J. Ammerman and L. L. Cavalli-Sforza, "A Population Model for the Diffusion of Early Farming in Europe," in C. Renfrew (ed.), *The Explanation of Culture Change: Models in Prehistory* (London: Duckworth, 1973), pp. 335-58.

It should be noted that each of these models offers ample scope for archaeological documentation (or refutation) in any particular case. Archaeology today is good at reconstructing past diets and at following the development of farming in any area. It is good at isolating the evidence for the collapse of early state societies (when such collapses occurred). It is effective in studying early trade routes, and effective also in the study of ranked societies and the recognition of elites. Moreover, radiocarbon dating very often today offers the opportunity of dating such changes rather precisely. What is of course very much less certain is the linkage that one would wish to establish between the archaeological evidence and the linguistic. It is upon that argument that the nub of the matter sometimes rests.

In the Indo-European case I have argued that the so-called kurgan invasions are largely illusory and that attention should be directed instead at the much earlier period (some three thousand years before) when farming developed in Europe.[23] The archaeological evidence is abundant for this topic, and it leaves little doubt that the essential domesticates — wheat, barley, sheep, and goat — came first to Europe (to Greece) from Anatolia. I would argue therefore that it is from this area that the first proto-Indo-European speakers came to Europe and thus that some sort of pro-Indo-European language was spoken in central Anatolia some nine or ten thousand years ago. Most archaeologists would agree that there was indeed a "wave of advance," very much as argued by the Ammerman/Cavalli-Sforza model, from southeast Europe along the Danube into central and towards north Europe. But M. Zvelebil and K. V. Zvelebil have stressed that the contribution of the indigenous population to the development of the new economy should not be forgotten,[24] and that component was clearly of significance. Nonetheless, the argument seems to me for the Indo-

[23] C. Renfrew, *Archaeology and Language: The Puzzle of Indo-European Origins* (London: Jonathan Cape, 1987).

[24] M. Zvelebil and K. V. Zvelebil, "Agricultural Transition and Indo-European Dispersals," *Antiquity* 62 (1988), 57–83.

European question a valid one, at least in its broad outlines.[25] We can now go on to see that the general approach may well apply very much more widely.

Explaining World Linguistic Diversity

The foregoing discussion clears the way for a return to the specific features of human diversity, seen in geographic terms. For I shall suggest that, using the archaeological perspective developed in the preceding consideration, it is possible to propose an outline historical sequence that will account for the pattern of language families as they are distributed in the world today. Moreover, the genetic evidence can be called into play to give some possibility of testing whether the proposals, made initially on archaeological and linguistic grounds, are borne out by the further category of evidence.

As I see it, the pattern of the world's languages today may be explained in terms of four principal processes, with linguistic divergence and in other circumstances convergence also always at work in the background. The first process is initial colonisation. The second process represents a late phase of initial colonisation in northern areas following the conclusion of the last ice age. The third process is elite dominance, which seems of paramount significance only in one or two cases. And the fourth and particularly important process is that of farming dispersal, a special case of the subsistence/demography model.

Farming dispersal has emerged recently as a process of widespread significance for the discussion of the distribution of a number of language families. Its role in promoting the dissemination of the Indo-European languages has been briefly outlined above. And I have suggested that a closely comparable case may be made for the Afroasiatic languages, for the Dravidian languages, and for the Altaic languages, with a different part of the nuclear farm-

---

[25] A. Dolgopolsky, "More about the Indo-European Homeland Problem," *Mediterranean Language Review* 6 (1993, in press).

ing area of the Near East acting as the homeland area for each.²⁶ Such a proposal would tie in very well with the suggestion emerging from the Nostratic hypothesis that all these languages are related within a single macrofamily.

The role of farming and of new technology in the spread of the Bantu languages has been made by a number of scholars (the Bantu languages form an important part of the Niger-Kordofanian languages of fig. 1).²⁷ Peter Bellwood, in a series of major articles, has stressed the importance of agriculture in a number of the world's language families, most particularly the Austronesian languages, including Polynesian.²⁸ And Charles Higham has recently made the case with great clarity for the Austroasiatic languages of southeast Asia, linking the dissemination of these with the dispersal of rice cultivation.²⁹

In each instance the logic of the argument is the same.³⁰ There are several areas in the world where indigenous wild plants (and sometimes animals) have been successfully domesticated. In each case this local development of farming has offered the opportunity for a settled way of life, with a greater population density and a greater intensity of production per unit area. When the farming "package" of plant and animal domesticates, along with the skills to exploit them, has proved to be suitable for transference to new ecological niches, then this has emerged as a very expansive

[26] C. Renfrew, "Before Babel: Speculations on the Origins of Linguistic Diversity," *Cambridge Archaeological Journal* 1 (1991), 3–23.

[27] D. W. Phillipson, "Archaeology and Bantu Linguistics," *World Archaeology* 8 (1976), 65–82; idem, "The Spread of the Bantu Languages," *Scientific American* 236 (1977), 106–14.

[28] P. Bellwood, "Foraging towards Farming: A Decisive Transition or a Millennial Blur?" *Review of Archaeology* 11–12 (1990), 14–24; idem, "The Austronesian Dispersal and the Origins of Languages," *Scientific American* 265 (1991), 88–93; idem, "Prehistoric Cultural Explanations for Widespread Language Families," paper delivered to the conference Archaeology and Linguistics: Understanding Ancient Australia, Darwin, July 8–12, 1991.

[29] C. Higham, unpublished paper.

[30] C. Renfrew, "Archaeology, Genetics and Linguistic Diversity," *Man* 27 (1992), 445–78.

economy. This offers a paradigm case, then, of the subsistence/ demography model for language replacement discussed earlier. In some cases there was indeed a kind of "wave of advance" that carried population increase, the new farming economy, and a new language over large areas. Figure 2 gives a sketch indication of some of the cases where farming dispersal appears to have taken place and has probably been accompanied, to a significant extent, by language replacement.

Certainly there are other areas where a local transition to farming has not in fact proved to be particularly expansive. This seems to be so for New Guinea, where very early cultivation was not accompanied by any striking outward expansion. The explanation here may be in part ecological and geographical: there is no major neighbouring land mass with climatic conditions suitable for the propagation of cultivation of New Guinea type (although the

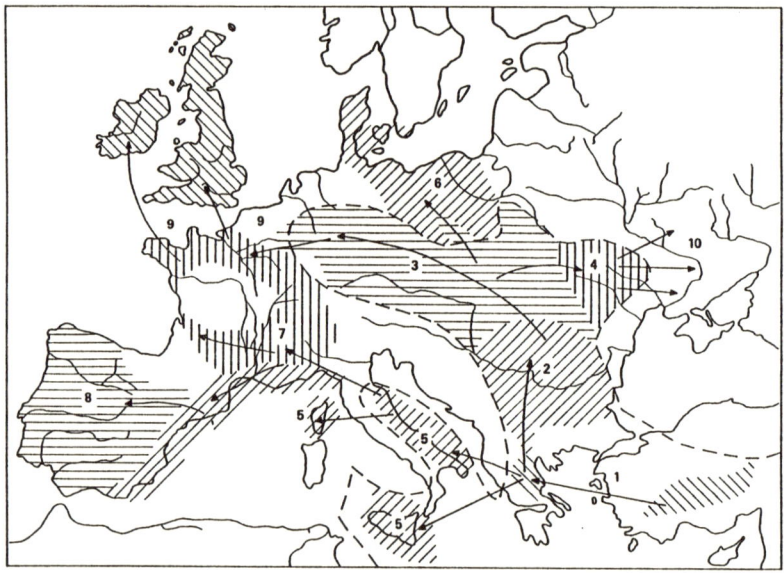

FIGURE 2. Farming dispersals in Europe and the spread of proto-Indo-European languages. Episodes 1 to 5 by demic diffusion (ca. 6500–5000 B.C.). Succeeding episodes involved both local movements of farmers and the acculturation of indigenous population.

precise conditions militating against its propagation to north Australia are still under discussion). Likewise, the early cultivation of plants in Peru does not seem to have been followed by any very rapid and widespread outward expansion. But the Peruvian case is complicated by the extreme altitude range, so that within a few miles there can be a very considerable range of ecological variability.

Armed with some insight into the considerable significance globally of processes of farming dispersal, it is possible to offer a very hypothetical account of a possible sequence of events through which the present configuration of diversity in the world may have come about.[31]

1. In the first place were *initial colonisation* processes, from about 100,000 years ago onwards. On the "out of Africa" model for our species, these would involve the radiation of the human species from Africa to Asia and beyond from that early time. There is evidence for *Homo sapiens sapiens* in Australia earlier than 40,000 years ago, and plausible but as yet unconfirmed indications of a very much earlier occupation in parts of South America some 20,000 years earlier. But it is not central to my argument that the colonisation of America took place so early, nor indeed that the developmental process for our species took place exclusively in Africa, although this does seem likely.

What we can suggest is that the Khoisan languages of Africa (whether or not together constituting a valid macrofamily) have occupied the space that they now occupy in Africa since the early development and colonisation phase, which there may well be some 100,000 years ago. Likewise, the Australian, "Indo-Pacific," and "Amerind" language areas (whether or not the terms denote valid macrofamilies) are likewise the result of initial peopling

---

[31] For a fuller discussion, see C. Renfrew, "World Languages and Human Dispersals: A Minimalist View," in J. A. Hall and I. C. Jarvie (eds.), *Transition to Modernity: Essays on Wealth, Power and Belief* (Cambridge: Cambridge University Press, 1992), pp. 11–68.

during the Pleistocene period. And of course many other areas of the globe will have been populated at that time, although the linguistic traces have often been obliterated by language replacement processes. The languages of the Caucasus and the isolated Basque language of north Spain may well be isolated pockets that survive from this early colonisation phase.

2. Processes of *farming dispersal* then represent the next major phase. They have been discussed briefly above (and are indicated in fig. 2), so that it may not be necessary to review them further here. Their contribution is, however, crucial to the picture. For the distribution of languages in the world today is emphatically not one of simple initial colonisation plus ensuing processes of divergence (and some convergence) as a result of nearly 100,000 years of consolidation in place. On the contrary, it is the very much more recent processes of farming dispersal, all in the past 10,000 years, that have made the greatest impact upon the world map.

3. At the end of the Pleistocene period, some 10,000 years ago, new climatic conditions prevailed, allowing the *late initial colonisation of northern areas* previously not inhabitable. So it is from that time that a number of northern language families date (Uralic-Yukaghir, Chukchi-Kamchatkan, Eskimo-Aleut, Na-Dene).

4. *Elite dominance* replacements are perhaps surprisingly rare, when viewed from this global perspective of language families, although of course within families there will be many cases where the locations of individual languages were determined by elite dominance processes. One of the most prominent elite dominance cases, interestingly, not only applies to the Indo-European case but was probably dependent upon mounted nomads, very much as the traditional view criticised here had maintained. But in this case it is the eastern Indo-European languages (that is to say, the Indo-Iranian languages) that are involved. A second major case is the analogous one of the Altaic languages. There initial distribution may well have been determined by the development first of farm-

ing and then of simple nomad pastoralism. But the development of mounted warfare some time after 1,000 B.C. must have had a very significant effect upon the steppe lands of Central Asia, and it is to that process that the present distribution of the Altaic languages (extending as far west as Turkey) must be attributed. Finally, the modern distribution of the Sino-Tibetan languages is dependent not only upon the farming dispersal processes of the neolithic and bronze age, but also upon elite dominance, whereby southern China came under imperial control in the Han and later periods.

5. And finally, in this review of the main phases of linguistic change, one must mention again the great colonial expansions of the past 400 years. Spanish and Portuguese are now among the dominant languages of Central and South America, and English in North America and Australia and other areas, while French and German and Dutch also have had their place in colonial history.

This brief and hypothetical outline offers what may prove to be an approximation of the sequence of processes that have shaped the language map of the world into its present form. It should be noted that there are cultural as well as linguistic implications.

First, the expansionist languages of the past five centuries have all been Indo-European. For it is historically the case that the colonial expansion was centred in Europe.

Second, it is the case that urban communities have in general spoken languages belonging to those families whose distributions belong to phase 2, the episode of farming expansion. But that is not a surprising observation, since urban civilisation nearly always rests upon a firm agricultural base. Ancient Egyptian was an Afroasiatic language, and most of the early civilisations of the Near East spoke Semitic languages (with the notable exception of Sumerian). Hittite, of course, was an Indo-European language, along with Greek and Roman (but probably not Etruscan). The Chinese civilisation and languages likewise developed within a farming context.

One notable exception to this general rule is offered by the Altaic languages, but the civilisation of the Mongols was based upon mobility, and this was a very special case. The situation is a little more complicated in the Americas, however, since the early farming practices there were less expansionist in their nature.

The Evidence from Genetics

This clear (if still entirely tentative) historical sequence can now be brought into relationship with the genetic evidence. Already a number of useful studies have focussed upon some aspect of the vast range of human diversity in order to illuminate possible correlations with linguistic groups.

At present the molecular genetic evidence comes essentially from the study of samples (often blood samples) derived from living and recent populations. There is indeed the hope that improved extractive and analytical techniques, probably based upon the polymerase chain reaction, will allow the study of the genetic composition of very much older human samples obtained from archaeological excavation. Obviously the whole study will benefit greatly from the time depth that such procedures might allow, and there is good hope that this will indeed prove feasible. Already useful nucleotide sequences have been obtained from tissue from an Egyptian mummy and from other ancient specimens.

At present, however, most of the relevant data come from studies of living populations. Such studies obviously tell us in the first place about the present rather than about the past. But there are several ways in which inferences about the past can quite plausibly be made using these modern samples.

The first and most obvious approach is to use gene frequency maps based upon data for blood groups and other polymorphisms. A very considerable body of data is now available, drawn from biochemical studies conducted upon a good sample of human populations around the world, and for many years these have been used to produce maps, each showing on a global scale the variation in the frequency of occurrence of a particular gene. The interpretation of such maps is not easy, since the patterns they depict are rarely simple. Some of the changes may be adaptive, reflecting, for instance, responses to different climatic conditions. But the genes that are likely to be of the greatest historical interest are those that change only very slowly over time. These are the ones that are not actively selected for or against. A very good example, the distribution of the Rhesus negative gene, has been discussed by A. E. Mourant and by L. L. Cavalli-Sforza.[32] This is a simpler map than many, and it shows a high frequency of occurrence of Rhesus negative in northern Spain, in very much the areas where the Basque language is spoken today. It is tempting to suggest a causal connection between the two and to suggest that a high Rhesus negative frequency was a characteristic of the original population in this area, ancestral to the modern Basque speakers. As noted above, Basque is not an Indo-European language, and it is possible that its ancestor was indeed spoken very much more widely in western Europe before the advent of the first Indo-European-speaking farmers at the onset of the neolithic. Such an argument makes perfectly good sense in genetic terms.

Most gene frequency maps do not, however, lend themselves to so clear an explanation. Indeed, they often show complex patterns of variation that are no doubt the result of a whole series of processes that have affected the genetic composition of the population over the years.

A more sophisticated approach is to use quite elaborate statistical techniques to pool the information used in the maps for the various genes and to seek to draw composite conclusions, rather than working with just one map at a time. Robert Sokal and his colleagues have done precisely this for the gene frequency maps

---

[32] A. E. Mourant, A. C. Kopec, and K. Domaniewska-Sobczak, *The Distribution of the Human Blood Groups* (Oxford: Oxford University Press, 1976); L. L. Cavalli-Sforza, "The Basque Population and Ancient Migrations in Europe," *Munibe (Antrop. Arqueol. Supl.)* 6 (1988), 129–37.

of Europe, undertaking a principal components analysis.[33] They found that the first (most important) component did indeed show a cline from southeast Europe towards the northwest. Such a pattern would be consistent with a significant genetic input at some time from the southeast, and they have interpreted this as supporting the view that there was indeed a major episode of demic diffusion, probably to be associated with the coming of farming to Europe from Anatolia some 8,000 years ago. This does not in itself prove that those first immigrant farmers spoke a proto-Indo-European language, as I have suggested, but it does at least serve to corroborate that the coming of farming to Europe was indeed a process with significant demographic consequences, and to this extent it is in harmony with the farming dispersal explanation offered here for the Indo-European language family.

Comparable statistical studies on a geographically wider scale have been undertaken by Guido Barbujani and his colleagues, who find some support for the spread of farming outwards from other areas of the Near East with comparable demographic consequences.[34] These could, as I have suggested, be associated with the diffusion of the Afroasiatic, Elamo-Dravidian, and Altaic language families.

The genetic data from living populations need not, however, be analysed solely by geographic analyses of this kind. Another very interesting approach has been to bring together genetic and linguistic data at an earlier stage, and to "label" each molecular sample with the language or language family appropriate to the donor. As noted earlier, it is possible to develop a classification of the samples, based on the similarity or dissimilarity of the genetic patterning obtained for each, and then to produce a classi-

---

[33] R. R. Sokal, N. L. Oden, and A. C. Wilson, "New Genetic Evidence Supports the Origin of Agriculture in Europe by Demic Diffusion," *American Journal of Physical Anthropology* 80 (1991), 21–38.

[34] G. Barbujani and A. Pilastro, "Genetic Evidence on Origin and Dispersal of Human Populations Speaking Languages of the Nostratic Macrofamily," *Proceedings of the National Academy of Sciences of the USA* 90 (1993, in press).

ficatory tree (a phenetic dendrogram) to illustrate it. In some circumstances it is reasonable to suggest that the classificatory tree (which is, of course, based upon observations made in the present) may well approximate the hypothetical evolutionary family tree for the genetic feature under consideration.

Cavalli-Sforza and his colleagues have offered an ambitious classification, based upon the genetic evidence (from classical genetic markers) for human populations in different parts of the world, identified in terms of the language family to which the sample donors belonged.[35] This tree is in many respects in harmony with the outline history set out here in the last section, supporting the view that there was an initial dispersal of our species out of Africa (probably rather more than 100,000 years ago) and a subsequent initial colonisation process such as I have outlined above. Very significantly, the populations that, following the discussions above of farming dispersals, one would expect to be closely related genetically *are* in most cases shown to be closely related. This pioneering exercise will have to be carried through in very much greater detail, and it would be premature at present to draw sweeping conclusions from the apparent corroboration by the genetic data of the picture that I have outlined. What this early exercise does, however, show is that the modern genetic data can indeed be brought to bear fruitfully upon the issue in this kind of way.

At this point also one should mention the great possibilities offered by the very precise sequencing of nuclear DNA and of mitochondrial DNA that has now become possible. Here the analysis is undertaken upon a sample from a human individual, and the tree of similarities and differences that is compiled as a result of the analyses is a tree showing relationships between se-

---

[35] L. L. Cavalli-Sforza, A. Piazza, P. Menozzi, and J. Mountain, "Reconstruction of Human Evolution: Bringing Together Genetic, Archaeological and Linguistic Data," *Proceedings of the National Academy of Sciences of the USA* 85 (1988), 6002–8; L. L. Cavalli-Sforza, "Genes, Peoples and Languages," *Scientific American* 265 (1991), 72–78.

lected human individuals (on the basis of the features studied) rather than similarities and differences between whole populations as in the case just considered. Important work in Polynesia based upon nuclear DNA studies is offering strong corroboration for the farming dispersal model for the colonisation of Polynesia,[36] which archaeologists and linguists were already proposing on the basis of their own studies. And ambitious work using mitochondrial DNA has been used to support the "out of Africa" model for the dispersal (by initial colonisation) of our own species, *Homo sapiens sapiens*.[37] The statistical basis for some of this work has been called into question in a rather technical dispute about maximum parsimony trees,[38] and it would seem that the outcome of the mitochondrial DNA study is not as clear-cut as had at first been claimed. But once again there is little doubt that the genetic evidence, collected from living populations, can indeed be used to make informative statements about the ancestral relationships of those populations. Naturally the genetic evidence deals with genetic relationships, and, as we have seen, there is no easy one-to-one correlation between these and relationships between languages.

In every case the interpretation of the data in one field has to be undertaken with extreme caution when applied to another field. But the potential relationships are indeed there. And so they should be, for there must be a single historical reality, in human terms, that underlies the patternings that we see today in the archaeological findings, in the linguistic distributions, and in the genetic evidence.

---

[36] J. S. Wainscoat et al., "Evolutionary Relationships of Human Populations from an Analysis of Nuclear DNA Polymorphisms," *Nature* 319 (1986), 491–93; idem, "Geographic Distribution of Alpha- and Beta-Globin Gene Cluster Polymorphisms," in P. Mellars and C. B. Stringer (eds.), *The Human Revolution: Behavioural and Biological Perspectives on the Origins of Modern Humans* (Edinburgh: Edinburgh University Press, 1989), pp. 31–38.

[37] A. C. Wilson, M. Stoneking, and R. L. Cann, "Ancestral Geographic States and the Peril of Parsimony," *Systematic Zoology* 40 (1991), 363–65.

[38] D. R. Maddison, "African Origin of Human Mitochondrial DNA Reexamined," *Systematic Zoology* 40 (1991), 355–63; A. R. Templeton, "Human Origins and Analysis of Mitochondrial DNA Sequences," *Science* 255 (1992), 737.

The synthesis that I have presented may certainly be regarded at this stage as both premature and uncertain. But what we can, I think, begin to learn from the exercise is that it may soon be feasible to offer a historical outline of this kind that will give valid insights into human diversity simultaneously in cultural, linguistic, and genetic terms. When that stage is reached we shall have learnt a great deal about human variability.

Conclusion

Many of the ingredients of what I have set out here may be regarded as somewhat speculative, and certainly the synthesis as I have offered it is a tentative one. But there is little doubt in my mind that a synthesis of some kind will become available soon. For even if there is still disagreement between the "lumpers" and the "splitters" among linguists, the archaeologists will certainly be looking for insights into the processes by which cultures and languages change. It may be that, in laying stress upon farming dispersals, I have gone too far. But the advance of archaeology will soon allow a clearer picture of the development of farming in different parts of the world. And certainly the dating techniques now available do allow such developments to be securely dated. Unfortunately, dating linguistic change is a much more difficult matter, on which there is very little agreement.

But what really gives grounds for hope, and for feeling that the issues we are discussing are more than mere speculation, is the development of molecular genetics, and its application to these questions. It cannot be too clearly stressed that genetic descent is not the same as linguistic descent: we have debated the circumstances in which the two may coincide and in which they may differ. But we can now follow lines of descent using molecular genetics, and we can hope that very soon the same techniques, applied to ancient human remains, will give us new insights into the genetic constitution of earlier populations.

So if the specific synthesis that I have offered you must be regarded as entirely tentative, I think we can suggest that a synthesis of some kind, perhaps in some ways like this, will be available in a couple of decades.

And what has this to say for us in relation to human values? Here I would prefer discretion to valour. It was Chairman Mao who said, "Let the past serve the present." But I am not sure that this instrumentalist view of the past — which is certainly shared by some of my postmodernist colleagues in archaeology — is a very wise one. We have seen the past too readily pressed into the service of the present not only by Marxists but by the Nazis, as I indicated earlier. So this evening I will draw no facile conclusions.[39]

What I will say is that I believe an understanding of human diversity can only lead to a greater respect for human diversity. All humans today belong to a single species, *Homo sapiens sapiens*, with only a limited range of genetic diversity. The much greater range of linguistic diversity depends upon a series of factors, some of which I have tried to outline. Those affecting cultural diversity are in several ways different, but farming origins seem to have had consequences of crucial relevance to both.

The genetic differences that exist are subtle. Genetic drift ensures that populations that become cut off from one another increasingly diverge genetically. Thus human populations on different continents, no longer part of the same breeding continuum, will come to differ genetically. The term "race" has little more meaning than that.

Ethnicity is something different — it is dependent less on genetic differences, on "race," than on cultural differences, including language, and more particularly upon how these are perceived by the participant.

Ethnicity will be the subject of my second lecture. We shall see that it is rooted in the kinds of human diversity that we have been

---

[39] I am grateful to all those who commented on this paper at the Tanner seminar, and in particular to the invited discussant, Dr. Alison Wylie.

considering — a diversity whose origins we are on the brink of understanding.

II. WHO WERE THE GREEKS? A PROBLEM OF ETHNICITY

Archaeology and Ethnicity

On this occasion let us pursue further the theme of "Archaeology and Identity" by asking what seems a rather simple question: "Who were the Greeks?" It is not a new question. Indeed, in 1930 Sir John Myres published a celebrated book of precisely this title.[1] But to define exactly *who* a group of people were, or who they are, turns out to be a rather difficult matter, raising complex issues about identity and ethnicity.

It is these issues that I now want to confront. In asking "Who were the Greeks?" I am posing, or intend to pose, a general question, of some topicality. It is, in some senses, the same kind of question as "Who were the Celts?" or "Who are the Serbs?" or "Who were the Jews?" Or we can insert any ethnic name at will: the Maori, the Navajo, the Pueblo people, the Scots, the Irish: all those resonant ethnic names, where history mingles with mythology, where language and culture overlap, where religion and identity converge.

My title "Who were the Greeks?" is, in reality, rich in ambiguity. Don't we all know the answer? The Ancient Greeks lived in Ancient Greece, before the Roman period. They wrote the Classics, initiated philosophical speculation, drama, lyric poetry, and the theoretical sciences, and created the "classical style" in sculpture and painting, reaching the summit of their intellectual achievement in the Athens of Pericles in the 5th century B.C., and the peak of their expansion more than a century later with the conquests of Alexander the Great in the Near East, Egypt, Iran, and even north India.

---

[1] J. L. Myres, *Who Were the Greeks?* (Berkeley: University of California Press, 1930).

We know all that. But *who* were they? That question is often taken to mean "Where did they come from?" The question is one of identity. And the reason it is important even today is that it is one of corporate or national identity: it is one of ethnicity.

It is easy to give an example of the critical role of such questions in the practical world of today. At the time of writing one province of the former Yugoslavia, centred upon Skopje (and formerly denominated "Macedonia" within Tito's Yugoslavia) has proclaimed political autonomy, independence. It is supported in this internationally, and there is widespread sympathy for their wish to be free of domination by the Serbs. But this new state insists upon calling itself "Macedonia," a position implacably opposed by the Greek government and people. For them "Macedonia" is a Greek term, going right back to the days of the kings of Macedonia, of whom the most famous was Alexander the Great himself. Two of the provinces of north Greece are today called (East and West) "Macedonia." The Greeks fear that to concede the term "Macedonia" to the Republic of Skopje would open the way to expansionist claims upon Thessaloniki, the great northern city of Greece, and on adjoining areas — territorial claims that have indeed been advanced by their neighbours to the north in the past. "What is Greece?" "What is Macedonia?" "Who were the Greeks?" — these are again burning questions. And when we speak in this way of ethnicity we are touching upon even more sensitive issues that underlie armed violence at the present time. Who are the Serbs, the Croatians, the Bosnians, the Kurds, the Tamils, the Irish, the Armenians, the Ossetians, the Tibetans — or, to go back fifty years, the Aryans?

It is not exactly nationalism that is the curse of our times, but that special kind of group sentiment that leads men and women to feel their collective identity so strongly that they will fight for it, and kill for it, and even undertake in its name the abomination "ethnic cleansing," that new Serbian contribution to our vocabulary.

In the past most writers, including most archaeologists, have assumed that in seeking the origin of an ethnic group, like the Greeks, they were asking, in effect, "Where did they come from?" It was assumed that before the days of cities and civilisation the Greeks were a tribal group, or perhaps several related tribes. For linguistic reasons, which we will come to in a moment, it was believed that they arrived in Greece from the north: "Immigrants from the North," as the title of the relevant chapter from the *Cambridge Ancient History* puts it.[2] Archaeologists therefore sought to find traces in the archaeological record of the "Coming of the Greeks." Any exotic artefact, any new pottery style, was examined in case it might prove to be an indicator of this prehistoric migration.

But archaeology has in recent years turned away from this "migrationist" view of history — this notion that nearly all significant changes are to be attributed to the arrival of new groups of people. Instead archaeologists have come to analyse rather more closely processes of change, social and economic, by which societies come to be transformed. On this processual view it may not follow that there was indeed any "Coming of the Greeks." In fact I shall argue that Sir John Myres was right when he said that "the Greeks were ever in process of becoming."[3]

It is true to say also that anthropologists have turned away from the "tribal" view of society, in which nonurban communities were automatically conceived as dividing themselves into well-articulated tribal groups.[4] Certainly it was convenient for colonial administrators in the last century to divide the map into named tribes. Preferably these would be tribes with chiefs — chiefdoms — to facilitate orderly government. These administrators often suf-

[2] R. A. Crossland, "Immigrants from the North," in *Cambridge Ancient History* I, 2. 3rd ed. (Cambridge: Cambridge University Press, 1971), pp. 824–76.

[3] Myers, *Greeks*, p. 538.

[4] J. Helm (ed.), *Essays on the Problem of Tribe* (Seattle: American Ethnological Association, 1968).

fered from the "take me to your leader" syndrome, assuming that if they asked with sufficient pertinicity for a tribal name (and to be taken to meet the "chief" of the "tribe") the natives would oblige.

But my former colleague Jack Goody has documented a very clear case of the converse in the Northwest of the Gold Coast (i.e., Ghana) in West Africa in his book *The Social Organisation of the LoWiili*. As Goody puts it:

> Compounds are scattered unevenly across the countryside in such a way that it is difficult to tell where one settlement ends and the next begins. There was no centralized political system before the advent of the British. . . . Cultural changes take place imperceptibly like dialects merging into one another. But when we examine the system of group designations used in this region, we find that it is based not upon a series of exclusive tribal names but upon a 'directional' system in which a number of contiguous peoples refer to themselves obliquely by two names.
>
> It will be obvious that such system introduces many complications for the outside observer. To be a member of a western European society, it is almost inconceivable that a person should not be aware of his 'nationality', whether he is French or Italian, Fulani or Ibo. Therefore, in making enquiries among these peoples, the responses of their informants have often been channelled into a similar mould.[5]

There is no clear tribal name for these West African people. "The reason for the existence of such a system appears to be the lack of any pronounced hiatus in the social relations of neighbouring peoples sufficient to arouse the consciousness of unity necessary for the emergence of a group name."[6] Indeed the name by which they are commonly called is a rather hilarious misnomer. Ethnographers asked in one place, "What do you call those people over

---

[5] J. Goody, *The Social Organisation of the LoWiili*, 2nd ed. (Oxford: Oxford University Press, 1967), p. 17.

[6] Ibid., p. 19.

there?" and wrote down the answer, taking it to be a kind of tribal name. Sometimes they were puzzled when they travelled some way westwards to ask the people in question what they called the people to their west, to be given much the same answer. In fact the group name that they had written down was not a true group name or ethnonym at all. It simply meant "the folks over there to the west."

The essential point here is that ethnicity — the existence of well-defined social groups or tribes, with names of their own for themselves — is not a universal. It is a matter of degree. And to project a well-defined ethnicity onto the prehistoric past may be a serious error. Chiefdoms, especially militaristic chiefdoms, do emerge in various parts of the world and are likely to have a clear self-identity. But they do so in fairly well-defined circumstances. In Europe I believe it was in the iron age — that is to say, during the first millennium B.C. — that one can discern the widespread rise of militaristic chiefdoms in the archaeological record and perhaps at this time that identity came to be defined through ethnicity.

This, I believe, is an important point. When we look at non-urban societies, the first question should not be "Which were the ethnic groups?" but rather "To what extent were there any social units or ethnic groups above the purely local level?"

Armed with these initial thoughts, we can now return to our case study, the Greeks.

Defining the Greeks

We all know a Greek sculpture when we see one. The ideals for the representation of human form, both male and female, were already established in Greece by the fifth century B.C. They were decisive in their influence upon Roman art, and influential once again during the Italian Renaissance, so that the Greek ideal of beauty became a norm for western civilisation until very recent times. It is an ideal towards whose subversion much of the art of the present century has been devoted.

Greek civilisation offers other undisputed indicators in the archaeological record, the surviving material culture. The Doric temple, for instance, was a feature of the acropolis or other sanctuary area of nearly every Greek city, at home both in the Aegean and in the colonies of Sicily and Magna Graecia. Perhaps the most important of all, the Greek alphabet (although derived from the Phoenician script of the Levant) was the medium for Greek literacy, and hence the basis for so much of Greek civilisation. To form a reliable view of the geographical extent of Greek civilisation, for instance in the fifth century B.C., it is sufficient to plot on a map the occurrence of some of these convenient indicators or perhaps the distribution of those city-states minting and issuing coins.[7] For the *polis*, the city-state, was the typically Greek governmental form, the original home of "politics," and coinage too had its inception in the Aegean.

When Sir John Myres wrote *Who Were the Greeks?* in 1930, he was asking, or trying to ask, a question essentially dealing with origins. For him "Who are you?" meant "Where do you come from?" or "How do you come to be here?"

Generations of archaeologists have indeed posed this question in relation to the Greeks. Most have taken as their starting point, naturally enough, such insights as they could obtain from the most ancient historical writers.

It transpires, however, that the early writings of the Greek historians give no very clear account of Greek origins. For them, history began with the first Olympiad in the year 776 B.C. Before that was a period documented only by shadowy traditions for which the best evidence came from the genealogies of some of the noble families of Greece. Before that again was the "Heroic Age" described in the Homeric epics.

---

[7] C. Renfrew and M. Wagstaff (eds.), *An Island Polity: The Archaeology of Exploitation in Melos* (Cambridge: Cambridge University Press, 1982), p. 5 with fig. 1.3.

Certainly the three main groups of dialects of the Greek language (the Aeolic, the Ionic, and the Doric) have since the times of the early Greek historians given rise to a variety of origin theories. Many of these refer to Hellen, the legendary ancestor of the Hellenes, and to his sons Aeolus, Dorus, and Xuthus (who was regarded by the Ionians as their common father in the national pedigree).[8]

It is generally the case that the origin theories or myths of a community or nation tend to be couched in terms of the migrations of tribes, often notionally led by a prominent figure from whom the tribe took its name. (Often, however, these eponymous heroes are evidently fictitious and in reality are constructed from the tribal name itself.) Such is the case for many biblical origin myths. In the Greek case the tribes are usually regarded as intrusive to Greece, sometimes seen as succeeding in the area a rather shadowy group, named the "Pelasgians." In other instances (notably for the Athenians) groups can be regarded as autochthonous, where necessary taking up the Greek language from incoming Greeks. Much weight has sometimes been placed upon the statement of Herodotus that before the Dorians came south to the Peloponnese they lived in the Pindus (i.e., northwest Greece); this assertion has given rise to an extensive scholarly literature about a supposed Dorian "invasion."

Until recently many scholars have sought to find direct indicators in the archaeological record — specific artefact types or styles of pottery decoration — which could serve as a material proof of the "Coming of the Greeks" or of the "Dorian Invasion." It is the case that Aegean civilisation went into a marked decline, both in Crete and in Mainland Greece, at the end of the bronze age. This was the so-called Dark Age before the emergence of Greek civilisation proper that culminated in the classical period of the fifth century, after a succession of periods or phases termed by the ar-

[8] Myres, *Greeks*, p. 335.

chaeologist "geometric," "archaic," and "orientalising." The Dark Age has often been seen as a hiatus, and the new features that followed it, including new burial rites and specific artefact forms found accompanying burials (such as the dress pins known as fibulae), were often regarded as intrusive and hence as potential indicators of incoming Greeks or Dorians and as possible clues by which skilled archaeological analysis might infer the home area of these "immigrants from the north."

Martin Bernal has discussed very effectively in his *Black Athena* the historical and sometimes racist assumptions that may have underlain this general preference among European scholars for a northern provenance for the incoming Greeks, rather than a Near Eastern or an African one.[9]

Sir John Myres looked to a very much earlier period than the end of the bronze age (around 1000 B.C.) for the evidence of immigrants. He laid emphasis instead upon a particular kind of wheelmade grey pottery from the Greek middle bronze age nearly a millennium earlier (around 1900 B.C.), frequently known to scholars as "Minyan ware." This scholarly name itself offers an example of the thought patterns of the nineteenth century. It was first recognised at the site of Orchomenos, well known for the great Mycenaean *tholos* tomb generally termed the "Treasury of Minyas," after the mythological hero notionally buried there. Here the principle of eponymy is extended even to pottery! It is interesting also that this particular ceramic ware was the subject of the very first published paper by the great archaeologist V. Gordon Childe, whose "On the Date and Origin of Minyan Ware" was published in 1915.[10] Much of his working life was indeed devoted to the attempted reconstruction of migrations and folk movements that would, he hoped, give a clue not only to the identity of the

---

[9] M. Bernal, *Black Athena: The Afroasiatic Roots of Classical Civilisation* (London: Free Association Press, 1987).

[10] V. G. Childe, "On the Date and Origin of Minyan Ware," *Journal of Hellenic Studies* 35 (1915), 196–207.

Greeks but also of the elusive Indo-Europeans. His major work on this theme *The Aryans* was published in 1926,[11] and much the same preoccupation underlay his last major work of detailed archaeological scholarship, *Prehistoric Migrations in Europe*.[12]

It is, of course, now more than a century since the discoveries of Heinrich Schliemann, first at Troy and then at Mycenae, caught the imagination of the scholarly world. The finds from the Shaft Graves of Mycenae made it natural that the late bronze age civilisation that he brought to light would be known as "Mycenaean." Scholars soon realised that it was this, the first urban civilisation of mainland Europe, that laid the foundations for the iron age civilisation of Greece that was to follow. Some assumed that the Mycenaeans were to be regarded as pre-Greek and that, as mentioned above, the Greeks came into Greece at the end of the bronze age, sometime after 1100 B.C.

The matter was further complicated at the end of the last century with the discovery by Sir Arthur Evans of the ruins of the great palace of Knossos in Crete, a principal centre of the civilisation that Evans was to term "Minoan." At Knossos he unearthed numerous inscribed clay tablets, written in various scripts. The most recent, and the most numerous, were inserted in what he termed the "Linear B" script, which he naturally supposed recorded the otherwise unknown Minoan language.

It came as a surprise to the scholarly world, therefore, when in 1956 Michael Ventris with the collaboration of John Chadwick published *Documents in Mycenaean Greek*,[13] proving beyond reasonable doubt that the language recorded in the Linear B tablets was in reality an early form of Greek.

All of this forms part of the background to our inquiry. For it is relevant here to stress the existence of a whole related frame-

---

[11] V. G. Childe, *The Aryans: A Study of Indo-European Origins* (London: Kegan Paul, Trench and Trubner, 1926).

[12] V. G. Childe, *Prehistoric Migrations in Europe* (Oslo: Aschehoug, 1950).

[13] M. G. F. Ventris and J. Chadwick, *Documents in Mycenaean Greek* (Cambridge: Cambridge University Press, 1956).

work of assumptions that has largely guided the development of thinking and has thus had a determining influence upon the course of research: this complex of issues may be referred to as the Indo-European problem.

The Language Factor and the Indo-European Problem

In my first lecture I stressed the importance for the development of historical linguistics of the recognition by Sir William Jones, two hundred years ago, of a family of languages that we have come to call Indo-European. We saw in that lecture how the traditional view, as advocated by Gordon Childe and more recently and very effectively by Marija Gimbutas, holds that the Indo-European homeland lay to the north of the Black Sea, in the steppe lands of southwest Russia and the Ukraine. They argued that the proto-Indo-European expansion out of that area (or the kurgan invasions, to use Gimbutas's terminology) took place at about the beginning of the early bronze age, perhaps in several waves.

Now the point here is that Greek is certainly an Indo-European language. If the first Indo-European speakers did not reach Greece until that time, around 3000 B.C., then the first Greek speakers could not have arrived earlier. Indeed it has been argued that the first Greek speakers were the first Indo-Europeans to reach Greece.

Naturally on this view it is plausible to see the Greeks as immigrants and speak of a "homeland" for them. In this context "the Greeks" can be taken to mean these early immigrants, speaking a very early form of the Greek language. Some writers, such as M. Sakellariou, have developed these ideas in great detail.[14]

My own view is that there is no good evidence for these supposed kurgan migrations. As argued previously, I would suggest that the only pan-European episode of sufficient significance to account for the arrival of a proto-Indo-European language or languages and hence a change of speech across nearly all of Europe is the coming of farming. On this view, a form of proto-Indo-

[14] M. Sakellariou, *Les Proto-Grecs* (Athens: Ekdotike Athenon, 1980).

European speech would reach Greece before 6000 B.C. with the first farmers, and other parts of Europe in succeeding centuries, and finally reach the north Atlantic by 4000 B.C. The Greek language would have developed from its proto-Indo-European ancestor, a process taking place gradually within the territories of what is today Greece after the arrival of the first proto-Indo-European farmers.

But it is important to stress that this very long-term view of things is not an option for those who are constrained by the conventional Childe or Gimbutas view of the Indo-European dispersal to look for a "Coming" of Indo-Europeans (who might well already be speaking an early form of the Greek language) at a time definitely later than the beginning of the bronze age. In fact the choices if one follows that timetable are rather few. For if, by common consent, we accept the Mycenaeans as Greek, and their first flowering is taken to be the Shaft Grave period at Mycenae around 1600 B.C. (which is generally assumed to inaugurate the late bronze age), then this *adventus Graecorum* must, within such a framework of assumptions, be set either during the early or middle bronze ages. For a variety of reasons, well surveyed by Roger Howell,[15] Minyan ware is no longer favoured as the distinguishing feature of the intruders and of their material culture. But it is easy to discern the line of argument that led the late Professor J. L. Caskey to choose, as a possible indicator of the "Coming of the Greeks," the phase of destructions that he believed terminated the Early Helladic II period in the Argolid, and the succeeding new pottery styles associated with Early Helladic III at Lerna and other sites.[16] There is little else by way of material evidence, however, to make such a suggestion plausible: it arises purely from that rather tight framework of assumptions that insists that there

[15] R. J. Howell, "The Origins of the Middle Helladic Culture," in R. A. Crossland and A. Birchall (eds.), *Bronze Age Migrations in the Aegean* (London: Duckworth, 1973), pp. 73–99.

[16] J. L. Caskey, "Greece, Crete and the Aegean Islands in the Early Bronze Age," *Cambridge Ancient History* I, 2, pp. 771–807.

must have been an incursion into Greece of Greek speakers at a time point situated between the end of the neolithic (and the first "kurgan" dispersals from north of the Black Sea) and the time of the Shaft Graves of Mycenae. In my own view the arguments result in what is virtually a *reductio ad absurdum* of the initial assumptions. The kurgan invasion theory simply does not work.

My own preference, therefore, is for a much longer time frame, so that the first Indo-European speakers could enter Greece at a much earlier date, leaving open the question of the subsequent evolution or inception of the Greek language itself (which I would assume to have taken place within Greece). For we cannot escape the well-established status of Greek as an Indo-European language, and the ultimate relevance of the Indo-European problem. Mention must be made at this point, however, of a further body of evidence that has generally been interpreted within the *arriviste* framework for the Greeks already discussed and criticised.

In 1928 J. B. Haley and C. W. Blegen published an interesting and important article in which they drew attention to the possible archaeological and historical significance of those place names in Greece that had already been recognised by other scholars as being unintelligible in the Greek language and thus almost certainly derived from some other, non-Greek language.[17] Given the prevailing assumptions just reviewed concerning a relatively late arrival in Greece of Greek speakers, it made sense to identify these names simply as "pre-Greek," implying that this hypothetical and unknown language was spoken in Greece before the "arrival" there of the first Greek speakers. The names in question typically end in the suffix *-ssos* (e.g., Parnassos) or *-nthos* (e.g., Tirynthos). Moreover, they are found (and were found in classical times) not only in the Greek mainland and in western Anatolia but in Crete, the Cyclades, and other Aegean islands. Haley and Blegen pointed

---

[17] J. B. Haley and C. W. Blegen, "The Coming of the Greeks," *American Journal of Archaeology* 32 (1928), 141–54.

out that, as far as was then known, there were no neolithic settlement sites in the Cycladic islands. They thus came to postulate at least two waves of immigration. The first, with the inception of the early bronze age, would be responsible for this distribution of "pre-Greek" place names; the second, at some later date, would bring about the arrival of the first Greeks.

My own first modest iconoclasm in this field was to discover and excavate (in collaboration with John Evans) a neolithic settlement in the Cycladic islands: Saliagos near Antiparos.[18] As I pointed out at the time,[19] this discovery transformed the constraints of the Haley/Blegen chronology, since the non-Greek place names could now certainly go back to the neolithic period. In my own view today, it is quite possible that they may find their origin earlier, even before the arrival of the farmers who introduced the neolithic. But I think perhaps a more likely explanation is that these names, while not indeed Greek, do nonetheless represent an early form of the Indo-European language that came to be spoken in Greece during the neolithic period, which was itself ancestral to the Greek language as it later developed. It has previously been suggested that these names may be related to the Luwian language of early western Anatolia.[20] Luwian, like Hittite, belongs to the Anatolian family of Indo-European languages. But it may be more appropriate to see these names as related to a "pre-Luwian" era just as they are generally regarded as "pre-Greek."

In this way, by examining the assumptions imposed upon our study by the traditional view of Indo-European origins, we can see that the linguistic evidence may be open to very different interpretation, working within a greatly extended time scale.

---

[18] J. D. Evans and C. Renfrew, *Excavations at Saliagos near Antiparos*, British School at Athens supplementary vol. 5 (London: Thames and Hudson, 1968).

[19] C. Renfrew, "Crete and the Cyclades before Rhadamanthus," *Kretika Chronika* 18 (1964), 137.

[20] L. R. Palmer, *Mycenaean and Minoan: Aegean Prehistory in the Light of the Linear B Tablets* (London: Faber and Faber, 1961), pp. 232–50.

Interaction: The Growth of a Koine

The argument that I am seeking to develop is, as will already be clear, that there was no "Coming of the Greeks," and that early Greek culture and civilisation grew up, in the Aegean, in very much the areas where we later see them in the iron age with the dawn of full, alphabetic literacy in the archaic period and where, in the main, they have existed ever since. As I have indicated, the linguistic evidence does not in fact require us to think in terms of immigration, although it has often been interpreted in that way. It is appropriate now to suggest how the "Greekness" of Greek culture may have come about, may gradually have emerged, in this area. Certainly this quality goes in its scope far beyond the Greek language alone and is also reflected in the material culture.

My own work on the origins of Aegean civilisation has led me to believe that its inception is indeed to be seen largely in local terms. Here I am thinking first of the two bronze age civilisations, the Minoan and the Mycenaean, which undoubtedly laid the foundations for what was to follow. As I have argued in *The Emergence of Civilisation*,[21] it was already in the early bronze age of the Aegean that many of the crucial processes were set in train that were to culminate a millennium later in the palaces of the Mycenaean world and in the late palace period of Crete. Indeed the very geographical scope of these bronze age civilisations may be seen to have been governed to a significant degree (as Myres and others had foreseen) by the extent of true Mediterranean climate and hence of Mediterranean vegetation, notably the olive and the vine, upon which they so notably depended.[22] It was in the early bronze age that viticulture first became well established in the Aegean, and, despite some recent arguments to the contrary, the evidence still seems to me to suggest that the same is true of olive cultivation.

[21] C. Renfrew, *The Emergence of Civilisation* (London: Methuen, 1972).
[22] Ibid., p. 48.

Certainly it is the case that it was during the early bronze age (in its second Early Bronze II phase) that bronze metallurgy expanded throughout the Aegean, and with it the trade in metal goods (of gold and silver as well as copper and bronze), so notably that it is possible to speak of an "international spirit" abroad at the time. Distribution maps of metal finds of recognisably Aegean forms (Cycladic and Minoan as well as Helladic) in the early bronze age already prefigure the distribution and extent of the Minoan and Mycenaean civilisations a millennium later.[23]

But we can go back even before the bronze age in recognising in the Aegean the emergence of an interaction zone, that is to say, a region where persistent trading contacts may be documented. For already during the early neolithic period the distribution of obsidian originating from the Cycladic island of Melos documents that seafarers from the Peloponnese and from Crete were obtaining this useful raw material from its Melian source.[24] Artefacts in obsidian are commonly found on every early farming site known in Crete and in southern Greece as well as throughout the Cycladic islands. They occur commonly in Thessaly and more sparingly to the north in neolithic Macedonia.

What may have begun in the early neolithic period as quite a restricted pattern of trading contact certainly emerged as a thriving "common market" in the early bronze age. Already at that time certain artefact types, such as the Cycladic folded-arm figure, indicate that these contacts were of more than purely commercial significance. Indeed by the Late Bronze I period,[25] around 1450 B.C., some of the pottery products of Crete and the mainland, represented by the so-called Marine style, are so similar that it takes a ceramic specialist of great experience to tell them apart.

Yet it is not until the full Mycenaean period (in the Late Helladic IIIB phase of the thirteenth century B.C.) that one can

[23] Ibid., pp. 330–31 with fig. 16.7.
[24] Renfrew and Wagstaff, *Island Polity*, p. 192 with fig. 15.4.
[25] Ibid., p. 226 with fig. 16.2.

begin to speak of unity, at least when considering pottery styles. By this time the palaces of Minoan Crete were no more (or at least they were no longer major political centres). The material culture had now become so uniform that it is possible to think in political terms of a possible Mycenaean occupation of Crete (hence the presence there of Linear B tablets written in what is now seen as essentially the Mycenaean language). These are still areas of archaeological controversy, but it is not necessary here to resolve every question to see the validity of the general point that is being made. This unity was diminished in the Late Helladic IIIC period, the twelfth century B.C., when various regional ceramic styles reflect what may have been a weakening of political unity (which should not, even in the Late Helladic IIIB period, be exaggerated purely on the grounds of uniform ceramic styles). And it is further weakened with the disintegration of the Mycenaean world after about 1060 B.C.

When urban civilisation re-emerged in the iron age of the eighth and seventh centuries B.C. it was in very much the same areas that we have been discussing for the bronze age. This area of common culture, the *koine* whose development one can discern throughout the bronze age, which culminated in the thirteenth century B.C., was very much re-established after an interlude of some two centuries. During that intervening "Dark Age" we see very little evidence of urban life in the Aegean.

From Mycenaean to Geometric: Continuity in the Dark Age

There is no doubt that the last century and more of the Mycenaean world was a time of serious and prolonged decline. In Crete the decline had begun very much earlier, with the destruction and abandonment of many of the Minoan palaces at the end of the Late Minoan IB period, perhaps around 1450 B.C. But only after 1100 B.C. was there apparently a widespread abandonment of sites in much of the Aegean, with the apparent extinction of urban living and (it would seem) the total loss of literacy. The causes of this decline are not well understood. But today it is generally attributed to internal factors on the one hand (perhaps associated with agricultural overexploitation) and to a decline in international trade on the other. It is now less widely held that armed attack by outsiders might have played a significant causal role, although the power vacuum left by the decline of the palace centres may well have left open the way to various opportunists on the fringes of the Mycenaean world. This was probably a rather typical case of system collapse,[26] rather than an instance of the dramatic overthrow of one civilisation by another or of barbarian incursion.

Many scholars have emphasised the debt which the new geometric and archaic Greece of the first millennium B.C. owed to the preceding Mycenaean world, and the evidence for linguistic continuity, discussed earlier, has lessened the temptation to think in terms of significant immigration at this time. There is, however, one field, that of Mycenaean and Greek religion, where some Indo-Europeanist scholars have thought in terms of a hiatus.

I well recall giving a seminar in Oxford some years ago, shortly after excavating a sanctuary of the Mycenaean period at the site of Phylakopi on the Cycladic island of Melos. I had described the interesting new evidence there that suggests elements of continuity in religious practice across the intervening Dark Age, between the very late Mycenaean finds from the late levels at Phylakopi and some of the early sanctuary sites of the succeeding geometric period in various parts of the Aegean. Professor Christopher Hawkes, a man of both great erudition and considerable force of expression, evinced dissatisfaction with my continuity arguments. For did not everyone know that the Greek pantheon was an Indo-European pantheon, presided over by Zeus himself, with a preponderance of male deities, in contrast to the pre-Greek Mycenaean

[26] C. Renfrew, "System Collapse as Social Transformation: Catastrophe and Anastrophe in Early State Societies," in C. Renfrew and K. L. Cooke (eds.), *Transformations: Mathematical Approaches to Culture Change* (New York: Academic Press, 1979), pp. 481–506.

religion, with its repertoire of female cult statues? The Indo-European argument was here reasserting itself, but this time in the context of religion rather than of language.

It was at this point that I myself became dissatisfied and formed the view that it would be necessary firmly to grasp the Indo-European nettle and to set out to reject those constricting thought frameworks that were putting such unacceptable constraints upon the reconstruction of Aegean prehistory.

Already Martin Nilsson, many years earlier, had emphasised the Minoan-Mycenaean roots of Greek religion.[27] Our discovery of several terracotta male figures and figurines at Phylakopi in a late Mycenaean context and of imported bronze statuettes depicting a male figure in the well-known "smiting god" position introduced, almost for the first time, a strong male element into the repertoire of Mycenaean religious statuary.[28] This and other arguments led me to challenge the notion of religious hiatus at this time.

If one surveys the long prehistory of cult in the Aegean, from the early neolithic with its characteristic rather plump figurines, through the diversity of the later neolithic (with the beginning of burial in cemeteries), and then to the early bronze age, with its marked increase in formal burial practices and in the offering of grave goods, one sees what may be regarded as a number of profound transformations in cult practice. The development of the Minoan palace religion and its later demise with the end of the palaces, to be followed by a very rustic version of the foregoing, seem excellent examples of what may be regarded as *transformations* in cult practice and no doubt also in religious beliefs. In each case what follows owed a great deal to what went before, but the

[27] M. R. Nilsson, *The Minoan-Mycenaean Religion and Its Survival in Greek Religion*, 2nd ed. (Lund: Skrifter utgivna av Kungl. Humanistiska Vetenskapssamfundet i lund 9, 1950).

[28] C. Renfrew, *The Archaeology of Cult: The Sanctuary at Phylakopi*, British School at Athens supplementary vol. 18 (London: Thames and Hudson, 1985), pp. 420–25.

two are recognisably different. In some cases at least it is unlikely that there was very significant foreign input. What was taking place was more the result of internal processes than of any response to external influences. These arguments need developing in detail.[29] But the conclusion to which they lead is clear: relatively rapid change is not in itself an indication of outside influence, nor indeed of discontinuity. Each case must be carefully examined on its merits and interpreted accordingly.

It must be admitted that the whole phenomenon of religious change is one that is very little understood by archaeologists or anthropologists, even in more recent times. The study of material culture undoubtedly offers scope for more systematic inferences about early cult practices than have been achieved in the past, but the study of religious change on the basis of archaeological material has hardly yet been undertaken in a systematic manner. Yet I would suggest that already we know enough to indicate that profound restructurings in religious beliefs and in religious iconography can take place quite rapidly and without any necessary significant input from outside.

Certainly it is the case, as Christopher Hawkes implied, that the Minoan and Mycenaean religions have generally been characterised on the basis of their iconography as predominantly female-oriented, while the traditional view of "Indo-European religion" (if such a term is warranted) is one of a male-dominated pantheon. I am myself skeptical, however, of the validity of the second point and indeed of the whole notion of a coherent "Indo-European" character of the religions of the European bronze age, whether or not there may have been general affinities much earlier, in the neolithic period. Moreover, the deities of ancient Greece do not in general have Indo-European names,[30] and there seems

[29] Ibid., pp. 397ff. and 431ff.
[30] S. Zimmer, "The Investigation of Proto-Indo-European History: Methods, Problems, Limitations," in T. L. Markey and J. A. C. Greppin (eds.), *When Worlds Collide: Indo-Europeans and Pre-Indo-Europeans* (Ann Arbor: University of Michigan Press, 1990), pp. 332-33.

little that is superficially "Indo-European" about most of them. Nor, conversely, is there any logical argument to deny Indo-European status to the deities of the Mycenaean religion simply on the grounds that they seem to have been predominantly female.

These are complex matters. Clearly, significant changes took place between the eleventh and the eighth centuries B.C. But, as I have argued, it does not follow that the transformation that occurred had an external origin. Certainly there is nothing here that suggests some form of major discontinuity that has to be associated with the arrival of Greeks or of Dorians.

In summary, then, it is important to observe that the civilisation of the Greeks of the sixth and fifth centuries B.C. had antecedents that go back very much earlier. The Greek language, as we have seen, was certainly spoken by the thirteenth century B.C., and the language and the religion both had precursors that may go back as far as the early neolithic period in the seventh millennium B.C. What is advocated here, then, is an evolutionary view rather than a migrationist one for the origins of Greek ethnicity. But to say this does not by any means exhaust the import of the initial question: "Who were the Greeks?" To deal with this more adequately, it is now necessary to return to the more general question of the nature of ethnicity that we raised at the outset.

Ethnicity Reconsidered

It is necessary at this point to analyse rather more closely what it is that we mean by "Greeks." Emphasis has been laid so far upon the Greek language, and to some extent upon continuities or discontinuities in the development of religion. We have seen also how the material culture of each phase in Greek prehistory was to some extent the natural successor of that of the preceding phase, and how a recurrent pattern of trading and other interactions is seen within the Aegean from very early times. But we have not so far sought to define rather more precisely what it is that we mean by ethnicity.

Even before doing so, it is pertinent to note that for the Greeks of classical Greece their citizenship within a particular city-state represented their principal political and communal affiliation. Indeed, as we shall see, in a very real sense it was this that represented their "ethnicity" at least as much as any sense of being collectively Greek. Before the Peloponnesian War, it is fair to say, one was citizen before one was a Greek, and before the Persian Wars this applies *a fortiori*. Homer rarely speaks of Hellenes (i.e., Greeks) at all.

The modern anthropologist lists a series of factors, all of them relevant to the definition of ethnicity:

1. shared territory or land;
2. common descent or "blood";
3. a common language;
4. community of customs or culture;
5. community of beliefs or religion;
6. self-awareness, self-identity;
7. a name (ethnonym) to express the identity of the group; and
8. a shared story (or myth) that tells the legend of the origin of the group and of its vicissitudes from remote antiquity to the present.

We have discussed aspects of the first five of these factors. It remains to place some emphasis upon the remaining three, all of which relate to self-awareness, to a sense of self-identity. For ultimately ethnicity is what people believe it to be. An important part of the belief is a perception of the "otherness" of others — the outsiders, the barbarians, the people who are not us.

Several of these points (specifically nos. 2 to 5) were emphasised by Herodotus (VIII, 144) when he spoke of "the kinship of all Greeks in blood and speech and the shrines of gods and the sacrifices that we have in common and the likeness of our way of life." It is convenient to note how many of these points are indicated in a more recent definition of ethnicity:

> Ethnos . . . can be defined as a firm aggregate of people, historically established on a given territory, possessing in common relatively stable particularities of language and culture, and also recognising their unity and difference from other similar formations (self-awareness) and expressing this in a self-appointed name (ethnonym).[31]

Fortunately the written records from Greece, from the Homeric epics onwards, give a series of insights into notions of self-identity among the Greeks, and in keeping with the approach adopted here it is perfectly possible to take an "evolutionary" view of this concept also. Certainly by about 400 B.C., if we look at a map of the area occupied by Greek city-states, like that prepared by Kirsten,[32] we can be confident that their citizens would certainly have considered themselves to be "Greek." There was no overall political unity at this time, even if, following the Peloponnesian War, many of the cities were effectively under Athenian control. But all can be regarded as members of a common *ethnos*.

Today, however, we can doubt whether the inhabitants of what we call Greece ever thought of themselves as a unity before the Trojan War (if indeed the Trojan War has some historical reality and is more than the poetic invention suspected by some sceptics).[33] It is not clear that Minoan Crete was ever unified politically,[34] and there is no plausible suggestion that there was a politi-

---

[31] Y. V. Bromley and V. I. Koslov quoted by T. Dragadze, "The Place of the 'Ethnos' in Soviet Anthropology," in E. Gellner (ed.), *Soviet and Western Anthropology* (London: Duckworth, 1980), p. 162.

[32] E. Kirsten, *Die Griechische Polis als historisch-geographisches Problem des Mittelmeerraumes* (Bonn: Fera. Dümmlers, 1956), fig. 13.

[33] M. I. Finley, "The Trojan War," *Journal of Hellenic Studies* 84 (1964), 1–9.

[34] J. F. Cherry, "Polities and Palaces: Some Problems in Minoan State Formation," in C. Renfrew and J. F. Cherry (eds.), *Peer Polity Interaction and Socio-Political Change* (Cambridge: Cambridge University Press, 1986), p. 24.

cally unified Mycenaean Empire. The evidence of the Linear B tablets of Pylos shows that the geographical boundaries of the polity can be situated within the western Peloponnese,[35] and there is no evidence for economic or political organisation of a kind that would have united the various palatial centres. Greece during Mycenaean times was a land of kingdoms or principalities, in that sense rather like mediaeval Italy. This impression is certainly very much that conveyed by Homer (although the epics took shape in post-Mycenaean times, and it is widely recognised that in some respects they reflect Greece in the geometric rather than in the Mycenaean period). The *Iliad* shows the expeditionaries coming together for military purposes but otherwise very much under the command of their local leaders (Agamemnon, Nestor, Odysseus, and so on). Thucydides (I, 3) in his account of the Peloponnesian War makes very much this point:

> Before the Trojan War, Hellas, as it appears to me, engaged in no enterprise in common.... Homer ... nowhere uses this name [Hellenes] of all or indeed of any of them except the followers of Achilles.... And he has not used the term Barbarians either. For the reason as it seems to me that the Hellenes on their part had not yet been separated off so as to acquire one common name by way of contrast.

Earlier I referred to the Mycenaean *koine* of the Late Helladic IIIB period, as reflected mainly in the pottery, extending over much of the southern Aegean. Certainly there are other widespread indicators of "community of customs or culture," and the distribution of stone-built round tombs (tholoi) offers a good example. But the uniformity is far from complete. For instance, the little female figurines in the "psi" form so characteristic of the Late Helladic IIIC period of the Argolid have a much more re-

---

[35] J. F. Cherry, "Investigating the Political Geography of an Early State by Multi-dimensional Scaling of Linear B Tablet Data," in J. Bintliff (ed.), *Mycenaean Geography* (Cambridge: British Association for Mycenaean Studies, 1977), pp. 76–83.

stricted distribution than that of the pottery of broadly "Mycenaean" style: they are scarcely found in Crete.[36] Moreover, there were, as far as we can tell, no sanctuaries in the Mycenaean period that enjoyed the pan-Greek popularity that great centres like Delos, Delphi, or Dodona enjoyed from the geometric period onwards. There are no good grounds, then, for thinking that the various communities that we collectively think of and term "Mycenaean" actually considered themselves as constituting some sort of unity in this sense. There is an analogy here with our own practice as historians or as archaeologists of referring to the late iron age inhabitants of northwestern Europe as "the Celts." For there is absolutely no evidence that they used this or indeed any other term to describe themselves collectively.[37] The Mycenaeans, like the Celts, are in this sense a modern construct. It is likely that their various self-identities focussed primarily upon the functioning polities, centered upon the palaces and citadels such as Mycenae, Pylos, Athens, and so forth. It is entirely uncertain whether they had any larger sense of collective identity.

As we have seen, the Mycenaean *koine* lost some of its uniformity (judging mainly by the pottery) in the late Helladic IIIC period, and then disintegrated in the centuries that followed. Certainly, in the geometric period, from the eighth century B.C., the position must have been very much as Thucydides described it. Many common elements in the art and material culture soon developed, several of them recognisably the result of innovation by and imitation of the leading centres, such as Athens or Corinth.

It was not until the foundation of the Olympic Games, traditionally set in 776 B.C., that any common endeavour is recorded. The Hellanodikai, who regulated the Games, represent the first appearance of any panhellenic authority. They are first attested around 600 B.C.

[36] Renfrew, *Archaeology of Cults*, p. 418.

[37] C. Renfrew, *Archaeology and Language: The Puzzle of Indo-European Origins* (London: Jonathan Cape, 1987), chapter 9.

We may suggest that there were three decisive influences that led to the formation of Greek self-awareness, to the formation of what we might call a Greek *ethnos*. (We should note in passing that the term *ethnos* itself was used by the Ancient Greeks to refer to much smaller groups, the tribal units of Greece. This point is well illustrated by the map prepared by A. M. Snodgrass,[38] which adds the *ethne* to the *poleis* shown by Kirsten.) This is not to overlook the shared language, or the elements of shared religion and material culture, which, as we have seen, can be traced back so very much earlier. These indications of unity along several dimensions were the ingredients out of which Greek ethnicity was shaped. But what we are tracing now is indeed the development of that essential insight of self-awareness without which those elements of unity could not have come together to form a true Greek ethnicity.

The first influence was undoubtedly Homer, perhaps the decisive force in the crystallisation of Greek consciousness. Homer, it can be argued, played a major role in offering an origin myth, a shared history, to which all Greeks could subscribe. In this context it does not in the least matter whether or not the Trojan War took place. What matters is that the Greeks, throughout the region documented in the maps (for instance by Kirsten or Snodgrass) indicating the extent of Greek culture, believed it to have taken place and recognised the deities described by Homer, and the general history and indeed the poetry itself, as their own.

The second was the institution of the panhellenic games, with the competition for honours among Greek cities, and the exclusion of those who were not Greek. Even if the traditional date for the origin of the Olympic Games has been set too early, as A. Mallwitz has argued,[39] and they did not begin until around 700 B.C., this

[38] A. M. Snodgrass, *Archaic Greece: The Age of Experiment* (London: J. M. Dent, 1980), p. 45 with fig. 9.

[39] A. Mallwitz, "Cult and Competition Locations at Olympia," in W. J. Raschke (ed.), *The Archaeology of the Olympics* (Madison: University of Wisconsin Press, 1988), p. 99.

was the first time that being Greek was used as a decisive criterion for inclusion or exclusion. The other homes of the periodic games — Delphi, Isthmia, Nemea— and the other major sanctuaries of the Greeks (including Dodona and Delphi as well as Ionian centres like Samos and Ialysos) all become the focus of attention for pilgrims and other travellers, setting up new patterns of interaction tending to promote community. And the elements of intercity rivalry and competition that the periodic games cleverly harnessed were perhaps the first manifestations of the peer-polity interaction that resulted in the construction of the treasuries of individual cities at Olympia and Delphi, and very soon in the competitive construction of ever larger and more impressive temples in the various cities themselves.[40]

The third unifying influence was the Persian War. There is nothing like attack from outside to mould diversity into unity. If ethnicity is an awareness of "us" — we, the Greeks — it is brought about most effectively by military threat from "them" — the barbarians. We have already touched upon the unifying effects of common military endeavour in mentioning the (possibly fictitious) Trojan War. And it should be remembered that most anthropologists agree that one of the most frequent causes of state formation is external military threat. There can be no doubt that the common endeavour of the Greek cities, acting together for the first time against the Persians, brought about a new level of Greek self-awareness. That this process continued in the aftermath of the Persian campaigns has been argued very effectively by Edith Hall in the *Inventing the Barbarian: Greek Self-Definition through Tragedy.*[41] She shows clearly how important the theatre was not only in reflecting but in establishing in fifth-century Greece the dichotomy between "them" and "us": Persians and Greeks.

[40] A. M. Snodgrass, "Interaction by Design: The Greek City State," in C. Renfrew and J. F. Cherry (eds.), *Peer Polity Interaction and Socio-Political Change*, pp. 47–58.

[41] E. Hall, *Inventing the Barbarian: Greek Self-Definition through Tragedy* (Oxford: Clarendon Press, 1989).

Constructing Greek Ethnicity

It should be clear by now that the answer to the question "Who were the Greeks?" can take different forms. If we are speaking of the origins of the Greek language it can, as we have seen, take us far back. To quote the leading authority, John Chadwick:

> To ask when the Greeks reached Greece may well be a meaningless question. We have no evidence to prove that Greek existed as a separate language before its speakers were established in Greece, and some indications to the contrary.[42]

Chadwick would place the emergence of Greek from its proto-Indo-European precursor *in Greece* during the bronze age. I have suggested above that this process took place earlier, *in Greece*, during the late neolithic period.

But if you mean full ethnic awareness, full ethnicity, a time when people would recognise each other not simply as Knossians, or Pylians, or Corinthians, or Athenians, but as Greek, as Hellenes, then this came much later. It began, in effect, with Homer, and was developed by the panhellenic games and the emergence of the great sanctuaries. It came to fruition with the Persian Wars.

If then we have to fix a decisive moment for the emergence of Greek ethnicity, it will not be the "Coming of the Greeks" but, as observed by several classical authors, the foundation of the Olympic Games. As Lysians began his Olympic Oration (*Olympiakos*) in 338 B.C.:

> Among many noble feasts, gentlemen, for which it is right to remember Heracles, we ought to recall the fact that he was the first, in his affection for the Greeks, to convene this contest. For previously the cities regarded each other as strangers.[43]

---

[42] J. Chadwick, "The Prehistory of the Greek Language," *Cambridge Ancient History* II, 2, p. 816.

[43] Lysias, *Olympic Oration*, XXXIII, 520.1, translated by W. R. M. Lamb, Loeb Classical Library (London: Heinemann, 1976).

We do not need to accept the myth of the divine (or heroic) foundation of the games to see the pertinence of the last sentence.

Pericles, in his celebrated oration a century and a half earlier, could proclaim Athens to be the School of Greece, and there he gives voice to a vision of Greek unity that later took political reality with the conquests of the Macedonian kings. Indeed the Macedonian period was one when political reality and ethnic polemic came to be intermixed in a manner all too familiar to modern ears. Isocrates was one of those orators who was very willing to construct a picture of the historic past to suit the political needs of the time, so that it is not altogether unfair to describe him as a propagandist, a term that, despite his undoubted loyalty to the Athenians, one could never apply to Thucydides. But it was Isocrates, nonetheless, who in his Olympic *Panegyricus* in 380 B.C. took the catholic sentiments of Pericles and broadened them to make the notion of "Greek" designate something beyond simple ethnicity as we have defined it.[44] He gave expression to a wider idea, whereby Greek might imply a cultural affiliation that all might aspire to share, whatever their origin:

> She [i.e., Athens] has brought it about that the name 'Hellenes' suggests no longer a race but an intelligence, and that the title 'Hellenes' is applied rather to those who share our culture than to those who share a common blood.

This insight of Isocrates underlies the aspiration of most of those who have found classical Greece a rewarding subject of study, from the time of the Renaissance down to the present day. Classical scholarship became, of course, central to the whole notion of learning and indeed of science in the western world. It was also central to the educational system of every European country. So our own image of the Greeks comes to us not directly from the textual sources, and still less from the archaeological remains, but

---

[44] Isocrates, *Panegyricus*, 51, translated by G. Norlin, Loeb Classical Library (London: Heinemann, 1928).

from a cultural tradition that still tends to equate the classics and the ideal.

That is the great tradition of classical scholarship. But we should not forget that other great tradition, this time an unbroken one, which has also been a powerful influence over the centuries. Here I am referring, of course, to the Greek Orthodox Church, as well as its sister churches in the orthodox tradition. Literacy, theology, and scholarship continued in an unbroken tradition, for even after the fall of Constantinople, the Orthodox Church continued to play a crucial role within the Aegean, and the Russian Orthodox Church a comparable one further north. Obviously it conserves and disseminates a rather different worldview, but it is one that has no less a claim to be called Greek.

And third, if we are following the strands of Greekness down to the present day, we should consider again the land of Greece, its government and its people, who very naturally consider themselves to be the inheritors of the ancient Greeks and who sometimes tend to reject, in consequence, those elements of their own more recent history (for instance, the centuries of Slav settlement) that do not conform to that self-image.

If Greek ethnicity is something that was first constructed in the three or four centuries following the foundation of the Olympic Games — and constructed out of ingredients that, as we have seen, have a far greater antiquity — it is not something whose definition ended with the assimilation of Greece into the Roman Empire. The Renaissance, the Orthodox Church, the Greek War of Independence, the Neo-Classical movement, and all manner of subsequent events have ensured that the image of Greece has never been a constant one. "Who were the Greeks?" is a question that can never find a definitive answer.

Identity: The Responsibility of Ethnicity

What we have seen, then, in the Aegean may be described as a clear case of the emergence of ethnicity, of ethnogenesis.

In Greece we have long, enduring continuities, indications of which may be discerned even across the significant transformations and restructurings in society that undoubtedly do occur. It may be suggested that the gradual evolution of the Greek language from its proto-Indo-European predecessor is one of these. During the bronze age we see the development of Aegean interactions not only in the sphere of trade (not least in metals) but also at the religious and symbolic level. The emergence of the Minoan palaces was followed by that of the mainland. But even with the collapse of Minoan power around 1400 B.C., and then of Mycenaean power two centuries later, we can discern elements of continuity across the ensuing Dark Age. The Greece of the protogeometric and geometric periods, although reconstituted, is quite recognisably the offspring of its bronze age predecessor. New elements are there, but like the male representations at Phylakopi, their origins can be traced back to the bronze age world in many cases.

These, then, are the ingredients: continuities in language, in culture, in religion, in territory, in descent, and very probably also in mythology. But the final, special ingredient, which is the *sine qua non* of ethnicity, is group identity, self-awareness. I have suggested that, while smaller units had their identities and ethnicities, the notion that all the lands that became Greece and their people (which is the same as to say all the lands where Greek was spoken) belonged together as a unit, the territory of the Hellenes, probably did not emerge until the seventh century B.C. The newly transformed Greek religion then took definitive shape, aided by and reflected in the epics of Homer. And the Olympic Games gave the first opportunity to express and to develop a panhellenic ideal.

Greek ethnicity is not, after all, incredibly ancient, nor lost in the mists of time. On the contrary it was, for the Ancient Greeks, something relatively recent, which came about only two or three centuries before the Athens of Pericles. Indeed it reached its definitive form only during and after the great external threat of the Persian Wars in the fifth century B.C.

There is, I feel, a lesson here for today. We are not the passive inheritors of a dominating and determining past, where the sins of the fathers will be visited upon their children for generation after generation. On the contrary, in large measure we choose our own ethnicity, collectively and to some extent individually. That is perhaps no very radical doctrine to announce in a nation that only a few years ago celebrated its Bicentenary. But it is less obvious in those parts of the world where individuals see their own identity as predetermined for them by their membership in groups that themselves appear to be the unchanging and unchangeable products of a remote past.

Most ethnicities are, and always have been, constructs. They rest upon myths of origin and myths of identity that, for good or ill, manipulate the ingredients of human diversity in the fields that we have considered.

It takes clarity of mind, and sometimes courage, to question these myths, to question the received identity that the past seems to offer. But to make war, to kill in the name of such a myth, of such a received identity, is to surrender responsibility for one's own actions to a past that is possibly misconceived. Already in 380 B.C. Isocrates offered a way forward, of breaking the chains that shackle us to a burdensome past. When he indicated that the name Greek (or Hellenes) "suggests no longer a race but an intelligence" and is "applied rather to those who share our culture than to those who share a common blood," he stated clearly, probably for the first time, that ethnicity is a matter of choice, not merely of inheritance, and by implication that the responsibility for that choice is ours. Had the world learnt that lesson fifty or more years ago there might have been no Second World War, and certainly no Holocaust. Had Europe learnt it only two or three years ago we would have been spared that special new barbarity of the 1990s: "ethnic cleansing."

As thinking people, we have each the opportunity and the duty of examining our inheritance and of recognising that we cannot absolve ourselves from the responsibility for our acts by invoking the past: ultimately the responsibility is our own.[45]

---

[45] I am most grateful to all those who participated in the Tanner seminar following my lectures, and in particular to Dr. Ian Morris, the invited discussant, for helpful comments on the original text of the paper.

THE TANNER LECTURERS

1976–77

OXFORD	Bernard Williams, Cambridge University
MICHIGAN	Joel Feinberg, University of Arizona *"Voluntary Euthanasia and the Inalienable Right to Life"*
STANFORD	Joel Feinberg, University of Arizona *"Voluntary Euthanasia and the Inalienable Right to Life"*

1977–78

OXFORD	John Rawls, Harvard University
MICHIGAN	Sir Karl Popper, University of London *"Three Worlds"*
STANFORD	Thomas Nagel, Princeton University

1978–79

OXFORD	Thomas Nagel, Princeton University *"The Limits of Objectivity"*
CAMBRIDGE	C. C. O'Brien, London
MICHIGAN	Edward O. Wilson, Harvard University *"Comparative Social Theory"*
STANFORD	Amartya Sen, Oxford University *"Equality of What?"*
UTAH	Lord Ashby, Cambridge University *"The Search for an Environmental Ethic"*
UTAH STATE	R. M. Hare, Oxford University *"Moral Conflicts"*

1979–80

OXFORD	Jonathan Bennett, University of British Columbia *"Morality and Consequences"*
CAMBRIDGE	Raymond Aron, Collège de France *"Arms Control and Peace Research"*
HARVARD	George Stigler, University of Chicago *"Economics or Ethics?"*

MICHIGAN	Robert Coles, Harvard University *"Children as Moral Observers"*
STANFORD	Michel Foucault, Collège de France *"Omnes et Singulatim: Towards a Criticism of 'Political Reason' "*
UTAH	Wallace Stegner, Los Altos Hills, California *"The Twilight of Self-Reliance: Frontier Values and Contemporary America"*

1980–81

OXFORD	Saul Bellow, University of Chicago *"A Writer from Chicago"*
CAMBRIDGE	John Passmore, Australian National University *"The Representative Arts as a Source of Truth"*
HARVARD	Brian M. Barry, University of Chicago *"Do Countries Have Moral Obligations? The Case of World Poverty"*
MICHIGAN	John Rawls, Harvard University *"The Basic Liberties and Their Priority"*
STANFORD	Charles Fried, Harvard University *"Is Liberty Possible?"*
UTAH	Joan Robinson, Cambridge University *"The Arms Race"*
HEBREW UNIV.	Solomon H. Snyder, Johns Hopkins University *"Drugs and the Brain and Society"*

1981–82

OXFORD	Freeman Dyson, Princeton University *"Bombs and Poetry"*
CAMBRIDGE	Kingman Brewster, President Emeritus, Yale University *"The Voluntary Society"*
HARVARD	Murray Gell-Mann, California Institute of Technology *"The Head and the Heart in Policy Studies"*
MICHIGAN	Thomas C. Schelling, Harvard University *"Ethics, Law, and the Exercise of Self-Command"*
STANFORD	Alan A. Stone, Harvard University *"Psychiatry and Morality"*

UTAH	R. C. Lewontin, Harvard University *"Biological Determinism"*
AUSTRALIAN NATL. UNIV.	Leszek Kolakowski, Oxford University *"The Death of Utopia Reconsidered"*

1982–83

OXFORD	Kenneth J. Arrow, Stanford University *"The Welfare-Relevant Boundaries of the Individual"*
CAMBRIDGE	H. C. Robbins Landon, University College, Cardiff *"Haydn and Eighteenth-Century Patronage in Austria and Hungary"*
HARVARD	Bernard Williams, Cambridge University *"Morality and Social Justice"*
STANFORD	David Gauthier, University of Pittsburgh *"The Incompleat Egoist"*
UTAH	Carlos Fuentes, Princeton University *"A Writer from Mexico"*
JAWAHARLAL NEHRU UNIV.	Ilya Prigogine, Université Libre de Bruxelles *"Only an Illusion"*

1983–84

OXFORD	Donald D. Brown, Johns Hopkins University *"The Impact of Modern Genetics"*
CAMBRIDGE	Stephen J. Gould, Harvard University *"Evolutionary Hopes and Realities"*
MICHIGAN	Herbert A. Simon, Carnegie-Mellon University *"Scientific Literacy as a Goal in a High-Technology Society"*
STANFORD	Leonard B. Meyer, University of Pennsylvania *"Music and Ideology in the Nineteenth Century"*
UTAH	Helmut Schmidt, former Chancellor, West Germany *"The Future of the Atlantic Alliance"*
HELSINKI	Georg Henrik von Wright, Helsinki *"Of Human Freedom"*

1984–85

OXFORD	Barrington Moore, Jr., Harvard University *"Authority and Inequality under Capitalism and Socialism"*
CAMBRIDGE	Amartya Sen, Oxford University *"The Standard of Living"*
HARVARD	Quentin Skinner, Cambridge University *"The Paradoxes of Political Liberty"*
	Kenneth J. Arrow, Stanford University *"The Unknown Other"*
MICHIGAN	Nadine Gordimer, South Africa *"The Essential Gesture: Writers and Responsibility"*
STANFORD	Michael Slote, University of Maryland *"Moderation, Rationality, and Virtue"*

1985–86

OXFORD	Thomas M. Scanlon, Jr., Harvard University *"The Significance of Choice"*
CAMBRIDGE	Aldo Van Eyck, The Netherlands *"Architecture and Human Values"*
HARVARD	Michael Walzer, Institute for Advanced Study *"Interpretation and Social Criticism"*
MICHIGAN	Clifford Geertz, Institute for Advanced Study *"The Uses of Diversity"*
STANFORD	Stanley Cavell, Harvard University *"The Uncanniness of the Ordinary"*
UTAH	Arnold S. Relman, Editor, *New England Journal of Medicine* *"Medicine as a Profession and a Business"*

1986–87

OXFORD	Jon Elster, Oslo University and the University of Chicago *"Taming Chance: Randomization in Individual and Social Decisions"*

CAMBRIDGE	Roger Bulger, University of Texas Health Sciences Center, Houston "*On Hippocrates, Thomas Jefferson, and Max Weber: The Bureaucratic, Technologic Imperatives and the Future of the Healing Tradition in a Voluntary Society*"
HARVARD	Jürgen Habermas, University of Frankfurt "*Law and Morality*"
MICHIGAN	Daniel C. Dennett, Tufts University "*The Moral First Aid Manual*"
STANFORD	Gisela Striker, Columbia University "*Greek Ethics and Moral Theory*"
UTAH	Laurence H. Tribe, Harvard University "*On Reading the Constitution*"

1987–88

OXFORD	F. Van Zyl Slabbert, University of the Witwatersrand, South Africa "*The Dynamics of Reform and Revolt in Current South Africa*"
CAMBRIDGE	Louis Blom-Cooper, Q.C., London "*The Penalty of Imprisonment*"
HARVARD	Robert A. Dahl, Yale University "*The Pseudodemocratization of the American Presidency*"
MICHIGAN	Albert O. Hirschman, Institute for Advanced Study "*Two Hundred Years of Reactionary Rhetoric: The Case of the Perverse Effect*"
STANFORD	Ronald Dworkin, New York University and University College, Oxford "*Foundations of Liberal Equality*"
UTAH	Joseph Brodsky, Russian poet, Mount Holyoke College "*A Place as Good as Any*"
CALIFORNIA	Wm. Theodore de Bary, Columbia University "*The Trouble with Confucianism*"
BUENOS AIRES	Barry Stroud, University of California, Berkeley "*The Study of Human Nature and the Subjectivity of Value*"

MADRID	Javier Muguerza, Universidad Nacional de Educación a Distancia, Madrid "*The Alternative of Dissent*"
WARSAW	Anthony Quinton, British Library, London "*The Varieties of Value*"

1988–89

OXFORD	Michael Walzer, Institute for Advanced Study "*Nation and Universe*"
CAMBRIDGE	Albert Hourani, Emeritus Fellow, St. Antony's College, and Magdalen College, Oxford "*Islam in European Thought*"
MICHIGAN	Toni Morrison, State University of New York at Albany "*Unspeakable Things Unspoken: The Afro-American Presence in American Literature*"
STANFORD	Stephen Jay Gould, Harvard University "*Unpredictability in the History of Life*" "*The Quest for Human Nature: Fortuitous Side, Consequences, and Contingent History*"
UTAH	Judith Shklar, Harvard University "*American Citizenship: The Quest for Inclusion*"
CALIFORNIA	S. N. Eisenstadt, The Hebrew University of Jerusalem "*Cultural Tradition, Historical Experience, and Social Change: The Limits of Convergence*"
YALE	J. G. A. Pocock, Johns Hopkins University "*Edward Gibbon in History: Aspects of the Text in The History of the Decline and Fall of the Roman Empire*"
CHINESE UNIVERSITY OF HONG KONG	Fei Xiaotong, Peking University "*Plurality and Unity in the Configuration of the Chinese People*"

1989–90

OXFORD	Bernard Lewis, Princeton University "*Europe and Islam*"

CAMBRIDGE	Umberto Eco, University of Bologna *"Interpretation and Overinterpretation: World, History, Texts"*
HARVARD	Ernest Gellner, Kings College, Cambridge *"The Civil and the Sacred"*
MICHIGAN	Carol Gilligan, Harvard University *"Joining the Resistance: Psychology, Politics, Girls, and Women"*
UTAH	Octavio Paz, Mexico City *"Poetry and Modernity"*
YALE	Edward N. Luttwak, Center for Strategic and International Studies *"Strategy: A New Era?"*
PRINCETON	Irving Howe, writer and critic *"The Self and the State"*

1990–91

OXFORD	David Montgomery, Yale University *"Citizenship and Justice in the Lives and Thoughts of Nineteenth-Century American Workers"*
CAMBRIDGE	Gro Harlem Brundtland, Prime Minister of Norway *"Environmental Challenges of the 1990s: Our Responsibility toward Future Generations"*
HARVARD	William Gass, Washington University *"Eye and Idea"*
MICHIGAN	Richard Rorty, University of Virginia *"Feminism and Pragmatism"*
STANFORD	G. A. Cohen, All Souls College, Oxford *"Incentives, Inequality, and Community"* János Kornai, University of Budapest and Harvard University *"Market Socialism Revisited"*
UTAH	Marcel Ophuls, international film maker *"Resistance and Collaboration in Peacetime"*

YALE	Robertson Davies, novelist *"Reading and Writing"*
PRINCETON	Annette C. Baier, Pittsburgh University *"Trust"*
LENINGRAD	János Kornai, University of Budapest and Harvard University *"Transition from Marxism to a Free Economy"*

1991–92

OXFORD	R. Z. Sagdeev, University of Maryland *"Science and Revolutions"*
CALIFORNIA	
LOS ANGELES	Václav Havel, former President, Republic of Czechoslovakia (Untitled lecture)
BERKELEY	Helmut Kohl, Chancellor of Germany (Untitled lecture)
CAMBRIDGE	David Baltimore, former President of Rockefeller University *"On Doing Science in the Modern World"*
MICHIGAN	Christopher Hill, seventeenth-century historian, Oxford *"The Bible in Seventeenth-Century English Politics"*
STANFORD	Charles Taylor, Professor of Philosophy and Political Science, McGill University *"Modernity and the Rise of the Public Sphere"*
UTAH	Jared Diamond, University of California, Los Angeles *"The Broadest Pattern of Human History"*
PRINCETON	Robert Nozick, Professor of Philosophy, Harvard University *"Decisions of Principle, Principles of Decision"*

INDEX TO VOLUME 15, 1994

THE TANNER LECTURES ON HUMAN VALUES

Afanassjew, Jury, 181
Africa: human evolution and, 313, 314; language families in, 295, 297
Afroasiatic language family, 297
agriculture: Aegean civilizations and viticulture, 330; demographic and economic change in neolithic Europe, 302, 303; development of and language change, 303–8, 326–27; European Community and French, 269; urban civilization and language change, 309
Algeria: de Gaulle's policy in, 255; immigration from to France, 265; nationalist revolt, 250, 280
Alsace-Lorraine: French nationalism and loss of, 236
Altaic language family, 308–9, 310
Amerind language family, 297, 307–8
Ammerman, A. J., 302
Anatolia: agriculture and proto-Indo-European language, 303, 312; origins of Greek language, 329
anthropology: definition of ethnicity, 337
antisemitism: French Revolution and, 225
Appeal to Autonomy: as theory of normativity, 25–26
Arabs: European oppression of, 9–10
Arafat, Yasser, 5, 13
archaeology: cognitive and questions of identity, 285–86; ethnicity of classical Greeks, 317–46; genetics and study of culture process, 289
Aristotle, 50, 72–73, 86, 105
Atlan, Henri, 130
Australian language family, 307–8
Australopithecus, 291

authority: realism as theory of normativity, 32–33; as source of obligation, 85–86; voluntarism as theory of normativity, 29–30

Bacterial genetics, 123, 136
Baier, Annette, 198
Baltimore, David, 128–29
Bantu languages, 305
Barbujani, Guido, 312
Barrès, Maurice, 238–39, 240, 241
Barruel, Abbé, 229
Basque language, 308, 311
Bavaria: Communist revolution of 1919, 164
Beadle, George, 123
Beaker culture, 299
beliefs: Hume's theory of morality, 61, 62; moral realism and, 46–47
Bellwood, Peter, 305
Bendixen, Ludwig, 152
Bentham, Jeremy, 73
Berlin, Isaiah, 281
Bernal, Martin, 324
Bernstein, Eduard, 156, 157–58
Bernstein, Leonard, 185–86
Biedenkopf, Kurt, 209
Biermann, Wolf, 200
Bill of Rights, American, 148
biology: genetic determinism and history of, 115–37
Blacks: French Revolution and concept of nation, 225
Blegen, C. W., 328–29
Bloch, Marc, 192

[357]

Bolshevism: establishment of control over Eastern Europe, 154; government duplicity, 149–50, 160–61; Lenin and revolutionary regime in Russia, 162–68; World War I and, 144

Bonard, Louis de, 224

Bosnian civil war, 144, 287–88, 318

Boveri, Theodore, 136

Brandt, Willy, 189

Braudel, Fernand, 262

Brecht, Bertolt, 9, 203

Brenner, Sidney, 129

Briand, Aristide, 159

Brink, David, 42, 117, 120

Brissot, Jacques-Pierre, 226

Britain: censorship during World War I, 152; European Community and national sovereignty, 272; policy of appeasement, 173–74

Bukharin, N. I., 166

Burke, Edmund, 147

Butler, Joseph, 33, 55, 85

capitalism: Eastern European revolutions of 1989, 183–84

Carlyle, Thomas, 146n

Caskey, J. L., 327–28

categorical imperative: as law of free will, 81–82

causality: Kant on free will, 80–81

Causasus, languages of, 308

Cavalli-Sforza, L. L., 302, 311, 313

Celts: collective identity, 340

censorship: European during World War I, 152

Chadwick, John, 325, 343

Charlot, Jean, 253

Chateaubriand, François-Auguste-René de, 228–29

Chaunu, Pierre, 264

Chevènement, Jean-Pierre, 259

Childe, V. Gordon, 298, 324–25, 326, 327

Churchill, Winston, 174

citizenship: French education and, 235; French Revolution and concept of nation, 225–26, 228

civil rights, Israeli record on, 14–15

Clarke, Samuel, 21, 24, 30–31, 33–34, 41, 43

class: French society and concept of nation, 234–35

Clemenceau, Georges, 236, 242

Cold War: origins of in post-1945 period, 175–84

colonialism: Arabs as victims of, 10, 13–14; and French nationalism, 236–38, 250, 255; linguistic change, 309; Palestinian concept of Zionism, 13–14; tribal view of society, 319–20

communism: early appeal of, 166–68; establishment of government in East Germany, 202–3; French nationalism and, 244, 245; government distortion of truth, 147; postwar appeal of in France and Italy, 177

communitarianism: conception of the person, 90–91

Comte, Auguste, 276

Constant, Benjamin, 229

convergence: concepts of in science and ethics, 64, 69

Council of People's Commissars, 155

counternationalism: French movement, 238–42

Crick, F., 123–26

culture: archaeology and study of process, 289, 298–304; French national identity and, 262, 266–67, 277–78; nationalism of French Revolution, 220–21

Cycladic islands: neolithic settlement sites in, 329

Dahrendorf, Gustav, 203

Danton, Georges-Jacques, 227

David, Eduard, 156

Davidson, Eric, 130

Delcassé, Théophile, 241

Delors, Jacques, 208

Déroulède, Paul, 240

developmental biology: history of, 115–37
diversity, human: explanations of world linguistic diversity, 304–10; genetics and, 288–91, 310–15; language and culture process, 298–304; origin of language families, 291–98
Dix, Otto, 160
DNA: archaeology and studies of mitochondrial and nuclear, 313–14; genetic determinism, 123–26, 127
Dolgopolsky, Aharon, 295
Dönhoff, Marion Countess, 211
Dreyfus Affair, 148, 238, 241
Drumont, Edouard, 238–39
Dulles, John Foster, 157
Dumont, Louis, 251n
Dunn, John, 212
Dunn, L. C., 134
duty: Hume on morality and, 56–57

Eastern Europe: peaceful revolutions of 1989, 143–47, 182–84; totalitarianism in postwar era, 179–82
economics: of European Community in postwar era, 178; France and European Community, 268; French nationalism and global system, 277–78; Middle East and European system, 7–8; reunification of Germany and, 189–90, 191–94, 209; of Weimar Germany, 160
education: immigration and French national identity, 263, 265; Republican citizenship and French, 235
Eisner, Kurt, 155, 158
elites: and language change, 301, 308–9
embryology: genetic determinism and history of, 116–37
emotivism: theory of ethics, 66–67
Enlightenment: nationalism of French revolutionaries, 220; tenets of liberalism, 148
Eshkol, Levi, 11
Eskimo-Aleut language family, 297
ethics. See normativity

ethnicity: archaeology and identity of classical Greeks, 317–46; as social construct, 347–48
Etkind, Efim, 181
Europe: agriculture and demographic-economic change in neolithic period, 302, 303, 326–27; French policy of integration, 250; iron age and elite-dominated social groups, 301, 321; origins of Cold War, 175–84; response of political elites to Hitler, 173–74. See also Eastern Europe; European Community; Germany
European Community: building of Western European collectivity, 178–79; French national identity and, 267–78
Evans, Sir Arthur John, 325, 329
evolution, human: emerging picture of, 291

fascism: and French nationalism in 1930s, 244–46; pre-World War II period and, 168–74; World War I and rise of in Europe, 159–68; World War II and, 174–75
Fatherland party, 153–54
femininity: as evaluative concept, 72
Ferry, Jules, 236, 237
Fischer, Fritz, 159
Foner, Eric, 194
foreign policy: de Gaulle and French nationalism, 253–55
France, nationalism: development of national consciousness, 219; European Community and national identity, 267–78; and de Gaulle, 251–60; and global system, 274–78; immigration and national identity, 260–67; in postwar era, 177, 248–51; present status of, 278–82; under Republic, 228–42; revolutionaries of 1789, 220–28; and World War I, 242–45; and World War II, 179, 246–48
Frankfurt, Harry, 82n
free market: negative aspects of, 184
free-rider problem: Hume's theory of morality, 57

free will: categorical imperative as law of, 81–82; Kant on causality and, 80–81
French Revolution, 220–28, 279
Freud, Sigmund, 70, 155, 190
Fustel de Coulanges, Numa Denis, 236

Gambetta, Léon, 233, 234
Garen, Alan, 133
de Gaulle, Charles: agricultural policy, 269; European Community and Luxembourg compromise, 267; nationalism in postwar era, 248–49, 251–60; pragmatism of, 274; Resistance and influence of, 247–48
Gellner, Ernest, 275, 286
gender: sexual reproduction and genetic determinism, 135–37
genetics: genetic determinism and history of biology, 115–37; human diversity and, 288–91; linguistic groups and, 310–15; network models of, 132
Geremek, Bronislaw, 146
Germany: European Community and reunification of, 269; formation of government following World War I, 154–57; Hitler's rise to power in, 171–73; response to outcome of World War II, 150–51; reunification of and postunification period, 185–214; right-wing movements after World War I, 153–54; submarine warfare during World War I, 161; Weimar Republic, 157–58, 160; World War I and government duplicity, 149–50, 151–53; World War I and rise of fascism in, 170–71
Gewirth, Alan, 93
Ghana: precolonial political system and concept of ethnicity, 320–21
Ghandi: philosophy of nonviolence, 181
Gimbutas, Marija, 299, 326, 327
Girondins, 226–27
Giscard d'Estaing, Valéry, 257, 264
global system: French nation-state and, 274–78
God: voluntarism as theory of normativity, 26–30
Goldschmidt, Richard, 135n

Goody, Jack, 320
Gorbachev, Mikhail, 144–45, 187
government: repression of truth, 147
Greece, classical: archaeology and ethnicity of, 317–46; sentimentalist theory of morality, 64
Greek Orthodox Church, 345
Greenberg, Joseph, 295, 297
Greenfield, Liah, 251n
Grosz, George, 160
Grotius, Hugo, 21, 26
Guinea: de Gaulle and decolonization, 255
Guizot, François, 229

Habermas, Jürgen, 210
Hacking, Ian, 120
Hacks, Peter, 205
Haecker, V., 135
Haley, J. B., 328–29
Hall, Edith, 342
Harrison, Ross, 121
Havel, Václav, 145, 146, 181, 214
Havemann, Robert, 200
Hawkes, Christopher, 333–34, 335
Hawks, Israeli, 6–7, 8
Hegel, Georg Wilhelm Friedrich, 82n
Heine, Heinrich, 187
heredity, definitions of, 115–16
Herodotus, 323, 337–38
Higham, Charles, 305
Hirsch, Albert, 199
history and historians: conspiracy of silence on Germany and World War I, 158–59; current French historiography, 279–81; early writings of classical Greek, 322–23; French education and Republican citizenship, 235; de Gaulle and French, 252, 256; Homer and Greek identity, 341; migrationist view of, 319; obligation of to the present, 185; role of nationalism in French, 229–32, 279
Hitler, Adolf, 157, 171–75, 186
Hobbes, Thomas, 21–22, 26–30, 32, 102
Holborn, Hajo, 185

Holocaust, 174
Homer, 337, 339, 341, 343, 346
Homo erectus, 291
Homo sapiens sapiens, 291, 307, 314
Honecker, Erich, 190, 204
horse, domestication of, 299, 300
Howell, Roger, 327
human nature: realist theory of morality, 63; reflective endorsement theory of normativity, 77; sentimentalist theory of morality, 50; Williams on ethics, 70
Hume, David, 25, 33, 35, 50, 51–64, 71–72, 73–76
humility: moral judgments and, 54
Hungary: Communist revolution in 1919, 164
Hussein, Saddam, 12–13
Hutcheson, Francis, 25, 61–62, 104n

identity: archaeology and ethnicity of classical Greeks, 317–46; cognitive archaeology and questions of, 285–86; communitarianism and normative theory, 91; conception of and theory of morality, 83–85, 88–89, 92–93; culture process and human diversity, 298–304; European Community and French national, 267–78; genetics and human diversity, 288–91; immigration and French national, 260–67; language families and, 291–98, 304–15; present status of, 278–82; religion and collective, 286–87; war and collective, 287–88
immigration: and French national identity, 260–67
Indo-European language family, 292–93, 308
Indo-Pacific language family, 297, 307–8
integrity: obligation and concept of, 84–85
Islam: French debate on immigration, 262, 264–65; Israeli-Palestinian conflict and fundamentalism, 9
Isocrates, 344, 347
Israeli-Palestinian conflict, 3–17

Italy: postwar appeal of communism, 177; rise of fascism in, 169–70

Jaurès, Jean, 149, 237, 244
Jews: European oppression of, 9–10, 12; exclusion of from French nation, 225, 232; French counternationalist movement and, 239; World War II and Holocaust, 174; World War II and Vichy regime, 247, 280
Jones, Sir William, 291–93, 294, 326
Judt, Tony, 177
justice: Hume on morality, 56–57; Rawls's concept of, 88

Kant, Immanuel, 25, 34, 37–38, 76, 77, 80, 83, 91–92
Kauffman, Stuart, 131
Kautsky, Karl, 155
Khoisan language family, 297, 307
Khrushchev, Nikita, 180
Kirsten, E., 338
Kohl, Helmut, 189, 190
Kopelev, Lev, 176
Koppel, Moshe, 130
KOR (Committee for Defense of Workers' Rights), 181
Krenz, Egon, 188
Krieger, Leonard, 213
Kronstadt uprising (1921), 165
Kuwait, 12

Lafontaine, Oskar, 190
La Guardia, Fiorello, 167n
language: groups of dialects in Greek, 323; normativity and private, 94–100, 101–4. *See also* Linguistics, historical
Lateran Treaty of 1929, 170
Lavisse, Ernest, 235
law: moral in Kantian system, 81–82; voluntarism as theory of normativity, 26–30
League of Nations, 159, 242
Lenin, V. I., 161–68
Le Pen, Jean-Marie, 257–58, 266
Lewontin, Richard, 127–28

liberalism: conception of the person, 90; Enlightenment and European, 148; formula of inalienable individual rights, 221, 223

life: normativity and value of, 101–6

linguistics, historical: archaeology and ethnicity of classical Greeks, 317–46; and concept of race, 290–91; culture process and human diversity, 298–304; explanations of diversity, 304–10; genetic evidence in, 310–15; origins of language families, 291–98

Louis XIV, 223–24

Luwian language, 329

Luxemburg, Rosa, 163

Lysians, 343–44

Maastricht treaty, 258–60, 270–73

Macedonia, modern use of place name, 318

Mackie, John, 39–40, 43–44, 108

Maistre, Joseph de, 224

Mallory, J. P., 299

Mallwitz, A., 341

Mandeville, Bernard, 22, 23

Mann, Thomas, 203

Mao Zedong, 316

market economy: reunification of Germany, 193–94

Marne, battle of, 152

Marshall Plan, 177

Marx, Karl, 155

masculinity: as evaluative concept, 72

Masur, Kurt, 188

Matteotti, Giacomo, 169

Maurras, Charles, 238–40, 241

Maziére, Lothar de, 189, 199

McCarthyism, 167n, 176–77

Medawar, Peter, 125

Meinecke, Friedrich, 159

Meir, Golda, 5

metaphysics: realism as theory of normativity, 34–35

Michelet, Jules, 230–32, 235, 239, 251–52, 259

Michnik, Adam, 146, 181

Mielke, Erich, 196

Mill, John Stuart, 25, 148

Millerrand, Alexandre, 241

Milosz, Czeslaw, 166, 181

Minoan civilization: decline of, 323–24, 346; origins of classical Greek culture, 325, 330–36; political organization, 338–40

Mirabeau, Honoré de, 225

mitochondrial DNA studies, 313–14

Mitterrand, François, 257, 266, 268

modernization: French nationalism and, 253, 267, 268

Modrow, Hans, 188

molecular biology: genetic determinism, 123, 128–29, 133

Mollet, Guy, 250

Monnet, Jean, 177–78

Monod, Jacques, 128

Moore, G. E., 24

morality. *See* normativity

Morgan, T. H., 116, 117, 122

Mourant, A. E., 311

Muller, H. J., 118, 119

Muller, Heiner, 200

multiculturalism: French national identity and, 262, 265

Mussolini, Benito, 169–70

Mycenaean civilization: origins of classical Greek culture, 324, 325, 327, 330–36, 346; political organization, 338–40

Myres, Sir John, 317, 319, 322, 324

myths: classical Greece and origin, 323; Eastern European revolutions of 1989, 183; ethnicity and violence, 347; postwar Germany, 151

Na-Dene language family, 297

Nagel, Thomas, 25, 42, 43, 48, 93, 94, 98, 104n

Napoleon, 228

nation: definition of, 217, 218; French revolutionaries of 1789, 220–28

National Front, French, 257–58

nationalism: collective identity and violence, 318; definition of, 217–18, 222; present status of in Europe, 183
——— French: European Community and, 267–78; global system and, 274–78; in postwar era, 248–51; present status of, 278–82; under Republic, 228–42; revolutionaries of 1789, 220–28; World War I and, 242–45; World War II and, 246–48
National Socialism: establishment of totalitarian rule, 172–73; ethnic identity, 288; government duplicity, 149–50, 160–61
naturalism: theory of normativity, 101–2
Nazism: present divisions among Germans, 195. See also Fascism; Hitler, Adolf; National Socialism
Needham, Joseph, 131
Neo-Nazis, German, 212
New Guinea: language families, 293, 294
Nichols, Johanna, 294
Nietzsche, Friedrich, 192–93
Niger-Kordofanian language family, 297
Nijhout, H. F., 130
Nilsson, Martin, 334
Noiriel, Gérard, 265
Nora, Pierre, 280
normativity: definition of, 22; Hume's theory of, 51–64, 73–76; Korsgaard's theory of, 78–107; overview of philosophical positions on, 24–26, 77, 107–8; realism as theory of, 30–48, 107; reflective endorsement method, 49–51, 107–8; voluntarism as theory of, 26–30, 107; Williams's theory of, 64–73
nuclear DNA studies, 313–14
Nusslein-Volhard, Christianne, 133

obligation: authority as source of, 85–86; identity and, 84–85; Korsgaard's theory of morality, 88–93; to others in normative theory, 93–101; realism as theory of normativity, 31–33, 40–41; voluntarism as theory of normativity, 26–30
Olympic Games (classical Greece), 340, 341–42, 343–44, 346

Ophul, Max, 179
oppression: victims of, 9–10, 12
origin myths: classical Greece, 323, 341
Orwell, George, 146, 168

Palestine National Movement, 13
Palestinians. See Israeli-Palestinian conflict
patriotism: definition of, 218
Pauker, Anna, 180
Paxton, Robert, 279
peace movement, Israeli, 11
Péguy, Charles, 241, 242
Peloponnesian War, 339
Pericles, 344
Persian Gulf War, 8, 12–13
Persian Wars (classical Greece), 342, 343, 346
Peru, early agriculture in, 307
Plato, 86–87
Poincaré, Raymond, 241, 242, 243
Poland: Soviet brutality during World War II, 150
Polynesia: models of colonization, 314
Pompidou, Georges, 257
prescriptivism: theory of ethics, 66–67
Price, Richard, 21, 24, 33–34
Prichard, H. A., 23, 24, 34, 40, 43, 58, 59, 65n
pride: moral judgments and, 54
procedural moral realism, 36–39
propaganda: Hitler on use of, 171–72
psychoanalytic theory: Williams on ethics, 70
psychology: of German reunification, 192–93, 209
Pufendorf, Samuel, 21, 26–30, 31
Puritan Revolution, 146n
Putnam, Robert, 212

race: genetics and concept of, 288–91
Railton, Peter, 42
Rathenau, Walther, 153
Rawls, John, 25, 37, 59n, 88–89

realism: criticism of Hume's theory of morality, 58–59; criticism of sentimentalist theory of morality, 63; reflective endorsement method of normativity, 50; as theory of normativity, 24–25, 30–48, 77, 107

Reconstruction, American Civil War, 194

reflective endorsement: Hume, Williams, and Kant on morality, 76; morality and human nature, 77; as theory of normativity, 25, 49–51, 107–8

reflexivity: Hume's theory of morality, 61, 63; Williams on ethics, 72–73

Reich, Jens, 200, 201, 211

relativism: concepts and conceptions in theory of normativity, 89–90; Kant's Formula of Humanity, 91–92

religion: and collective identity, 286–87; Minoan-Mycenaean roots of Greek, 333–36

Renan, Ernest, 236

Renouvier, Charles, 229

Resistance: French in World War II, 246–48, 251

Revanche: French nationalism, 236

revolutions: Eastern European of 1989, 143–47, 182–84. *See also* Russian Revolution

Richelieu, Cardinal, 223–24

rights: and claims in Israeli-Palestinian conflict, 3–4

Robespierre, Maximilien de, 226–27, 238

Rocard, Michel, 264

Ross, W. D., 24

Rousseau, Jacques, 221–22, 223

Ruhlen, Merritt, 297

Rushdie, Salman, 9

Russian Orthodox Church, 345

Russian Revolution, 144, 154, 162, 163, 243–44

Sakellariou, M., 326

Sakharov, Andrei, 181

Sanskrit language, 292

Sartre, Jean-Paul, 177

Schiffer, Eugen, 156

Schmidt, Helmut, 211

Schnapper, Dominique, 264

Schotté, Oscar, 134

Schrödinger, Erwin, 125

Schumacher, Kurt, 203

Schuman, Robert, 177–78

Schuman Plan, 178

Schumpeter, Joseph, 210

Séguin, Philippe, 259

Seignobos, Charles, 235

self-determination: Palestinians' right of, 4, 14

sentimentalism: Hume's theory of morality, 51–64; reflective endorsement method of normativity, 50

Serbs: Bosnian civil war and ethnic cleansing, 287–88, 318

sexual reproduction: gender and genetic determinism, 135–37

Shannon, Claude, 124

Shklar, Judith, 276

Sieyès, Joseph, 222, 223, 224, 225

Sino-Tibetan language family, 309

skinheads: Neo-Nazism in Germany, 212

Skopje, Republic of: Macedonia and independence movement, 318

Slansky, Rudolf, 180

slavery: French Constitution of 1791, 225–26

Snodgrass, A. M., 341

social contract: French Revolution and concept of, 221–22

socialism: establishment of Communist state in East Germany, 202–3; French nationalism, 243–44, 245

Sokal, Robert, 311–12

Solidarity movement, 181

Soviet-German Pact of 1939, 150, 167n

Soviet Union: emergence of Cold War, 176–84; establishment of Communist state in East Germany, 202–4; German invasion of, 174, 175; Lenin and revolutionary regime, 162–68; show trials of mid-1930s, 150; totalitarianism in postwar era, 179–82. *See also* Russian Revolution

Spanish Civil War, 161

Spemann, Hans, 121
Spinelli, Altiero, 177–78
Stalin, Josef, 167n, 176, 180
Stolpe, Manfred, 199
Stresemann, Gustav, 159
Sturtevant, Alfred H., 122
substantive moral realism, 36–39
Svitych, Illich, 295
Switzerland: during World War II, 175
sympathy: Hume's theory of, 57–58

Tatum, Edward, 123
technology: connection between terror and, 179n; and language change, 302
Thierry, Augustin, 230
Third World: sentimental left and, 11–12, 13
Thomas, René, 131
Thucydides, 212, 339, 340
Tocqueville, Alexis de, 237
Todorov, Tzvetan, 220, 232, 237
Touchard, Jean, 252n
trade: Aegean civilizations in early bronze age, 331; language change and, 301
tragedy: Israeli-Palestinian conflict as, 16
Trilling, Lionel, 150
Trojan War, 338–39, 341, 342
Trotsky, Leon, 162, 163n
Trubetzkoy, N. S., 294, 300
truth: normative concetps, 47–48; repression of by governments, 147

United Nations, 176
urban communities: Aegean cultures and decline of, 332–33; language families and, 309
utilitarianism: Bentham's theory of morality, 73, 74–76; as naturalistic form of realism, 42; pleasure and pain in ethical theory, 102

values: human diversity and collective identity, 287–88; Korsgaard's theory of normativity, 101–6; realism as theory of normativity, 41–42; Williams's theory of ethics, 70
Venture, Michael, 325

Versailles, Treaty of, 157, 159
Vichy regime, 246–47, 279, 280
voluntarism: theological and Hume's theory of morality, 62; as theory of normativity, 24, 26–30, 77, 107

Waddington, C. H., 131, 132
war: collective identity and violence, 287–88, 347
Watson, J. D., 123–26
Webb, Sidney and Beatrice, 166
Weber, Eugen, 233, 234, 241
Weber, Max, 148, 154
Weimar Republic, 157–59, 160, 186
Weismann, August, 115
Weizsäcker, Richard von, 211
Whitehead, Alfred North, 131
Williams, Bernard, 25, 50–51, 64–73, 89, 90
Wilson, E. B., 136
Wilson, Woodrow, 154, 157
Wittgenstein, Ludwig, 94–100, 101–4
Wolf, Christa, 200–201
Woodger, J. H., 131
Woodward, C. Vann, 185
World War I: Bolshevik peace settlement, 163–64; formation of German government following, 154–57; German attitudes at beginning of, 151–53; government deception in Europe, 143–44, 146–47, 149; legacy of and fascism in Germany, 170–71; and rise of fascism in Europe, 159–68; submarine warfare, 161; World War II as continuation of, 174
World War II: German reaction to outcome of, 150–51; Hitler and course of, 173–75; postunification Germany and, 195

Yonnet, Paul, 264n
Yugoslavia: civil war in former, 144, 287–88, 318

Zinoviev, Grigory, 162
Zionism, 13–14
Zvelebil, K. V. and M., 303